101 EXERCISES IN PSYCHOLOGICAL TESTING AND ASSESSMENT
Third Edition

Ronald Jay Cohen
St. John's University

Mayfield Publishing Company
Mountain View, California
London • Toronto

International Standard Book Number 1-55934-429-6

Manufactured in the United States of America
10 9 8 7 6 5 4 3 2 1

Mayfield Publishing Company
1280 Villa Street
Mountain View, CA 94041

To the Student

This book was developed for use by students taking a course variously described as "psychological testing," "psychological assessment," and "tests and measurement," and is designed to supplement textbook study and in-class lecture material with hands-on laboratory exercises. Chapters in this book generally correspond to the order of the coverage of topics presented in *Psychological Testing and Assessment: An Introduction to Tests and Measurement* (Cohen, Swerdlik, & Phillips, 1996). And while it is heartily recommended that this guide be used as a companion to the Cohen et al., text, it is possible to use it in conjunction with other psychological testing texts with no ill effects.

As you are no doubt aware, the term *learning* is both a noun and a verb. Sequentially in one's experience, learning may initially be a verb (as in "learning new material"), and a noun later (as in "calling upon one's learning"). However, it is also true that old learning facilitates new learning and so arguments about the prominence of new versus old learning take on a kind of chicken-or-the-egg impossibility of resolution. Regardless, learning is an active process that requires deliberate effort in both storing information and maintaining readiness for instant retrieval. In my experience, one of the best ways to facilitate the process of learning is to mentally "work out" with the learning. This means, among other things, that one tries to link what is currently being learned to past learning, generate new and novel ideas related to the learning, and think critically about it.

Elsewhere, I have written about what I termed "generative thinking," or *the goal-oriented intellectual production of new or creative ideas* (Cohen, 1994, p. 13). As implied in this definition, there is little that is random about generative thought. Generative thinking may have different objectives, including a better understanding of a new concept. A philosophy guiding the development of the exercises in this book is that the best way for you to grasp measurement principles is to do more than merely be able to define them. Rather, it is imperative that you expand and build on these principles, mentally play with them, and in the process discover for yourself this beginnings of the extent of their meaning. Although this book contains some exercises of the familiar drill-and-review

format, the vast majority of the exercises require mental extension beyond the bounds of what is presented in the Cohen et al. (1996) text.

On occasion, an instructor who has used a prior edition of this book has asked me why I used the format I did; that is, why I did not write a workbook that was dedicated in whole to drill-and-review types of exercises. My response is grounded in terms of the degree of intellectual challenge the work poses to the student (as well as the author of the workbook—myself). It would be a relatively simple matter, and a wholly unchallenging one at that, to prepare a drill-and-review-type of workbook. In all candor, I probably would find such a task tedious. It is likewise my hunch that serious students assigned to complete such exercises might also find the work tedious and singularly unrewarding. Ideally, the student in an upper-level course such as measurement will learn key material primarily from lecture and the textbook, not from a workbook such as this. This book should serve as a stimulus for one's personal expansion of the learning experience that begins in the classroom. Creating a series of exercises designed to foster generative thinking with regard to psychological testing and measurement represented an intriguing challenge for me. It is my hope that these exercises will represent an intriguing challenge for you as well. And to the extent that one construes intellectual challenge as fun, I must admit to having had some fun in creating these exercises. To the extent that completing these exercises is intellectually intriguing for you, perhaps you too will have some fun with them.

In addition to providing a stimulus for generative thought, seven objectives guided the development of this work. Each of these objectives are similar to, or extensions of, the objectives that guided the preparation of the Cohen et al. (1996) textbook. They are as follows:

1. to provide students with "do-able" laboratory exercises pertinent to basic measurement concepts, the better for them to achieve (a) a sense of personal mastery with respect to such concepts, (b) personal experience in relevant data manipulations, and (c) the ability to understand and relate to technical terms in professional journals, test manuals, and test reports. In addition to

step-by-step illustrations of the use of various statistics employed in the context of testing, there is also ample opportunity for you to be creative in developing applications of measurement principles;

2. to go beyond assisting the student in the acquisition of course content as presented in the primary text by stimulating depth of understanding of the theory and practice of psychological measurement;

3. to make students eager to pick up their psychological testing textbook—to the extent that such a feat is possible—by involving students in the subject matter;

4. to blend theoretical and applied material in a way designed to provide the student with a rationale for (and a "hands-on feel" of) the assessment process. In the interest of maintaining the confidentiality of published materials, and in an effort to avoid "armchair analyses" and inappropriate generalization from data, all such exercises are accomplished using tests and test items constructed by students themselves or by other means (such as by the use of the mock personality inventory in Appendix A);

5. to provide case illustrations of the wide range of "real world" contexts in which psychological tests are used;

6. to provide both in-class as well as out-of-classroom type tasks and exercises, many of which will be appealing to students who are at virtually any point along the continuum of experience and sophistication with psychological tests;

7. to help balance an appreciation of the science of psychological measurement as it exists today with a healthy, realistic degree of self-criticism and a vision of the challenges that lay ahead.

Some of the exercises can be completed in class by yourself. Some of the exercises will require some out-of-class activity. For example, the "Pick-A-Test" exercise that is presented in most chapters beginning with Chapter 9 requires that you select a test that you might like to learn more about, and then do some library research.

In Chapters 3 through 7, many of the exercises entail the calculation of statistics commonly used in measurement. Step-by-step illustrations of the computations of many of these statistics are evident throughout these chapters, each such illustration designed to facilitate learning. While it is true that all the "real world" user of virtually any statistic needs to know is how to select, run, and enter data into the right computer program, these step-by-step calculation exercises cannot help but lead to a better conceptual understanding of the problem-solving process.

In some instances, an exercise might contain reprinted material from some article relevant to testing—the better to serve as a stimulus for thoughtful discussion. In other exercises, it will be you who is called upon to put your own background and experience to work (along with what you've learned from your text) and, in essence, write an "article" relevant to testing; of course such

writing need not be of publishable quality though it should, at a minimum, bear your own unique imprimature.

During the course of a semester it is a safe assumption that your instructor will *not* assign every single exercise; there simply isn't time. Your instructor's preference may be to concentrate attention on the psychometric foundations of testing, in which case you may spend the bulk (if not all) of your time with Chapters 1 through 7. Alternatively, your instructor may focus the course more on applied phenomena and you may spend more time on the later chapters in this book. If in skimming through this book you find a particular exercise that you think you would really enjoy—and find a valuable learning experience—you may want to bring it to the attention of your instructor.

And now, three tips in using this book:

1. *Be prepared!* Know what will be required of you—a week or two in advance, if possible—and be ready. A sharpened pencil with an eraser, some unlined paper for calculations, some graph paper and a straight edge (6-inch rule will do) for graphing, a pocket calculator, and lined, single sheet paper suitable for essay-type writing, are standard equipment for these laboratory exercises. Being prepared also means having read the chapter in your textbook that was assigned prior to the class meeting and being prepared to raise any questions that you have on the material.

2. *Maintain team spirit.* Many of the exercises require you to work with one or more of your classmates; root for them as you would like them to root for you. "Winning" in such team exercises is analogous with "learning" and it is essential for an atmosphere conducive to "winning" to be maintained from the start of the semester to the end.

3. *Take notes.* To maximize the benefit you derive from completing the exercises in this book, make a habit of jotting down any aspect of the exercise—or the concepts involved—for which a bit more explanation would be helpful. Don't hesitate to raise these notes in class; your instructor is there to help and it's up to you to use that valuable resource to the fullest.

At the end of each chapter in this book, there is a four-question test on material from the corresponding chapter in Cohen et al. (1996). Referred to as the 4-Question Challenge, this test is designed to help you sample the degree to which you have retained the material in the chapter. In addition, this brief test can itself be employed in a firsthand exploration of how data from one test or series of tests (such as a score on the 4-Question Challenge) relates to data from another test or series of tests (such as your midterm and/or final examination). As you learn more about numerically gauging the relationship between two or more tests, you may want to test the hypothesis that a strong, positive correlation exists between students' scores on the 4-Question Challenge and midterm and/or final course grade. Here's hoping that this hypothesis is confirmed, and that you are greatly enriched for your efforts.

Ronald Jay Cohen

ACKNOWLEDGMENTS

Thanks to my Sponsoring Editor at Mayfield Publishing, Frank Graham, for creating an environment in which a new and innovative approach to psychological testing and assessment could be developed. For their part in the production-related efforts in the service of that same dedication to innovation, thanks to April Wells-Hayes at Mayfield Publishing and Robin Lockwood at Lockwood & Associates. Sincere thanks also to my longtime friend, Mark Swerdlik for his assistance in tracking down research papers, and for his helpfulness in the field testing of some of these exercises with students. Thanks to Lou Primavera and Bernie Gorman for their preparation of an addendum on factor analysis to previous editions of the main text; the addendum proved helpful in factor analysis related writing in this book. Thanks to Suzanne M. Phillips for contributing exercise 84 and assisting directly or indirectly in part to the writing of all of the Pick-A-Test exercises, as well as exercises 22, 32, 33, and 100. Thanks to Barry Loigman, and other participants of the 1995 *Teaching of Psychology* meeting in St. Petersburgh Beach, Florida who used the two previous editions of this book, and proffered a wealth of useful suggestions for improvement.

Thanks to the Museum of Modern Art Film Still Archives and the courtesies extended by, in alphabetical order, Cinerama Releasing Corporation, Columbia Pictures Corporation, the Geffen Film Company, the Ladd Company, MGM, Orion Pictures, Paramount Pictures, RKO Pictures, Twentieth Century-Fox Film Corporation, United Artists, Universal Pictures, and Warner Brothers.

Finally, thanks to Edith, Harold, Barbara, Richard, Alan, Susan, Harrison, and Sheena for their support through the years.

REFERENCES

Cohen, R. J. (1994). *Psychology & adjustment: Values, culture, and change.* Needham Heights, MA: Allyn & Bacon.

Cohen, R. J., Swerdlik, M. E., & Phillips, S. M. (1996). *Psychological testing and assessment: An introduction to tests and measurements.* Mountain View, CA: Mayfield Publishing Company.

Brief Contents

To the Student   *iii*

PART 1: AN OVERVIEW   *1*

1. Psychological Testing and Assessment   *3*
2. Historical, Cultural, and Legal/Ethical Issues   *10*

PART 2: THE SCIENCE OF PSYCHOLOGICAL MEASUREMENT   *19*

3. A Statistics Refresher   *21*
4. Norms, Correlation, and Regression   *37*
5. Reliability   *68*
6. Validity   *76*
7. Test Development   *95*

PART 3: THE ASSESSMENT OF INTELLIGENCE   *109*

8. Intelligence and Its Measurement   *111*
9. Tests of Intelligence   *121*
10. Preschool and Educational Assessment   *130*

PART 4: PERSONALITY ASSESSMENT   *169*

11. Objective Methods and Overview   *171*
12. Projective Methods   *187*
13. Other Personality and Behavioral Measures   *197*

PART 5: TESTING AND ASSESSMENT IN ACTION   *203*

14. Clinical and Counseling Assessment   *205*
15. Neuropsychological Assessment   *222*
16. The Assessment of People with Disabling Conditions   *228*
17. Industrial/Organizational Assessment   *233*
18. Consumer Assessment   *243*
19. Computer-Assisted Psychological Assessment   *249*

APPENDIX A: The Mid-Pawling Personality Inventory (MPPI)   *255*

APPENDIX B: A Glossary of Measurement Terms   *257*

SOURCES   *266*

Contents

To the Student   *iii*

PART 1: AN OVERVIEW   *1*

1. PSYCHOLOGICAL TESTING AND ASSESSMENT   *3*

Exercise #1
On Measurement   *5*

Exercise #2
Testing or Assessment?   *5*

Exercise #3
The Process of Assessment   *6*

Exercise #4
The Interviewer/Interviewee
Interaction   *7*

Exercise #5
Behavioral Assessment   *7*

Exercise #6
Getting Information about Tests   *8*

2. HISTORICAL, CULTURAL, AND LEGAL/ETHICAL CONSIDERATIONS   *10*

Exercise #7
Psychological Testing and Assessment in
Historical Perspective   *12*

Exercise #8
The Cohen Chicken Soup Essay   *12*

Exercise #9
The Nonverbal Interview   *13*

Exercise #10
Guidelines for Using Psychological
Tests   *13*

Exercise #11
The Test Purchaser Qualification
Form   *14*

Exercise #12
A Legal/Ethical Roundtable   *14*

Exercise #13
Another Legal/Ethical Roundtable   *15*

PART 2: THE SCIENCE OF PSYCHOLOGICAL MEASUREMENT   *19*

3. A STATISTICS REFRESHER   *21*

Exercise #14
Scales of Measurement in Everyday
Life   *23*

Exercise #15
Reviewing Descriptive Statistics   *23*

Exercise #16
Accumulating Data on a Mock Personality
Inventory   *31*

4. NORMS, CORRELATION, AND REGRESSION   *37*

Exercise #17
Transformed Scores: Percentiles   *39*

Exercise #18
Standard, Standardized, and Normalized
Standard Scores   *44*

Exercise #19
Stanines, SAT/ACT, and Grade-Equivalent
Scores   *47*

Exercise #20
Norms   *57*

Exercise #21
The Pearson *r*   *58*

Exercise #22
"Hello" to Rho   *61*

Exercise #23
Other Coefficients of Correlation   *62*

Exercise #24
An Exercise in Regression   *64*

5. RELIABILITY   *68*

Exercise #25
The Concept of Reliability   *70*

Exercise #26
Test-Retest and Interscorer
Reliability   *71*

Exercise #27
Using the Spearman-Brown
Formula   *71*

Exercise #28
Understanding Internal Consistency
Reliability   *74*

6. VALIDITY   *76*

Exercise #29
The Concept of Validity   *78*

Exercise #30
The Quantification of Content
Validity   *78*

Exercise #31
Predicting a Criterion Score   *79*

Exercise #32
The Multitrait-Multimethod Matrix   *82*

Exercise #33
Factor Analysis and the Correlation
Matrix   *87*

Exercise #34
Factor Analysis and Construct
Validity   *89*

Exercise #35
"Fairness" and "Bias"   *90*

7. TEST DEVELOPMENT   *95*

Exercise #36
The Test Development Process   *97*

Exercise #37
Scaling the Bounds of
Consciousness   *100*

Exercise #38
Guttman Scaling   *101*

Exercise #39
Item Analysis: Quantitative
Methods   *102*

Exercise #40
Item Analysis: Qualitative
Methods   *105*

Exercise #41
Writing "Good" Items   *106*

PART 3: THE ASSESSMENT OF INTELLIGENCE   *109*

8. INTELLIGENCE AND ITS MEASUREMENT   *111*

Exercise #42
The Concept of Intelligence   *113*

Exercise #43
Interpreting IQ Scores   *113*

Exercise #44
"Mental Age"   *115*

Exercise #45
Successive and Simultaneous
Processing   *117*

Exercise #46
Rating the Gifted   *117*

Exercise #47
Grappling with Some Measurement
Issues   *117*

Exercise #48
More Issues, More Grappling   *119*

9. TESTS OF INTELLIGENCE   *121*

Exercise #49
Tests of Intelligence   *123*

Exercise #50
Tailoring Without Needles or Thread   *123*

Exercise #51
Factor Analysis and Tests of Intelligence   *124*

Exercise #52
Much Ado About Mensa   *124*

Exercise #53
Create an Alternative Measure of Intellectual Ability   *127*

Exercise #54
Administering the MALS   *127*

Exercise #55
Pick-A-Test: Tests of Intelligence   *128*

10. PRESCHOOL AND EDUCATIONAL ASSESSMENT   *130*

Exercise #56
Preschool Assessment: Physical Development   *132*

Exercise #57
Preschool Assessment: Cognitive Development   *132*

Exercise #58
Preschool Assessment: Language and Social Development   *133*

Exercise #59
Assessment in the Schools   *134*

Exercise #60
Standardized Achievement Tests   *150*

Exercise #61
Firsthand Portfolio Assessment   *165*

Exercise #62
Authentic Assessment . . . Really!   *165*

Exercise #63
Pick-A-Test: Preschool and Educational Measures   *165*

PART 4: PERSONALITY ASSESSMENT   *169*

11. OVERVIEW AND OBJECTIVE METHODS   *171*

Exercise #64
"Personality" and Its Assessment   *173*

Exercise #65
George Washington's 16 PF   *173*

Exercise #66
Empirical Criterion Keying—California Style   *178*

Exercise #67
Clinical Versus Actuarial Prediction   *179*

Exercise #68
Personality Test Scales   *181*

Exercise #69
"Just Your Type"   *183*

Exercise #70
Pick-A-Test: Personality Tests   *183*

12. PROJECTIVE METHODS   *187*

Exercise #71
Understanding and Using Projective Techniques   *189*

Exercise #72
The Holtzman Inkblot Technique   *190*

Exercise #73
The Szondi Test   *192*

Exercise #74
The Psychometric Soundness of Projective Methods   *194*

Exercise #75
Pick-A-Test: Projective Personality Measures   *194*

13. OTHER PERSONALITY AND BEHAVIORAL MEASURES   *197*

Exercise #76
The Q-Sort and the Concept of
Self   *199*

Exercise #77
Situational Performance Measures   *199*

Exercise #78
Behavioral Observation   *200*

Exercise #79
Pick-A-Test: Measures of Specific Aspects
of Personality   *200*

PART 5: TESTING AND ASSESSMENT IN ACTION   *203*

14. CLINICAL AND COUNSELING ASSESSMENT   *205*

Exercise #80
The Interview as a Tool of
Assessment   *207*

Exercise #81
The Case Study   *208*

Exercise #82
Behavioral Observation II   *216*

Exercise #83
P. T. Barnum and the MPPI   *216*

Exercise #84
The Multitrait-Multimethod Matrix
Revisited   *219*

Exercise #85
Pick-A-Test: Clinical Measures   *219*

15. NEUROPSYCHOLOGICAL ASSESSMENT   *222*

Exercise #86
The Neuropsychological
Examination   *224*

Exercise #87
Interview with a
Neuropsychologist   *225*

Exercise #88
Pick-A-Test: Neuropsychological
Tests   *225*

16. THE ASSESSMENT OF PEOPLE WITH DISABLING CONDITIONS   *228*

Exercise #89
Administering, Scoring, and Interpreting
Nonstandardized Psychological
Tests   *230*

Exercise #90
Assessing Adaptive Behavior   *230*

Exercise #91
Pick-A-Test: The Assessment of People
with Disabling Conditions   *231*

17. INDUSTRIAL/ ORGANIZATIONAL ASSESSMENT   *233*

Exercise #92
Assessment of Personnel   *235*

Exercise #93
Test Profiles   *235*

Exercise #94
Another Day, Another Profile   *236*

Exercise #95
Your Personality Suits You for Work
As . . .   *239*

Exercise #96
Pick-A-Test: Industrial/Organizational
Assessment   *240*

18. CONSUMER ASSESSMENT   *243*

Exercise #97
Taste-Tests   *245*

Exercise #98
Psychographics   *245*

**19. COMPUTER-ASSISTED
PSYCHOLOGICAL
ASSESSMENT**   *249*

Exercise #99
Computer-Assisted Psychological
Assessment   *251*

Exercise #100
Computer-Assisted Educational
Assessment: The Case of the
GRE   *251*

Exercise #101
Pick-A-Test: Computer-Assisted Test
Products   *253*

**APPENDIX A: THE MID-PAWLING
PERSONALITY INVENTORY
(MPPI)   255**

**APPENDIX B: A GLOSSARY OF
MEASUREMENT
TERMS   257**

SOURCES   266

PART

1

AN OVERVIEW

Chapter 1

Psychological Testing and Assessment

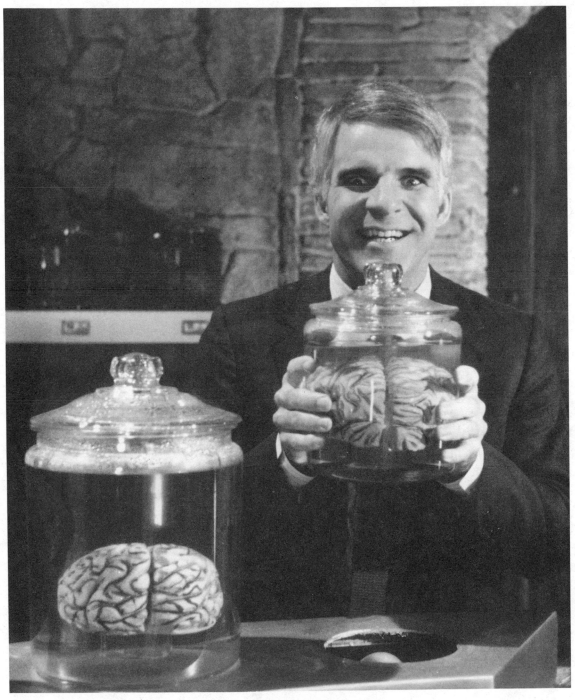

Are Two Brains Better Than One?

Many important questions and issues arise in discussions of the nature and measurement of psychological variables—none of which are raised by Steve Martin in The Man With Two Brains.

Outline for Chapter 1 of Cohen et al. (1996)
PSYCHOLOGICAL TESTING AND ASSESSMENT

Testing and Assessment
Testing and Assessment Defined
The Tools of Psychological Assessment
   The test
   The interview
   The case study
   The portfolio
   Behavioral observation
   Other tools
12 Assumptions in Psychological Testing and Assessment
   Assumption 1: Psychological traits exist.
   Assumption 2: Psychological traits can be quantified and measured.
   Assumption 3: Various approaches to measuring aspects of the same thing can be useful.
   Assumption 4: Assessment can provide answers to some of life's most momentous questions.
   Assumption 5: Assessment can pinpoint phenomena that require further attention or study.
   Assumption 6: Various sources of input enrich and are part of the assessment process.
   Assumption 7: Various sources of error are part of the assessment process.
   Assumption 8: Tests and other measurement techniques have strengths and weaknesses.
   Assumption 9: Test-related behavior predicts non-test related behavior.
   Assumption 10: Present-day behavior sampling predicts future behavior.
   Assumption 11: Testing and assessment can be conducted in a fair and unbiased manner.
   Assumption 12: Testing and assessment benefits society.

Who, What, and Why?
Who are the Parties?
   The test developer
   The test user
   The testtaker
   Society at large
What Type of Settings Is Assessment Conducted in and Why?
   Educational settings
   Counseling settings
   Clinical settings
   Business settings
   Other settings

Evaluating the Quality of Tests
What Is a "Good" Test or Assessment Procedure?
   Reliability
   Validity
   Other considerations
Reference Sources for Test Information
   Test catalogues
   Test manuals
   Test reviews

CLOSE-UP:
Computer Assisted Psychological Assessment

EVERYDAY PSYCHOMETRICS:
Psychometrics Defined

EXERCISE 1
ON MEASUREMENT

OBJECTIVE

To encourage generative thinking on the subject of measurement in general.

BACKGROUND

Commodities of daily life are measured in familiar units. It is commonplace to measure, for example, gasoline by the gallon, fruit by the pound, and waistlines by the inch. Perhaps because we deal with these types of measurement so frequently, we tend to take measurement for granted. In the study of psychological testing and assessment, however, little about the process of measurement can be taken for granted. A variety of skills and knowledge must be brought to bear in the development of meaningful measures, as well as in the administration and interpretation of those measures.

YOUR TASK

Write a brief essay on the subject of measurement. In that essay, discuss your thoughts on the subject of measurement in general—your essay need not relate to measurement in psychology. Give your imagination free reign, developing interesting concepts that have anything at all to do with measurement. Your essay can be well researched with references to the scholarly literature. You may choose instead to write an essay that is more informal, freewheeling, even humorous. Or, like the sample essay that follows, your essay may combine such features. You may wish to write your own original essay before reading the one below.

ON MEASUREMENT

Measuring a variable such as distance seems simple. All you need is a ruler, yardstick, tape measure, or some such device. Of course, it wasn't always that way. The first tools used to measure distance were probably stones, branches, or parts of one's own body. For example, one widely used measure of distance was the *cubit,* defined as the length between an adult's elbow and the outstretched middle finger. For the purposes of "standardization," the length of some body part of a royal personage could be used. An Egyptian royal cubit, for example, is equal in length to seven palms and presumably was "standardized" on a pharaoh with very long arms. The standard measure of length in the United States—the foot—is based on the length of an English king's foot.

During the Renaissance in Italy, common units of measurement included the *passo* (pace), the *piede* (foot), and the *pollice* (the width of the thumb). The exact length of each of these measures might vary a bit not only from town to town but from trade to trade; an architect's *passo* might differ from that of an engineer's (Hart, 1962). It was as late as 1861 that the metric system of measurement first became obligatory in Italy. And it was as late as 1975 that the United States Congress passed into law the Metric Conversion Act. After the passage of that law, it was expected that the United States would join the rest of the world in using that system of measurement. However, the metric system never caught on here. Today Americans do little more metrically than "quaff soft drinks and liquor from liter bottles" and "watch 100-meter sprints" (Beathard, 1994).

Even the metric system, as simple as it seems to be, isn't really that simple. Consider in this context the length of a meter; how long is it, *really*? In 1875, 17 nations met to ratify a treaty at a meeting called the Convention of the Meter. The nations agreed that a meter would be equal in length to a platinum bar to be stored in a vault at the International Bureau of Weights and Measures in France. However, concerns about possible changes in an atom or two of the platinum bar standard led to a redefinition of the length of a meter in 1960. Another international meeting was convened, this one attended by representatives from 38 countries. A meter was defined as "1,650,763.73 vacuum wave-lengths of monochromatic orange light emitted by krypton atom of mass 86." The platinum bar idea was a lot simpler.

No, not even the measurement of simple things is as simple as it may appear at first blush. And measuring psychological variables such as intelligence, assertiveness, or potential to commit violent acts—well, that's a whole other story unto itself.

EXERCISE 2
TESTING OR ASSESSMENT?

OBJECTIVE

To enhance understanding of the semantic distinction between the terms *psychological testing* and *psychological assessment.*

BACKGROUND

The semantic difference between the terms *psychological testing* and *psychological assessment* is not always straightforward, not even to psychologists. This exercise is designed to compel you to think about the difference.

YOUR TASK

From your own understanding of the distinction between "testing" and "assessment," how would you classify each of the following activities? Why?

• An undergraduate student and part-time test proctor administers the Miller Analogies Test (MAT) to a group of students in the university's counseling center.

• A man suffers neurological loss caused by an on-the-job accident that he claims was the result of the negligence of his employer. A court refers the man to a neuropsychologist to evaluate the extent of the loss, if any. The neuropsychologist administers a battery of psychological tests and submits a written report of the findings to the court.

• A man suffers neurological loss caused by an on-the-job accident that he claims was the result of the negligence of his employer. A court refers the man to a neuropsychologist to evaluate the extent of the loss, if any. The neuropsychologist seeks out and obtains case study material in an effort to evaluate the man's neuropsychological intactness prior to the date of the accident. The neuropsychologist interviews the man with respect to observations made from the case study material, as well as related matters. A series of tests to determine the nature and extent of any impairment are administered, and a report of the findings is submitted to the court.

• An experimental psychologist devises and uses a "tongue taste dispenser" apparatus to investigate aspects of the perception of taste in humans. After experiencing each of ten different tastes, subjects are asked to describe verbally each of the taste sensations.

• A comparative psychologist uses the "tongue taste dispenser" to investigate taste perception in chimpanzees. After experiencing each of the ten different tastes, a group of trained raters rate each subject for positive or negative effect, as indicated by facial expression.

• A social psychologist studies the phenomenon of obedience to authority by means of an apparatus that leads research subjects to believe that they will dispense electric shocks to other research subjects upon the experimenter's commands.

• A psychologist exploring alternative definitions of "intelligence" studies the "street smarts" of adolescent subjects by means of in-school, in-home, and on-the-street observation and evaluation of subjects' interactions.

• A personality psychologist seeks an answer to the question "Do people with eating disorders have distorted images of their body?" by studying a sample of patients who have eating disorders and a matched sample of subjects who do not. The methodology of the study calls for the administration of paper-and-pencil tests of body image distortion, as well as interviews with family members, friends, and other associates of the subjects.

• A personnel psychologist evaluates a candidate's suitability for a position as the manager of a multimillion-dollar mutual fund by interviewing the candidate, evaluating the candidate's employment history and record and letters of reference, and reviewing the candidate's record of civic involvement and recreational interests.

• An auto manufacturer pondering whether to name its latest model car "Exacta" refers this question to a consumer psychologist. The consumer psychologist administers a specially devised series of tests to a sample of people who have expressed interest in purchasing a car within the next month. This series is made up of a word-association test (subjects are asked to say the first thing that comes into their mind when they hear the word "Exacta" as well as other automobile-related words), figure drawings (people are asked to draw and then explain the picture of the car they envision when they hear that the car is called an "Exacta"), and a picture/story-telling test in which they are asked to make up a story upon being exposed to pictures involving "Exacta" in various types of situations.

• A graduate research assistant proctors a computer administration of two tests: one that is a general measure of personality and another that surveys vocational interests. Immediately after the administration of the two tests, the computer scores the answer sheets and spews out a written narrative that summarizes the results, integrates and analyzes the findings from the two tests, and makes recommendations of possible vocational pursuits on the basis of the findings.

Although the semantic border between "testing" and "assessment" may appear clear, it can quickly become blurry, and people may differ as to whether some of the vignettes cited above illustrate instances of "psychological testing" or "psychological assessment."

EXERCISE 3
THE PROCESS OF ASSESSMENT

OBJECTIVE

To enhance understanding of the tools of the assessment process and the role of each of the parties in that process.

BACKGROUND

The tools of the assessment process include the following:

• the test
• the interview
• the case study
• behavioral observation, and
• others

The parties to the assessment process include the following:

- the test developer
- the test user, and
- the test taker

YOUR TASK

Suppose that you are an independent distributor for a company that produces natural herbs that are represented to help students study more effectively by lessening debilitating anxiety. For the sake of example, let's call this natural herb company "Cramway." As a Cramway representative who also happens to be interested in psychological measurement, you design a study to measure the effect the Cramway product has on students' anxiety. Your study design is of the pre/post variety; anxiety will be measured before beginning the Cramway program, and seven days after Cramway products have been ingested on the prescribed regimen. Now all you need is something to measure the construct of anxiety; something to measure how anxious a person characteristically is on any given day.[1]

1. Of the tools of assessment available to you, which one (or more) do you think you would use? Which wouldn't you use? Why?
2. From what you've read in your text so far, as well as drawing on your own opinions and beliefs, explain the rights and responsibilities of each of the parties in the assessment process with respect to your anxiety assessment project.
3. This question, if assigned by your instructor, will require a bit of research in the university library. Using reference books, periodicals, and related sources of information about (as well as reviews of) tests and measurement procedures, decide on your top three selections for use as a measure of anxiety in your Cramway study. Explain why you chose the instruments or procedures you did.

EXERCISE 4
THE INTERVIEWER/INTERVIEWEE INTERACTION

OBJECTIVE

To better understand how an interviewer's personality can influence the conduct of an interview.

_____

[1]Technically, the construct being referred to here is the *trait* of anxiety— this in contrast to the more transient *state* of anxiety.

BACKGROUND

Think of how various interviewers you have seen or heard on television or radio conduct their interviews; two interviews conducted with the exact same objectives in mind, sometimes even with much the same questions, might yield different data due to characteristics of the interviewer.

YOUR TASK

One student will volunteer to play an interviewee while another will volunteer to take on the role of any well-known celebrity interviewer. The more adept the latter student is at impersonating the celebrity, the more fun this exercise will be. Different teams of students, one playing the role of the celebrity interviewer, the other playing the role of the (student) interviewee will get up in front of the class and execute an interview. The interviewer's initial prompt to the interviewee will be "Tell me about the happiest time of your life," and follow-up questions will probe the who, what, where, and how of whatever is described. The role of the "audience" is to note the differences in the interviewer's style of interviewing.

If you're having difficulty thinking of the role of a celebrity you'd like to play, how about one of these: David Letterman, Ted Koppel, Bryant Gumble, Geraldo Rivera, Barbara Walters, Larry King, Joan Lunden, Phil Donahue, Oprah Winfrey, Peter Jennings, Dan Rather, Ricki Lake, Connie Chung, Montel Williams, or Jay Leno.

EXERCISE 5
BEHAVIORAL ASSESSMENT

OBJECTIVE

To enhance understanding of, and promote generative thinking about, behavioral assessment.

BACKGROUND

Deinstitutionalization and the placement of children and adult psychiatric patients into community-based facilities created a need for a means by which staff could monitor progress made in skills necessary for independent living. Behavioral checklists, such as the "Emptying Garbage" scale (Roth & Hermus, 1980, p. 89) in Figure 1-1, can provide such a means. For this scale, note that the behavior of taking out the garbage has been broken down into a series of individual behaviors. "Goes to garbage can" and "Takes full bag from garbage can" are two short-range behavior objectives that when both attained,

Figure 1-1

The Taking-Out-the-Garbage Checklist. Deinstitutionalization and the placement of children and adult psychiatric patients into community-based facilities created a need for behavioral checklists by which the facility staff gauges the progress of developmentally disabled individuals. Rudimentary skills necessary for independent living—such as taking out the garbage—are tracked via checklists such as the one below. This checklist came from the "Housekeeping Skills" section of a book of behavioral checklists, with other sections such as "Personal Management," "Kitchen Skills," "Street Safety," "Travel Training," "Leisure Skills," and "Community Skills." (Source: Roth & Hermus, 1980, p. 89)

BEHAVIORAL PROGRAMMING SCALE

Name of Client: Instructor: Date:

EMPTYING GARBAGE

LRO   SRO Behavior   Daily Recordings

		M	T	W	Th	Fri	Weekly total	Criteria met? (Yes = +, No = −)
1	**Removing Garbage**	░	░	░	░	░	░	
	A. Goes to garbage can.							
	B. Takes full bag from garbage can.							
2	**Disposing of Garbage**	░	░	░	░	░	░	
	C. Takes bag of garbage to trash can.							
	D. Opens trash can.							
	E. Places garbage in trash can.							
	F. Closes trash can.							
3	**Lining Can with New Bag**	░	░	░	░	░	░	
	G. Goes to closet.							
	H. Takes new garbage bag.							
	I. Takes bag to garbage can.							
	J. Places bag in can.							
	K. Pushes bag into can.							
	L. Overlaps bag top over can top.							

LRO = Long-range behavior objective
SRO = Short-range behavior objective
     Enter "1" through "7" in appropriate box to indicate client's level of skill. Criterion is met when a score of "7" is achieved four times out of five for two consecutive trial periods.

meet the long-range behavior objective of "Removing Garbage."

YOUR TASK

After studying the "Emptying Garbage" behavioral programming scale, create your own behavioral programming scale. Your scale should take some relatively simple behavior necessary for independent living, and then break it up into its component behaviors.

EXERCISE 6
GETTING INFORMATION ABOUT TESTS

OBJECTIVE

To experience firsthand what is involved in gathering information and making decisions about a psychological test.

BACKGROUND

Test catalogues, test manuals, test reviews, and published research on psychological tests can help prospective users make informed decisions regarding such instruments and procedures. To answer questions such as "Is this test appropriate for this use with this population?" test users need more than intuition; they need facts.

YOUR TASK

You are a psychologist employed in a university counseling center. The dean has decided that the university is going to build and operate a community child day-care center. The dean has placed you in charge of hiring all of the caretakers at the center. Further, the dean wonders aloud whether all serious candidates for jobs at the new center should be screened for psychopathology with a test called the Minnesota Multiphasic Personality Inventory-2 (MMPI-2). The dean asks you to report back with your written opinion regarding the pros and cons of using the MMPI-2 for this purpose.

1. What sources would you use to gather information to respond to the dean's mandate?
2. What questions would you hope to have answered in your sources about the MMPI-2?
3. What other types of tests or assessment procedures might you wish to include in the process of hiring day-care workers? Why?
4. Write your report to the dean.

REFERENCES

Beathard, R. (1994, June 26). Excited? Just remember metric. *The New York Times*, p. F11.

Hart, I. B. (1962). *The world of Leonardo da Vinci.* New York: Viking.

Roth, M. R., & Hermus, G. P. (1980). *Developmental plan handbook for community skills training* (2nd ed.). New York: Developmental Press.

THE 4-QUESTION CHALLENGE

In general, this self-administered test samples material from the beginning, middle, and end of each chapter in your textbook. The questions are very straightforward and in some instances represent verbatim excerpts from the book. This "Challenge" may help to serve as a rough gauge of how well you are attending to all of the material in each chapter.

After reading a chapter in your textbook, take the corresponding 4-Question Challenge. Give yourself 1 point for each correct answer. If all four items are answered correctly, your score will be 4. Do your best on these tests over the course of the term. Then note how your final grade in this course corresponds to your 4-Question Challenge average.

Here is your first 4-Question Challenge:

1. Which does not belong?
   (a) Henry
   (b) Geraldo
   (c) Byte
   (d) Carat
2. A television producer hires a director for a new show after viewing samples of the director's work on other television shows. Using the language of psychometrics, we could say that the director was hired on the basis of
   (a) a portfolio assessment
   (b) a behavioral assessment
   (c) a case study evaluation
   (d) an interview
3. Which is an assumption inherent in the assessment enterprise?
   (a) Various sources of error are part of the assessment process.
   (b) Computer assessment is superior to more traditional methods.
   (c) One source of information input is superior to multiple sources.
   (d) Future behavior predicts present or past behavior.
4. If you needed a current, unbiased evaluation of a well-known psychological test, which would be the best source to consult?
   (a) *Who's Who in Psychological Assessment?*
   (b) the test's published manual
   (c) *The Eleventh Mental Measurements Yearbook*
   (d) the test publisher's current catalogue

Chapter 2

Historical, Cultural, and Legal/Ethical Considerations

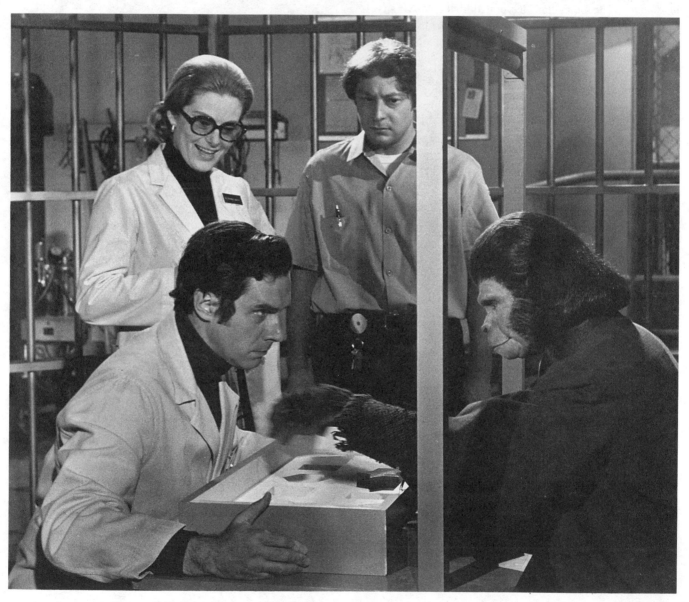

The work of Charles Darwin (1859) conferred new scientific respectability on experimentation with animals—but not quite this much respectability.

Outline for Chapter 2 of Cohen et al. (1996)
HISTORICAL, CULTURAL, AND LEGAL/ETHICAL CONSIDERATIONS

An Historical Perspective
  Antiquity to the Nineteenth Century
  The Nineteenth Century
  The Twentieth Century
    The measurement of intelligence
    The measurement of personality
    Measurement in various settings

Culture and Assessment
  Verbal Communication
  Non-verbal Communication
  Evaluative Standards

Legal/Ethical Considerations
  The Concerns of the Public
  The Concerns of the Profession
    Test-user qualifications
    Testing people with disabilities
    Computerized test administration, scoring, and interpretation
  The Rights of Testtakers
    The right of informed consent to testing
    The right to be informed of test findings
    The right to have the least stigmatizing label
    The right to have findings held confidential
  Psychological Tests in the Courtroom

CLOSE-UP:
  Tests, Assessment, and Culture

EVERYDAY PSYCHOMETRICS:
  Test Use, Base Rates, and Jury Impressions

EXERCISE 7
PSYCHOLOGICAL TESTING AND ASSESSMENT IN HISTORICAL PERSPECTIVE

OBJECTIVE

To enhance understanding of enterprise of psychological testing in historical perspective.

BACKGROUND

Since antiquity there has been, as Tyler (1965, p. 3) put it, "a need for some way of organizing or systematizing the many-faceted complexity of individual differences." Through the years that societal need may have manifested itself in questions as diverse as "Who is best qualified for this task?" "Who is a witch?" and "Who shall be placed in a special class?"

YOUR TASK

1. (a) How might psychological tests be brought to bear on three current problems or issues that you hear or read about in the media?
   (b) How might analogous or similar questions or issues have manifested themselves at various times in history—ancient times, the "Dark Ages," and the Renaissance—and how might society in those times have addressed them?
   (c) How might analogous or similar questions or issues manifest themselves in primitive societies today and how might those societies address them?
2. This is another one of those questions that if assigned, will—unless you're a walking storehouse of historical facts—necessitate a trip to the library.

If, in answering Part 1 of this exercise, a question you raised pertained to the measurement of school children's intelligence, you may know that people such as Alfred Binet, Lewis M. Terman, and Maud A. Merrill are some of the historic personages who have concerned themselves with similar questions. If you raised a question about the emotional fitness of military recruits, you may know that psychologist Robert Sessions Woodworth dealt with just that issue during the First World War. Your task in this library assignment is to select a historical figure who raised a question similar to one of the five that you listed, and complete a brief biography on that individual. While keeping it brief, make certain your biography includes at least a little detail on how the individual approached and dealt with the question of interest.

EXERCISE 8
THE COHEN CHICKEN SOUP ESSAY

OBJECTIVE

To provide a firsthand experience with the multicultural nature of contemporary society, and illustrate the need for cultural sensitivity in test development.

BACKGROUND

There are almost as many recipes for chicken soup as there are ethnic backgrounds. People from different Asian cultures may like to season their soup with soy sauce or curry. For many people from Arabic cultures, fresh lemon juice is an indispensable ingredient. Which recipe for chicken soup is best? It is all a matter of personal preference and taste. If you were the judge in an international chicken soup tasting contest, you might choose the variety of soup that tasted most like the one you have traditionally been served. Then again, you might go for some wildly different entry from another culture.

YOUR TASK

Except for a panel of three students acting as judges, the entire class, or small groups within it, will hold a "Chicken Soup Challenge." Each participant will write down his or her recipe for chicken soup. Vegetarians may take an alternate form of this test by committing to writing their best recipe for vegetable soup. From all of the recipes, the panel of judges will select the best soup recipe. A spokesperson for the judging panel will explain why the winning recipe won. Then it's time for a debate between the judges and the rest of the participants—who may very well question why their recipe submission did not win top honors. The task for everyone will then be to come up with a set of culturally sensitive rules for judging essays in future contests. For the purposes of illustration, here is the recipe for Dr. Cohen's Chicken Surprise*:

Ingredients
3 pound boiler-fryer chicken
2 quarts cold water
2 celery stalks with leaves (cut up)
2 carrots (cut up)
1 leek (cut up)
1 small onion (cut up)
1 sprig parsley
1 teaspoon salt (optional)

---

*It is always a surprise to me when this soup comes out tasting the same way twice.

Place whole chicken, including giblets (except liver), and all other ingredients in a very large pot. [Reminder based on my own culinary experience: Don't forget to remove the wax paper envelope with the giblets from inside the chicken!] Heat to boiling, remove foam, and then reduce heat. Simmer for about $1\frac{1}{2}$ hours or until meat parts easily from bone. Remove meat from bones and skin, and place in separate container. Cover soup in a container and refrigerate for at least 12 hours. Skim congealed fat from soup prior to reheating, and add chicken.

EXERCISE 9
THE NONVERBAL INTERVIEW

OBJECTIVE

To sensitize students to the role of nonverbal factors in an interview.

BACKGROUND

Many nonverbal behaviors "speak" even "louder" than spoken words about what an interviewee may be thinking or feeling. For example, sweaty palms may betray anxiety as might hyperventilation.

YOUR TASK

Students will form teams of two, with one student playing the role of the interviewer and the other interviewee. The students will role-play any interviewer-interviewee they care to attempt (for example, psychologist-patient, news reporter-president, etc.) and work together to prepare in advance a list of a half-dozen or so interview questions. The questions should lend themselves to nonverbal as well as verbal responses. The team should also prepare in advance a list of the nonverbal answers that the interviewee will be trying to convey in response to each of the questions. The nonverbal response may be the same or different from the verbalized one. Volunteer interviewer-interviewee teams will perform their interviews before the entire class. After each performance, the task for the rest of the class will be to guess the nonverbal response to each of the questions. After all of the interviews, a discussion on the role of nonverbal behavior during the interview will follow.

EXERCISE 10
GUIDELINES FOR USING PSYCHOLOGICAL TESTS

OBJECTIVE

To better appreciate the concerns of psychologists, educators, and others with responsibility for developing, selecting, administering, scoring, and interpreting psychological tests.

BACKGROUND

The concern of the American Psychological Association (APA) with respect to the use of psychological tests dates at least as far back to 1895, the year the infant APA organized its first committee on mental measurement. Since that time, various guidelines regarding tests and testing have been published in numerous APA publications including *Standards for Educational and Psychological Testing*.

YOUR TASK

1. Solely from what you know now, list the guidelines that you feel the profession should be addressing with respect to all aspects of tests and testing. Include guidelines with respect to the following areas:
   (a) test development and construction;
   (b) the publication of tests and accompanying technical manuals;
   (c) administration of tests;
   (d) scoring of tests;
   (e) interpretation of tests;
   (f) the use of tests in specific contexts such as clinical, educational, counseling, and employment testing;
   (g) the testing of linguistic minorities; and
   (h) the testing of people who have disabling conditions.
2. Write down your responses to each of the questions above. You may wish to save your answers at this stage in your learning about psychological testing and then compare your responses to these same questions as you near completion of the course. Should your responses to each of these questions be the same or very similar at both stages of the proposed pre/post design, it's a good bet that either *(a)* or *(b)* below are true:
   (a) You exhibit a keen acumen for the field of psychological testing; you were aware of many of the issues in the field even at the initial stages of your measurement course.

(b) You were not very aware of the issues in the field of psychological testing in the initial stages of your measurement course, and you weren't that much ahead of the game by the end of the course.

Of course if your responses are *not* the same or similar at both stages of the pre/post design, then a third alternative *(c)* may be applicable (particularly if your responses are demonstrative of a growing sophistication with the field):

(c) You have benefited from this course in ways that you now can't even anticipate, enriched your fund of information about tests and the process of testing, and made everyone around you (including your instructor) very proud.

EXERCISE 11
THE TEST PURCHASER QUALIFICATION FORM

OBJECTIVE

To sensitize students to the position of test publishers and other distributors of professional psychological tests.

BACKGROUND

In recent years, test publishing companies have voluntarily begun to make mandatory the completion of a test purchaser qualification form as a condition of the sale of certain tests. Currently, however, there is no one uniform test purchase form.

YOUR TASK

Design a "Uniform Psychological Test Purchase Qualification Form" to be used by all publishers of psychological tests. *Hint*: At a minimum, you will want to include on your form information about the prospective purchaser's education, licensure/certification, professional association memberships, and education, training, and experience with regard to testing and assessment. You may require the purchaser to make a statement regarding the intended use of the psychological test. After you have completed the form, write a brief message to the prospective purchaser explaining the reasons you require such information prior to selling the test.

EXERCISE 12
A LEGAL/ETHICAL ROUNDTABLE

OBJECTIVE

To provide a forum for the debate of various ethical and legal issues attendant to the professional practice of psychological testing.

BACKGROUND

Professionals in the field of psychology are presently grappling with a number of questions and issues regarding the use of psychological tests—questions and issues that will ultimately impact on (if not shape the way) psychological testing is carried out in the future. Some of the topics under debate are listed below.

YOUR TASK

This exercise is an oral exercise, an in-class "roundtable." And, in the spirit of a roundtable, begin by moving the furniture so that all of your chairs form a large circle. If your classroom happens to be one of those that is equipped with fixed-position chairs and desks please do not attempt to execute the previous instruction.

Imagine now that you are all members of the State Board for Psychology and that you have assembled to come to some resolution regarding some outstanding issues. Your instructor is the chair of the committee, and he or she will read the questions below aloud and then ask follow-up questions as she or he deems necessary. Everyone in the class—everyone on the board, that is—should be given the opportunity to be heard on each one of the issues before the board. For this reason, the board chair may elect to select one board member to answer the question posed, and then, moving in clockwise fashion, listen to what, if anything, other board members have to add.

- Minimally, what information should be contained in a test manual?
- What are the minimal requirements for standardizing a standardized test?
- Who should be allowed to purchase psychological tests? Why?
- Who should be allowed to use psychological tests? Why?
- How should rules regarding the purchase and/or use of psychological tests be enforced?
- What procedures in administering, scoring, and interpreting tests should be followed when testing people with disabling conditions?

- What procedures in administering, scoring, and interpreting tests should be followed when testing culturally or linguistically different people?
- What rights should be listed under the "Test Taker's Bill of Rights"? Why?

EXERCISE 13
ANOTHER LEGAL/ETHICAL ROUNDTABLE

OBJECTIVE

Continue the discussion of issues related to the practice of psychological testing by focusing here on cases of alleged malpractice.

BACKGROUND

Below is a sampling of actual legal cases as summarized in *Malpractice: A Guide for Mental Health Professionals* (Cohen, 1979).

YOUR TASK

Continuing the roundtable discussion as described in the previous exercise, one participant will read aloud one of the case summaries below. Immediately after each case is read, discuss in round-robin fashion some of the legal or ethical issues that you believe are important with respect to the case. What are the possible implications of these decisions for the practice of psychological testing?

TARASOFF V. REGENTS OF UNIVERSITY OF CALIFORNIA
118 Cal. Rptr. 129; 529 P.2d 553 (California, 1974)*

Tatiana Tarasoff was murdered by Prosenjit Poddar. Poddar had been in therapy with psychologist Dr. Lawrence Moore at the Cowell Memorial Hospital of the University of California at Berkeley. Poddar had made known to Moore his intention to kill an unnamed girl two months prior to the murder. After conferring with psychiatrists Gold and Yandell, Moore had written a letter to campus police chief William Beall requesting the assistance of the police department in securing Poddar's confinement. Dr. Harvey Powelson, the chief of the department of psychiatry at the hospital, asked Beall to return Moore's letter and

directed that all copies of the letter and Moore's other notes on the case be destroyed. Powelson also "ordered no action to place Prosenjit Poddar in seventy-two-hour treatment and evaluation facility." After Tatiana was murdered, her parents brought suit against Doctors Moore, Powelson, Gold, and Yandell, Police Chief Beall, four campus police officers, and the Regents of the University of California as the employer of all of the other defendants.

The Supreme Court of California ruled that a psychotherapist has a duty to warn endangered third parties of their peril. The court recognized that many therapy patients make idle threats, and it acknowledged the need for privacy in therapist/patient communications. However, it ruled that screening the idle from the genuine threats was a matter of professional judgment and that the public interest superseded the individual patient's interest under certain conditions. It said:

First, defendants point out that although therapy patients often express thoughts of violence, they rarely carry out these ideas. Indeed the open and confidential character of psychotherapeutic dialogue encourages patients to voice such thoughts, not as a device to reveal hidden danger, but as part of the process of therapy. Certainly a therapist should not be encouraged routinely to reveal such threats to acquaintances of the patient; such disclosures could seriously disrupt the patient's relationship with his therapist and with the persons threatened. In singling out those few patients whose threats of violence present a serious danger and in weighing against this danger the harm to the patient that might result from revelation, the psychotherapist renders a decision involving a high order of expertise and judgment.

[5] The judgment of the therapist, however, is no more delicate or demanding than the judgment which doctors and professionals must regularly render under accepted rules of responsibility. A professional person is required only to exercise "that reasonable degree of skill, knowledge, and care ordinarily possessed and exercised by members of [his] profession under similar circumstances." (Bardessono v. Michels (1970) 3 Cal.3d 780, 788, 91 Cal. Rptr. 760, 764, 478 P.2d 480, 484.) As a specialist, the psychotherapist, whether doctor or psychologist, would also be "held to that standard of learning and skill normally possessed by such specialist in the same or similar locality under the same or similar circumstances." (Quintal v. Laurel Grove Hospital (1964) 62 Cal.2d 154, 159–160, 41 Cal.Rptr. 577, 580, 397 P.2d 161, 164.) But within that broad range in which professional opinion and judgment may differ respecting the proper course of action, the psychotherapist is free to exercise his own best judgment free from liability; proof, aided by hindsight, that he judged wrongly is insufficient to establish liability.

In other words, the fact that a decision calls for considerable expert skill and judgment means, in effect, that it be tested by a standard of care which takes account of those circumstances; the standard

---

*The complete text of the significant decision in this case, including the majority opinion by Justice Tobriner and a dissenting opinion by Justice Clark, appears in the appendix to Cohen (1979). Also included in the appendix is an excerpt from Dr. Moore's letter to Police Chief Beall.

used in measuring professional malpractice does so. But whatever difficulties the courts may encounter in evaluating the expert judgments of other professions, those difficulties cannot justify total exoneration from liability.

Second, defendants argue that free and open communication is essential to psychotherapy (see In re Lifschutz (1970) 2 Cal.3d 415, 431–432, 85 Cal.Rptr. 829, 467 P.2d 557); that "Unless a patient . . . is assured that . . . information [revealed by him] can and will be held in utmost confidence, he will be reluctant to make the full disclosure upon which diagnosis and treatment . . . depends." (Sen. Committee on the Judiciary, comments on Evid. Code, §1014.) The giving of a warning, defendants contend, constitutes a breach of trust which entails the revelation of confidential communications.

We recognize the public interest in supporting effective treatment of mental illness and in protecting the rights of patients to privacy (see In re Lifschutz, *supra*, 2 Cal.3d at p. 432, 85 Cal.Rptr. 829, 467 P.2d 557), and the consequent public importance of safeguarding the confidential character of psychotherapeutic communication. Against this interest, however, we must weigh the public interest in safety from violent assault. The Legislature has undertaken the difficult task of balancing the countervailing concerns. In Evidence Code section 1014, it established a broad rule of privilege to protect confidential communications between patient and psychotherapist. In Evidence Code section 1024, however, the Legislature created a specific and limited exception to the psychotherapist-patient privilege: "There is no privilege . . . if the psychotherapist has reasonable cause to believe that the patient is in such mental or emotional condition as to be dangerous to himself or to the person or property of another and that disclosure of the communication is necessary to prevent the threatened danger."

[6] The revelation of a communication under the above circumstances is not a breach of trust or a violation of professional ethics; as stated in the Principles of Medical Ethics of the American Medical Association (1957) section 9; "A physician may not reveal the confidences entrusted to him in the course of medical attendance . . . *unless he is required to do so by law or unless it becomes necessary in order to protect the welfare of the individual or of the community*." (Emphasis added.) We conclude that the public policy favoring protection of the confidential character of patient-psychotherapist communications must yield in instances in which disclosure is essential to avert danger to others. The protective privilege ends where the public peril begins.

CLARK V. GERACI
29 Misc.2d 791; 208 N.Y.S.2d 564 (New York, 1960)

The plaintiff in this case was a civilian who worked for the Air Force as an accountant. He had taken off time from work owing to respiratory difficulties that stemmed from his alcoholism. In response to an official request for information concerning the causes of the plaintiff's absences, the defendant psychiatrist revealed that the plaintiff had a drinking problem (despite the fact that the plaintiff had explicitly objected to the revelation of that information). The plaintiff was subsequently fired from his job, and he brought suit against the doctor for breach of confidentiality.

The court recognized that breach of doctor-patient confidentiality is an actionable offense, but it declined to find in favor of the plaintiff in this case. The court held that the plaintiff had probably lost his job not because of the mere revelation of confidential material, but because of repeated absences from work. Furthermore, the court held the doctor's duty to the United States government to be above the doctor's duty to the patient.

BERRY V. MOENCH
8 Utah 2d 191; 331 P.2d 814; 73 A.L.R.2d 315 (Utah, 1958)

Berry was a patient seen by Dr. Moench, a psychiatrist, seven years prior to this litigation. Berry was about to remarry, and the father of his bride-to-be asked a Dr. Hellewell to write Dr. Moench to find out information about Berry. Hellewell wrote to Moench, specifically stating that the reasons he was soliciting information about Berry was to advise the father of the prospective bride-to-be. Dr. Moench's letter to Hellewell said that Berry had been diagnosed as "manic depressive depression in a psychopathic personality." Moench went on to offer the following advice in his letter:

> My suggestion to the infatuated girl would be to run as fast and as far as she possibly could in any direction away from him. . . . Of course, if he doesn't marry her, he will marry someone else and make life hell for that person.

Berry brought suit against Moench for breach of confidentiality. The court found in favor of the defendant, holding that the parents of the woman Berry was dating were concerned only with the welfare of their daughter and that that concern was a sufficient interest to legally protect. The court wrote that, according to generally accepted standards of decent conduct, "the privilege exists if the recipient has the type of interest in the matter, and the publisher stands in such a relation to him that it would reasonably be considered the duty of the publisher to give the information."

SCHWARTZ V. THIELE
242 Cal. App. 2d 799; 51 Cal. Rptr. 767 (California, 1966)

Judith Schwartz's suit against psychiatrist David A. Thiele alleged that they were strangers when they met in a restaurant parking lot about 9:30 in the morning. As stated in the court record, Judith and her sister "after having had breakfast at a restaurant in the city of Los Angeles, were walking to her automobile (when) the defendant, a total stranger to the plaintiff, and without her consent, purported to make an examination of plaintiff as to her mental illness." Exactly why Thiele had occasion to "examine" Schwartz or what, in fact, transpired in the parking lot is not clear from the court record:

> In the case at the bench, so far as it may be determined from the pleading, the defendant had some contact with the plaintiff, the exact nature of which is not disclosed.

After that contact, Thiele wrote a letter to the psychiatric department of the Superior Court of Los Angeles County stating that Schwartz was mentally ill and that she was likely to injure herself or others if not immediately hospitalized. After receiving the letter, a judge of the superior court signed an order appointing a physician to examine Schwartz. The court-appointed physician tried, through Schwartz's lawyer, to arrange an appointment for an examination. However, Schwartz was examined by her own physician, who did not find her to be mentally ill.

Schwartz's suit against Thiele claimed $100,000 in damages. She alleged that her right of privacy had been invaded and as a consequence of that invasion she had suffered "great mental pain and physical suffering, humiliation, annoyance, and mortification" and she had been exposed to "public ridicule and disgrace."

The court found in favor of the defendant, holding him immune from liability and noting that there was no publication of the letter. The court further stated:

> The restraint and treatment of persons who are mentally ill is a matter of public concern. If a person in good faith and for probable cause makes a written statement to an agency charged with the duty of enforcement of the law, designed to give such agency information upon which it can conduct an investigation, such a communication is not an invasion of the right of privacy of the person who is the subject of the communication.

Charouleau v. Charity Hospital of New Orleans
319 So.2d 464 (Louisiana, 1975)

A patient was seen in a public hospital emergency room by a physician who referred the case to psychiatry. While a psychiatric resident was interviewing the patient, the patient took a revolver from her purse and pointed it at the resident. The resident took the gun from the woman, determined it was unloaded, and handed it back to the woman "to establish a rapport." The woman told the resident that she had previously been admitted to this hospital and that she was seeking admission now to rid herself of a drug abuse problem. The resident told the patient that she would not be committed to an institution against her will, and he proceeded within the patient's view to write a note stating that it was his opinion that the woman could benefit from prolonged hospitalization. The resident did not review the patient's chart, which could have been obtained from the records room, and he did not instruct anyone to keep an eye on the patient. He escorted her to the admission desk and instructed her to sit down and wait for the clerk to return. As well as can be determined, the patient took her chart sometime after the resident dropped her off, straying from the admission area. The patient was found dead the following morning in a hospital toilet, from a self-inflicted bullet wound.

The patient's husband brought suit against the resident and the hospital. The case against the resident was settled out of court, but the hospital contended that it could not be held legally culpable as the proximate cause of the patient's death. The plaintiff charged that the hospital negligently had a resident instead of a psychiatrist in the emergency room, that it did not have a procedure for direct admission into psychiatry, that it allowed psychiatric patients to stray from admission, that it did not prevent patients from seeing their own charts, and that it did not have a policy of reviewing the past records of potentially suicidal patients.

The court did not find the defendant hospital culpable, because as a matter of course previous records are not examined in emergency-room treatment, in order to expedite dispositions. The court found the admissions procedure used by the defendant hospital to be much the same as in comparable hospitals and did not find compelling evidence that the hospital was the proximate cause of the patient's death.

In Re Sterilization of Moore
221 S.E.2d 307 (North Carolina, 1976)

A director of a county's Department of Social Services requested the court to order authorization for the sterilization of a minor who, according to a psychological report, had a full scale IQ of under 40. The constitutionality of the order was challenged. Citing the opinion of the United States Supreme Court in *Buck v. Bell* (47 S.Ct. 584), the Supreme Court of North Carolina held that: A state does have the right to sterilize a retarded or insane person provided that the sterilization is not prescribed as punishment, the policy is applied equally to all persons, and notice and hearing are provided; according to mental health laws, the interest of the unborn child is sufficient to warrant the sterilization of a retarded individual; and, further, the People also have the right to prevent the procreation of children who will become a burden on the State.

REFERENCES

Cohen, R. J. (1979). *Malpractice: A guide for mental health professionals.* New York: The Free Press.

Darwin, C. (1859). *On the origin of species by means of natural selection.* London: Murray.

Standards for educational and psychological testing. (1985). Washington, DC: American Psychological Association.

Tyler, L. E. (1965). *The psychology of human differences.* (3rd ed.). New York: Appleton-Century-Crofts.

THE 4-QUESTION CHALLENGE

1. The historical significance of competitive examinations in China during the Chan dynasty has to do with
   (a) cross-cultural and longstanding difficulties in hiring reliable postal workers.
   (b) the perpetuation of nepotism in hiring for civil service positions.
   (c) evidence of a reverse discrimination hiring policy in existence since 1115 B.C.
   (d) evidence of concern for psychometric principles thousands of years ago.

2. Cultural sensitivity in test development is manifested by
   (a) panels of experts who review test items for discriminatory content.
   (b) reliability studies exploring differences in test score as a function of mode of administration.
   (c) validity studies exploring differences in test score as a function of mode of administration.
   (d) All of the above

3. The Code of Fair Testing
   (a) grew out of the work of a 1992 Congressional subcommittee on test publisher practices.
   (b) specifies obligations of test developers and test users with regard to various areas.
   (c) specifies obligations of testtakers under statutory truth-in-testing laws.
   (d) All of the above

4. According to the *Standards,* all of the following are rights of testtakers except:
   (a) the right not to have privacy invaded
   (b) the right to be informed of test findings
   (c) the right to a nonstigmatizing diagnosis
   (d) the right of informed consent to testing

THE SCIENCE
OF PSYCHOLOGICAL
MEASUREMENT

Chapter 3

A Statistics Refresher

It's Enough to Make You Faint!

Some people are overwhelmed by the thought of working with numbers. But numbers are not only a part of the 1926 Fritz Lang film Metropolis, *they're also a part of the everyday world of psychological assessment; the key to not being overwhelmed begins with a mastery of some basic statistical concepts.*

Outline for Chapter 3 of Cohen et al. (1996)
A STATISTICS REFRESHER

Scales of Measurement
Nominal Scales
Ordinal Scales
Interval Scales
Ratio Scales
Measurement Scales in Psychology

Describing Data
Frequency Distributions
Measures of Central Tendency
The arithmetic mean
The median
The mode
Measures of Variability
The range
The interquartile and semi-interquartile range
The average deviation
The standard deviation and variance
Skewness
Kurtosis

The Normal Curve
Area Under the Normal Curve

Standard Scores
z Scores
T Scores
Other Standard Scores
Normalized standard scores

CLOSE-UP:
Error of Measurement and the True Score Model

EVERYDAY PSYCHOMETRICS:
The Normal Curve and Psychological Tests

EXERCISE 14
SCALES OF MEASUREMENT IN EVERYDAY LIFE

OBJECTIVE

To gain greater familiarity with various scales of measurement by generating some original examples.

BACKGROUND

In your textbook, scales of measurement are discussed in the context of psychological testing and assessment. However, examples of nominal, ordinal, interval, and ratio scales can be found in everyday life. Here are some examples:

Nominal scales. Perhaps the most common example of nominal measurement is the number printed on a football jersey. The number is there for the purpose of identifying the player. It cannot meaningfully be added to, subtracted from, or multiplied or divided by any other number.

Ordinal scales. Have you ever been to a wine tasting and been asked to rank order various wines from least favored to most favored? If so, you have had firsthand experience with ordinal measurement. Although rank-ordering is permitted with ordinal measurement, remember that no implication is made regarding how much greater one ranking is than another. It would be statistically incorrect to say that a wine ranked first was twice as good as the wine ranked second, three times as good as the wine ranked third, and so on. There is no absolute zero point in an ordinal scale; without individual units of measurement, zero is without meaning. All of the wines being ranked have some taste and no wine has absolutely no taste.

Interval scales. As with ordinal scales, interval scales contain no absolute zero point. As an illustration, consider the measurement of temperature. Zero degrees Fahrenheit is not indicative of the complete absence of temperature. Because there is no absolute zero point on the Fahrenheit scale, it would not be meaningful to make statements in terms of ratios. While we can say that the difference between 20 and 40 degrees Fahrenheit is the same as the number of degrees difference as 75 and 95 degrees Fahrenheit, we cannot accurately say that 40 degrees is twice as hot as 20 degrees.

Ratio scales. A ratio scale for measuring temperature is the Kelvin scale. Unlike the Fahrenheit or centigrade scales, the Kelvin scale has a true zero point. On the Kelvin scale, 0 degrees is the temperature at which molecular activity ceases. One can legitimately state that 20 degrees Kelvin is twice as warm (or half as cold) as 10 degrees Kelvin, because equal intervals exist between the numbers on the scale and the scale has a true zero point.

YOUR TASK

Provide additional examples of nominal, ordinal, interval, and ratio measurement from everyday life. Explain why each of your examples qualifies as that type of measurement. If you cannot think of an everyday example for any particular scale of measurement, make up your own scale.

EXERCISE 15
REVIEWING DESCRIPTIVE STATISTICS

OBJECTIVE

To obtain firsthand experience in describing a distribution of data using descriptive statistics.

BACKGROUND

Like other exercises in this book, this one contains step-by-step illustrations designed to explain the calculation of selected statistics typically used in the fields of psychological and educational measurement. In general, a model of calculations is provided and it is then up to you to calculate those same statistics, in the same way, using similar data.

In Table 3-1 you will find raw scores on a hypothetical 100-item, multiple-choice test where one point was awarded for each correct answer and all scores could range from 0 (none correct) to 100 (all correct). The scores for the 25 students in the class are also illustrated in the form of a frequency distribution (Table 3-2), a grouped frequency distribution (Table 3-3), a frequency polygon (Figure 3-1), a histogram (Figure 3-2), and a bar graph (Figure 3-3)—one in which it has been assumed for the purpose of illustration that a raw score of 65 or higher had been arbitrarily set in advance to be a passing grade.

MEASURES OF CENTRAL TENDENCY

Let's now calculate the arithmetic mean, the median, and the mode—the *measures of central tendency*—for this distribution of test scores.

The Mean

The *mean*, denoted by the symbol $\overline{X}$ (and pronounced "X bar") is equal to the sum of the observations (or test

Table 3-1

Data from Your Measurement Course Test

Student	Score (number correct)
Judy	78
Joe	67
David	69
Miriam	63
Valerie	85
Diane	72
Henry	92
Gertrude	67
Paula	94
Martha	62
Bill	61
Homer	44
Robert	66
Michael	87
Brandon	76
Mary	83
"Mousey"	42
Barbara	82
John	84
Donna	51
Uriah	69
Leroy	61
Ronald	96
Vinnie	73
Patty	79

Table 3-2

Frequency Distribution of Scores From Your Test

Score	f (frequency)
96	1
94	1
92	1
87	1
85	1
84	1
83	1
82	1
79	1
78	1
76	1
73	1
72	1
69	2
67	2
66	1
63	1
62	1
61	2
51	1
44	1
42	1

Table 3-3

A Grouped Frequency Distribution

Class Interval	Frequency
96–100	1
91–95	2
86–90	1
81–85	4
76–80	3
71–75	2
66–70	5
61–65	4
56–60	0
51–55	1
46–50	0
41–45	2

Figure 3-1

Data From Your Measurement Course in a Frequency Polygon

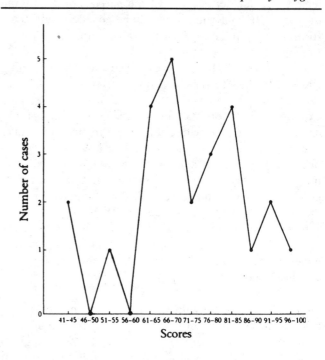

scores in this case) divided by the number of observations. Symbolically written, the formula for the mean is: $\overline{X} = \overline{\Sigma}X/n$ where the Greek uppercase sigma (Σ) represents "summation," X is a test score, and n is equal to the number of observations or test scores. An arithmetic mean can also be calculated from a frequency distribution. The formula for calculating the mean from grouped data is as follows:

$$\overline{X} = \frac{\Sigma fX}{n}$$

Figure 3-2

Data From Your Measurement Course in a Histogram

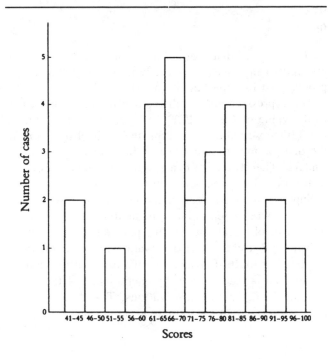

Figure 3-3

Data From Your Measurement Course in a Bar Graph

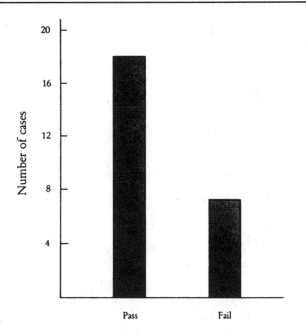

where *f* is the corresponding frequency of the occurrence of a score. The step-by-step process is as follows:

Step 1

List each of the observations—each test score, or *X* in this case—in the first column.

Step 2

List the corresponding frequency of each score in an adjacent column, thus creating a frequency distribution.

Step 3

Multiply each score by its corresponding frequency.

Step 4

Add the products obtained in Step 3 above—that is, add all of the *fX*'s.

Step 5

Divide the number (*n*) of measurements or scores—the total of the frequencies.

Inserting the test score data into the computation procedures listed for each of the steps listed above and the computation of the mean for the grouped data would look like this:

X	f	fX
96	1	1(96) = 96
94	1	1(94) = 94
92	1	1(92) = 92
87	1	1(87) = 87
85	1	1(85) = 85
84	1	1(84) = 84
83	1	1(83) = 83
82	1	1(82) = 82
79	1	1(79) = 79
78	1	1(78) = 78
76	1	1(76) = 76
73	1	1(73) = 73
72	1	1(72) = 72
69	2	2(69) = 138
67	2	2(67) = 134
66	1	1(66) = 66
63	1	1(63) = 63
62	1	1(62) = 62
61	2	2(61) = 122
51	1	1(51) = 51
44	1	1(44) = 44
42	1	1(42) = 42
	$\Sigma f = 25$	$\Sigma fX = 1803$

$$\overline{X} = \frac{1803}{25} = 72.12$$

The Median

The *median* is the middle score in a distribution and the simplest way of determining its value in a distribution of 25 scores would entail listing the scores in ascending (or descending) magnitude and then locating the center:

96

94

92

87

85

84
83
82
79
78
76
73
72
69
69
67
67
66
63
62
61
61
51
44
42

The *median* is the middle score in a distribution, and the by way of a 2-step process: (1) listing all of the data (including repeating scores) in order of magnitude—in increasing or decreasing order, and (2) finding the value of the middle observation. For an odd number of observations, the median is the value of the $([n + 1]/2)^{th}$ observation.

In the present example, let's begin by arranging the data in increasing order of magnitude:

42
44
51
61
61
62
63
66
67
67
69
69
72
73
76
78
79
82
83
84
85

87
92
94
96

Having done that we can now solve for the median, referred to in some statistical writings as $\tilde{X}$ ("X tilde," pronounced like the "tilda" in "Matilda").

The expression above tells us that the median is equal to the value of $([n + 1]/2)^{th}$ observation or the value of the 13th observation. Counting the 13th observation in the distribution of scores we've been working with we find 72. Therefore, we can say that the median of this distribution is 72, or put another way, $\tilde{X} = 72$.

Suppose that instead of an odd number of observations, our task was to calculate the median from an even number of observations. For the purposes of illustration, let's add 97 to the list of observations, thereby raising n in this case to 26. For an even number of observations, the median is equal to the arithmetic mean of the $(n/2)^{th}$ and the $[(n/2) + 1]^{th}$ observations. The data listed in increasing order of magnitude are as follows:

42
44
51
61
61
62
63
66
67
67
69
69
72
73
76
78
79
82
83
84
85
87
92
94
96
97

The value of the $(n/2)^{th}$ observation is the value of the $(26/2)^{th}$ or 13th observation. The 13th observation is equal to 72.

The value of the $[(n/2) + 1]^{th}$ observation is the value of the $[(26/2) + 1]^{th}$ or 14th observation. Here, the 14th observation is equal to 73.

We can now solve for the value of the median as follows:

$$\tilde{X} = \frac{72 + 73}{2} = 72.5$$

Just before moving on from our discussion of the median to a discussion of another measure of central tendency, the mode, let's take note of the case where there are repeated scores at the median. For example, suppose the 14th observation in the data above was not 73 but 72. The $(n/2)^{th}$ or 13th observation would still be 72. However, the $[(n/2) + 1]^{th}$ or 14th observation is now also 72 (instead of 73). The solution for the median in this instance would be as follows:

$$\tilde{X} = \frac{72 + 72}{2} = 72$$

The Mode

The *mode* is the most frequently occurring score in a distribution of scores. In the distribution of measurement test scores we've been using, there is no *one* score that is *the* most frequently occurring score. Three scores (69, 67, and 61) are "the most frequently occurring." In this instance then, we would say that the distribution is *trimodal*; it has three modes.

MEASURES OF VARIABILITY

Variability is an indication of how scores in a distribution are scattered or dispersed. Statistics that describe the amount of variation include the range, the interquartile range, the semi-interquartile range, the standard deviation, and the variance.

The Range

The *range* of a distribution is equal to the difference between the highest and lowest scores. In the present example, it is equal to the difference between the highest (96) and lowest (42) scores, or 96 − 42. Performing the subtraction, we find the difference to be 54; we therefore say that the test scores in this distribution had a range of 54.

The Interquartile and Semi-interquartile Ranges

Conceptually, the calculation of an interquartile range entails the division of a distribution of observations—in the present example test scores—into four quarters so that 25% of the test scores fall into each of the quarters; the interquartile range (IR) is equal to the difference between

the score at the third quartile (Q_3) and the score at the first quartile (Q_1). The *semi*-interquartile range is simply the IR divided by 2.

Some calculation is necessary to determine the value of Q_1 and Q_3 so that IR can be determined. To calculate Q_3 we may use the following formula:

$$Q_3 = U_{ri} - \left[\left(\frac{C_{ri} - .75n}{f_{ri}} \right) (W_{ri}) \right]$$

U_{ri} is the upper real limit of the relevant interval
C_{ri} is the cumulative frequency of the relevant interval
f_{ri} is the frequency of the relevant interval
W_{ri} is the width of the relevant interval

Note that in this formula for the computation of the third quartile that .75 is a constant; this is so because we are computing the point at or below which 75% of the scores fall. The "relevant interval" is the first class interval where the cumulative frequency is greater than or equal to .75n—or in this case, greater than or equal to (.75)(25), or 18.75.

The calculation of Q_1 is similar to the calculation of Q_3 except that the constant in the expression np is .25 and not .75. This is because we are calculating the point at or below which 25% of the scores fall:

Table 3-4

Calculating an Interquartile Range (IR)

	Score	Frequency	Cumulative Frequency	
	96	1	24 + 1 = 25	
	94	1	23 + 1 = 24	
	92	1	22 + 1 = 23	
	87	1	21 + 1 = 22	
	85	1	20 + 1 = 21	
	84	1	19 + 1 = 19	
Q_3	81	1	18 + 1 = 19	Q_3
	82	1	17 + 1 = 18	
	79	1	16 + 1 = 17	
	78	1	15 + 1 = 16	
	76	1	14 + 1 = 15	
	73	1	13 + 1 = 14	
Q_2	72	1	12 + 1 = 13	Q_2
	69	2	10 + 2 = 12	
	67	2	8 + 2 = 10	
	66	1	7 + 1 = 8	
Q_1	63	1	6 + 1 = 7	Q_1
	62	1	5 + 1 = 6	
	61	2	3 + 2 = 5	
	51	1	2 + 1 = 3	
	44	1	1 + 1 = 2	
	42	1	1 + 0 = 1	

For Q_3 the relevant interval is the first class interval where the cumulative frequency is greater than or equal to .75n. In

Table 3-4 *Continued*

this example, the relevant interval is the first class interval where the cumulative frequency is greater than or equal to:

$$(.75)(25), \text{ or } 18.75.$$

Thus, the relevant interval is 83, when the cumulative frequency is 19.

For Q_1, the relevant interval is the first class interval where the cumulative frequency is greater than or equal to $.25n$. In this example, the relevant interval is the first class interval where the cumulative frequency is greater than or equal to:

$$(.25)(25), \text{ or } 6.25$$

Thus, the relevant interval is 63 when the cumulative frequency is 7.

The calculations for Q_3 and Q_1 are shown below:

$$Q_3 = 83.5 - \left[\left(\frac{19 - 18.75}{1}\right)(1)\right]$$

$$= 83.5 - [(.25)(1)]$$

$$Q_3 = 83.5 - .25 = 83.25$$

$$Q_1 = 63.5 - \left[\left(\frac{7 - 6.25}{1}\right)(1)\right]$$

$$= 63.5 - [(.75)(1)]$$

$$Q_1 = 63.5 - .75 = 62.75$$

Note: For Q_2, otherwise known as the median, the relevant interval is the first class interval where the cumulative frequency is greater than or equal to:

$$(.50)(25), \text{ or } 12.5.$$

Thus, the relevant interval is 72 where the cumulative frequency is 13:

$$Q_2 = 72.5 - \left[\left(\frac{13 - 12.5}{1}\right)(1)\right]$$

$$= 72.5 - [(.5)(1)]$$

$$Q_2 = 72.5 - .5 = 72$$

Knowing the value of Q_3 and Q_1 we can now solve for the value of IR in the present example:

$$IR = Q_3 - Q_1$$

$$IR = 83.25 - 62.75$$

$$IR = 20.5$$

What if we had used the distribution of test scores as they appear in Table 3-3 (instead of as they appear in Table 3-2)? Do you think Q_1, Q_2, and Q_3 would come out to be exactly the same? Now do the calculations; the answer may surprise you.

In essence, the interquartile range is a measure of variability that conveys information about the middle part of a distribution of scores—the scores between the 25th and 75th percentiles. In many test manuals, you may come across a reporting of the variability of scores not in terms of the interquartile range but rather in terms of the semi-interquartile range (one-half the interquartile range). The reporting of one-half the interquartile range is done to convey information about how far, on average, the 25th percentile lies from the median of the distribution,

Figure 3-4

A Quartered Distribution

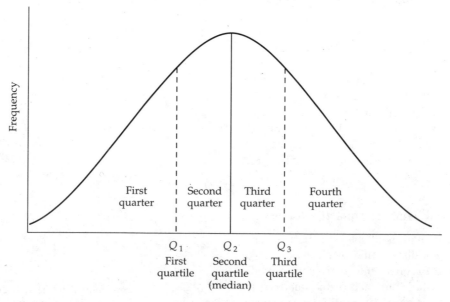

and how far, on average, the 75th percentile lies from the median of the distribution. The semi-interquartile range is perhaps used most frequently when data in the distribution of test scores are highly skewed.

The Average Deviation

The *average deviation* (AD) is equal to the sum of the deviation scores divided by the total number of scores. The formula for the AD is as follows:

$$AD = \frac{\Sigma|X - \overline{X}|}{n} = \frac{\Sigma|x|}{n}$$

where the lowercase italicized "x" signifies a scores's deviation from the mean (obtained by subtracting the mean from the score). The bars on each side of the *x* indicate that the number should be read as its absolute value—devoid of a positive or a negative sign (though positive for practical purposes). All of the deviation scores are then summed and divided by the total number of scores. In Table 3-5 we calculate the AD for the distribution of test scores we've been working with.

While the AD is used relatively rarely as a measure of variation, the computation of an AD provides a good conceptual introduction to a much more widely used

Table 3–5

Calculating an Average Deviation

X	X − $\overline{X}$	$\|X - \overline{X}\|$ or $\|x\|$
96	96 − 72.12 = 23.88	23.88
94	94 − 72.12 = 21.88	21.88
92	92 − 72.12 = 19.88	19.88
87	87 − 72.12 = 14.88	14.88
85	85 − 72.12 = 12.88	12.88
84	84 − 72.12 = 11.88	11.88
83	83 − 72.12 = 10.88	10.88
82	82 − 72.12 = 9.88	9.88
79	79 − 72.12 = 6.88	6.88
78	78 − 72.12 = 5.88	5.88
76	76 − 72.12 = 3.88	3.88
73	73 − 72.12 = .88	.88
72	72 − 72.12 = − .12	.12
69	69 − 72.12 = − 3.12	3.12
69	69 − 72.12 = − 3.12	3.12
67	67 − 72.12 = − 5.12	5.12
67	67 − 72.12 = − 5.12	5.12
66	66 − 72.12 = − 6.12	6.12
63	63 − 72.12 = − 9.12	9.12
62	62 − 72.12 = −10.12	10.12
61	61 − 72.12 = −11.12	11.12
61	61 − 72.12 = −11.12	11.12
51	51 − 72.12 = −21.12	21.12
44	44 − 72.12 = −28.12	28.12
42	42 − 72.12 = −30.12	30.12

$$\Sigma = 287.12 \quad AD = \frac{287.12}{25}$$
$$= 11.4848$$

measure of variability, the last one we will discuss in this chapter. . . .

The Standard Deviation

The *standard deviation* (SD) is a measure of variability that is equal to the square root of the average squared deviations about the mean. Stated another way, the SD is equal to the square root of the variance. The *variance* is equal to the arithmetic mean of the squares of the differences between the scores in a distribution and their mean.

Step-by-step general instructions for calculating the variance and a SD are followed by a step-by-step illustration of the calculation of the variance and the SD for the data in the distribution of the test scores we've been working with. Two methods referred to as "the deviation score formula" and the "raw score formula" are presented.

Step-by-Step Calculation of the Variance and Standard Deviation: The Deviation Score Formula

The deviation score formula is as follows. This formula requires the following six steps:

Step 1

Calculate the mean. $\qquad$ THE FORMULA $\overline{X} = \frac{\Sigma X}{n}$

Step 2

Calculate each deviation score. $\qquad (X - \overline{X})$

Step 3

Square each deviation score. $\qquad (X - \overline{X})^2$

Step 4

Sum the squared deviation scores. $\quad \Sigma(X - \overline{X})^2$

Step 5

Divide the sum of the squared deviations by the sample size. This measure, s^2, is the variance. $\qquad \frac{\Sigma(X - \overline{X})^2}{n}$

Step 6

Calculate the square root of the variance; the square root of s^2 is s, the standard deviation. $\qquad \sqrt{\frac{\Sigma(X - \overline{X})^2}{n}}$

Step-by-Step Calculation of the Variance and Standard Deviation: The Raw Score Formula

The raw score formula is as follows. This formula requires the following five steps.

Step 1

Square each raw score and sum them. $\qquad \Sigma X^2$

Step 2

Divide the summed raw scores by the number of raw scores. $\qquad \frac{\Sigma X^2}{n}$

Step 3

Calculate the mean of the raw scores and square it.

$$\left(\frac{\Sigma X}{n}\right)^2 = \overline{X}^2$$

Step 4

Subtract the squared mean from the quotient obtained in Step 2; this yields the variance.

$$\frac{\Sigma X^2}{n} - \overline{X}^2$$

Step 5

The square root of the variance is the standard deviation.

Refer to Table 3-6 for the actual calculations.

YOUR TASK

Collect data and then describe the data you've collected using descriptive statistics. The data you collect will be the height in inches of each of your classmates. List the names and heights—much as we listed the hypothetical measurement course scores and then do the following:

Table 3-6

Calculating the Standard Deviation Using Both the Raw Score and Deviation Score Formulas

				Calculations	
				Deviation Score Formula	Raw Score Formula
X	X^2	$X - \overline{X}$	$(X - \overline{X})^2$		
96	9216	23.88	570.2544	$\overline{X} = 72.12$	$\overline{X} = 72.12$
94	8836	21.88	478.7344	$\Sigma(X - \overline{X})^2 = 4972.64$	$\overline{X}^2 = (72.12)^2$
92	8464	19.88	395.2144		$= 5201.29$
87	7569	14.88	221.4144		
85	7225	12.88	165.8944	$\dfrac{\Sigma(X - \overline{X})^2}{n} = \dfrac{4972.64}{25}$	$\dfrac{\Sigma X^2}{n} = \dfrac{135005}{25}$
84	7056	11.88	141.1344		
83	6889	10.88	118.3744	$= 198.91$	$= 5400.2$
82	6724	9.88	97.6144		
79	6241	6.88	47.3344		
78	6084	5.88	34.5744	$\sqrt{198.91} = 14.10$	$\dfrac{\Sigma X^2}{n} - \overline{X}^2 = 5400.2 - 5201.29$
76	5776	3.88	15.0544		
73	5329	.88	.7744		$= 198.91$
72	5184	−.12	.0144		$\sqrt{198.91} = 14.1$
69	4761	−3.12	9.7344		
69	4761	−3.12	9.7344		
67	4489	−5.12	26.2144		
67	4489	−5.12	26.2144		
66	4356	−6.12	37.4544		
63	3969	−9.12	83.1744		
62	3844	−10.12	102.4144		
61	3721	−11.12	123.6544		
61	3721	−11.12	123.6544		
51	2601	−21.12	446.0544		
44	1936	−28.12	790.7344		
42	1764	−30.12	907.2144		

1. Create a frequency distribution.
2. Create a grouped frequency distribution.
3. Draw a frequency polygon of the data.
4. Draw a histogram of the data.
5. Draw a two-bar bar graph labeled "65 Inches or Over" and "64 Inches and Under."
6. Calculate the arithmetic mean, the median and the mode, and comment on which you feel is the best measure of central tendency in this instance.
7. Calculate the range, the interquartile range, and the average deviation.
8. Calculate the standard deviation using the raw score formula.
9. Calculate the standard deviation using the deviation score formula.
10. Discuss which measure of variability best describes the variability in the distribution and why.

EXERCISE 16
ACCUMULATING DATA ON A MOCK PERSONALITY INVENTORY

OBJECTIVE

To obtain firsthand experience in administering a (mock) personality test while accumulating test data (that will be manipulated in exercises to come).

BACKGROUND

Have you ever administered a personality test to anyone? The chances are good that at this stage in your career you probably have not—that is, until now. In Appendix A you will find a mock personality test—the Mid-Pawling Personality Inventory (MPPI). As part of this exercise, your task is to take on the role of test administrator. After you have administered it, file the test protocol (answer sheet) in a safe place; you will need to refer to it in future exercises.

YOUR TASK

Within the next week, "at your leisure," take a few minutes to administer the MPPI to someone of college age. As a class, decide on a way to achieve an approximately even balance between male and female testtakers; as you will see, the same number of testtakers in each group will be desirable for one facet of the upcoming data analysis.

The MPPI is a *mock* personality test—one which bears only some cosmetic resemblance at best to a real personality inventory. Still, in your capacity as test administrator (and

student of psychological measurement) there are three things that you must keep firmly in mind:

1. *Be professional.* Because the test isn't a real test and because responses to it do not really tell anything about the respondent one way or another, the temptation may exist to treat the exercise casually; *refrain from that temptation!* You will defeat the purpose of the exercise if you are joking or otherwise unprofessional in your approach. Remember that while testing and research data collection need not always be a solemn task—it can even be an enjoyable experience—it must never be treated as a joke.
2. *Obtain informed consent prior to testing.* In the present instance, "informed consent" simply means that a disclosure to the testtaker has been made with respect to the nature and purpose of the test as well as the use to which the findings will be put. Note that as part of the sample form for an informed consent to take the MPPI (below), it is also noted that the data will be neither confidential nor privileged.
3. *Fully debrief the testtaker at the time the testtaker is given feedback on the testing.* A full debriefing entails a complete description of the study, a full explanation of any deception that was part of the study, and an honest, straightforward response to any questions the testtaker has regarding the study. The bottom line here is that at the end of this study, the testtaker should not only feel good about having participated, but also might feel that he or she has learned something about the way students learn about testing.

Materials Needed for Administering the MPPI

The materials you will need for administering the MPPI are as follows:

- 1 copy of the test
- 1 test protocol
- 2 #2 pencils

Administration Instructions

The examiner places two #2 pencils down alongside face-up copies of the MPPI and the MPPI answer sheet and then says the following:

"Please read the following instructions along with me as they appear on your answer form while I read them aloud. The MPPI consists of 100 items, each item to be answered either True or False. While there is no formal time limit, do not take too long thinking about any one item; answer each item quickly with your first response —your first response is your best response. Answer all of the items without skipping any. Remember that there are no right or wrong answers to any of the questions so please feel free to give your first and uncensored response to each of the questions. Please use a number

2 pencil to blacken each of the answer grids and make sure that your responses are blackened fully while erasures are fully erased.

The MPPI is a test devised for the sole purpose of teaching students about the process of psychological testing. The test has not been shown to reliably or validly indicate anything about anyone's personality. Your responses to this test are neither confidential nor privileged; data from this as well as other tests will be used as part of a class exercise. We would, however, like you to use a code name for the purpose of taking this test; please enter that code name in the appropriate space below.

After testtakers have completed the last item, they are informed that you will be getting back to them sometime before the end of the term with feedback regarding the test. Indeed, you will be getting back to them, but what you tell them . . . well, that's the subject of a future exercise.

THE MID-PAWLING PERSONALITY INVENTORY (MPPI)

Directions:

The MPPI consists of 100 items, each item to be answered either "True" or "False." While there is no formal time limit, do not take too long thinking about any one item; answer each item quickly with your first response—your first response is your best response. Answer all of the items without skipping any. Remember that there are no right or wrong answers to any of these questions so please feel free to give your first and uncensored response to each of the questions. Please use a number 2 pencil to blacken each of the answer grids and make sure that your responses are blackened fully while erasures are fully erased.

The MPPI is a test devised for the sole purpose of teaching students about the process of psychological testing. The test has not been shown to reliably or validly indicate anything about anyone's personality. Your responses to this test are neither confidential nor privileged; data from this as well as other tests will be used as part of a class exercise. We would, however, like you to use a code name for the purpose of taking this test; please enter that code name now:

CODE NAME _____

Directions:

Answer each question either "True" or "False" by blackening the appropriate grid with a number 2 pencil.

1. T | | F | |	26. T | | F | |	51. T | | F | |	76. T | | F | |
2. T | | F | |	27. T | | F | |	52. T | | F | |	77. T | | F | |
3. T | | F | |	28. T | | F | |	53. T | | F | |	78. T | | F | |
4. T | | F | |	29. T | | F | |	54. T | | F | |	79. T | | F | |
5. T | | F | |	30. T | | F | |	55. T | | F | |	80. T | | F | |
6. T | | F | |	31. T | | F | |	56. T | | F | |	81. T | | F | |
7. T | | F | |	32. T | | F | |	57. T | | F | |	82. T | | F | |
8. T | | F | |	33. T | | F | |	58. T | | F | |	83. T | | F | |
9. T | | F | |	34. T | | F | |	59. T | | F | |	84. T | | F | |
10. T | | F | |	35. T | | F | |	60. T | | F | |	85. T | | F | |
11. T | | F | |	36. T | | F | |	61. T | | F | |	86. T | | F | |
12. T | | F | |	37. T | | F | |	62. T | | F | |	87. T | | F | |
13. T | | F | |	38. T | | F | |	63. T | | F | |	88. T | | F | |
14. T | | F | |	39. T | | F | |	64. T | | F | |	89. T | | F | |
15. T | | F | |	40. T | | F | |	65. T | | F | |	90. T | | F | |
16. T | | F | |	41. T | | F | |	66. T | | F | |	91. T | | F | |
17. T | | F | |	42. T | | F | |	67. T | | F | |	92. T | | F | |
18. T | | F | |	43. T | | F | |	68. T | | F | |	93. T | | F | |
19. T | | F | |	44. T | | F | |	69. T | | F | |	94. T | | F | |
20. T | | F | |	45. T | | F | |	70. T | | F | |	95. T | | F | |
21. T | | F | |	46. T | | F | |	71. T | | F | |	96. T | | F | |
22. T | | F | |	47. T | | F | |	72. T | | F | |	97. T | | F | |
23. T | | F | |	48. T | | F | |	73. T | | F | |	98. T | | F | |
24. T | | F | |	49. T | | F | |	74. T | | F | |	99. T | | F | |
25. T | | F | |	50. T | | F | |	75. T | | F | |	100. T | | F | |

Directions:

Answer each question either "True" or "False" by blackening the appropriate grid with a number 2 pencil.

1. T|| F||	26. T|| F||	51. T|| F||	76. T|| F||
2. T|| F||	27. T|| F||	52. T|| F||	77. T|| F||
3. T|| F||	28. T|| F||	53. T|| F||	78. T|| F||
4. T|| F||	29. T|| F||	54. T|| F||	79. T|| F||
5. T|| F||	30. T|| F||	55. T|| F||	80. T|| F||
6. T|| F||	31. T|| F||	56. T|| F||	81. T|| F||
7. T|| F||	32. T|| F||	57. T|| F||	82. T|| F||
8. T|| F||	33. T|| F||	58. T|| F||	83. T|| F||
9. T|| F||	34. T|| F||	59. T|| F||	84. T|| F||
10. T|| F||	35. T|| F||	60. T|| F||	85. T|| F||
11. T|| F||	36. T|| F||	61. T|| F||	86. T|| F||
12. T|| F||	37. T|| F||	62. T|| F||	87. T|| F||
13. T|| F||	38. T|| F||	63. T|| F||	88. T|| F||
14. T|| F||	39. T|| F||	64. T|| F||	89. T|| F||
15. T|| F||	40. T|| F||	65. T|| F||	90. T|| F||
16. T|| F||	41. T|| F||	66. T|| F||	91. T|| F||
17. T|| F||	42. T|| F||	67. T|| F||	92. T|| F||
18. T|| F||	43. T|| F||	68. T|| F||	93. T|| F||
19. T|| F||	44. T|| F||	69. T|| F||	94. T|| F||
20. T|| F||	45. T|| F||	70. T|| F||	95. T|| F||
21. T|| F||	46. T|| F||	71. T|| F||	96. T|| F||
22. T|| F||	47. T|| F||	72. T|| F||	97. T|| F||
23. T|| F||	48. T|| F||	73. T|| F||	98. T|| F||
24. T|| F||	49. T|| F||	74. T|| F||	99. T|| F||
25. T|| F||	50. T|| F||	75. T|| F||	100. T|| F||

─────────────────────── **THE 4-QUESTION CHALLENGE** ───────────────────────

1. Measurement using continuous scales
   (a) always involves error.
   (b) is always ordinal in nature.
   (c) is always normally distributed.
   (d) All of the above
2. The term "class intervals" is best associated with
   (a) socioeconomic status of a sample of testtakers.
   (b) a frequency distribution of testtaker scores.
   (c) a grouped frequency distribution of testtakers scores.
   (d) measures of central tendency and of variability.

3. Equal to the square root of the averaged squared deviations about the mean, this statistic is called
   (a) the range.
   (b) the standard deviation.
   (c) the average deviation.
   (d) the semi-interquartile range.
4. The normal curve
   (a) is bell-shaped.
   (b) has no skewness.
   (c) has a median and mode of the same value.
   (d) All of the above

Chapter 4

Norms, Correlation, and Regression

Correlation and the Full Moon

In Wolf, Jack Nicholson transforms into a werewolf when the moon is full. In fact, many published studies have noted an association between a full lunar presence and strange behavior. Under rigorous scrutiny, however, these studies have been found to be wanting with regard to the usage of appropriate correlational techniques (Rotton & Kelley, 1985). All of which brings us to the need for a sound understanding of the concept of correlation, a subject we take up after a consideration of standard scores and norms.

Outline for Chapter 4 of Cohen et al. (1996)
NORMS, CORRELATION, AND REGRESSION

Norms
    The Normative or Standardization Sample
    Types of Norms
        Percentiles
        Age norms
        Grade norms
        National norms
        National anchor norms
        Subgroup norms
        Local norms
    Fixed Reference Group Scoring Systems
    Norm-Referenced versus Criterion-Referenced Interpretation

Correlation
    The Concept of Correlation
    The Pearson r
    The Spearman rho
    Graphic Representation of Correlation

Regression .
    Multiple Regression
    Meta-Analysis

CLOSE-UP:
Pearson, Galton, Correlation, and Regression

EVERYDAY PSYCHOMETRICS:
Good Ol' Norms and the GRE

EXERCISE 17
TRANSFORMED SCORES: PERCENTILES

OBJECTIVE

To enhance understanding of and provide firsthand experience with transformed scores and, in particular, percentile scores.

BACKGROUND

Harold Seashore's brief article, "Methods of Expressing Test Scores," provides a succinct review and elaboration of some of the material contained in your textbook. It will be helpful to read it before proceeding to the material that follows on percentile scores.

• •

Methods of Expressing Test Scores

Harold G. Seashore

An individual's test score acquires meaning when it can be compared with the scores of well-identified groups of people. Manuals for tests provide tables of norms to make it easy to compare individuals and groups. Several systems for deriving more meaningful "standard scores" from raw scores have been widely adopted. All of them reveal the relative status of individuals within a group.

The fundamental equivalence of the most popular standard score systems is illustrated in the chart on the next page. We hope the chart and the accompanying description will be useful to counselors, personnel officers, clinical diagnosticians and others in helping them to show the uninitiated the essential simplicity of standard score systems, percentile equivalents, and their relation to the ideal normal distribution.

Sooner or later, every textbook discussion of test scores introduces the bell-shaped normal curve. The student of testing soon learns that many of the methods of deriving meaningful scores are anchored to the dimensions and characteristics of this curve. And he or she learns by observation of actual test score distributions that the ideal mathematical curve is a reasonably good approximation of many practical cases. He learns to use the standardized properties of the ideal curve as a model.

Let us look first at the curve itself. Notice that there are no raw scores printed along the baseline. The graph is generalized; it describes an idealized distribution of scores of any group on any test. We are free to use any numerical scale we like. For any particular set of scores, we can be arbitrary and call the average score zero. In technical terms we "equate" the mean raw score to zero. Similarly we can choose any convenient number, say 1.00, to represent the scale distance of one standard deviation.[1] Thus, if a distribution of scores on a particular test has a mean of 36 and a standard deviation of 4, the zero point on the baseline of our curve would be equivalent to a raw score of 36; one unit to the right, $+1\sigma$, would be equivalent to 40, $(36 + 4)$; and one unit to the left, -1σ, would be equivalent to 32, $(36 - 4)$.

The total area under the curve represents the total number of scores in the distribution. Vertical lines have been drawn through the score scale (the baseline) at zero and at 1, 2, 3, and 4 sigma units to the right and left. These lines mark off subareas of the total area under the curve. The numbers printed in these subareas are percents —*percentages of the total number of people.* Thus, 34.13 percent of all cases in a normal distribution have scores falling between 0 and -1σ. For practical purposes we rarely need to deal with standard deviation units below -3 or above $+3$; the percentage of cases with scores beyond $\pm3\sigma$ is negligible.

The fact that 68.26 percent fall between $\pm1\sigma$ gives rise to the common statement that in a normal distribution roughly two-thirds of all cases lie between plus and minus one sigma. This is a rule of thumb every test user should keep in mind. It is very near to the theoretical value and is a useful approximation.

Below the row of deviations expressed in sigma units is a row of percents; these show *cumulatively* the percentage of people which is included *to the left* of each of the sigma points. Thus, starting from the left, when we reach the line erected above -2σ, we have included the lowest 2.3 percent of cases. These percentages have been rounded in the next row.

Note some other relationships: the area between the $\pm1\sigma$ points includes the scores which lie above the 16th percentile (-1σ) and below the 84th percentile $(+1\sigma)$—two major reference points all test users should know. When we find that an individual has a score 1σ above the mean, we conclude that his score ranks at the 84th percentile in the group of persons on whom the test was normed. (This conclusion is good provided we also add this clause, at least subvocally: *if this particular group reasonably approximates the ideal normal model.*)

The simplest facts to memorize about the normal distribution and the relation of the *percentile* system to deviations from the average in sigma units are seen in the chart. They are

Deviation from the mean	-2σ	-1σ	0	$+1\sigma$	$+2\sigma$
Percentile equivalent	2	16	50	84	98

To avoid cluttering, the graph reference lines have not been drawn, but we could mark off ten percent sections of area under the normal curve by drawing lines vertically from the indicated decile points (10, 20, . . . 80, 90) up through the graph. The reader might do this lightly with a colored pencil.

---

[1] The mathematical symbol for the standard deviation is the lower case Greek letter sigma, or σ. These terms are used interchangeably in this article.

The Normal Curve, Percentiles, and Selected Standard Scores

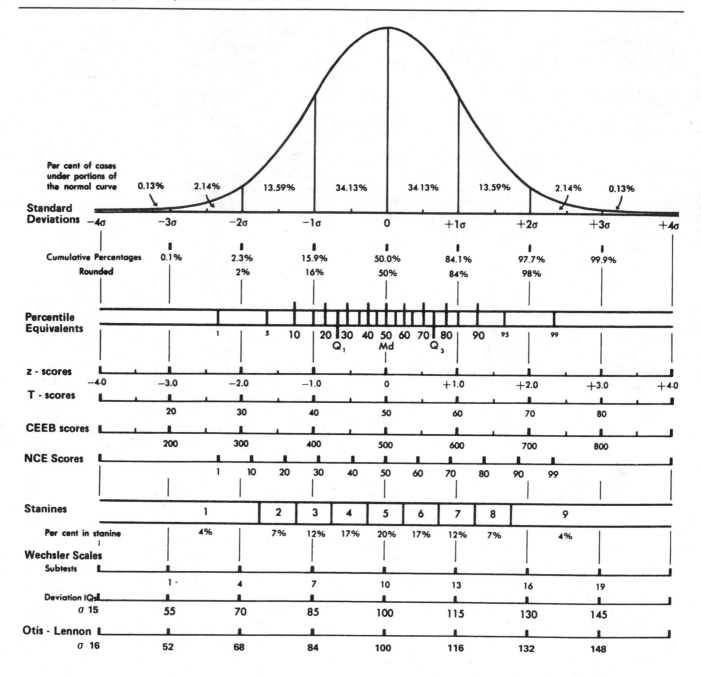

We can readily see that ten percent of the area (people) at the middle of the distribution embraces a smaller *distance* on the baseline of the curve than ten percent of the area (people) at the ends of the range of scores, for the simple reason that the curve is much higher at the middle. A person who is at the 95th percentile is farther away from a person at the 85th percentile in units of *test score* than a person at the 55th percentile is from one at the 45th percentile.

The remainder of the chart, that is, the several scoring scales drawn parallel to the baseline, illustrates variations

of the *deviation score* principle. As a class these are called *standard scores*.

First, there are the *z-scores*. These are the same *numbers* as shown on the baseline of the graph; the only difference is that the expression σ has been omitted. These scores run, in practical terms, from −3.0 to +3.0. One can compute them to more decimal places if one wishes, although computing to a single decimal place is usually sufficient. One can compute *z*-scores by equating the mean to 0.00 and the standard deviation to 1.00 for a distribution of any shape, but the relationships shown in this figure between the *z*-score equivalents of raw scores and percentile equivalents of raw scores are correct only for normal distributions. The interpretation of standard score systems derives from the idea of using the normal curve as a model.

As can be seen, T-scores are directly related to *z*-scores. The mean of the raw scores is equated to 50, and the standard deviation of the raw scores is equated to 10. Thus a *z*-score of +1.5 means the same as a T-score of 65. T-scores are usually expressed in whole numbers from about 20 to 80. The T-score plan eliminates negative numbers and thus facilitates many computations.

The College Entrance Examination Board uses a plan in which both decimals and negative numbers are avoided by setting the arbitrary mean at 500 points and the arbitrary sigma at another convenient unit, namely, 100 points. The experienced tester or counselor who hears of a College Board SAT-V score of 550 at once thinks, "Half a sigma (50 points) above average (500 points) on the CEEB basic norms. And when he hears of a score of 725 on SAT-N, he can interpret, "Plus $2\frac{1}{4}\sigma$. Therefore, better than the 98th percentile."

Yet another standard score is the recently developed Normal Curve Equivalent or NCE. This score, used primarily for reporting in federally funded programs such as Title I, has a mean of 50 and a standard deviation of 21.06. Note that this choice of mean and standard deviation will yield a range of scores from about 1 to 99. Note also that the T-scores, percentile ranks, and NCEs all have 50 as the mean reference point, a possible source of confusion to those who do not insist on careful labeling of data and of scores of individuals in their records.

Another derivative of the general standard score system is the *stanine* plan, developed by psychologists in the Air Force during the war. The plan divides the norm population into nine groups, hence "standard nines." Except for stanine 9, the top, and stanine 1, the bottom, these groups are spaced in half-sigma units. Thus, stanine 5 is defined as including the people who are within $\pm0.25\sigma$ of the mean. Stanine 6 is the group defined by the half-sigma distance on the baseline between $+0.25\sigma$ and $+0.75\sigma$. Stanines 1 and 9 include all persons who are below -1.75σ and above $+1.75\sigma$, respectively. The result is a distribution in which the mean is 5.0 and the standard deviation is 2.0.

Just below the line showing the demarcation of the nine groups in the stanine system there is a row of percentages which indicates the percent of the total population in each of the stanines. Thus 7 percent of the population will be in stanine 2, and 20 percent in the middle group, stanine 5.

Interpretation of the Wechsler scales depends on a knowledge of standard scores. A subject's raw score *on each of the subtests* in these scales is converted, by appropriate norms tables, to a standard score, based on a mean of 10 and a standard deviation of 3. The sums of standard scores on the Verbal Scale, the Performance Scale, and the Full Scale are then converted into IQs. These IQs are based on a standard score mean of 100, the conventional number for representing the IQ of the average person in a given age group. The standard deviation of the IQs is set at 15 points. In practical terms, then, roughly two-thirds of the IQs are between 85 and 115, that is, $\pm1\sigma$. IQs of the type used in the Wechsler scales have come to be known as *deviation IQs*, as contrasted with the IQ developed from scales in which a derived mental age is divided by chronological age.

Users of the Wechsler scales should establish clearly in their minds the relationship of subtest scaled scores and the deviation IQs to the other standard score systems, to the ordinary percentile rank interpretation, and to the deviation units on the baseline of the normal curve. For example, every Wechsler examiner should recognize that an IQ of 130 is a score equivalent to a deviation of $+2\sigma$, and that this IQ score delimits approximately the upper two percent of the population. If a clinician wants to evaluate a Wechsler IQ of 85 along with percentile ranks on several other tests given in school, he can mentally convert the IQ of 85 to a percentile rank of about 16, this being the percentile equal to a deviation from the mean of -1σ. Of course he should also consider the appropriateness and comparability of norms. It should also be noted here that many ability tests, especially group-administered paper-and-pencil tests such as the *Otis-Lennon School Ability Test*, use a standard deviation of 16, rather than 15, in computing their standard score indices.

Efficiency in interpreting test scores in counseling, in clinical diagnosis, and in personnel selection depends, in part, on facility in thinking in terms of the major interrelated plans by which meaningful scores are derived from raw scores. It is hoped that this graphic presentation will be helpful to all who in their daily work must help others understand the information conveyed by numerical test scores.

• •

While Seashore's article provides a brief overview of transformed scores in general, in this as well as succeeding exercises we will be focusing on specific transformed scores—beginning here with *percentiles*. As typically employed in the field of psychological testing, a percentile may be defined as a raw score that has been converted into an expression of the percentage of test-takers whose score falls below a particular raw score. Percentile scores are widely used in the manuals of—as well as other literature on—commercially published standardized tests. It is therefore incumbent upon the student of psychological testing to understand how they are used (as well as how they are *not* used).

Raw scores may be converted to percentiles through the use of the following formula:

$$P = n_L/N \times 100$$

where P = percentile, n_L = the number of scores lower than the score being converted to a percentile, and N = the total number of scores.

For practice with this formula, let's refer back to the distribution of the measurement class test scores that appeared in Table 3-1 and focus on Valerie's raw score of 85. The conversion of that raw score to a percentile would proceed as follows:

Step 1

Insert the value of n_L into the equation.

$$P = \frac{20}{N} \times 100$$

The value of n_L is found by simply counting the number of scores that were lower than Valerie's. In this case, $n_L = 20$.

Step 2

Insert the value of N into the equation.

$$P = \frac{20}{25} \times 100$$

In this example, N is equal to 25 since there were a total of 25 scores.

Step 3

Solve for P. $P = 0.80 \times 100 = 80$

The numerator (20) divided by the denominator (25) is equal to 0.80. The product of 0.80 multiplied by 100 is 80. We now know that Valerie's score falls at the 80th percentile.

YOUR TASK

1. Select any five other students from the distribution of test scores in Table 3-1 and convert their raw scores to percentiles.

2. Test your ability to make proper interpretations from percentile scores by circling either T for True or F for False for each of the 10 statements below. Since this test is provided as a learning experience for you—and not as an aid to your instructor's evaluation of you—make it a learning experience by jotting down any questions or comments that arise as you think about which answer is correct. Be sure to raise your questions or comments in class.

THE INTERPRETING PERCENTILE SCORES TEST*

ANSWER		ITEM	QUESTIONS/COMMENTS
T	F	1. Tim is a sixth grader. He obtained a percentile score of 70 in reading on a published standardized test. This means that Tim got 70 percent of the items correct.	
T	F	2. Mary got a raw score (not a percentile score) of 70 correct on reading. She is in Tim's sixth grade class. This score and Tim's percentile score of 70 indicate that Mary and Tim both are good readers.	
T	F	3. Susie, a third grade student, scored at the 30th percentile in arithmetic at the end of the school year. Scores this low are regarded as failing, and therefore Susie should be retained for another year in arithmetic instruction so that she will not be handicapped in the future.	
T	F	4. Bill received a percentile score of 90 at the beginning of the year and moved up to a percentile score of 99 by the end of the year. Jim, similarly, moved from the 50th percentile to the 59th. They made about equal progress.	

---

* John R. Hills, "Interpreting Percentile Scores," From *Hills Handy Hints*. Reprinted by permission of the publisher, National Council on Measurement in Education, Washington, D.C.

ANSWER		ITEM	QUESTIONS/COMMENTS

T   F   5. There is little difference between Sally's score of the 98th percentile and Jeanne's score of the 99.9th percentile, but there is a large difference between Rebecca's 84th percentile and Sally's 98th percentile.

T   F   6. Mrs. Henderson is the new Principal at Hartford Elementary. She set as her goal getting every pupil up to the 50th percentile within 4 years of her arrival at Hartford Elementary. With diligent effort and full cooperation from the staff and administration, this is a reasonable goal for most modern schools.

T   F   7. Mrs. Henderson wants to evaluate the standing of each grade in Hartford Elementary by comparing Hartford students' achievement with the average achievement in a representative sample of elementary schools in the nation. She obtains the percentile scores for each second grade pupil in reading and averages them. The average of these percentiles is the percentile rank for her schools' second graders.

T   F   8. Mr. Brown learns that Mrs. Henderson wants to compare the performance of each grade in Hartford with other schools. He is correct in claiming that unless the test publisher provides norms on school means, comparisons of Hartford means with the mean performances in other schools cannot be made.

T   F   9. While Rebecca scored at the 84th percentile on the reading test, Helmut scored only at the 75th percentile. Clearly Rebecca is a better reader than Helmut.

T   F   10. Miss Spolano is the school counselor at Hartford. She claims that scores on the reading test should not be reported as percentiles, but as percentile bands. However, the percentile banks are so wide for Gretchen, from the 37th percentile to the 58th percentile, that only by getting the percentile score itself do you have an accurate measure of how well Gretchen reads.

EXERCISE 18
STANDARD, STANDARDIZED, AND NORMALIZED STANDARD SCORES

OBJECTIVE

To enhance understanding of, as well as provide firsthand experience with, standard scores.

BACKGROUND

As generally used in the field of psychological testing, the term *standard score* refers to a raw score that has been converted from one scale into another scale—the latter typically being one that is more widely used and interpretable—that has some arbitrarily set mean and standard deviation. A z-score, for example, is a raw score that has been transformed to a scale that has a mean set at 0 and a standard deviation set at 1. To illustrate this, consider the following example. Todd, a senior at a prestigious university, earned a score of 90 on a test of Greek literature, a score of 62 on a test in chemical engineering, and a score of 50 on a test of floral arrangement. With that information—the raw scores—alone, what can you say about Todd's performance on these tests? The answer here is that you can't say very much. Oh, you might suspect that Todd was a Renaissance man with quite varied academic and artistic interests—either that or someone who is vocationally unfocused and in need of counseling. But without knowing more information about where these raw scores place Todd's performance within the total distribution of raw scores for each of these tests, it would be impossible to draw any meaningful conclusions regarding his relative performance in each of these areas.

Suppose that the scores for all three of the tests were approximately normally distributed and that (1) the distribution of the Greek literature scores had a mean of 100 and a standard deviation of 10, (2) the distribution of chemical engineering test scores had a mean of 50 and a standard deviation of 12, and (3) the distribution of floral arrangement test scores had a mean of 50 and a standard deviation of 15. Now, what statements can be made regarding Todd's relative performance on each of these three tests?

Todd did best on the chemical engineering test; his raw score of 62 falls at a point one standard deviation above the mean. Todd's next best score was on the floral arrangement test; his raw score of 50 falls exactly at the mean of the distribution of scores. And finally there is Todd's performance on the Greek literature test; his raw score of 90 falls at a point one standard deviation below the mean. Converting Todd's raw scores to a scale that has a mean of 0 and a standard deviation of 1—that is,

converting Todd's raw scores to z-scores—we can say that Todd achieved a z-score of +1 on the chemical engineering test, a z-score of 0 on the floral arrangement test, and a z-score of −1 on the Greek literature test. The general formula used to transform raw scores into z-scores entails subtracting the mean from the raw score and dividing by the standard deviation. The general formula is as follows:

$$z = \frac{X - \overline{X}}{s}$$

where z is the value of the obtained standard score,

X is the value of the raw score to be transformed,
$\overline{X}$ is the value of the mean of the distribution of raw scores, and
s is the value of the raw score distribution standard deviation.

Now let's use this formula to convert Todd's raw score of 62 on the chemical engineering test to a z-score (just to make sure that a raw score that lies exactly one standard deviation above the mean does indeed transform to a z-score of +1):

$$z = \frac{X - \overline{X}}{s} = \frac{62 - 50}{12} = 1$$

Standard scores may be used to compare performance of different testtakers on different tests. Suppose we wanted to know if Todd's score on his Greek literature test was better than Mousey's score on his measurement examination. You will recall that Mousey earned a raw score of 42 on the test, and that the mean and standard deviation of the test were respectively 72.12 and 14.10. Using the general formula (above) and presuming for the purpose of this illustration that the scores on this test were distributed normally, let's now convert Mousey's raw score of 42 to a standard score:

$$z = \frac{X - \overline{X}}{s} = \frac{42 - 72.12}{14.10} = -2.136$$

Having calculated a value of z that is greater than −2, it can be seen that Mousey's score on the examination fell more than two standard deviations below the mean. We can therefore say Todd's performance on his Greek literature test was superior to that of Mousey on the measurement examination.

While z-scores are relatively simple to use, they are not without computational disadvantages. Because a z-score can be equal to 0 or can be negative, certain types of data manipulations with them become awkward. It is also a fact of life that many testtakers (as well as parents of testtakers) bristle at hearing their test scores reported as negative numbers. How would you feel if you were told that your score on your last measurement examination was −2.136? For these reasons (as well as others), alternative standard score systems have been developed to linearly transform z-scores (as well as raw scores) to a scale that does not contain negative numbers. Such systems are all "standard" to the extent that both the mean and the standard deviation of the new scale have been arbitrarily set. The general formula for linearly converting a z-score to a new standardized score (NSS) may be expressed as follows:

$$NSS = ASD(z) + AM$$

where NSS is the new standardized score,

ASD is the value of the arbitrarily-set standard deviation, z is the value of the standard score to be transformed, and AM is the value of the arbitrarily-set mean.

As an example, let's convert a z-score of 1 to a "new" score on a "new" scale. Let's set the new scale to have a mean of 50 and a standard deviation of 10. And let's christen all scores derived on this scale as T scores—this out of respect and esteem for psychologist E. L. Thorndike. Using the formula presented above, the "New Standardized Score" (NSS) or "T" score equivalent of a z-score of 1 could be calculated as follows:

$$NSS = ASD(z) + ASM$$

$$T = 10(1) + 50$$

$$T = 60$$

By the way, W. A. McCall beat us to the development of T scores by 70 or so years—right down to naming the scale after Professor Thorndike. But take heart; there are many new scales just waiting to be created. Use the formula above to convert a z-score of 1 to a new scale— call this new scale any name you wish—that has a mean set of 1,000 and a standard deviation set at 300. What is the value of a z-score of 1 on this scale? the value of a z-score of –1? the value of a z-score of –2.136? What is the z-score equivalent of a score of 1600 on this new scale?

The general formula used to linearly convert a raw score to a new standardized score may be expressed as follows:

$$NSS = ASD\left(\frac{X - \overline{X}}{SD_x}\right) + ASM$$

where NSS is the value of the new standardized score,

ASD is the value of the arbitrarily-set standard deviation, X is the value of the raw score to be converted, $\overline{X}$ is the value of the mean of the raw scores, SD_x is the value of the standard deviation of the raw scores, and ASM is the arbitrarily-set mean.

Suppose we wanted to convert Mousey's raw score of 42 (from the class examination data distribution that had a mean of 72.12 and a standard deviation of 14.10) to a

new standardized score that had a mean of 1,000 and a standard deviation of 300. Using the formula above, and presuming again that the class examination data were approximately normal in their distribution, the calculation of the new standard score would proceed as follows:

$$NSS = ASD\left(\frac{X - \overline{X}}{SD_x}\right) + ASM$$

$$NSS = 300\left(\frac{42 - 72.12}{14.10}\right) + 1,000$$

$$NSS = 300\left(\frac{-30.12}{14.10}\right) + 1,000$$

$$NSS = 300\,(-2.136) + 1,000$$

$$NSS = -640.851 + 1,000$$

$$NSS = 359.149$$

Mousey's raw score of 42 converted to the new standardized score is 359.149.

Some of the terms used by clinicians, researchers, test manual and book authors have not been entirely consistent—or standard—with respect to systems of standard scoring. Thus for example, some test manuals and books reserve the term *standard score* only for use with reference to z-scores; raw scores (as well as z-scores) linearly transformed to any other type of "standard" scoring systems—that is, transformed to a scale with an arbitrarily set mean and standard deviation— are differentiated from z-scores by the term *standardized*. Thus while a z-score would be referred to as a "standard score," a T score would be referred to as a "standardized score." Another point of terminology (and potential source of confusion) which you should be aware of concerns the term "normalized standard score" (also sometimes referred to simply as a "normalized score"). An explanation follows with reference to Figure 4-1.

The normal curve is, for all intents and purposes, a theoretical abstraction; while it exists in theory, one would be hard put to find "real world" test (or any other) data that were distributed in a perfectly normal fashion. While many such "real world" distributions of data— particularly those containing very large numbers of observations—may come close to being normally distributed, none are truly normal frequency distributions; one requirement in this regard would be that the tails of the curve never touch the base line but only approach it as they trail off into infinity in either direction. When data are said to be normally distributed, what is really meant, in most (if not all) cases, is that the data are *approximately* normally distributed. The concept of a normal curve, even if it is only a theoretical abstraction, is very useful; the normal frequency distribution is a well-known

Figure 4-1

The Normal Curve and Some Transformed Score Equivalents

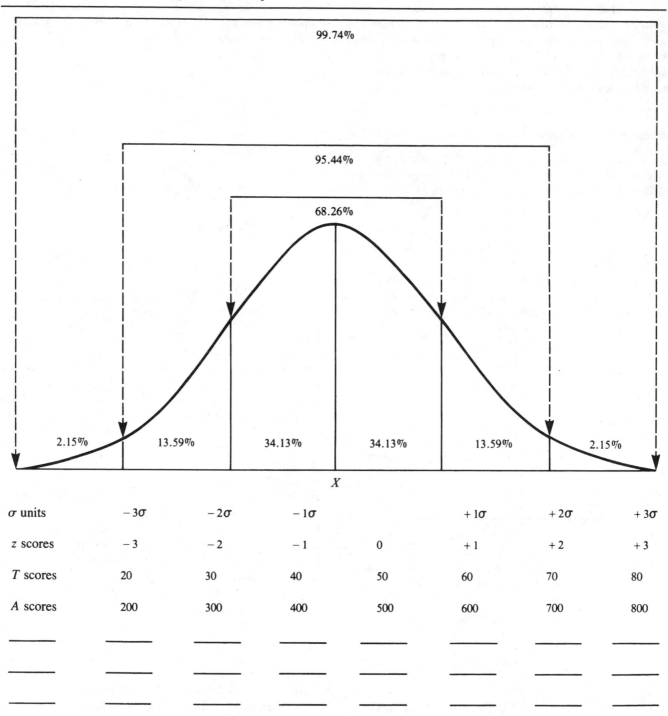

σ units	−3σ	−2σ	−1σ		+1σ	+2σ	+3σ
z scores	−3	−2	−1	0	+1	+2	+3
T scores	20	30	40	50	60	70	80
A scores	200	300	400	500	600	700	800

entity from which data can be easily interpreted, compared, and manipulated. And if test users have data that are not distributed normally, it may well be to their advantage to use statistical procedures to transform the data into a normal form—to "normalize" the data.

Assume for the moment that a test user has a distribution of test scores (on a variable we'll call V) which is not distributed normally. And assume further that the test user has good reason to believe that V is actually normally distributed in the population and that the present (non-normal) distribution was only an artifact of something such as poor sampling or a poor instrument of measurement. Provided some other technical assumptions are met, the test user may wish to use statistical procedures to "normalize" the distribution of data. Conceptually, such normalization may involve the stretching and pulling of a skewed curve to approximate the shape of a normal curve. A *normalized standard score scale* is a scale of standard scores that corresponds to a distribution of observations that has been "molded" to approximate the normal curve. If this scale has a mean arbitrarily set at 50 and a standard deviation arbitrarily set at 10, a given score on this scale might be referred to as a *T* score.

In practice, test manual and book authors, as well as others, have been somewhat casual in their labeling of various standard scoring systems. The best way for a test user to determine, for example, if a *T* score referenced in a test manual is a normalized standard score or simply a standardized score, is to look for reference to this point in the manual itself (or, if such references are lacking, contact the test publisher).

One last point about "stretching," "pulling," and "molding" data to approximate a normal distribution. You may know from personal experience that when you've had to stretch, pull, or in other ways attempt to mold your body into a garment, say a pair of jeans, the jeans didn't fit, feel, or wear the same as when you didn't have to go to such heroics to get into them. There's an analogy there somewhere with respect to test data; technical problems may arise as a function of your fashioning of a normal distribution. For example, highly skewed data "forced" into a normal shape may yield distorted images of the distances between certain raw scores.

YOUR TASK

1. Approximately what percentage of the test scores were higher than Mousey's? Lower?
2. Approximately what score would Mousey's raw score be equal to as a *T* score? As an *A* score?
3. Select five other scores from the class examination data, convert them to *z*-scores, indicate where they fall on the graph (by drawing them in similar to the way we've drawn in Mousey's score on Figure 4-1), and answer Questions 1 and 2 above with respect to each of these five scores.
4. Explain the differences between each of the following three terms as they have been used in the measurement literature:
   (a) standard score
   (b) standardized score
   (c) standard normalized score
5. Devise and give a name to 3 new standardized scoring systems and fill in the blank spaces in Figure 4-1 for each of them. Next, determine what Mousey's measurement examination test score would be in terms of these new standardized scores.

Frequency distributions of data may vary widely; some, for example, give a lopsided appearance with the majority of cases piled up to the left or right of center. Other distributions of data vary in appearance from being as peaked as a triangle to as flat as a rectangle. But amidst the peaks, valleys, and plateaus of the graphs of other frequency distributions stands the bell-shaped normal frequency distribution or normal curve—a distribution that can be defined precisely mathematically (Hays, 1973) and a standard by which to compare other frequency distributions. The measurement of many human physical and psychological characteristics yields frequency distributions that approximate the normal frequency distribution; this is especially true when highly reliable and valid measuring tools are employed with large samples. When test data do not yield a normal frequency distribution, the test user may attempt—provided certain technical assumptions permit—to statistically transform the data to fit the normal curve. Because so much is known about the normal frequency distribution, data in this form tend to be easier to interpret. In Figure 4-1 there are some standard and standardized score equivalents for various points along the normal curve (the blank spaces are there for you to insert values for your own standardized scoring systems.)

EXERCISE 19
STANINES, SAT/ACT, AND GRADE-EQUIVALENT SCORES

OBJECTIVE

To enhance understanding of and sharpen interpretation skills with respect to converted scores such as stanines and SAT/ACT scores as well as scores expressed as grade-equivalents.

BACKGROUND

Researchers during World War II developed a standardized score with a mean of five and a standard deviation of approximately two. Divided into nine units, this "standard nine" scale was referred to as a *stanine*. Today, stanines are employed, among other settings, in many school systems for recording data into students' permanent records. And while we're on the subject of data in student records, data from standardized educational tests are often recorded in converted scores called grade equivalents, and data from college entrance exami-nations such as those administered by American College Testing (ACT) and Educational Testing Service—including the Scholastic Aptitude Test (SAT)—are recorded in standardized scores called *A* scores.

Following is a brief article prepared by The Psychological Corporation, explaining what stanines are and how they are used and a ten-item True/False test on stanines.

• •

Stanines and Their Computation for Local Use

The interpretation of test results for purposes of comparison and evaluation is an important feature of the educative process. In order that this may be effectively done, it is necessary to transform the raw scores obtained through testing into some kind of derived scores. There are various methods of doing this of which the three most commonly used are conversions to percentile ranks, grade equivalents, and stanines. This latter method was first used extensively by the military during World War II as a system for transforming masses of test data into one simple and workable form. The stanine scale (short for STAndard-NINE scale) transforms data into values ranging from 1 to 9, and thus makes possible the translation of various kinds of information into one-digit scores, comparable in form and easily added to develop composite scores.

The advantages of this simple nine-point scale are equally valid in the field of education, and stanines have now come into widespread use as a means of interpreting individual raw scores on many types of tests. Stanine groupings are coarse enough to prevent overinterpretation of small differences, yet they differentiate sufficiently for most practical purposes.

THE NATURE OF THE STANINE SCALE

Like other commonly used statistical means of expressing scores, the stanine scale is dependent on the assumption that the measured trait is distributed normally in the general population, so that a graphic representation of that distribution would closely approximate the so-called bell-shaped curve. In a normal raw-score distribution, the greatest number of cases are concentrated near the middle while the remaining cases are distributed symmetrically on either side, decreasing as the distance from the center becomes greater. It follows that, within the limits imposed by a particular raw-score distribution, transformed stanine scores can be expected to conform to the proportions of this normal curve with a fixed percent of cases (rounded) falling within each of the nine stanine classifications. This is illustrated in Figure 1.

In this scale, raw scores are converted to scores ranging from 1 (low) to 9 (high) with a mean of 5 and a standard deviation (S.D.) of 2.[1] Each stanine (except 1 and 9) is $\frac{1}{2}$ S.D. in width, the middle stanine of 5 extending from $\frac{1}{4}$ S.D. below to $\frac{1}{4}$ S.D. above the mean. As may be noted in Figure 1, the normal (bell-shaped) curve never quite touches the base line, since extreme

---

[1] The mean of a group of scores, or numbers, is the arithmetic average. The standard deviation is a statistical unit indicating the degree to which the scores tend to spread out or vary.

Figure 1

Stanines and the Normal Curve

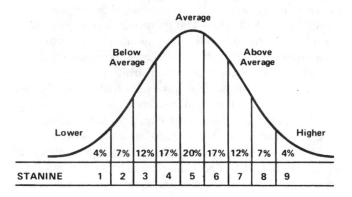

scores in stanines 1 and 9 extend considerably beyond $\frac{1}{2}$ S.D. The top of stanine 8, in terms of distance from the mean, is $+ 1\frac{3}{4}$ S.D. and marks off approximately 46 percent of the 50 percent of cases above the mean. Stanine 9, then, includes all the remaining cases (roughly the top 4%) no matter how far from the mean they may extend. Similarly, stanine 1 extends downward indefinitely from $1\frac{3}{4}$ S.D. below the mean.

Stanines can be described quantitatively as follows:

9 Very superior
8 Superior
7 Considerably above average
6 Slightly above average
5 Just average
4 Slightly below average
3 Considerably below average
2 Poor
1 Very poor

Occasionally it is desirable to use larger groupings. For this purpose, stanines 1, 2, and 3 are generally considered low; stanines 4, 5, and 6, average; and stanines 7, 8, and 9, high.

Unlike grade equivalents or percentile ranks, stanines 2 through 8 are equally spaced steps in the scale—that is, a stanine 8 is as much better than a stanine 6 as a stanine 5 is better than a 3. Because of this characteristic, the scale is particularly appropriate for making comparisons among scores or for profiling scores of individuals. The scale is also well adapted to use by the teacher in grouping students for instruction and has the advantage of de-emphasizing insignificant differences among pupils' scores.

It must be remembered, however, that whenever gross groupings are made from more finely expressed measures, there are bound to be sharp divisions *between* steps. This drawback is inherent to the stanine system. For example, assume that raw scores 10 to 15 are included within stanine 8, and 16 to 19 within stanine 9; a raw-score difference of just one point could change the stanine classification. Thus, a raw score of 15 would place a student at the upper end of stanine 8, whereas one additional raw-score point would have placed the same student in stanine 9, at its lower end. Since there is an inescapable error of measurement in any test score, such a small difference as one raw-score point could be due entirely to chance. Therefore, in comparing several *stanine* scores for an individual, differences of only one stanine should *not* be regarded as significant.

APPROPRIATE USES OF STANINES

Wherever it is possible to arrange data in rank order—from highest (or best) down to lowest (or poorest), stanines may be used. Consequently, they are not only useful in expressing test scores but in tabulating teachers' rankings, performance ratings, and similar data. Stanines obtained from the distribution of any such scores may be compared with those obtained from any other set, provided, of course, the data are derived from the *same group of individuals*. For example, arithmetic stanines may be compared with reading stanines; mental ability stanines may be compared with achievement stanines. From these data, bivariate (two-way) charts, graphically depicting the relationship between two measures, can easily be constructed. These charts may be used either for visual identification of atypical cases or as the first step in computing a correlation coefficient. Figure 2 is an example of such a chart.

Because stanine scales always have the same mean and variability (standard deviation), stanines obtained from the same group on various measures may be combined into composite scores for use in prediction. For instance, stanines from a prognostic test may be combined with those derived from previous grades and teachers' ratings to form a composite predictor of success in a foreign language.

An individual profile of a pupil's scores on several measures may easily be constructed. Such a profile will almost automatically indicate the pupil's standing within the total group in each area measured. That same profile may also be used to portray the pupil's relative strengths and weaknesses from one area to another. It should be noted again, however, that in interpreting stanine scores, *only differences of 2 or more stanines should be regarded as significant*. National stanine norms provided by a test publisher can, of course, be used in profiling scores from the various subtest areas *in a single test battery,* but the test user should remember that only when stanines are based on the *same* population will comparisons between them be valid. On the other hand, *locally* developed stanines, if available, may be used to profile scores from tests whose standardization populations were *not* the same and whose *national* stanines are therefore not directly comparable.

Figure 2

Bivariate Chart Showing the Relationship between ALP Mathematics Composite Prognostic Stanines and Metropolitan Mathematics Problem Solving Stanines for the Eighth Grade in One Community

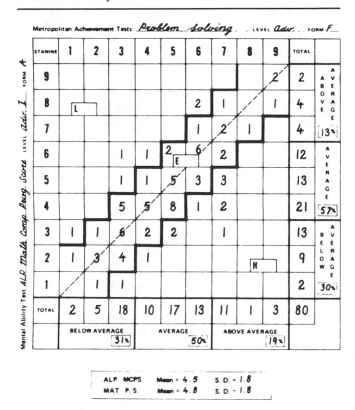

Reporting pupil progress to parents can be easily and effectively done through the use of stanines. In fulfilling this important responsibility, it is critically important that reports be presented in a comprehensible form that will help home and school work together effectively toward the education of each child. Stanines can be more readily understood by parents than other types of transformed scores. They are less liable to serious misinterpretation than are grade equivalents, for example, and, because there are only nine levels, they do not give the impression that measurement is more precise than it really is, as is the case with percentile ranks of 100 differentiated scores.

Counseling and guidance of pupils in educational and vocational decision-making may be greatly enhanced by the use of graphic representations of the pupil's performance on a wide variety of measures. The stanine system is admirably adapted to this type of profiling.

ESTABLISHING LOCAL NORMS IN TERMS OF STANINES

The use of *local* score distributions or norms has long been advocated by professional test publishers as a useful adjunct to national norms. The techniques for establishing some types of local norms are quite complex. The stanine system, however, simplifies the process, and local distributions of scores expressed as stanines offer distinct advantages. The use of local stanines makes it possible to compare individual performance across all of the locally administered standardized tests. When the local stanines are based on a comparatively large group, such as all pupils in a given grade within the system, subgroups of the total may also be compared in terms of these local stanines. Two or more measures given to the same group—measures on which the scores have been translated into local stanines—may be plotted on bivariate (two-way) charts. Finally, local stanine norms may be established for distributions of scores on measures for which no national normative data are available, such as locally constructed tests and teachers' ratings.

The basic decision to be made before any computation can be done concerns the selection of an appropriate group on which to base the stanine scale. This is critical since the stanine system assumes that the raw-score distribution approximates normality. If a small group, such as a classroom, were chosen, it would be highly unlikely that it would reflect a normal distribution of the trait being measured. At what point, then, is a group large enough to make reasonable an assumption of normal distribution? This is difficult to answer, but it is significant that the scoring service of The Psychological Corporation cautions against the development of local norms for groups of less than 100 pupils per grade level.

Even with a group of 100 or more, it is important to look at the distribution of raw scores to see whether there is a severe restriction in their range, or whether scores pile up at the top or bottom rather than in the middle. If the score distribution departs significantly from normality in either of these respects, great caution must be exercised both in the computation of stanines and in their interpretation.

In computing local stanines, it is always preferable to work with raw scores, rather than any type of transformed scores, so that none of the precision of the original data will be lost in translation. The first step is to determine the theoretical number of cases that should be assigned to each stanine level. This is done by multiplying successively the total number of cases in the distribution by the theoretical percent of cases at each stanine level.

In the example given in Figure 3, the total number of cases has been arbitrarily set at 325. The theoretical percents for each stanine have been transferred from Figure 1, where they are shown just above the line at the base of the curve. Theoretical frequencies are shown in the third column: for stanine 9, .04 × 325 = 13, for stanine 8, .07 × 325 = 22.75 (23), etc. Note that the theoretical percent desired at each stanine has been rounded to a whole percent and that rounding is also necessary in determining the theoretical frequencies. If, due to rounding, the theoretical frequencies do not add to the actual number of cases in the distribution, an adjustment must be made.

Figure 3

Frequency Desired at Each Stanine Level for a Group of 325 Scores

STANINE	Theoretical Percent	Theoretical Frequency
9	4	13
8	7	23
7	12	39
6	17	55
5	20	65
4	17	55
3	12	39
2	7	23
1	4	13
Total	100 %	325

It rarely happens that a distribution of raw scores can be divided *exactly* according to the theoretical percents. (Only if the scores constitute a precisely normal distribution would this be true.) Therefore, the assignment of scores to stanine levels is unlikely to be precisely in accordance with the theoretical values. Above all, it must be remembered that *everyone having the same raw score must be assigned the same stanine.*

A COMPUTATIONAL EXAMPLE

Assigning stanine values to a given set of raw scores becomes a relatively simple procedure. Figure 4 shows an example of a completed worksheet for computing the reading stanines for a single grade level within a single community. The total number of cases is again 325. The directions below list the steps involved in preparing this worksheet.

Step 1

Arrange test papers or answer sheets in rank order from high to low. Note the highest and the lowest obtained scores, and on the worksheet, set up the scale of the Raw Score column to cover this range.

Step 2

In the adjacent column of frequencies (f), opposite each raw score, write the number of individuals who, by actual count, obtained that score.

Figure 4

Sample Worksheet for Assigning Actual Stanine Values to a Group of 325 Scores

XYZ Reading Test Intermediate Battery Form Q in Grade 5			
Raw Score	f	Actual Frequency	STANINE
42	1		
41	1		
40	2	17	9
39	6		
38	7		
37	4		
36	9	27	8
35	4		
34	10		
33	7		
32	13	39	7
31	19		
30	11		
29	14	53	6
28	16		
27	12		
26	13		
25	11	64	5
24	18		
23	22		
22	16		
21	11		
20	14	53	4
19	12		
18	13		
17	14	35	3
16	8		
15	9		
14	6		
13	3	24	2
12	6		
11	2		
10	3		
9	2		
8	2		
7	2	13	1
6	1		
5	0		
4	0		
3	0		
2	1		
Total	325	325	

(A) points to row 25/24.

Step 3

Add the frequencies in column f and write the total at the bottom of the column. This is shown to be 325.

Step 4

Starting at the bottom of column f, count off the scores in Stanine 1; in this case, it is possible to include just 13 scores, the exact theoretical frequency for this group. Draw a line to mark off these scores tentatively as Stanine 1, and enter the number 13 in the Actual Frequency column.

Step 5

For Stanine 2, the theoretical frequency is 23. A choice must be made here between $6 + 3 + 6 = 15$ (too few) or $6 + 3 + 6 + 9 = 24$, only one too many. Since the latter choice is preferable, scores of 12 through 15 are included, and a line is drawn between 15 and 16 to mark off Stanine 2.

Step 6

Work upward, marking off Stanines 3 and 4. Notice that in this example, the tentative actual frequencies are 35 and 53. In marking off Stanine 3, 35 cases have been included, although ideally there should be 39. However, to include the next score (19), another 12 cases would have to be added, making 47, and the original 35 is closer to the desired 39 than is 47. To this point, Stanines 1 through 4, 125 cases have been included where 130 were desired.

Step 7

Now mark off Stanine 5. In the example, 64 cases have been included rather than the theoretical 65, but adding either 12 or 16 would spoil the shape of the curve. Check the midpoint in Stanine 5 (between 24 and 25 at A). The actual number of cases assigned to this point is 165, closely approximating $\frac{1}{2}$ of 325, or 162.5.

Step 8

Now continue counting off the frequencies for Stanines 6, 7, 8, and 9. After having made a tentative assignment, make any adjustments necessary to bring the actual frequencies at each level into the closest possible agreement with the theoretical frequencies.

Step 9

Check the symmetry of the stanine assignment; there should be about the same number of cases in Stanines 1 and 9, 2 and 8, 3 and 7, 4 and 6. In the example, the greatest discrepancy is between the 17 and 13 of Stanines 9 and 1 respectively. A possible adjustment would be to shift the 7 cases at score 38 from Stanine 9 to Stanine 8. This would leave 10 cases in Stanine 9, slightly closer to the 13 in Stanine 1, but Stanine 8 would now include 34 cases. Shifting the 10 at score 34 would leave the desired 24, but neither Stanine 7 nor 6 could absorb these ten extra cases. The logical conclusion is to leave the allocations as first set up.

It can easily be seen that the smaller the group and the less precisely normal the distribution of their scores, the more difficult is the task of assigning stanines and the more subjective is the judgment involved. However, it is important to note that a discrepancy between actual and theoretical frequencies is of less consequence at the extremes than it is in the middle range of the table, since the stanine assignment of fewer pupils is affected.

• •

YOUR TASK

Test your understanding of stanines as well as SAT/ACT scores and grade-equivalent scores by taking the three ten-item tests that follow.[1] Circle either Y for Yes or N for No for each of the questions in the Yes/No tests and either T for True or F for False for each of the statements in the True/False test.

Since these tests are provided as a learning experience for you—and not as an aid to your instructor's evaluation of you—make it a learning experience by jotting down any questions or comments that arise as you think about which answer is correct. Be sure to raise your questions or comments in class.

THE STANINE SCORE INTERPRETATION TEST

ANSWER	ITEM	QUESTIONS/COMMENTS
Y N	1. Mary is a sixth grader. She received a stanine score of zero on her standardized test in mathematics. This means that Mary's score was very low compared to other sixth graders. Is that correct?	
Y N	2. Bill received a stanine score of 5 on the same standardized mathematics test that Mary took. He is also in the sixth grade. The score of 5 means that Bill is doing average work in mathematics, and he would be at the 50th percentile for sixth graders. Is that correct?	
Y N	3. Pedro received a stanine score of 6.5 on the mathematics test. This score should be interpreted as being midway between the sixth and seventh stanines.	
Y N	4. Cindy is in the same class as Bill, Mary, and Pedro. On the mathematics test, she received a stanine score of 9. Her mother wants to know just how high that score is—what percent of pupils perform less well than Cindy. Ms. Billingsley tells Cindy's mother that 96 percent of students in Cindy's grade performed less well than Cindy. Is this an accurate statement of Cindy's percentile rank?	
Y N	5. Alfonso's stanine score is 7. Mr. Rivera is more familiar with standard scores than stanines. He asked Ms. Billingsley how many standard deviations above the mean a stanine score of 7 was. Ms. Billingsley immediately responded, "One." Does Ms. Billingsley have a trick for remembering such things so well?	

---

[1] "Interpreting Stanine Scores," "Interpreting SAT & ACT Scores," and "Interpreting Grade-Equivalent Scores," all by John R. Hills from *Hills Handy Hints* published by and reprinted with the permission of the National Council on Measurement in Education, Washington, D.C.

ANSWER		ITEM	QUESTIONS/COMMENTS
Y	N	6. Mr. Rivera decided that Ms. Billingsley really knew her stanines. So he pushed his luck and asked her what percent of students got stanine scores of 7. Ms. Billingsley thought for a moment. Then she replied, "In a normal distribution, 12 percent of the scores will be in the seventh stanine." Taken aback by the speed of her response, Mr. Rivera asked whether another trick was involved. Was there?	
Y	N	7. Mr. Tatnall overheard the conversation between Ms. Billingsley and Mr. Rivera and decided to contribute another guide. He suggested that stanines were the same as deciles. So, he said, the first stanine would be the same as the first decile, the second stanine and the second decile would be equivalent, and so on. Is Mr. Tatnall correct?	
Y	N	8. Mr. Rivera decided to ask one more question. He has found that most of his students receive the same stanine scores in the fifth grade that they got in the fourth grade or even the third grade. He concluded that they are not making much progress in school. Is that correct?	
Y	N	9. Mr. Tatnall asked what should he do about Patricia, who went down from the fifth stanine last year to the fourth stanine this year in reading comprehension? Should Mr. Tatnall be worried about this?	
Y	N	10. Mr. Rivera then asked about his student Elena, whose stanine score in reading comprehension went up from the fourth stanine to the sixth stanine. Is that big a difference important?	

THE SAT/ACT INTERPRETATION TEST

ANSWER		ITEM	QUESTIONS/COMMENTS
Y	N	1. Donald told Mr. Henkin, the counselor at Burnside High School, that he had just received his Scholastic Aptitude Test (SAT) scores and that his Verbal (V) and Mathematical (M) scores were both about	

ANSWER	ITEM	QUESTIONS/COMMENTS
	400. He was disappointed because those scores are well below average. Is the average SAT score 500?	
Y N	2. Mary told her best friend, Susie, that her SAT score was 900. Susie was impressed, because her scores were only V of 450 and M of 450. Did Mary perform better than Susie?	
Y N	3. Jeremy received his SAT scores and his ACT scores in the mail. His ACT scores were much lower than his SAT scores. He had two SAT scores (495 and 515) but his ACT report had 5 scores, with numbers such as 17 and 18. Adding all 5 ACT scores together won't produce a total as high as one of the SAT scores. Did he perform less satisfactorily on the ACT?	
Y N	4. Susie added together her V and M scores on the SAT and got a total of 1225. She looked at her ACT scores of 22, 23, 21, and 23, and expected them to add up to 89, but her ACT composite score is only 22. Has her ACT composite been calculated incorrectly?	
Y N	5. Harold took both the SAT and the ACT. He estimated that for college-going students the SAT score mean is about 450 and the ACT score mean is about 17. However, he got ACT scores with an average near 20, but his SAT scores are only around 400. Is something wrong because he is above the mean on one test but below the mean on the other?	
Y N	6. Tulawney, the star student of Burnside High School, took both the SAT and the ACT in the fall of her senior year. She scored near 700 on each of the SAT scores and near 25 on each of the ACT scores. She had so much fun taking these tests and did so well that at the next opportunity she took them both again. To her dismay, her scores on both the SAT and the ACT were lower on the second testing. She went to Mr. Henkin to find out what was wrong, and he told her not to worry. She should have expected her scores to be lower on the second testing. Is Mr. Henkin correct?	

ANSWER		ITEM	QUESTIONS/COMMENTS

Y   N

7. Willie took the SAT one year and got a Verbal score of 450. He was not satisfied, so he studied vocabulary diligently for a year and then took the test again. His Verbal score went up to 500. He recommended to everyone that they study vocabulary the way he did because his score improved so much after only one year. Is Willie's vocabulary study responsible for his improved SAT Verbal score?

Y   N

8. Sue Ellen wants to go to college very much, but her ACT composite score in her junior year was only 11. In order to raise that score, she studied diligently during the next year. She wanted to raise her achievement in natural science, social science, and mathematics because ACT tests include questions based on high school courses in those areas. When she took the ACT again, her composite went up to 14. The school principal, on hearing this, asked at a faculty meeting whether this kind of diligent study should be prescribed for all students who have low ACT scores. Mr. Henkin said that Sue Ellen's experience did not justify such a conclusion. Her improvement might readily have occurred without the extra study. Is that true?

Y   N

9. Elijah took the Preliminary Scholastic Aptitude Test (PSAT) in his junior year and received a V score of 65 and an M score of 63. He asked Donald to help him decide what these scores mean. Donald said that they were very low. Donald was disappointed in his SAT scores, which were about 400, but that is much higher than scores of only 65 and 63. Then Elijah went to Sue Ellen for advice. She had been thrilled to get her ACT score composite up to 14 after a year of hard work. She said that scores in the sixties were very high. Elijah had been influenced by a statistician, so he concluded that if one person said his scores were low and the other said they were high, the scores must be about average. Is that correct?

ANSWER		ITEM	QUESTIONS/COMMENTS
Y	N	10. Mr. Livingston, the Commissioner of Education, is working hard to improve education in his state. He looked at the mean SAT scores for students in his state this year and found them little different from last year. Have his efforts been fruitless because the mean SAT scores did not increase?	

THE GRADE-EQUIVALENT SCORES INTERPRETATION TEST

ANSWER		ITEM	QUESTIONS/COMMENTS
T	F	1. Tim is a sixth grader. He obtained a GE score of 9.2 in reading. This means that Tim scored well above average sixth graders on reading.	
T	F	2. A GE score for Tim of 9.2 means that he can read as well as ninth graders in the second month of the school year.	
T	F	3. Tim's GE score of 9.2 on reading means that when a group of ninth graders in their second month were tested on ninth grade reading material, they received scores equivalent to Tim's score.	
T	F	4. Tim's GE score of 9.2 on reading means that Tim could well be put in a class of ninth graders for material in which reading skills were important.	
T	F	5. Tim's 9.2 GE in reading means that in a flexible school in which children work on materials at their own level, Tim should be put into a ninth grade class for instruction in reading.	
T	F	6. Tim obtained a GE score of 7.3 in arithmetic on the same test battery from which his reading GE score was 9.2. This means that in reading Tim is nearly 2 years ahead of his performance in arithmetic.	
T	F	7. GE scores of 9.2 in reading and 7.3 in arithmetic indicate that Tim is farther ahead of his own class in reading than in arithmetic.	
T	F	8. Tim's GE of 9.2 in reading was from fall testing in the sixth grade. Tested in the spring, he received a GE score of 8.0. That indicates	

ANSWER   ITEM   QUESTIONS/COMMENTS

that his reading skills declined during that school year. Some effort should be expended to find out why and whether such losses can be expected to continue.

T   F   9. When tested in September, 30 percent of the students in Mr. Brown's fifth grade class got GE scores below 5.1. Something needs to be done to help his students reach grade level. Also, the third and fourth grade teachers should improve the instruction given to students before they reach Mr. Brown.

T   F   10. Jones Elementary School is an inner-city school. The Jones school mean GE score in reading in first grade was .6. The mean increased each year until by the sixth grade it was up to 3.2. Thus, the Jones mean was .4 year behind at the first grade and nearly 3 years behind by the sixth grade. Because the Jones students are falling farther behind the national average each year, the reading program, the teachers, and the administration are inadequate to meet the learning needs of the Jones school students.

EXERCISE 20
NORMS

OBJECTIVE

To enhance understanding of, and provide firsthand experience with, norms.

BACKGROUND

Given the many varied ways that tests can be constructed, knowledge of a raw score on a given test seldom provides enough information to make a meaningful interpretation of performance on the test. Raw scores that have been converted to *z, T, A, C,* sten, stanine, or other such scores tend to be more readily interpretable.[2]

However, given the fact that there exists for the purpose of reporting test scores such a wide variety of derived scales, it is imperative that test developers and writers of test manuals provide the users of such materials with information sufficient to understand the particular scale employed. *Norms* describe the performance on a test of a representative group of testtakers (the *normative* or *standardization* sample) and provide a context for interpreting testtakers' scores. Ideally, and in accordance with guidelines set forth in the *Standards* (1985), the description of a published, standardized test's norms should include, at a minimum, all of the following:

- a description of the scales used in reporting the scores of testtakers in the standardization sample as well as (1) the rationale for using the scales selected, and (2) a description of how the scaled scores were derived from the raw scores;
- a rationale for why raw scores and not scaled scores are being employed, if indeed that is the case;
- a description of the normative study including the year(s) in which the normative data were gathered. The description of the methodology should be in detail

---

[2] The *C* scale (see Guilford & Fruchter, 1978) is an 11-unit scale with a standard deviation of 2. A modified version of the *C* scale is the "standard ten" or *sten* scale (Canfield, 1951), a 10-unit *C* scale that has been used in tests such as the 16 PF.

sufficient to permit evaluation of its appropriateness. Specifically, a presentation of the sampling design, the normative sample, and descriptive statistics as well as response rates should be included; and,

• the normative sample should consist of people similar in many respects to the people a test user might wish to compare test performance on.

In addition, the section on norms in a published test manual might encourage users of the test to develop their own local norms.

YOUR TASK

Picture yourself as a professor in the measurement class at a hypothetical institution we'll call Western Hootsville University. And remember that data from Table 3-1 (how can you forget it?)? That's the data from the course in tests and measurement that *you* teach.

Your counterparts in the state university system, that is, the professors who teach the same course at Eastern Hootsville University, Northern Hootsville University, and Southern Hootsville University, all think that the test from which the data from Table 3-1 were derived is the greatest thing since sliced bread. You have letters on your desk from each of these three instructors asking not only for a copy of your precious exam, but the norms to go with it—this so each of the professors can see how their respective students stack up against those at Western. Being the magnanimous person that you are, you write back that you will send them not only the exam but also an exemplary set of norms to go with it.

And by this point you have no doubt gleaned that your assignment in this task is to create an exemplary set of norms for your class's test data. While you will have to employ your creative imagination in writing about such aspects of the norms as your description of the "standardization sample," you can be quite concrete about other matters such as the descriptive statistics. To the best of your ability, make the description of the norms you create look and "feel" similar to the section on norms that you might find in the manual of a well-standardized published test. If you have no idea what such a section might look like, consult the manuals of some standardized tests.

EXERCISE 21
THE PEARSON r

OBJECTIVE

To enhance understanding of, and provide firsthand experience with, the calculation and interpretation of a coefficient of correlation—specifically, the Pearson *r*.

BACKGROUND

Correlation is an expression of the degree of correspondence between two things. A coefficient of correlation (*r*) expresses a linear relationship between two variables. More technically, it reflects the degree of concomitant variation between a single independent variable (an *X* variable) and a single dependent variable (a *Y* variable). The *coefficient of correlation* is the numerical index that expresses this relationship; it tells us the extent to which *X* and *Y* are "corelated." The most commonly used coefficient of correlation is a statistic developed by Karl Pearson referred to alternatively as the Pearson *r*, *r*, or the Pearson product-moment correlation coefficient.

A sound understanding of the concept of correlation is essential to the study of psychological testing. As we will see in the following chapter on the subject of reliability, a correlation coefficient is the statistical tool used to describe the relationship between one's score on a test and one's score on a re-test with the same instrument. And then again in the chapter on the subject of validity, we will see how, for example, a correlation coefficient is used to describe the relationship between an observed score on a test and the "true score."

YOUR TASK

1. Create a scatterplot.

Regardless of the primary text you are using in this course, you will no doubt find coverage of the use of a *scatterplot* or *scatter diagram*—a graph—to describe the correlation that exists between two variables. Refer to that material in order to create a scatterplot of the data described below.

Student	Number of Hours Spent Preparing	Final Exam Score
Malcolm	23.0	98
Heywood	16.0	92
Mervin	0.5	45
Zeke	12.0	80
Sam	9.0	76
Macy	10.0	57
Elvis II	1.0	61
Jed	14.0	88
Jeb	8.5	70
Leroy	15.0	90

The final examination data for the second graduating class—a total of ten students—enrolled in a new trade school called the "Home Study School of Elvis Presley Impersonators" follow. Adjacent to the final examination score (which no doubt was a take-home test) is the actual number of hours each student spent studying and otherwise preparing for the exam. What

A Scatterplot of Study Time and Final Examination Scores

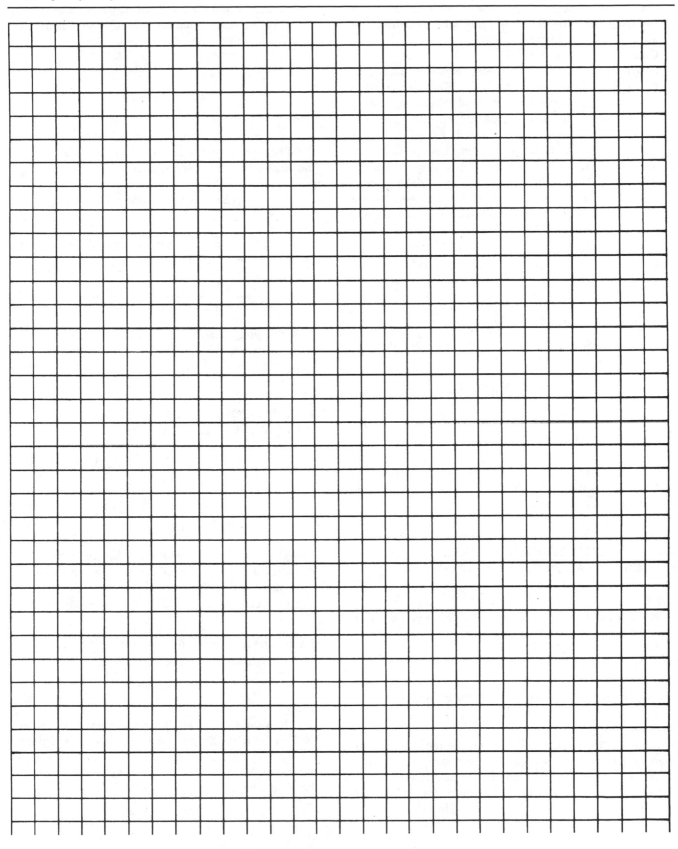

is the direction and magnitude of the correlation between time spent in preparation and score on the final examination? Use your scatterplot to estimate an answer to this question.

2. Calculate and interpret a Pearson r.

How strong is the relationship between number of hours spent in preparation for the final examination and raw score on that examination? What is the nature of the direction of that relationship—positive or negative? The Pearson r is the most widely used of several alternative measures of correlation. It is the statistical tool of choice when the relationship between the variables is linear and when the two variables being correlated are continuous (that is, they can theoretically assume any value). What follows are two formulas used to calculate a Pearson r, one to be used with deviation scores, the other to be used with raw scores. Each formula is explained in step-by-step fashion; all you have to do is the setting-up and the calculations.

The Deviation Score Formula

The deviation score formula for calculating the Pearson r is as follows:

$$r = \frac{\Sigma(X - \overline{X})(Y - \overline{Y})}{\sqrt{\Sigma(X - \overline{X})^2 \Sigma(Y - \overline{Y})^2}}$$

Applying the formula above to the study of time/final examination data and letting X equal the number of hours studied, and Y equal the score on the final examination, a Pearson r can be calculated using the step-by-step procedure described below.

THE DEVIATION SCORE FORMULA FOR CALCULATING THE PEARSON r

Step 1

Set up a table with the following 7 headings, one next to the other, across the top:

$$X, \; Y, \; x, \; y, \; xy, \; x^2, \text{ and } y^2$$

Step 2

List the values for X next to the corresponding values for Y in the table.

Step 3

Calculate the mean for $X(\overline{X})$ and the mean for $Y(\overline{Y})$ and then use this information to calculate deviation scores (x and y) for each value of X and Y. Recall that a deviation score is found by subtracting from each value the mean of its respective distribution ($X - \overline{X}$, and $Y - \overline{Y}$).

Step 4

Multiply each x by its corresponding y and sum all of the products.

$$\Sigma[(x)(y)] = 949.2$$

Step 5

Square each x and then sum all of the squares. Do the same for the corresponding values of y—square each of them and then sum all of the squares.

$$\Sigma x^2 = 416.4$$

$$\Sigma y^2 = 2678.1$$

Step 6

Multiply one sum of the squared deviation scores by the other sum of the squared deviation scores and find the square root of their product.

$$\sqrt{(\Sigma x^2)(\Sigma y^2)} = 1056.0118$$

Step 7

Substitute the values you have calculated for the appropriate terms in the formula and solve for the Pearson r.

$$r = \frac{949.2}{\sqrt{(416.4)(2678.10)}} = \frac{949.2}{1056.0118} = .899$$

Now that you are an expert in the use of the deviation score formula, why not broaden your horizons by calculating the Pearson r using the raw score formula.

THE RAW SCORE FORMULA FOR CALCULATING THE PEARSON r

The raw score formula for calculating the Pearson r is as follows:

$$r = \frac{N\Sigma XY - (\Sigma X)(\Sigma Y)}{\sqrt{[N\Sigma X^2 - (\Sigma X)^2][N\Sigma Y^2 - (\Sigma Y)^2]}}$$

Applying the formula above to the study time/final examination data and letting X equal the number of hours studied, and Y equal the score on the final examination, a Pearson r can be calculated in the following way:

Step 1

Set up a table with the following 5 headings, one next to the other, across the top:

$$X, \; Y, \; XY, \; X^2, \text{ and } Y^2$$

Step 2

List the values for X next to the corresponding values for Y in the table. Sum all of the values for X and note that sum at the bottom of the X column. Sum all of the values for Y and note that sum at the bottom of the Y column.

$$\Sigma X = 109 \qquad \Sigma Y = 757$$

Step 3

Multiply each value of X by its corresponding value of Y and fill in the product in the corresponding place in the XY column. Sum all of these products to obtain ΣXY and note that sum at the bottom of the XY column.

$$\Sigma XY = 9200.5$$

Step 4

Square all of the values of X and then sum all of these values, noting the sum at the bottom of the X^2 column. Square all of the values of Y and then sum all of these values, noting the sum at the bottom of the Y^2 column.

$$\Sigma X^2 = 1604.5 \qquad \Sigma Y^2 = 59983$$

Step 5

Insert the appropriate numbers into the formula and solve for r.

$$r = \frac{10(9200.5) - (109)(757)}{\sqrt{[10(1604.5) - (109)^2][10(59983) - (757)^2]}}$$

$$r = \frac{9492}{\sqrt{[4164][26781]}} = \frac{9462}{10560.118} = .899$$

Regardless whether the deviation or the raw score formula is employed, you probably—hopefully—calculated the value of r to be .899. What does the calculated Pearson r of .899 mean? Is this number statistically significant given the size and nature of the sample? Could this result have occurred by chance? Explain with reference to Appendix B, "Critical Values of Pearson r."

EXERCISE 22
"HELLO" TO RHO

OBJECTIVE

To introduce, explain, and provide a computational example of rho.

BACKGROUND

Rho is a correlation coefficient used when one or both of the variables to be correlated are ordinarily scaled— that is, when one or both of the variables to be correlated is in the form of rank-order data. Note that while we refer to this statistic simply as rho for the sake of brevity, it has been referred to in numerous other ways in the psychometric literature including "Spearman's rho," "the Spearman rho," the "rank-order coefficient of correlation," and "the rank-difference correlation coefficient." The formula for rho is as follows:

$$\text{rho or } r_s = 1 - \frac{6\Sigma d^2}{n^3 - n}$$

Here d is equal to the algebraic difference in ranks for each object or persons in two distributions of ranks, and n is the sample size (or the number of pairs of ranks).

Note that rho is often symbolized with the usual symbol for a correlation coefficient (r) along with an italicized s subscript, the s standing for Spearman.

While the formula for rho is of course different than the formula for the Pearson r, you should understand, as Nunnally (1978, p. 134) pointed out, that rho is "only a shortcut version" of the Pearson r and "the results obtained by applying rho are exactly the same as those obtained by applying . . . [the Pearson r] to two sets of ranks." By the way, it is also true that two other indices of correlation, the phi coefficient and the point-biserial coefficient (both to be discussed subsequently), are also special cases of the product-moment correlation; thus, r, rho, phi, and the point-biserial coefficients of correlation are in the mathematical sense identical.

An example of the type of situation in which rho would be employed in the correlational analysis is the case where two trained behavioral observers rank each of 25 children in a classroom on the variable "hyperactivity." Rho would be used to determine how much agreement there was between the raters. Two personnel managers might rank-order 20 job applicants with respect to suitability for employment; again, rho would be used to obtain an index of the level of agreement. Nunnally (1978, pp. 134–135) reviewed other types of data analysis situations where rho might be employed.

What better way is there to illustrate what's involved in calculating rho than some "hands-on" data analysis. Imagine that 10 would-be beauty school attendees take a beauty school's qualifying examination in order to determine whether they will be accepted for training. Some of the 10 applicants are male, some are female, some eventually take jobs in the world of cosmetology, while others explore ways to become licensed travel agents or dental hygienists. Understand that while some of this information—such as entry or nonentry into the field of beauty—may seem irrelevant at the moment, we will shortly be using it to further illustrate correlational concepts.

The beauty school accepts all 10 applicants contingent on their ability to finance (or have the government finance) their tuition, and once everyone's all paid up, six weeks of rigorous and intensive training begins. At the conclusion of training, and with a plethora of courses

Student	Sex	Entered Into a Career in Beauty?	"A" Score	"B" Score
1. Randy	Male	NO	86	84
2. Shelly	Female	YES	91	93
3. Terry	Male	YES	75	77
4. Robin	Female	NO	64	61
5. Sandy	Female	NO	73	75
6. Leslie	Male	YES	82	80
7. Chris	Female	NO	79	81
8. Kim	Male	YES	79	76
9. Francis	Male	NO	88	85
10. Freddy	Female	YES	80	89

such as Advanced Hair Streaking, Blow Drying 101, and Independent Study in Pedicure, a final examination is administered. Included in the table below are demographic information and career disposition information, as well as raw score (number of items correct) on the beauty school's pre-admission qualifying test (Test A) and post-training final examination (Test B). For the record, both tests are of the 100-item, short-answer variety with one point awarded for each correct answer.

YOUR TASK

Is there a relationship between the pre-admission score on the qualifying examination and the comprehensive end-of-course examination? If so, how would you describe it? Ordinarily, a Pearson r would be calculated to determine the answer to this question—given that we have interval-level data to work with (the test scores), and not merely rankings. However, for the purpose of obtaining computational experience with rho, we (i.e., you) will convert these data into ranks; and that's Step 1.

Step 1

To solve for r_s, begin by placing the data into ranked form if it is not already in ranked form.

You are going to get a little—not much, just a little—help in getting started. Fill in the blank spaces below for the beauty school data:

Student	"A" Score	"B" Score	Rank Order of "A" Score	Rank Order of "B" Score
1. Randy	86	84	3	4
2. Shelly	91	93	—	—
3. Terry	75	77	—	—
4. Robin	64	61	—	—
5. Sandy	73	75	—	—
6. Leslie	82	80	—	—
7. Chris	79	81	—	—
8. Kim	79	76	—	—
9. Franics	88	85	—	—
10. Freddy	80	89	—	—

Step 2

Believe it or not, the worst is over and it's all downhill from here. All you need do is subtract each "B" ranking from its corresponding "A" ranking to obtain a d score. Once you've obtained the d score, square it. Now sum the squares.

Step 3

Solve for rho.

Having calculated rho, what can you say about the relationship between scores on the beauty school's pre-instruction and post-instruction tests?

For more practice with rho, respond to the following two questions.

1. Professors Go and Nogo team-teach a seminar in ethics to ten students. The students in this ethics seminar recently took a midterm examination that consisted of one essay question. As an initial step in evaluating their students' work, the two professors have each rank-ordered the papers, assigning the number 1 to the best paper and the number 10 to the worst. Using Spearman's rho, calculate a coefficient of correlation between the two professors' rankings. What does rho tell us about the respective judgments of Go and Nogo?

	Professor Go	Professor Nogo
Tiffany	5	3
Levelor	1	2
Harley	4	4
Macy	9	7
Dreyfus	8	8
Scotch	2	1
Andersen	10	9
Visine	7	10
Hershey	3	6
Chrysler	6	5

2. Seven students complete the hypothetical "Reading Rank-Order Test" (RROT) twice, with the second test administration conducted two weeks after the first. The RROT does not provide a score for each student. Rather, the tests produce a rank-ordering of the students in terms of the reading ability evidenced on the test. On the first administration of the test, Kimba did best, followed by Julep, Steve, Edie, Nodu, Ike, and Tina. On the second administration, Julep did best, followed by Steve, Kimba, Tina, Ike, Edie, and Nodu. After completing the values for the table that follows, calculate Spearman's rho. What can you conclude from these data?

Student	Test	Retest
Kimba		
Julep		
Nodu		
Steve		
Edie		
Tina		
Ike		

EXERCISE 23
OTHER COEFFICIENTS OF CORRELATION

OBJECTIVE

To introduce and gain some firsthand experience with other coefficients of correlation.

BACKGROUND

In addition to r and rho, there are times when, because of the nature of the data or the sample, other correlation coefficients may be employed. These other coefficients include the biserial r, the point-biserial r, the tetrachoric r, and the phi coefficient.

Denoted by the symbol r_b, the biserial r is appropriate when the two variables to be correlated are continuous in nature, but one of the two has been arbitrarily dichotomized. Inherent in the formula for the calculation of the biserial r is a correction for the arbitrary dichotimization of the dichotomized variable; the result is an estimate of the Pearson r that would have been obtained had the data not been dichotomized.

Referring back to the beauty school example, let's suppose we arbitrarily classify all scores of 65 or over on the final examination as "Pass" and all scores of 64 or under as "Fail." And now let's further suppose that we wished to correlate score on test "A" (see Exercise 22) with pass/fail status on test "B." The appropriate coefficient of correlation to calculate would be r_b. As another example of the way in which biserial correlation may be used, consider the case of a teacher or researcher interested in performance on one item of a test—was the item passed or failed?—in relation to score on the entire test; a right-wrong test item may be viewed as an artificially dichotomized measure of whatever is being assessed by the test as a whole. Biserial correlation coefficients are frequently calculated (or approximated) by means of tables designed for that purpose; should you have occasion to calculate it by means of its formula, that formula (complete with an explanation on how to calculate it) can be found in advanced statistics texts (such as Lord & Novick, 1968).

Denoted by the symbol r_{pb}, the point-biserial r is a correlation coefficient appropriate for use with a variable that is continuous in nature (such as score on the entry level test for the beauty school) and another variable that is a true—not an arbitrary—dichotomy (such as sex of student). In the process of developing a test of ability, for example, we might use r_{pb} to examine the nature of the relationship between an individual item on a test (whether it was answered correctly or incorrectly) and the raw score (number scored as correct) on the entire test. To learn about the nature of the relationship between entry level test score and sex in the beauty school data, we would calculate r_{pb} as follows:

$$ r_{pb} = \sqrt{\frac{n_1 n_0}{N} \left(\frac{\overline{X}_1 - \overline{X}_0}{\sqrt{\Sigma(X - \overline{X})^2}} \right)} $$

Let's preface our explanation of the terms in the expression above by noting that whether an examinee is either male or female will have to be denoted by some quantitative code for "male" and "female." The simplest code we can think of for use here is "0" = male and "1" = female.

Having said that, we explain that in the expression above X represents the continuous variable (score on the entry level test), $\overline{X}$ is equal to the mean of all of the scores on the entry level test, and X_0 and X_1 are respectively representative of scores for male and female testtakers, while n_0 and n_1 are respectively representative of the number of male and female testtakers. N is equal to the total number of testtakers. Knowing all of that, your task is to solve for r_{pb} and then interpret your findings.

The tetrachoric r, denoted by the symbol r_t, is appropriate for use when the two variables to be correlated have been arbitrarily reduced to a dichotomy. The end product of the calculation of r_t approximates what the Pearson r would have been if the data had been continuous and the assumptions inherent in the use of the Pearson r had been met. Referring back to the beauty school example, suppose a score of 65 or over on each of the two tests was arbitrarily designated as a passing grade, while a score of 64 or under was arbitrarily designated as a failing grade. The tetrachoric r would be the appropriate statistic to determine the nature of the relationship that exists between passing or failing the entry level test and passing or failing the final examination. However, even the dean of the beauty school might shy away from calculating r_t once he or she found out how complicated a process it is (see Lord & Novick, 1968).

The phi coefficient, denoted by the Greek letter phi (ϕ) is a coefficient of correlation designed for use with true dichotomies. Referring one more time to the beauty school example, if you were interested in calculating the relationship between entry into the field of beauty and sex, the phi coefficient would be the correlation coefficient of choice. In test development, the phi coefficient is frequently employed to examine the nature of the relationship between correct/incorrect response on a particular item and some truly dichotomous variable (such as graduate/drop-out). In the following equation, let's assume that both of the dichotomous variables being correlated can be coded using the same type of 0/1 coding system we presented in our description of the point-biserial r. Now the phi coefficient of correlation for variables X and Y could be calculated using the following formula:

$$ \phi_{XY} = \frac{p_{(XY)1} - (p_{X1})(p_{Y1})}{\sqrt{(p_{X1})(1 - p_{X1})(p_{Y1})(1 - p_{Y1})}} $$

Here, $p_{(XY)1}$ represents the proportion of testtakers scoring "1" on both X and Y, p_{X1} represents the proportion of testtakers scoring "1" on X, and p_{Y1} represents the proportion of testtakers scoring "1" on Y. Applying the code system of 0 = male, 1 = female, and 0 = did not enter field of beauty and 1 = did enter field of beauty, and using X to denote the occupational disposition variable while using Y to denote the sex variable, we could set up the coding table used to calculate phi as follows:

Student	(Y) Sex	Sex Code	(X) Entered Field?	Field Code
RANDY	MALE	0	NO	0
SHELLY	FEMALE	1	YES	1
TERRY	MALE	0	YES	1
ROBIN	FEMALE	1	NO	0
SANDY	FEMALE	1	NO	0
LESLIE	MALE	0	YES	1
CHRIS	FEMALE	1	NO	0
KIM	MALE	0	YES	1
FRANCIS	MALE	0	NO	0
FREDDY	FEMALE	1	YES	1

YOUR TASK

1. What is the nature of the relationship between entry level test score and sex? What was the value of the point-biserial r you calculated?

2. What is the nature of the relationship between sex and entry into the beauty field in this study? What was the value of the phi coefficient you calculated?

EXERCISE 24
AN EXERCISE IN REGRESSION

OBJECTIVE

To enhance understanding of, and provide firsthand experience with, the concept of regression.

BACKGROUND

In the language of statistics, the definition of *regression* parallels that of its more usual definition of "reversion to some previous state"; in statistics, the reversion referred to is a reversion to the mean. In your text, you probably read about how a regression line is the line of best fit with respect to raw data expressed in the form of a scatterplot. Here we will try to approach the concept of regression from another perspective, focusing on what is actually meant by the concept of *reversion to the mean.* Consider now this hypothetical example:

This year, 100,000 people, each of whom is very much like John and Mary (in terms of variables such as age, socioeconomic status, and so forth), have taken a test called the "National Extraversion Text" (NET). The mean score (or "extraversion quotient"—EQ) for all those people was 100, and the standard deviation was 5. John's EQ according to the test was 110 and Mary's was 90.

Given that there is error inherent in the measurement of EQ scores, take a guess about the nature of the "true score" of John and Mary on the NET. Specifically, if you had to guess, would you say that John's "true score" is

probably higher or lower than 110? And what about Mary's "true score"? Would you guess that it was higher or lower than 90?

If you are like most people, you would guess that since the average score on the test is 100, John's "true score" is probably lower than 110. And using the same logic, you would probably guess that Mary's "true score" is higher than 90. If you in fact made such inferences, you have illustrated for yourself the concept of "regression to the mean."

Knowing no other information than an individual's raw score on a test (we'll refer to it as X), the group's mean score (we'll refer to it as $\overline{X}$), and a reliability estimate of the test (we'll refer to it as r_{xx}), we can obtain an estimate of the individual's true score ($\hat{T}$, read "T hat") on the test by using the following formula:

$$\hat{T} = r_{xx}(X - \overline{X}) + \overline{X}$$

Suppose then that the reliability estimate (r_{xx}) of the NET was .5; what would you estimate John's EQ score to be? How about Mary's? The predicted true score for John is 105 and the calculations follow below. You're on your own if you're curious about Mary's true EQ.

The predicted true score for John would be calculated as follows:

$$\hat{T} = .5(110 - 100) + 100$$

$$= .5(10) + 100$$

$$= 5 + 100$$

$$= 105$$

In psychological testing, the situation sometimes arises wherein we have knowledge of a score on one test (or one particular form of a test) and from that information we would like to predict to some criterion (such as a score on another test, a score on another form of the same test, or a gradepoint average). Consider in this context some data for scores found to be equivalent on the hypothetical "Helping Out Others Test" (HOOT) and another (hypothetical) test distributed by a European publisher, the "Rome Altruism Test" (RAT). Simply for the sake of convenience, let's label the HOOT scores as X and the RAT scores as Y:

HOOT (X)	RAT (Y)
10	10
30	20
50	30
60	40
70	50
80	60

Knowing that the scores on the two tests are related as indicated above, and knowing what a testtaker scored on one of these two tests, we would be able to calculate

—and thus predict with some accuracy—the testtaker's score on the other test. Exactly how accurate our prediction will be will depend on the nature of the correlation between the variables in question; the higher the correlation between the variables in question; the higher the correlation between the two variables—that is, the stronger the absolute (positive or negative) magnitude of the relationship between the variables—the more accurate our prediction.

The formula used to calculate the regression equation is the same as the equation for a straight line:[3]

$$\hat{Y} = a + bX$$

In the equation for the straight line, a is the Y intercept and b is the slope of the line (otherwise expressed as the change in Y divided by the change in X, or $\Delta Y/\Delta X$. In the regression equation, $\hat{Y}$ (the predicted value for Y—read as "Y hat") is substituted for Y and a and b are referred to as *regression coefficients*. In the regression equation,

$$a = \overline{Y} - b\overline{X}$$

and

$$b = \frac{n\Sigma XY - \Sigma X\Sigma Y}{n\Sigma X^2 - (\Sigma X)^2}$$

Suppose you knew that Hector's score on the HOOT was 78; what would you predict Hector's score on the RAT to be? To answer this question, you might proceed as follows:

Step 1

Set up a table that lists the values of X, the values of Y, and the values of XY and X^2. You will also need to determine the values of the expressions below:

- ΣY
- ΣX
- ΣX^2
- $(\Sigma X)^2$

We'll get you started by setting up the table and inserting the values X and Y.

X	Y	XY	X	X^2	Y^2
10	10				
30	20				
50	30				
60	40				
70	50				
80	60				

Step 2

Calculate b, using the following formula:

$$b = \frac{n\Sigma XY - (\Sigma X)(\Sigma Y)}{n\Sigma X^2 - (\Sigma X)^2}$$

Step 3

Solve for a, using the following formula along with the values you obtained in the prior two steps:

$$a = \overline{Y} - b\overline{X}$$

Step 4

Write the resulting regression equation. Thus to predict Hector's score on the RAT, given Hector's score on the HOOT ($X = 78$), we would solve for $\hat{Y}$ as follows:

$$\hat{Y} = a + bX$$

where b and a were the calculated values found in Steps 2 and 3 respectively, and $X = 78$.

Suppose now a revised form of the HOOT was published (the HOOT-R) and you could more accurately predict RAT scores by using a combination of HOOT and HOOT-R scores; because more than one score would be used to predict a criterion score a *multiple regression* equation would be necessary. And you will no doubt breathe a sigh of relief when we tell you that multiple regression is beyond the scope of this book.

YOUR TASK

1. Draw a scatterplot of the HOOT and RAT data presented above. Then draw in—without any calculations or reference to any formulas—what looks to you like the best "line of best fit" for the data.
2. If you knew that Hector's score on the HOOT was 78, what would you estimate his score on the RAT to be?

REFERENCES

Canfield, A. A. (1951). The "sten" scale—A modified C-scale. *Educational and Psychological Measurement, 11*, 295–297.

Guilford, J. P., & Fruchter, B. (1978). *Fundamental statistics in psychology and education.* (6th ed.). New York: McGraw-Hill.

Hays, W. L. (1973). *Statistics for the social sciences.* (2nd ed.). New York: Holt, Rinehart & Winston.

Lord, F. M., & Novick, M. R. (1968). *Statistical theories of mental test scores.* Menlo Park, CA: Addison-Wesley.

Nunnally, J. C. (1978). *Psychometric theory.* (2nd ed.). New York: McGraw-Hill.

Rotton, J., & Kelly, I. W. (1985). Much ado about the full moon: A meta-analysis of lunar-lunacy research. *Psychological Bulletin, 97*, 286–306.

Standards for educational and psychological testing. (1985). Washington, D.C.: American Psychological Association.

---

[3] Elsewhere you may have seen this same formula expressed in an alternate form: $Y = mx + b$.

Scatterplot of HOOT and RAT Data

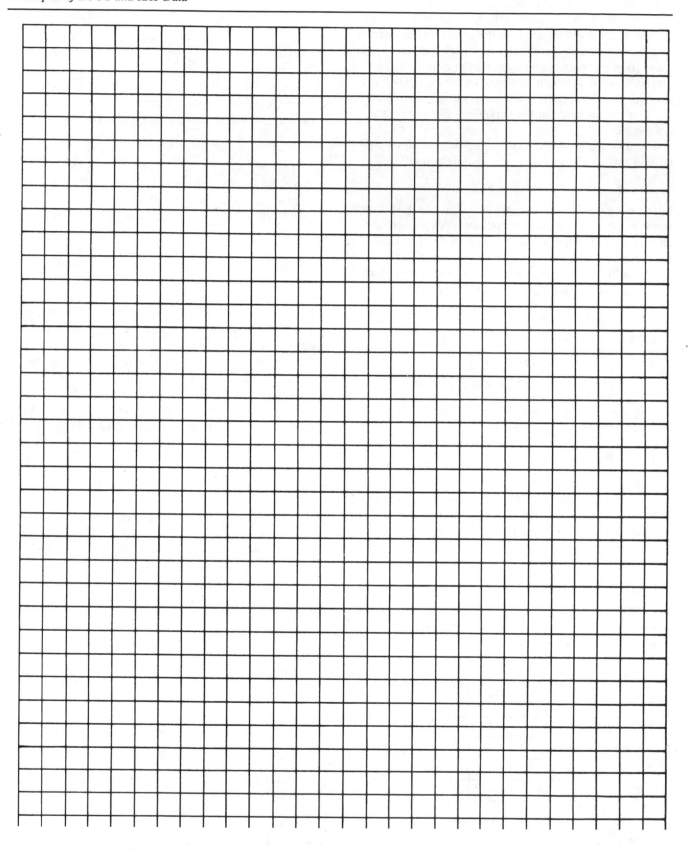

THE 4-QUESTION CHALLENGE

1. National anchor norms are designed to
   (a) "anchor" average test performance of one group to a later administration of the same test.
   (b) "anchor" average test performance of one group to another group elsewhere in the country.
   (c) "anchor" scores on one test to another test through the development of score equivalency tables.
   (d) compare test scores of a group of U.S. Navy officers to test scores of U.S. Naval Academy students.

2. Which is a criterion-referenced test?
   (a) the final spokesmodel competition on *Star Search*
   (b) an examination for entry into the electrician's union
   (c) a teacher-made midterm examination scored on a curve
   (d) None of the above

3. Correlation is an expression of
   (a) the degree and direction of correspondence between two things.
   (b) the degree and direction of correspondence between two independent variables.
   (c) cause and effect in a normal or approximately normal distribution.
   (d) the deviation of moments about the mean of a normally distributed distribution.

4. Meta-analysis is a term used to describe
   (a) a tendency of scores to fan out from the mean.
   (b) a graphic technique for representing regression.
   (c) a variant of psychoanalysis developed by Carl Jung.
   (d) a method for combining information across studies.

Chapter 5

Reliability

On Consistency in Measurement

How much consistency in measures of intelligence or personality would you expect to find between tests administered to this man (actor Albert Finney in Under the Volcano) *and those same tests administered a day or two after he's had a chance to "sleep it off"? What are the broader implications of this example with respect to the subject of test reliability?*

Outline for Chapter 5 of Cohen et al. (1996)
RELIABILITY

The Concept of Reliability
Sources of Error Variance
Test construction
Test administration
Test scoring and interpretation

Types of Reliability Estimates
Test-Retest Reliability Estimates
Parallel Forms and Alternate-Forms Reliability Estimates
Split-Half Reliability Estimates
The Spearman-Brown formula
Other Methods of Estimating Internal Consistency
The Kuder-Richardson formulas
Coefficient alpha
Measures of Inter-Scorer Reliability

Using and Interpreting a Coefficient of Reliability
The Purpose of the Reliability Coefficient
The Nature of the Test
Homogeneity versus heterogeneity of test items
Dynamic versus static characteristics
Restriction or inflation of range
Speed versus power tests
Criterion-referenced tests
Alternatives to the True Score Model

Reliability and Individual Scores
The Standard Error of Measurement
The Standard Error of the Difference Between Two Scores

CLOSE-UP:
The Reliability of the Bayley Scales for Infant Development

EVERYDAY PSYCHOMETRICS:
The Reliability Defense and the Breathalyzer Test

EXERCISE 25
THE CONCEPT OF RELIABILITY

OBJECTIVE

To enhance understanding of the concepts of *reliability* and *error variance*.

BACKGROUND

Broadly speaking, the concept of *reliability* as used in the context of psychological testing refers to the attribute of consistency in measurement. According to what is referred to as the *true score* model or theory, a score on a test reflects not only the "true" amount of whatever it is that is being measured (such as the true amount of an ability or the true amount of a particular personality trait), but also other factors including chance and other influences (such as noise, a troublesome pen—virtually any random, irrelevant influence on the testtaker's performance). A *reliability coefficient* is an index of reliability—one that expresses the ratio between the "true" score on a test and the total variance. We place the word "true" in quotes because, as Stanley (1971, p. 361) so aptly put it, a true score "is not the ultimate fact in the book of the recording angel." Rather, a *true score* on a test is thought of as the (hypothetical) average of all the observed test scores that would be obtained, were an individual to take the test over and over again, an infinite number of times. More technically, a true score is presumed to be the remaining part of the observed score, once the observed score is stripped of the contribution of random error. Recall that

$$X = T + E$$

where X represents an observed score, T represents a true score, and E represents an error score (a score due to random, irrelevant influences on the test). Now let's focus on the squared standard deviations—or variances (symbolized by lowercase sigmas)—of observed scores, true scores, and error scores. The formula that follows,

$$\sigma^2 = \sigma_{tr}^2 + \sigma_e^2$$

indicates that the total variance (σ^2) in an observed score (or a distribution of observed scores) is equal to the sum of the true variance (σ_{tr}^2) and the error (σ_e^2) variance.

The reliability of a test—denoted below by the symbol r_{xx} to indicate that the same ability or trait (x) is being measured twice—is an expression of the ratio of true to observed variance:

$$r_{xx} = \frac{\sigma_{tr}^2}{\sigma^2}$$

If all of the observed scores in a distribution were entirely free of error—and in essence equal to true scores—the calculated value of r_{xx} would be 1. If all of the observed scores in a distribution contained equal parts error and "true" ability (or traits, or whatever), the calculated value of r_{xx} would be .5. The lower range of a reliability coefficient is .00 and a coefficient of .00 would be indicative of a total lack of reliability; stated another way, such a quotient would be indicative of total error variance (and a total absence of any variance due to whatever it was that the test was supposed to have been measuring).

How is a reliability coefficient calculated? While the ratio presented above serves us well in theory, it tends not to be very useful in everyday practice. For most data, we will never know what the "true" variance is and so calculating a reliability coefficient is more complicated than the simple construction of the ratio above. The reliability of a test is typically estimated using the appropriate method from any of a number of existing methods. Before getting to specifics, however, let's go back to the expression indicating that the observed variance is equal to the true variance plus the error variance,

$$\sigma^2 = \sigma_{tr}^2 + \sigma_e^2$$

and rewrite that expression as follows,

$$\sigma_{tr}^2 = \sigma^2 - \sigma_e^2$$

and then substitute the resulting terms into the expression of the ratio of true to observed variances:

$$r_{xx} = \frac{\sigma^2 - \sigma_e^2}{\sigma^2}$$

Solving for r_{xx} we derive the following expression of test reliability:

$$r_{xx} = 1 - \frac{\sigma_e^2}{\sigma^2}$$

In practice, an estimate of reliability as reflected in a reliability coefficient is calculated by means of a coefficient of correlation such as the Pearson r or Spearman's rho—whichever is the appropriate statistic for the data. For example, if the reliability coefficient to be calculated is of the test-retest variety, you may wish to label scores from one administration of the test as the X variable, and scores from the second administration of the test as the Y variable; the Pearson r would then be used (provided all of the assumptions inherent in its use were met) to calculate the correlation coefficient—then more appropriately referred to as a "coefficient of reliability." Similarly, if the reliability coefficient to be calculated is a measure of interscorer reliability, you may wish to label Judge 1's scores as the X variable and Judge 2's scores as the Y variable and then employ either the formula for the Pearson r or the Spearman rho (the latter being the more appropriate statistic for ranked data). An exception to this general rule is the case where a measure of internal consistency is required; here, alternative statistics to r (such as coefficient alpha) may be more appropriate.

YOUR TASK

Answer these three questions in detail:

1. Is it possible to develop a test that will be totally free of error variance? Explain why or why not.
2. As an academic exercise, what if you wished to develop an ability-type test that in no way reflected the test-taker's ability? In other words, contrary to the question above where you asked whether it would be possible to develop a totally error-free test, here you are being asked if it is possible to develop a test that would reflect nothing but error.
3. Describe the role the concept of *correlation* plays in the concept of *reliability*.

EXERCISE 26
TEST-RETEST AND INTERSCORER RELIABILITY

OBJECTIVE

To enhance understanding of, and provide practical experience with, the computation of test-retest reliability and interscorer reliability.

BACKGROUND

As part of Exercise 21 you were made privy to final examination score data for a class from a new home study trade school of impersonation. Let's now suppose that one morning the chancellor of that school wakes up with a severe headache, terrible cramps, and a sudden interest in the area of psychometrics. And given this newfound interest, the chancellor insists that all of the school's ten students must re-take the same (take home) examination—this so that a coefficient of test-retest reliability can be calculated. Let's further suppose that only a week or so has elapsed since each of the students first took the (not so) final examination. All of the students comply and the data for the first administration of the final examination as well as its re-administration are presented below:

Student	Final Exam Score	Re-Test Score
Malcolm	98	84
Heywood	92	97
Mervin	45	63
Zeke	80	91
Sam	76	87
Macy	57	92
Elvis II	61	98
Jed	88	69
Jeb	70	70
Leroy	90	75

YOUR TASK

If you liked the exercise in Chapter 4 where you calculated what in essence was an alternate forms reliability coefficient, you should also like your task here: calculating a test-retest coefficient of correlation.

1. *(a)* Create a scatterplot of these data. Simply by "eyeballing" the obtained scatterplot, what would you say about the test-retest reliability of the final examination the school is using?
   (b) For the purpose of this illustration, let's assume that all of the assumptions inherent in the use of a Pearson r are applicable. Now use r to calculate a test-retest reliability coefficient. What percentage of the observed variance is attributable to "true" differences in ability on the part of the testtakers and what percentage of the observed variance is error variance? What are the possible sources of error variance?
2. Let's say that instead of final examination score and re-test data, the scores above represented the ratings of two former *Star Search* judges with respect to criteria like "general ability to impersonate Elvis Presley," "accent," and "nonoriginality." Re-labeling the data for the final examination as "Judge 1's Ratings," and relabeling the data for the re-test as "Judge 2's Ratings," rank-order the data and calculate a coefficient of interscorer reliability using Spearman's rho. To help get you started, a table you can use to convert the judge's ratings to rankings follows. After you've computed the Spearman rho, answer this question: What is the calculated coefficient of interscorer reliability coefficient and what does it mean?

Student	Judge 1 Rating	Judge 1 Ranking	Judge 2 Rating	Judge 2 Ranking
Malcolm	98	——	84	——
Heywood	92	——	97	——
Mervin	45	——	63	——
Zeke	80	——	91	——
Sam	76	——	87	——
Macy	57	——	92	——
Elvis II	61	——	98	——
Jed	88	——	69	——
Jeb	70	——	70	——
Leroy	90	——	75	——

EXERCISE 27
USING THE SPEARMAN-BROWN FORMULA

OBJECTIVE

To enhance understanding of, and provide firsthand experience with, the Spearman-Brown formula.

A Scatterplot of Test and Re-test Scores

A Scatterplot of the Ratings of Judge 1 and Judge 2

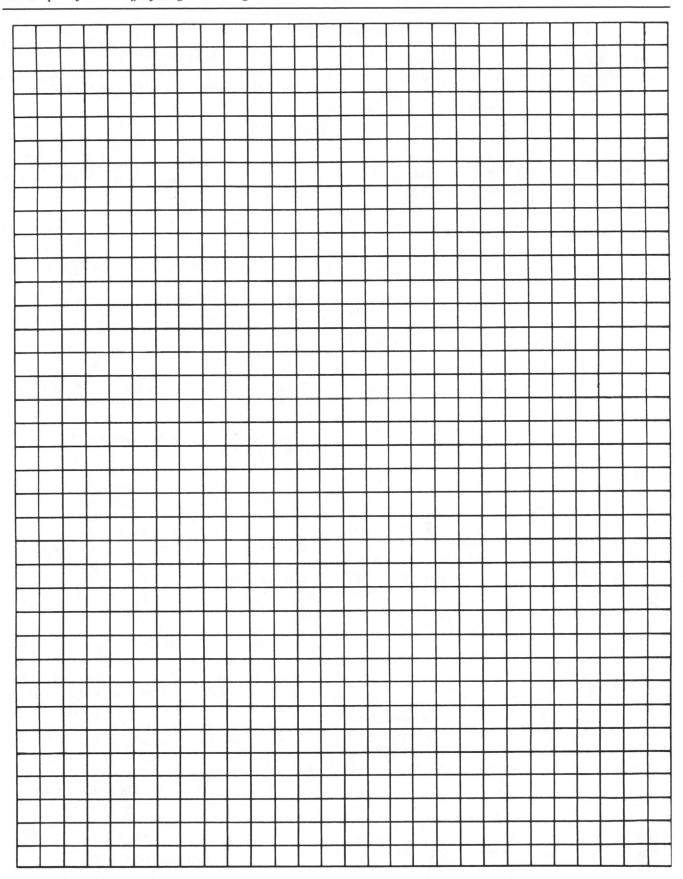

BACKGROUND

"What is the nature of the correlation between one-half of a test and the other?" "What will the estimated reliability of the test be if I shorten the test by a given number of items?" "What will the estimated reliability of the test be if I lengthen the test by a given number of items?" In answer to these and related types of questions, the appropriate tool is the Spearman-Brown formula.

Reduction in test size for the purpose of reducing test administration time is a common practice in situations where the test administrator may have only a limited amount of time with the testtaker. In the version of the Spearman-Brown formula used to estimate the effect of reducing the length of a test, r_{sb} is the Spearman-Brown formula, n represents the fraction by which the test length is being reduced, and r_{xy} represents the reliability coefficient that exists prior to the abbreviation of the test:

$$r_{sb} = \frac{nr_{xy}}{1 + (n-1)r_{xy}}$$

Let's assume that a test user (or developer) wishes to reduce a test from 150 to 100 items; in this case, n would be equal to the number of items in the revised version (100 items) divided by the number of items in the original version (150):

$$n = \frac{100}{150} = .67$$

YOUR TASK

1. Assuming the original 150-item test had a measured reliability (r_{xy}) of .89, use the Spearman-Brown formula to determine the reliability of the shortened test.
2. Now, how about some firsthand experience in using the Spearman-Brown formula to determine the number of items that would be needed in order to attain a desired level of reliability? Assume for the purpose of this example that the reliability coefficient (r_{xx}) of an existing test is .60 and that the desired reliability coefficient (r_{xx}) is .80. In the expression of the Spearman-Brown formula below, n is equal to the factor that the number of items in the test would have to be multiplied by in order to increase the total number of items in the test to the total number needed for a reliability coefficient at the desired level, r' is the desired reliability, and r_{xx} is the reliability of the existing test:

$$n = \frac{r'(1 - r_{xx})}{r_{xx}(1 - r')}$$

Thus, for example, if n were calculated to be 3, a 50-item test would have to be increased by a factor of 3 (for a total of 150 items) in order for the desired level of reliability to have been reached. Try one example on your own. Assume now for the purpose of example that a 100-item test has an $r_{xx} = .60$. In order to increase the reliability of this test to .80, how many items would be necessary?

EXERCISE 28
UNDERSTANDING INTERNAL CONSISTENCY RELIABILITY

OBJECTIVE

To enhance understanding of the psychometric concept of internal consistency reliability as well as methods used to estimate it.

BACKGROUND

This exercise is designed to stimulate thought about the meaning of an estimate of internal consistency reliability. Your instructor may assign one, all, or only some of the parts of this exercise.

YOUR TASK

1. In your own words, write a brief (about a paragraph or two) essay entitled "The Psychometric Concept of Internal Consistency Reliability."
2. Using your school library, locate and read three primary sources having to do with methods of obtaining an estimate of internal consistency. On the basis of what you have learned from these articles, rewrite the essay you wrote in Part 1, incorporating the new information. Your new essay should be no more than two pages.
3. A number of different methods may be used to obtain an estimate of internal consistency reliability. In a sentence or two, describe when each of the following would be appropriate:
   (a) the Spearman-Brown formula
   (b) coefficient alpha
   (c) KR-20
4. Each of the following statements is true. In one or two sentences, explain why this is so.
   (a) An internal consistency reliability estimate is typically achieved through only one test session.
   (b) An estimate of internal consistency reliability is inappropriate for heterogeneous tests.
   (c) An estimate of internal consistency reliability is inappropriate for speeded tests.
   (d) When estimating internal consistency reliability, the size of the obtained reliability coefficient depends not only on the internal consistency of the test, but on the number of test items.

REFERENCE

Stanley, J. C. (1971). Reliability. In R. L. Thorndike (Ed.), *Educational measurement*. (2nd ed.). Washington, D.C.: American Council on Education.

THE 4-QUESTION CHALLENGE

1. A coefficient of reliability is

   (a) a proportion that indicates the ratio between "true" score on a test and the total variance.

   (b) a proportion that indicates the ratio between a "universe" score and the total universe.

   (c) equal to the ratio between the variance and the standard deviation in a normal distribution.

   (d) None of the above

2. Test construction, test administration, and test scoring and interpretation are

   (a) the sole responsibility of a test publisher.

   (b) sources of error variance.

   (c) "facets" according to true score theory.

   (d) All of the above

3. A measure of a test's internal consistency reliability could be obtained through the use of

   (a) Kuder-Richardson formula 20.

   (b) Cronbach's coefficient alpha.

   (c) the Spearman-Brown formula.

   (d) All of the above

4. In contrast to a power test, a speed test

   (a) has a time limit designed to be long enough to allow all testtakers to attempt all items.

   (b) can yield a split-half reliability estimate based on only one administration of the test.

   (c) tends to yield score differences among testtakers that are based on performance speed.

   (d) tends to yield spuriously inflated estimates of alternate forms reliability.

Chapter 6

Validity

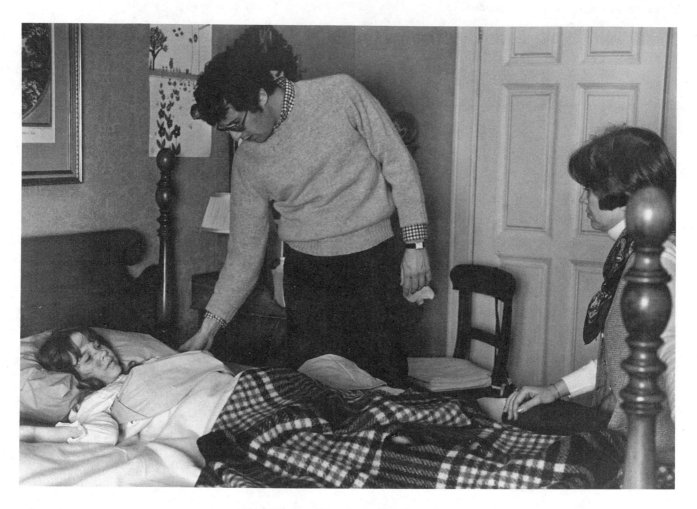

Is There an Exorcist in the House?

Why is the little girl in The Exorcist *acting strangely? After an exhaustive set of medical tests that fail to provide a satisfactory answer, the doctors in this movie refer the mother to the clergy for more diagnostic tests—the latter tests to explore the hypothesis that the girl is possessed. But stop a moment and think about how a test or measure that purported to measure the construct "possession" might be validated. Specifically, how might one attempt to establish the content, criterion-related, and construct validity of the test or measure?*

By the way, the photo above is not *a clip from* The Exorcist *but rather an on-the-set, between-takes shot of the little girl (actress Linda Blair), the concerned mother (actress Ellen Burstyn), and the film's director, William Friedkin.*

Outline for Chapter 6 of Cohen et al. (1996)
VALIDITY

The Concept of Validity
  Face Validity

Content Validity
  The Quantification of Content Validity

Criterion-Related Validity
  What Is a Criterion?
    Characteristics of a criterion
  Concurrent Validity
  Predictive Validity
    The validity coefficient
    Incremental validity
    Expectancy data
    Decision theory and test utility

Construct Validity
  Evidence of Construct Validity
    Evidence of homogeneity
    Evidence of changes with age
    Evidence of pretest/posttest changes
    Evidence from distinct groups
    Convergent evidence
    Discriminant evidence
    Factor analysis

Validity and Test Bias
  The Definition of "Test Bias"
    Rating error
    Test bias and the federal courts
  Fairness as Applied to Tests

CLOSE-UP:
  Factor Analysis: What It Is, How It's Done, and What to Do with It

EVERYDAY PSYCHOMETRICS:
Adjustment of Test Scores by Group Membership:
Fairness in Testing or Foul Play?

EXERCISE 29
THE CONCEPT OF VALIDITY

OBJECTIVE

To enhance understanding of, and provide firsthand experience with, the concept of validity.

BACKGROUND

The word *validity* as applied to a test refers to a judgment concerning how well a test does in fact measure what it purports to measure; more specifically, it is a judgment based on evidence about the appropriateness of inferences drawn from test scores. One way of conceptualizing validity has been with respect to the following three-category taxonomy:

Content validity
Criterion-related validity
Construct validity

Within the context of the three-category taxonomy, the validity of a test may be evaluated by (1) scrutinizing its content, (2) relating scores obtained on the test to other test scores or other measures, and (3) executing a comprehensive analysis of not only how scores on the test relate to other test scores and measures, but also how they can be understood within some theoretical framework for understanding the construct the test was designed to measure. These three approaches to validity assessment are not mutually exclusive; each should be thought of as one type of evidence that, with others, contributes to a judgment concerning the validity of the test. However, although all three types of validity evidence contribute to a unified picture of a test's validity, a test user may not need to know about all three types of validity evidence; depending upon the use to which a test is being put, one or another of these three types of validity evidence may not be as relevant as the next.

YOUR TASK

1. Select any psychological trait such as introversion, aggressiveness, independence—any one will do. Suppose now that someone has created a new test to measure whatever psychological trait you identified above. The new test appropriately enough is called "The Test of *[fill in the blank with the name of the trait]*."

    Because you are keenly interested in this particular psychological trait and want to know if indeed this new test is measuring what it purports to measure, you begin writing a proposal for a grant to conduct a test validation study. *Validation* is the process of gathering

and evaluating validity evidence; one speaks, for example, of content validation strategies, criterion-related validation strategies, and construct validation strategies. Briefly outline what you plan to do in order to obtain content-, criterion-, and construct-related validity evidence.

Oh, and there is one other thing . . .

2. The concept of *face validity* refers more to what a test appears to measure than to what the test actually measures; it in essence relates to a judgment concerning how relevant the items appear to be to the subject matter of the test. If a test definitely appears to measure what it purports to measure "on the face of it," it could be said to be high in face validity. Face validity, according to the 1974 *Standards for Educational and Psychological Testing*, is not an acceptable basis for interpretive inferences from test scores.[1] Still, face validity is important to the extent that it exerts an influence on the way the testtaker approaches the testing situation. Include in your description of content-, criterion-, and construct-related validation strategies, how you might attempt to determine whether the new test was high or low in face validity.

EXERCISE 30
THE QUANTIFICATION OF CONTENT VALIDITY

OBJECTIVE

To enhance understanding of, and provide firsthand experience with, the concept of content validity.

BACKGROUND

Content validity refers to a judgment concerning how adequately a test samples behavior representative of the universe of behavior the test was designed to sample. In many instances the determination of whether or not a test is content valid depends upon the opinion of a panel of experts or judges. Thus for example, a panel of experts in the area of shyness might be called upon to determine if a test of shyness adequately samples the universe of shy/not shy-type behaviors.

Lawshe (1975) developed what he called a *content validity ratio (CVR)* to be used in conjunction with ratings made by a panel of experts. For example, suppose a panel of experts were called upon to decide whether

---

[1] See page 26 in that edition of the *Standards*. By the way, we cited that edition and not the 1985 revision of the *Standards* because the term *face validity* isn't even mentioned in the section on validity in the latter edition.

skill in (or knowledge of) a particular area as measured by a test item was essential to the performance of a job. And let's say the panelists could rate the behavior tapped by the test item as either essential, useful but not essential, or not necessary. The more panelists who perceived the item as essential, the greater the degree of content validity. The formula for the CVR is as follows:

$$CVR = \frac{n_e - N/2}{N/2}$$

Here, n_e is equal to the number of panelists indicating "essential," and N is the total number of panelists. When fewer than half the total number of panelists indicated "essential," the CVR will be negative. If exactly half of the panelists indicate "essential," the CVR will be zero. And when more than half but not all the panelists indicate "essential," the CVR will range between .00 and .99.

In content-validating a test, the content validity ratio is calculated for each item. The items for which agreement could have occurred by chance are eliminated. The table below from Lawshe (1975) provides the minimum CVR values needed for significance at the .05 level. In the case where there are 10 panelists, an item would need a minimum CVR of .62 for significance at the .05 level.

YOUR TASK

In order to provide you with some firsthand experience with the calculation of a CVR, imagine the following scenario. An experimental psychologist by the name of Nussbaum has devoted her research life to addressing questions such as (1) why so many Ph.D.'s seem to have problems correctly spelling and punctuating "Ph.D." and (2) the associations people have to various smells. In the

Table 6-1

Minimum Values of the Content Validity Ratio for Significance at p = .05 (one-tailed test)

Number of Panelists	Minimum Value
5	.99
6	.99
7	.99
8	.75
9	.78
10	.62
11	.59
12	.56
13	.54
14	.51
15	.49
20	.42
25	.37
30	.33
35	.31
40	.29

latter context, she has been developing a new test to measure associations conjured by different scents and has called upon a panel of 20 experts (all of whom are Ph.D.'s with a well-documented ability to spell and punctuate their degree appropriately) to assist in the project. The test, christened the Nussbaum Olfactory Schedule (NOS), contains 50 items—each of which entails the administration of a stimulus smell (such as a rose, pine, and lemon-scented dishwashing liquid). Each item is rated by each expert as imparting either a "unique smell," "an odor with some potential," or "a totally not unique smell." The idea here is to assemble items with unique smells. The ratings for the first five items appear below. Using the symbol n_u to indicate the number of panelists judging a particular item or stimulus to be unique, and calculating the CVR for each item, determine whether you would include each of these items in the NOS and explain why.

Item 1: 9 of the judges rated it unique.
Item 2: 10 of the judges rated it unique.
Item 3: 12 of the judges rated it unique.
Item 4: 14 of the judges rated it unique.
Item 5: 17 of the judges rated it unique.

EXERCISE 31
PREDICTING A CRITERION SCORE

OBJECTIVE

To enhance familiarity and provide firsthand experience with the process of predicting a criterion score.

BACKGROUND

One important application of the validity coefficient is its use in predicting a criterion score. Suppose for example that on the basis of a college entrance examination, a college admissions officer seeks to predict what an applicant's grades might look like at the end of the first semester of college.

You will recall that in general, as r_{xy} approaches 1.00, prediction accuracy increases; as r_{xy} approaches 0.0, prediction accuracy decreases. In order to be able to predict individual criterion scores, the test user or test developer needs validation data from a representative sample of a defined population—predictor test scores (which we will refer to as X scores) as well as criterion scores (which we will refer to as Y scores). One procedure for calculating an estimated criterion score (referred to as Y' and pronounced "Y prime") entails the following:

- computation of the respective means and standard deviations of X and Y;

- substitution of the appropriate values into a formula for the linear regression equation; and
- solving the equation to determine the value of Y'.

If the relationship between the two variables (the test score and the criterion score) is linear, a linear regression for prediction of the criterion such as outlined below may be employed.

Step 1

Determine the specific regression equation from the general formula based on the data by substituting the respective means and standard deviations of X and Y into the general formula. The general formula for predicting a criterion score is

$$Y' = \left[(r_{xy}) \left(\frac{s_y}{s_x} \right) (X - \overline{X}) \right] + \overline{Y}$$

where Y' = the estimated criterion score
r_{xy} = the Pearson r
s_y = the standard deviation of the criterion scores
s_x = the standard deviation of the predictor scores
X = an individual predictor score
$\overline{X}$ = mean of the predictor scores
$\overline{Y}$ = mean of the criterion scores

After the means and standard deviations are substituted into the general formula, the equation reduces to: $Y' = aX + b$ in which a and b are, as we noted in Chapter 4, regression coefficients. Also as we noted in Chapter 4, the reduced equation is recognizable as the equation for a straight line.

Step 2

Choose one individual test score. Substitute the score for X and solve for Y'.

To predict any criterion score from any test score, repeat Step 2. Mathematically, one can also predict the test score (X) from a knowledge of the criterion score (Y).

As an example, let's assume a high school guidance counselor has conducted a validation study of a hypothetical test we will call the "Freshman Grade Predictor" (FGP). The counselor has before him the last year's class of students' FGP scores obtained while the students were still seniors in high school. The counselor also has before him the students' grade-point indexes for their first year of college (for those students who attended college). If the tests scores on the FGP are indeed valid for predicting freshman grades, then the test will be a boon to the counselor with respect to the counseling of future classes of students (as well as advising school officials) on sundry matters (such as those regarding the placement of students in accelerated, average, or remedial classes).

Letting X stand for a score and Y stand for a "score" on the predictor (actually grade-point average), let's assume that counselor observed the following:

r_{xy} = .89   This is an expression of a correlation coefficient though in the present context it would more appropriately be referred to as a *validity coefficient*. It expresses the coefficient of correlation that exists between the predictor and criterion variables.

s_y = .6   The standard deviation of grade-point averages for the first year of college-level work is .6.

s_x = 10   The standard deviation of FGP test scores is 10.

$\overline{X}$ = 50   The mean of FGP test scores is 50.

$\overline{Y}$ = 2.0   The mean grade-point average for the first year of college work is 2.0.

The general formula for the regression equation and the appropriate substitutions are as follows:

$$Y' = \left[(r_{xy}) \left(\frac{s_y}{s_x} \right) (X - \overline{X}) \right] + \overline{Y}$$

$$Y' = \left[(.89) \left(\frac{0.6}{10.0} \right) (X - 50) \right] + 2.0$$

$$Y' = [(.89)(.06)(X - 50)] + 2.0$$

$$Y' = [(.05)(X - 50)] + 2.0$$

$$Y' = [.05X - 2.5] + 2.0$$

$$Y' = .05X - .5 \qquad \text{(a)}$$

The reduced equation (a) is the regression equation with which we can now predict freshman grade-point average with knowledge of only a single test score.

Assume now that this is a new school year. The counselor needs all the help he can get to answer this question: Should Paul be placed in an accelerated class? The overall grade-point average of students in the accelerated class is 3.0. Paul's score on the FGP was 80. Knowing Paul's test score, the counselor can estimate Paul's freshman grade-point average; this may be one—and only one—bit of information used to decide if Paul should indeed be placed in an accelerated class. The validation study had indicated that the validity coefficient between FGP test scores and freshman grade-point average is .89. Substituting Paul's test score into the regression equation obtained from the validation study we obtain the following:

$$Y' = .05X - .5$$

$$Y' = .05(80) - .5$$

$$Y' = 3.5$$

The counselor estimates Paul's freshman grade-point average to be about 3.5. The next question the counselor needs answered is "How accurate is this estimate?" The standard error of estimate (s_{est}) comes into play here.[2] This statistic allows one to determine how much of the score is attributable to error in the statistical sense (recall that "error" is the difference between the observed score and the predicted score) and its formula is as follows:

$$s_{est} = s_y \sqrt{1 - r_{xy}^2}$$

where s_{est} = standard error of estimate,
s_y = standard deviation of the criterion score, and
r_{xy} = the correlation (validity) coefficient.

Using the data from the example above:

$$s_y = .6$$

$$r_{xy} = .89$$

$$s_{est} = .6\sqrt{(1 - .89^2)}$$

$$= .6\sqrt{1 - .792}$$

$$= .6\sqrt{(.208)}$$

$$= .6(.456)$$

$$= .27$$

What is the meaning of the .27 we obtained? To interpret this result, recall that with respect to units of the standard error of measurement:

±1 = approximately 68% of the area under the normal curve
±2 = approximately 95% of the area under the normal curve
±3 = approximately 99.7% of the area under the normal curve

Similarly, with regard to a predicted score and the standard error of estimate, the approximate probabilities are as follows:

68% that the predicted score will occur within ±1 s_{est}
95% that the predicted score will occur within ±2 s_{est}
99.7% that the predicted score will occur within ±3 s_{est}

If Paul's predicted grade-point average (Y') were 3.5 with $s_{est} = .27$, the probability is 95% that his actual grade-point average would fall within ±2 s_{est} of his predicted grade-point average, or 3.5 ± .54 (or between 2.96 and 4.04). If the correlation were higher, the standard error of estimate would be smaller and the interval within which a predicted score would be most likely to occur would be narrower. The guidance counselor will have to look to other sources such as teacher recommendations

---

[2] Sometimes expressed as $S_{y.x}$ and read "the standard deviation of Y for a given value of X."

in drawing his conclusion about placement in the accelerated class.

For the sake of example, let's consider the case wherein the FGP correlates almost perfectly with freshman grade-point average—where r_{xy} equals .99. The regression equation, assuming the means and standard deviations for X and Y stayed the same as above, would be

$$Y' = \left[(r_{xy}) \left(\frac{s_y}{s_x} \right) (X - \overline{X}) \right] + \overline{Y}$$

$$Y' = \left[(.99) \left(\frac{.6}{10} \right) (X - 50) \right] + 2.0$$

$$Y' = [.0594X - 2.97] + 2$$

$$Y' = .0594X - .97$$

Paul's estimated criterion score based on a test score of 80 would be

$$Y' = .0594(80) - .9 = 3.782$$

and the standard error of estimate would be

$$s_{est} = s_y \sqrt{(1 - r^2)}$$

$$= .6\sqrt{(1 - .99^2)}$$

$$= .6\sqrt{(1 - .9801)}$$

$$= .6\sqrt{.0199}$$

$$= .6(.14)$$

$$= .08$$

We can see that with a correlation (validity) coefficient of .99, the counselor could be 95% confident that Paul's grade-point average would occur within ±2s_{est}, which is 3.77 ± .16—between 3.61 and 3.93. Notice the prediction interval is narrower than the one computed with the lower correlation coefficient of .89.

Now let's suppose the FGP did not correlate at all with high school grade-point average. With $r_x = 0.0$, the regression equation reduces to $Y' = \overline{Y}$:

$$s_{est} = s_y \sqrt{1 - r^2}$$

$$= .6\sqrt{1 - 0.0^2}$$

$$= .6\sqrt{1}$$

$$= .6(1)$$

$$= .6$$

With reference to these data, one could say with 95% confidence that Paul's high school grade-point average would occur within ±2(.6) (or between 0.8 and 3.2).

The three examples cited to illustrate the relationships between the correlation (validity) coefficient and the standard error of estimate may be summarized as follows:

r_{xy}	s_{est}	Predicted Criterion Range at 95% Confidence Level
.89	.27	2.8 to 3.8
.99	.08	3.6 to 3.9
.00	.60	0.8 to 3.2

Note that as r_{xy} approaches 1.00, the standard error of estimate shrinks, and the interval within which the criterion score is likely to occur also shrinks. Stated another way, as r_{xy} approaches 1.00, the more precisely we can predict the range within which a criterion score is likely to occur.

To use s_{est} meaningfully as a measure of error in predicting criterion scores, the XY relationship should not only be linear but the variances of the respective X and Y distributions should not be significantly different from one another. One easy though imprecise way to assess linearity is by drawing a scatterplot of the data. If the cloud of dots appears to bend (and you aren't suffering from visual defects or hallucinations, and haven't been drinking or otherwise had your state of consciousness altered), suspect nonlinearity of the data. The scatterplot may also reveal unequal variances, a condition known as *heteroscedasticity* (*hetero* means "different"; *scedastic* means "scatter"). Heteroscedasticity occurs when there is wider variability in criterion performance among, for example, the high-scoring testtakers as compared with the low-scoring testtakers. The resulting scatterplot is wider toward one end of the bivariate distribution. Figure 6-1 provides an example of heteroscedastic data. Chronological age is the X variable; mental age as determined by performance on the hypothetical "National Intelligence Test" (NIT) is the Y variable. The wider variability at the upper end suggests there is wider variation in mental age among the (chronologically) older testtakers.

In this exercise we have examined and illustrated statistical considerations with respect to the relationship between two variables (correlation) and the prediction of one variable from another (regression). As you are—or should be—aware, corresponding statistical techniques exist for use with more than one predictor variable; these corresponding techniques are multiple correlation and multiple regression. If, for example, we were trying to predict married subjects' criterion performance on a "life satisfaction test" (LST), we might administer a number of different (predictor) tests—perhaps the following three: a marital satisfaction test, a job satisfaction test, and a self-satisfaction test. After administering these three tests as well as the criterion LST to a sample of respondents, the results from a multiple correlation might indicate that the self-satisfaction test is more highly correlated with the criterion than the other two tests and should therefore be "weighted" more heavily in the multiple regression equation. Of course, it's a lot more complicated than that, and the interested reader is referred to any of the many current statistics texts that discuss in detail the techniques of multiple correlation and multiple regression.

YOUR TASK

Walk in the shoes of the guidance counselor described above and decide whether another candidate for accelerated class placement, Karla, should or should not be placed in the accelerated class. Karla's score on the FGP was 86, r_{xy} was equal to .75, and s_y was equal to .87. After you give your answer, provide a word or two about how sure you are.

EXERCISE 32
THE MULTITRAIT-MULTIMETHOD MATRIX

OBJECTIVE

To enhance understanding of how a multitrait-multimethod matrix (Campbell & Fiske, 1959) can function to provide insights regarding the convergent and discriminant validity of the methods used.

BACKGROUND

In the example that follows, values for three traits as obtained by three methods will be inserted into a matrix of correlations. The template for insertion of these values is presented in Table 6-2, and a step-by-step description of the insertion of the values is presented in Tables 6-3 through 6-8.

YOUR TASK

After reading the description of the multitrait-multimethod that follows, respond to questions 1 and 2 at the end of this exercise.

THE MULTITRAIT-MULTIMETHOD MATRIX

"Multitrait" means "two or more traits" and "multimethod" means "two or more methods." The multitrait-multimethod matrix (Campbell & Fiske, 1959) is the matrix or table that results from correlating variables (traits) within and between methods. Values for any

Figure 6-1

Heteroscedastic scatterplot showing the relationship between chronological age and mental age as measured by the NIT

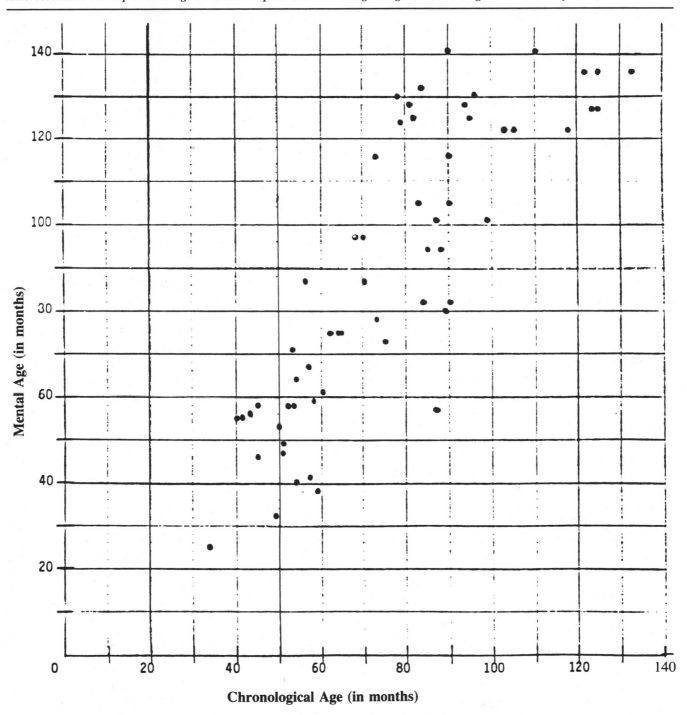

number of traits (such as aggressiveness or extraversion) as obtained by various methods (such as behavioral observation or a projective test) are inserted into the table, and the resulting matrix of correlations provides insight with respect to both the convergent and discriminant validity of the methods used. Table 6-2 provides a preview of the basic structure of the matrix when measures of three traits have been obtained by the use of three methods.

Let's suppose you have developed a test you wish to validate that purports to measure the trait "job satisfaction" (JS). Your test is a paper-and-pencil, self-report measure of satisfaction in the workplace. Using the multitrait-multimethod design, you would need to examine at least one other variable. You select marital satisfaction (MS) as a second trait to examine. "For good measure," you add a third trait to the experimental design: self-satisfaction (SS), a trait you define as the comfort and

Table 6-2

Basic Structure of a Multitrait-Multimethod Matrix for Three Traits Assessed by Three Methods

	Method 1			Method 2			Method 3		
	Trait 1	*Trait 2*	*Trait 3*	*Trait 1*	*Trait 2*	*Trait 3*	*Trait 1*	*Trait 2*	*Trait 3*
Method 1									
Trait 1	.								
Trait 2	.	.							
Trait 3	.	.	.						
Method 2									
Trait 1	.	.	.	.					
Trait 2	.	.	.	.	.				
Trait 3	.	.	.	.	.	.			
Method 3									
Trait 1	.	.	.	.	.	.	.		
Trait 2	.	.	.	.	.	.	.	.	
Trait 3	.	.	.	.	.	.	.	.	.

satisfaction one has with oneself alone, including personal comfort and satisfaction with level of academic, financial, and social achievement. If strong correlations were found to exist between measures of JS, MS, and SS, you might conclude that all three of these measures were actually measuring the same thing, a construct you might call "general life satisfaction." Alternatively, moderate correlations among these traits assessed by the instruments you are using would suggest that while all three may be components of general satisfaction, each also contributes something unique; each represents a viable trait separate and distinct from the others.

As illustrated in Table 6-3, the three methods you have elected to use are (1) a self-report rating scale, (2) a spouse rating scale, and (3) a peer questionnaire; each of the three types of satisfaction traits we are interested in will be assessed by each one of these methods. This means, for example, that a measure of "self-satisfaction" will be obtained not only by the subject himself or herself, but also by the subject's spouse (that is, how self-satisfied the spouse believes the subject to be) and by a peer of the subject.

The data required for insertion into the matrix include the following: reliability coefficients, validity coefficients, correlations between the different traits measured by the same method, and correlations between different traits measured by the different methods. In Table 6-4, along the diagonal we have labeled **a**, are the reliability coefficients for the three traits measured by the same method. Focusing on this part of the matrix we can see that the reliability coefficient of the self-report job satisfaction scale is .98; the reliability coefficient of the self-report marital satisfaction is .94, the reliability of self-satisfaction as measured by the peer questionnaire is .88, and so on. The reliability coefficients will typically be the highest values reported in the matrix.

Another part of the matrix contains correlations between different traits using the same method; it is highlighted

Table 6-3

A Multitrait-Multimethod Matrix for Three Measures of Satisfaction Assessed by Three Different Methods

	Self-report			Spouse Rating Scale			Peer Questionnaire		
	JS	*MS*	*SS*	*JS*	*MS*	*SS*	*JS*	*MS*	*SS*
Self-report									
JS	.								
MS	.	.							
SS	.	.	.						
Spouse rating scale									
JS	.	.	.	.					
MS	.	.	.	.	.				
SS	.	.	.	.	.	.			
Peer questionnaire									
JS	.	.	.	.	.	.	.		
MS	.	.	.	.	.	.	.	.	
SS	.	.	.	.	.	.	.	.	.

Table 6-4

Multitrait-Multimethod Matrix with Reliability Coefficients Inserted

	Self-report			Spouse Rating Scale			Peer Questionnaire		
	JS	MS	SS	JS	MS	SS	JS	MS	SS
Self-report									
JS	a .98								
MS	.	.94							
SS	.	.	.96						
Spouse rating scale									
JS	.	.	.	a .92					
MS	.	.	.	.	.89				
SS	.	.	.	.	.	.86			
Peer questionnaire									
JS	.	.	.	.	.	.	a .80		
MS	.	.	.	.	.	.	.	.85	
SS	.	.	.	.	.	.	.	.	.88

Table 6-5

Multitrait-Multimethod Matrix, with Correlations Between Different Traits Using the Same Methods Highlighted

	Self-report			Spouse Rating Scale			Peer Questionnaire		
	JS	MS	SS	JS	MS	SS	JS	MS	SS
Self-report									
JS	.								
MS	b .50	.							
SS	.42	.59	.						
Spouse rating scale									
JS	.	.	.	.					
MS	.	.	.	b .40	.				
SS	.	.	.	.60	.52	.			
Peer questionnaire									
JS	.	.	.	.	.	.	.		
MS	.	.	.	.	.	.	b .10	.	
SS	.	.	.	.	.	.	.50	.46	.

in Table 6-5 in the solid triangles labeled **b**. If tests are actually measuring different constructs, these correlations should be relatively low. Self-report measures of marital satisfaction and job satisfaction correlate .50—a fact that suggests that while they are measuring something in common, they are also both contributing unique information as well. Much the same could be said about the self-satisfaction measures, which also seem to fall in the .40 to .60 range.

A third part of the matrix contains the validity coefficients—designated in Table 6-6 along the **c** diagonals. Here we see the correlations between the same trait using different methods. For example, the validity coefficient

between job satisfaction by self-report and job satisfaction by spouse rating is .65; the validity coefficient between marital satisfaction by spouse rating and marital satisfaction by peer questionnaire is .72.

As illustrated in Table 6-7 a fourth component of the matrix contains correlations between different traits using different methods (**d** triangles). The value of these correlation coefficients will be among the lowest in the matrix if evidence of construct validity is deemed to be present.

The complete multitrait-multimethod matrix is presented in Table 6-8. For satisfactory evidence of construct validity, the validity coefficients (representing correlations between

Table 6-6

Multitrait-Multimethod Matrix with Validity Coefficients for the Same Trait Assessed by Different Methods

	Self-report			Spouse Rating Scale			Peer Questionnaire		
	JS	MS	SS	JS	MS	SS	JS	MS	SS
Self-report									
JS	.								
MS	.	.							
SS	.	.	.						
Spouse rating scale									
JS	**c** .65	.		.					
MS	.	.61	.	.	.				
SS	.	.	.66	.	.	.			
Peer questionnaire									
JS	**c** .59	.	.	**c** .69	.		.		
MS	.	.55	.	.	.72	.	.	.	
SS	.	.	.58	.	.	.68	.	.	.

Table 6-7

Multitrait-Multimethod Matrix with Correlations for Different Traits Assessed by Different Methods

	Self-report			Spouse Rating Scale			Peer Questionnaire		
	JS	MS	SS	JS	MS	SS	JS	MS	SS
Self-report									
JS	.								
MS	.	.							
SS	.	.	.						
Spouse rating scale									
JS	.	**d** .10	.15	.					
MS	**d** .02	.	.18	.	.				
SS	.04	.10	.	.	.	.			
Peer questionnaire									
JS	.	**d** .08	.11	.	**d** .00	.04	.		
MS	**d** .01	.	.09	**d** .00	.	.02	.	.	
SS	.06	.11	.	.02	.05	.	.	.	.

the same traits using different methods) in the **c** diagonal should be higher than correlations between different traits, same methods (**b** triangles); they should also be higher than correlations between different traits, different methods (**d** triangles). If job satisfaction correlated with marital satisfaction using different methods (validity coefficients), it should be higher than job satisfaction correlated with marital satisfaction by the same method. If the correlation between self-report job and marital satisfaction were higher than job satisfaction by self-report correlated with job satisfaction by peer questionnaire, one could assume that the scores on self-report

Table 6-8

A Sample Multitrait-Multimethod Matrix

	Self-report			Spouse Rating Scale			Peer Questionnaire		
	JS	MS	SS	JS	MS	SS	JS	MS	SS
Self-report									
JS	**a** .98								
MS	**b** .50	.94							
SS	.42	.59	.96						
Spouse rating scale									
JS	**c** .65	**d** .10	.15	**a** .92					
MS	**d** .02	.61	.18	**b** .40	.89				
SS	.04	.10	.66	.60	.52	.86			
Peer questionnaire									
JS	**c** .59	**d** .08	.11	**c** .69	**d** .00	.04	**a** .80		
MS	**d** .01	.55	.09	**d** .00	.72	.02	**b** .10	.85	
SS	.06	.11	.58	.02	.05	.68	.50	.46	.88

were affected substantially by some other factor common to the method (such as desire to respond in a socially desirable way).

1. A sports psychologist conducted a study dealing with the relationship between anxiety-before-the-game and athletic skill in high school football players. In the study, all varsity football players at Warren G. Harding High School rated themselves on two variables: anxiety-before-the-game and athletic skill. The Harding High football coaching staff rated all of the varsity football players on the same two variables. Surveying the multitrait-multimethod matrix that resulted, what might you conclude?

	Self-Evaluation		Coaches' Evaluation of Student	
	Anxiety	Skill	Anxiety	Skill
Self-Evaluation				
Anxiety	.95	—	—	—
Skill	.40	.80	—	—
Coaches' Evaluation of Student				
Anxiety	.77	.15	.86	—
Skill	.10	.15	.20	.71

2. A hypothetical study examined the relationship between SAT Verbal and Math scores, final grade in high school courses in math and English, and final grade in college courses in freshman math and English. The resulting multitrait-multimethod matrix follows below. A colleague in the English department has called on

you to share your expertise in psychometrics. Explain to your colleague the meaning of each of the coefficients in the matrix. Impart your thoughts on the reliability and validity of each of the scales based on the matrix. Conclude with a summary statement regarding the nature of the relationship between SAT Verbal and Math scores, final grade in high school courses in math and English, and final grade in college courses in freshman math and English.

	SAT		High School		College	
	Math	Verbal	Math	Verbal	Math	Verbal
SAT						
Math	.95	—	—	—	—	—
Verbal	.56	.96	—	—	—	—
High School						
Math	.77	.20	.80	—	—	—
Verbal	.18	.69	.55	.77	—	—
College						
Math	.73	.10	.78	.66	.40	—
Verbal	.17	.30	.80	.75	.80	.46

EXERCISE 33
FACTOR ANALYSIS AND THE CORRELATION MATRIX

OBJECTIVE

To enhance understanding of the role of the correlation matrix in the process of factor analysis.

BACKGROUND

A brief elaboration on the presentation of factor analysis in your text follows. Read it carefully before attempting to respond to the question that follows.

FACTOR ANALYSIS AND
THE CORRELATION MATRIX

A table of intercorrelations called a *correlation matrix* is a key element of a factor analysis. A matrix of correlations contains correlational information regarding two or more variables. The advent of high-speed data processing equipment makes possible the creation and analysis of a correlation matrix with hundreds of variables or more. In our model below (Table 6-9), there are only five variables (*A, B, C, D,* and *E*). As we will explain, these five variables could represent individual test items, tests, or test batteries. An assumption inherent in the application of a factor analysis is that the test items (tests or test batteries) are reliable and valid. The correlation between a variable and itself as represented in the matrix (for example, variable *A* in a row and variable *A* in a column) is always 1.

The five variables in our sample correlation matrix could represent five items on the same test. Alternatively, the five variables could represent a total of five items from different tests. The correlations between any two of the items imparts information regarding how the items are related. For example, a high positive correlation (.9) exists between variable *A* and variable *E*. Let's suppose that variables *A* and *E* both represent true/false items on a personality test. Variable *A* represents an item that reads, "I enjoy meeting new people," and variable *B* represents an item that reads, "Under the right circumstances, I can be the life of the party." The high correlation between the items tells us that in responding to these two items, testtakers tend to respond in the same way. Thus people who report that they enjoy meeting new people also report a potential of being the life of a party. People who report that they do not enjoy meeting new people also tend not to be the life of a party.

The five variables in our sample correlation matrix could represent composite scores on five different tests.

In another example, the five variables might represent composite scores as a result of the administration of five different groups of tests. The correlations between any two of the variables would then impart information regarding how the tests (or test groups) are related. For example, a low correlation (.04) exists between variable *B* and variable *D*. Let's suppose that variables *B* and *D* both represent composite scores on two different personality tests batteries. Variable *B* represents a composite score on a test battery called the Overall Assertiveness Tests (OATS), and variable *D* represents a composite score on a test battery called the Remarkable Creativity Tests (RCTS). The low correlation between the two test batteries tells us that there is no discernable relation between assertiveness and creativity. A highly assertive individual may or may not be creative, just as a highly creative person may or may not be assertive.

As its name implies, factor analysis entails "factoring" the correlations in the matrix. Factoring may be a familiar concept from algebra, where it involves a method of making a large, unwieldy algebraic expression more manageable by breaking it down into factors. Likewise, the correlation matrix in factor analysis is made more manageable by factoring. The objective is to wind up with a smaller number of factors than variables. In the example above wherein variables *A* and *E* were representative of true/false personality test items, a factor analyst might conclude that the two items tap a single factor labeled "introversion/extraversion." A "true" response on both of the items might earn the testtaker points toward a designation of "extraverted personality." A "false" response on both of the items might earn the testtaker points toward a designation of "introverted personality."

The actual process of factor analysis may take place in many different ways. Numerous methods exist for determining which correlations in the matrix yield common factors (such as introversion/extraversion in the example above), specific factors (not common to many of the variables), or factors that reflect error or unreliability in measurement (Comrey, 1992). In one approach, the factor analyst evaluates what is called the *scree criterion,* or what is perceived as a natural dividing point in the relative importance of the factors. You have probably engaged in a similar exercise if you have ever been involved in assigning grades based on a curve of test scores. As an example, let's say that the following scores represented the top ten scores in a particular class: 92, 92, 91, 90, 90, 89, 82, 81, 80 and 80. In deciding the number of *A*s to assign, one might look for clusters of scores, separated by gaps in the distribution. Here, depending on other factors, the grade of *A* might be assigned to the first six students, even if 89 and 90 are not usually considered to be in the *A* range. The grades from 89 to 92 seem to form a natural cluster, clearly separated from the next highest grades, which are in the low 80s. In a way, this is similar to what happens when

Table 6-9

A Sample Correlation Matrix for Variables **A, B, C, D,** *and* **E**

	A	B	C	D	E
A	1.00	.18	.32	.09	.90
B	—	1.00	.27	.04	.95
C	—	—	1.00	.28	.03
D	—	—	—	1.00	.02
E	—	—	—	—	1.00

the scree criterion is applied; clusters of factors that logically seem to go together are identified.

Another approach to determining which of many possible factors are common factors—an approach that is typically used along with the scree criterion—entails analysis of the *eigenvalues* (pronounced I-gen-values), or the numerical indices of the relative strength or importance of each factor. When the scores on two tests tend to vary together, the measures are said to "share variance." Factors that share a large amount of variance with the many measured variables have high eigenvalues and are likely to be viewed as common factors. Low eigenvalues indicate that the factor may be a specific factor or an error factor.

A detailed discussion of factor analytic procedures is beyond the scope of this book. Our modest objective here has been to provide but a first step in understanding the conceptual basis of this widely used but technically complex statistical tool.

YOUR TASK

What follows is a correlation matrix for four items (here labeled *W, X, Y,* and *Z*) on a True/False test of introversion/extraversion. Based on the data you observe, write four items on this test represented by *W, X, Y,* and *Z* and a brief explanation of why you wrote the items that you did.

Correlation Matrix for Variables **W, X, Y,** *and* **Z**

	W	X	Y	Z
W	1.00	.98	.97	.09
X	—	1.00	.99	.03
Y	—	—	1.00	.07
Z	—	—	—	1.00

EXERCISE 34
FACTOR ANALYSIS AND CONSTRUCT VALIDITY

OBJECTIVE

To enhance understanding of factor analysis and how this statistical tool can be used in the analysis of a test's construct validity.

BACKGROUND

Impulsivity is widely believed to be highly correlated with juvenile delinquency; juvenile delinquents tend to act on impulse rather than with a great deal of forethought. Consistent with this view, one might predict that a test designed to measure impulsivity, if it is indeed a

valid measure of impulsivity, would correlate highly with a measure of juvenile delinquency. But what if a measure of impulsivity did not correlate highly with delinquency? Would that measure automatically not be a valid measure of impulsivity? Before you answer, keep in mind that there may be different kinds of impulsivity. Some tests of impulsivity may be measuring cognitive impulsivity, and other tests may be measuring behavioral impulsivity. In fact, this is exactly what White, Moffitt, Caspi, Bartusch, Needles, & Stouthamer-Loeber (1994) found in their study of the construct validity of 11 measures of impulsivity.

YOUR TASK

Read the White et al. (1994) study with an eye toward learning about the use of factor validity in exploring the construct validity of tests. Then answer the following questions.

1. What criteria did White et al. use in selecting the tests of impulsivity they would use in their study?
2. What criteria did White et al. use in selecting subjects in their study?
3. After having collected their data, White et al. calculated correlations between the measures they used and organized their information in a correlation matrix. What kind of correlations would you have expected between the measures if all of the measures had defined impulsivity in the same way and were all valid measures of it?
4. What kind of correlations did White et al. calculate, and how did they explain this finding?
5. After factoring the correlation matrix, White et al. determined that four variables loaded on one factor they called "behavioral impulsivity." What were the four variables that loaded on that factor?
6. Continuing to factor, White et al. determined that six variables loaded on a second factor they called "cognitive impulsivity." What were these six variables?
7. White et al. noted that the two factors they derived may have more to do with the way impulsivity is measured than anything else. Behavioral impulsivity is a factor associated with impulsivity when impulsivity is measured by rating scales administered to observers (such as parents and teachers of impulsive subjects). Cognitive impulsivity is a factor more associated with tasks completed by the subjects themselves. Future factor analytic research could help to clarify the actual nature of the factors if (1) tasks can be identified that reflect behavioral impulsivity (and thus load on behavioral impulsivity), or (2) ratings can be made that reflect cognitive impulsivity (and thus load on cognitive impulsivity). Write a simple research outline to follow up on the White et al. study.
8. White et al. found that their measure of delinquency was significantly correlated with both of the impulsiv

factors derived from the factor analysis. The correlation was stronger with the Behavioral Impulsivity factor ($r = .44$) as compared to the Cognitive Impulsivity factor ($r = .16$). This suggests that studies that use measures that reflect the Behavioral Impulsivity factor are more likely to find that delinquency is related to impulsivity than are studies using measures that primarily reflect the Cognitive Impulsivity factor. In general, what do these findings tell us about the construct validity of the measures used in the White et al. study?

EXERCISE 35
"FAIRNESS" AND "BIAS"

OBJECTIVE

To enhance understanding of the terms *fairness* and *bias* as those terms are used in the field of psychological testing.

BACKGROUND

If an individual does not perform satisfactorily on a test and as a consequence is deprived of something he or she wants, it would not be unheard of for the individual to claim—almost reflexively—that the test was unfair. While some tests may indeed be unfair or "biased" in the psychometric sense (and other tests may be inherently fair and unbiased but used in an unfair way), responsible test developers, publishers, and users strive to serve the general good by promoting fair, unbiased tests.

YOUR TASK

Drawing on your own background and experience, your textbook, and the Psychological Corporation article that follows, answer the following three questions:

1. Describe in your own words a "fair test."
2. Describe in your own words a "biased test."
3. What can be done to eliminate unfair and biased tests?

• •

Fairness and the Matter of Bias

Lois E. Burrill, Ruth Wilson

Potential bias in standardized tests is a topic of great concern to test users. This concern can probably be traced back into the early twenties, but during the decade of the sixties, as the nation became acutely aware of racial discrimination and the denial of basic civil rights in many quarters, new issues were raised. Charges were made concerning the "fairness" of commercially developed

ability and achievement tests for many of the students in our schools.

The claim was made that the tests were designed for white, middle-class children, growing up in suburban communities. Thus, it was charged, the tests were inherently inappropriate, invalid, or unfair to pupils who are black, poor, or living in the inner core of our old urban centers. More recently, charges of "sex bias" have been added to the others. It has been claimed that tests support and reinforce the stereotypes of sex roles dominant in the middle-class culture, and thus penalize children who do not respond as required by these cultural patterns.

Unfortunately, there is at the present time no consensus in regard to what bias is or how to eliminate it. The word "bias" comes up in most of the discussions about fairness. However, this term is rarely defined in any precise or operational way. Like "creativity," bias seems to be a term that people believe they understand intuitively; yet they cannot easily formulate a definition. Faced with this dilemma, publishers such as The Psychological Corporation have attempted to deal with the concept of fairness—in all its complexity—in three different areas: first, fairness in relation to the normative information published for the test; second, fairness in the content of the actual test questions; and third, fairness in the way test results are used for decision making.

FAIRNESS AND THE QUALITY OF NORMS

Most publishers, including The Psychological Corporation, have taken great pains to ensure that national norms are truly representative of the nation as a whole. In order to do this, children of all ethnic groups, socioeconomic levels, and geographical regions are represented in their norms samples in the proportions in which they exist in the national population. Moreover, boys and girls from urban, suburban, and rural communities, large schools and small, public, parochial and independent schools, are included on the same proportional basis.

Precision has recently been added to this selective process through the use of census data based on school system boundaries rather than on political units. Thus, the charge that the norms for most tests are based entirely on the performance of middle-class whites simply is not true.

Although particular school systems may differ in composition from the total population, national norms have meaning and importance for all school systems. They describe one reality: the typical performance of the nation's school children. By so doing, they form an important frame of reference; they are a point of departure for decision making. It should be understood, however, that by virtue of their being a representative sampling of all the wide variations found in the United States, national norms present a composite picture of national performance, and there are few communities in the entire nation matching that composite picture across all comparisons. In many communities, the discrepancies between local characteristics and those represented as typical (by the norm) are, in fact, great.

Test publishers recognize this fact, and, today, test manuals report normative data carefully for all test users to examine. The care with which these data are collected is evidence of the usefulness of the norms that accompany the test and should be evaluated thoughtfully by the potential test user.

The danger here is in using only one frame of reference. National norms provide one important yardstick; others are also available, and each one adds a different dimension to the picture. Some test publishers collect and publish information concerning the performance of specific groups. Many provide scoring services designed to enable school systems to interpret their test scores in terms of local norms. Item analysis, matching test questions with specific instructional objectives, provides criterion-referenced interpretation. Test users are encouraged to use as many frames of reference as possible in interpreting test results.

FAIRNESS AND THE CONTENT OF THE TEST

One of the essential characteristics of a good test is *validity,* a technical testing term usually defined as "the degree to which a test measures what it is intended to measure." In nontechnical language, fairness and validity are roughly synonymous, so it is probably not coincidental that bias is often perceived in terms of test validity. Test validity is frequently broken down further into several categories: face validity—the appearance of measuring what is intended; predictive validity—the ability of the test to accurately predict a future performance or other criterion; and content validity—the adequacy of the sample of questions to assess the area being measured. For each of these types of validity or fairness, there are various ways of identifying invalidity or unfairness due to bias.

Face Validity—Facial Bias

The term "facial bias" has been coined recently to describe situations where particular words, pictures, item formats, or other characteristics of the test *appear* to disfavor some group, regardless of whether any statistical evidence can be collected to show that they actually affect scores on a test. In respect to facial bias, the following points need to be considered: 1) Is the question or its presentation offensive to some group? 2) Does the question "turn off" some children, either psychologically or emotionally? 3) Is the context of the question so alien to the child's experiential background that he or she is unable to answer a question that should not depend on that background?

These questions concern the "cultural fairness" of a test. It must be recognized that attempts to build tests that are "culture-free" have been unsuccessful. There are no differences among individuals in their responses to test questions that cannot be attributed, to some extent, to differences in culture; "Each of us lives in a somewhat different culture. Not only Eskimos and Africans but also Vermonters and Virginians, farmers and townspeople, boys and girls, even first-born and next born in the same family live in somewhat different 'cultures.' The differences are not equally great in all these instances, but they exist as differences in all cases, and they can be used to support the charge that any item that discriminates is unfair."[1] Since test scores that do not differentiate among individuals would be meaningless, the issue is not one of trying to eliminate all distinctions but rather of establishing controls for relevant cultural parameters.

Publishers are aware of possible sources of unintentional bias. For example, some items may appear to be more relevant to one geographic region than another; others may appear to favor males over females. These and many other aspects must be considered in item selection in order to produce an instrument that is sufficiently balanced to be appropriate for general use. The format of the test may influence the performance of children who are unfamiliar with the testing process; where several different types of items are included on one page, without being introduced by practice items, an unreasonable burden is placed on these children.

In meeting this responsibility, test publishers have given renewed and intensified attention to certain aspects of the traditional test-development enterprise. Until fairly recently, most standardized tests were constructed by white middle-class people, who sometimes clumsily violated the feelings of the test-takers without even knowing it. One could say that they were not so much culture biased as "culture blind." More recently, however, much has been done to modify test-development procedures in order to ensure the appropriateness of the final instruments for all the uses to which they may be put.

The Psychological Corporation has, for example, instituted staff training programs. Such matters as sensitivity to prejudice, stereotypes, and material offensive to particular groups; over- or underemphasis on the worth, capabilities, or importance of particular racial, religious, or ethnic segments of the national population; inclusion of minority as well as majority examples of worthy Americans in all areas of life and culture; and the delineation of life in contemporary urban environments, as well as rural, have become part of the criteria for judging the validity of test items. Artwork has been revised to eliminate the "mom, dad, two kids plus dog" stereotype of family composition. Adult figures include uncle, grandfather, or some other model as well as

---

[1] Ebel, Robert L., *Essentials of Educational Measurement.* Englewood Cliffs, N.J.: Prentice-Hall, Inc., 1972, p. 505.

"Father." Urban scenes are depicted in the artwork, and children and adults who are clearly minority group members are pictured.

Vocabulary is another area of concern. For example, in some proposed items, reviewers have found the term "black" used in ways that might be considered derogatory. Thus a story about a crow (described as a big, black bird) who stole shiny dimes was rewritten to eliminate the possible connection of "black" with "theft."

Staff members have been made aware of possible "sex bias." Steps have been taken to avoid the over- or under-representation of either sex group in test items and artwork or the portrayal of either sex in restricted or stereotypic roles. Recent test publications represent males and females with approximately equal frequency, exhibit a full range of activities and personality traits for both, and show mixed-sex activities. All types of work are presented positively, and both males and females are shown participating in a wide range of vocations and household situations.

Vocabulary places a limitation here, particularly at the primary grades. Curricular materials are "sex biased" in terms of presenting male nouns and pronouns at a generally earlier level than the corresponding female words. It is equally difficult to replace the gender-specific items with sexually neutral words at these lower levels. For example, curricular materials introduce the words "man," "policeman," "fireman," etc. in the primary grades, while alternate titles such as "human," "adult," "police officer," "fire fighter," etc. are not introduced before the fourth grade. Since test publishers adhere to the principle of using grade-controlled vocabulary, the problem of eliminating all "sex-biased" items is a complicated one.

In recent years, test publishers have included on their professional staff, both in full-time and consultant roles, persons who can advise in matters of "culture blindness." Materials in tests under development are reviewed by black people, Spanish-speaking Americans, and others who are familiar with the needs and styles of pupils from a variety of minority backgrounds, soliciting their reactions to any content that might be, unintentionally, inappropriate or offensive for some children.

Such consultants have a constructive role to play in each of the five major steps in test development. During the blueprinting stage, they review the outline or scheme of the tests and identify content of special pertinence or irrelevance to minority students. During content development, they make suggestions as to potential item bias, insensitive content, and unclear or potentially biased artwork. They also review plans for the statistical analysis of potential bias during item analysis and standardization stages. Finally, they review the final draft and suggest special needs of minority children as concerns test reporting.

Despite the continuing efforts made in this regard, no publishers can make an *a priori* statement that a given test is "not discriminatory." Matters of face validity or facial bias, whether ethnic, sex, geographic, socioeconomic, are essentially judgmental, rarely subject to psychometric or statistical proof. Although publisher and authors exert every possible effort to ensure that the content of the test itself, the questions asked, the language in which they are asked, the artwork, format and time limits are unbiased and free from prejudice, each agency selecting a test must make its own final judgmental decisions concerning its appropriateness for the particular group involved.

Predictive Validity—Bias of Selection/Prediction

Predictive validity refers to the accuracy with which scores on certain types of tests indicate future success in some area of learning or endeavor. Unfairness, prejudice, or discrimination in these test scores is known as bias of selection/prediction. A number of statistical procedures have been developed to identify this type of bias in tests that are being used for prediction or selection. The entire Spring 1976 issue of *Journal of Educational Measurement* was devoted to this important area of concern. Although these procedures will not be described in detail here, it is important to note that each procedure is based on somewhat different assumptions about the definition of what is fair or unbiased prediction. Further, they are contradictory in their results.

In this situation, it is not the statisticians or the researchers who must decide what is fair. There is a larger issue involved that must be decided by society as a whole. Then, appropriate statistical analysis can be used or new methods developed to assess whether or not a test is biased by *that* definition.

Content Validity—Item Bias

Until the mid-seventies, efforts to deal with facial bias and with bias in prediction received far greater attention than issues concerning item bias. This was probably due to the assumption that achievement test items—questions assessing what was taught in school—were unlikely to exhibit bias other than facial bias. However, for years, researchers have been struggling with the question of how to identify this kind of bias.

Item bias may occur when, for reasons not readily apparent even to trained editors or expert judges, a test question is shown to function for different groups in some systematically different way. Some critics of tests have claimed that for a test to be unbiased, each subgroup of interest (ethnic groups, the two sexes, etc.) must perform alike in regard to the mean score on each item of the test. This definition, of course, assumes that the groups are actually alike with respect to whatever is being measured by the test question, and that observed differences in score are, therefore, the results of an unfair item. Others anticipate that the groups may perform somewhat differently on individual questions, but insist that such differences should balance out over the test as a whole. Again, the groups are presumed to be equal in ability on the skill domain being tested by the set of items.

This assumption of equality is difficult to support, however, when it comes to achievement of ethnic minority groups. Even when the inherent ability or potential of the groups is assumed to be equal, one certainly cannot assume the groups have had equal opportunity to acquire the knowledges and skills in question. Indeed, to do so, and to eliminate items that show differences, might well have the effect of destroying the empirical evidence of the lack of equal educational opportunity or the need for improved instructional programs to right the balance.

The statistical or psychometric problem, then, has been to find ways of identifying which differences in performance are real (and need to be acknowledged) and which are the result of bias in the way the question is asked (and need to be corrected by changing or eliminating the question). A number of procedures have been proposed by researchers—each beginning with an attempt to define the kind of bias the method is intended to isolate.

One of the earliest of these approaches, and perhaps the most widely recognized, is that based on the psychometric notion of "interaction" between group membership and item performance. In this definition, it is assumed that a consistent difference in performance may not be due to bias, but that questions which have a far greater- or lesser-than-average difference between groups may be biased. Among the procedures using this approach, perhaps the best known is Angoff's delta plot procedure, described in Anastasi's measurement text.[2]

Another way of trying to identify item bias is based on the relationship of performance on each test question to performance on the test as a whole. When this statistic, known as item-test correlation, shows a significantly greater- or lesser-than-average difference between two groups, the item may be considered biased, according to this approach.

One of the most promising procedures explored during the 1970s was developed by Janice Scheuneman at The Psychological Corporation. This technique, known as modified chi-square analysis, defines lack of bias as follows: For population groups with the same total score on the test in which the item appears, the proportion of each group who respond correctly to an item will be the same. If this is not true, bias is suspected. Using this definition and standard statistical techniques, it is possible to determine the probability that a given item is unbiased. Where the probability is low, the item may need to be discarded.

The 1976 edition of the *Metropolitan Readiness Tests* was analyzed for ethnic bias, using this procedure, and all items suspected of bias were eliminated from the final forms. The procedure was also used in the development of the *Otis-Lennon School Ability Test*. These procedures, reported in the research literature, constitute one of the most comprehensive attempts on the part of any test publisher to reduce ethnic bias in their tests.

The procedures described above all rely on techniques and statistics developed from classical test theory. Recently a new approach to test construction and scaling has been explored by many publishers, including The Psychological Corporation. Known as latent-trait theory, this methodology also holds much promise for the identification of item bias. The psychometric characteristics of any test question may be portrayed graphically in the form of a curve, called the item-characteristic curve. Bias may be defined by this method as differences in the shape of that curve for various ethnic groups.

To utilize any of these statistical procedures for identifying item bias, the test constructor must be able to identify the group membership of the individuals involved in the item analysis. Of course, from a publisher's point of view, this identification is not an invasion of privacy, since scores are never assembled with the demographic data. In fact, ethnic, sex, and other demographic data are only used to generate the p-values, item-test correlations, and other data used to test for item bias. In the past, this requirement has caused considerable difficulty. Although schools and communities are anxious for evidence or proof that tests are not biased, they are very reluctant to permit collection of the data necessary to conduct the research. Thus, many tests are still not being examined for item bias, even though the publisher is anxious to do so and the necessary techniques are available.

FAIRNESS IN USE OF TESTS FOR DECISION MAKING

The validity of test results can be influenced adversely by the way in which the test is administered. Members of some minority groups often approach the testing situation with negative feelings about their chances of success. The teacher's own attitude when administering the test may produce tension, anxiety, or even hostility in some students. On the other hand, the teacher can encourage students to do their best by establishing an atmosphere of mutual trust and by emphasizing the fact that the purpose of testing is not merely to assign grades and check mastery but to help the students to profit by their own strengths and overcome their weaknesses.

Unfortunately, there have been flagrant examples of misuse of test information. Test publishers do not consider that their responsibility ends with the development of appropriate instruments. Rather, they are extending their efforts to provide the necessary guidelines for appropriate interpretation and use. In test manuals and accessory materials, comprehensive treatment is given to

---

[2] Anastasi, Anne, *Psychological Testing*. Fourth Edition. New York: Macmillan, 1976, pp. 222–224.

such matters as the nature of the particular tests, proper (and improper) inferences that may be drawn from test results, and cautions and limitations regarding the interpretation. In particular, information is given about how test results can be used in a number of concrete situations in urban centers, in specially funded projects, and the like. Issues of bias in interpretation and use have been addressed, not only in the test manuals, but also in service publications, professional papers, conferences, journal articles, etc.

In particular, it must be said clearly and frequently that achievement test scores are indicative information that must be used in conjunction with everything else a school knows about an individual. Test results must not be used to make inferences about the worth of individuals or, especially in the case of students who have suffered educational disadvantage, about their potential for learning. Test scores should be seen as formative, rather than summative, as warning signals rather than stop signs.

SUMMARY

In their efforts to eliminate bias from published tests, the makers of these instruments seek the cooperation of parents, community groups, and school boards, as well as school administrators and teachers. Although much has been done to define, analyze, and eliminate bias in test instruments, much remains to be done. Perhaps the greatest single achievement in this regard is the recognition of the problem and the realization that the common goal can only be gained through the combined efforts of test publishers and test users.

● ●

REFERENCES

Campbell, D. T., & Fiske, D. W. (1959). Convergent and discriminant validation by the multitrait-multimethod matrix. *Psychological Bulletin, 56,* 81–105.

Lawshe, C. H. (1975). A quantitative approach to content validity. *Personnel Psychology, 28,* 563–575.

Standards for educational and psychological testing. (1974). Washington, DC: American Psychological Association.

Standards for educational and psychological testing. (1985). Washington, DC: American Psychological Association.

White, J. L., Moffitt, T. E., Caspi, A., Bartusch, D. J., Needles, D. J., & Stouthamer-Loeber, M. (1994). Measuring impulsivity and examining its relationship to delinquency. *Journal of Abnormal Psychology, 103,* 192–205.

▬▬▬▬▬▬▬▬ THE 4-QUESTION CHALLENGE ▬▬▬▬▬▬▬▬

1. It's the degree to which an additional predictor explains something about the criterion measure not explained by predictors already in use. It is
   (a) construct validity.
   (b) content validity.
   (c) incremental validity.
   (d) concurrent validity.
2. It is a tool used by many personnel psychologists to learn about how much a new test can improve the employee selection process. It is
   (a) the content validity ratio.
   (b) the Taylor-Russell tables.
   (c) factor analytic methods.
   (d) the multitrait-multimethod matrix.
3. Which term does not belong?
   (a) halo effect
   (b) severity error
   (c) central tendency error
   (d) random error
4. Which would *not* be an effective tool for an affirmative action program?
   (a) a sliding band
   (b) within-group norming
   (c) differential cutoffs
   (d) elimination of eigenvalues

Chapter 7

Test Development

A Perfect "10"?

Dudley Moore finds Bo Derek to be a 10—presumably with respect to an overall rating of "beauty"—in the film of the same title. From a psychometric perspective, however, one might question the reliability and validity of the (mental) scale this man is using to arrive at such a rating. . . . Why? What are the problems attendant to the development of such a scale?

Outline for Chapter 7 of Cohen et al. (1996)
TEST DEVELOPMENT

Test Conceptualization

Test Construction
  Scaling
    Types of scales
    Scaling methods
  Writing Items
    Item formats
  Scoring of Items

Test Tryout
  What is a "Good" Item?

Item Analysis
  Item-Difficulty Index
  Item-Validity Index
  Item-Reliability Index
    Factor analysis and inter-item consistency
  Item-Discrimination Index
    Analysis of item alternatives
  Item-Characteristic Curves
    Latent-trait models
  Other Considerations
    Guessing
    Item fairness
    Speeded tests
  Qualitative Item Analysis
    The "think aloud" test administration
    Expert panels

Test Revision
  Cross Validation

CLOSE-UP:
  Anatomy of the Development of a Test:
  The Personality Research Form

EVERYDAY PSYCHOMETRICS:
  Psychometrics in the Classroom

EXERCISE 36
THE TEST DEVELOPMENT PROCESS

OBJECTIVE

To enhance understanding, stimulate thought, and provide firsthand experience with respect to the process of developing a psychological test.

BACKGROUND

Stated in general terms, the process of developing a test may be thought of as occurring in five stages:

1. Test Conceptualization
2. Test Construction
3. Test Tryout
4. Analysis
5. Revision

One can learn about the "nuts-and-bolts" of the test development process not only from descriptions in textbooks but from real-world accounts of the process in sources such as professional journals. For example, in an article entitled "A Sequential System for Personality Scale Development," psychologist/test author Douglas N. Jackson (1970) afforded readers an inside look at the process of developing the Personality Research Form. And in the reprinted article that follows, Abadzi and Florez (1981) describe not only the procedures used in developing their test, but the trials and tribulations as well.

YOUR TASK

Read the following article and then answer these questions with reference to it:

1. If the process of test development is conceptualized as occurring in five steps (test conceptualization, test construction, test tryout, item analysis, and test revision), identify each of these steps with reference to the Puerto Rico Self-Concept Scale.
2. With reference to each of the five steps in the test development process cited above, what questions do *you* have regarding the process of developing the Puerto Rico Self-Concept Scale; in other words, what would you like to know more about?
3. With reference to each of the five steps in the test development process cited above, what suggestions for future direction do you have to offer the authors of this test?

Constructing the Puerto Rico Self-Concept Scale: Problems and Procedures*

The Puerto Rico self-concept scale was developed for the purpose of assessing the relationship of self-concept with academic achievement and other school-related variables in Puerto Rico. An 88-item scale that can measure self-concept in the 4th, 7th, and 10th grades was constructed. Empirical criterion keying was used for the development of items that were also adapted to the phraseology used by local students. After small-group testing, the 264-item bank was administered to 2,445 students. Item analyses focused on item discrimination. Scores showed a low but significant correlation with previous year's grade point average. Overall scale reliability was .93. A 34-item short form had overall reliability of .84. Preliminary norms were prepared from existing data.

The educational community in the United States is becoming increasingly interested in the identification of personal variables that affect student performance. The self-concept of a student is considered an important variable related to academic achievement. Significant, though mostly moderate correlations have been demonstrated by several researchers, between measurements of self-concept and student grades (Bloom, 1976; Brookover, Patterson, & Thomas, 1962; Campbell, 1967; Fink, 1962; Gill, 1969; Gordon, 1966; Purkey, 1970).

Coppersmith (1967) considers the self-concept to be an individual's self-evaluation. More than 200 scales have been constructed that attempt to elicit this self-evaluation through various methods. Factor analyses carried out on some of the instruments indicate the presence of such factors as physical appearance, peer relations, school performance, leadership, and opinions about oneself (Muller & Leonetti, 1972; Richmond & White, 1971; Stanwyck & Felker, 1971).

There seems to be a continuous interaction between the self and academic achievement, each directly influencing the other (Purkey, 1970). In evidence of this intricate relationship, the Commonwealth of Puerto Rico, Department of Education, developed a project whose purpose was to measure the self-concept of Puerto Rican students and to study its interactions with academic achievement. Accordingly, specifications for a self-concept scale were set.

The scale to be constructed should (1) make possible the assessment of the relationship between student self-concept and academic performance; (2) identify students

*By Helen Abadzi and Sonia Florez and reprinted with permission from *Applied Psychological Measurement*.

Table 7-1

Reliability Coefficients for the Self-Concept Scale

Form and Coefficient	Grade			
	4th	*7th*	*10th*	*Overall*
Long form (88 items)				
K-R 20	.92	.94	.94	.93
Split-half	.92	.93	.93	.93
Short form (34 items)				
K-R 20	.85	.86	.86	.86
Split-half	.83	.87	.85	.85

with low self-concept at the 4th, 7th, and 10th grade level; and [sic] (4) measure changes from one grade level to the other. These specifications made it necessary to consider the development of a single form that could be used with 4th, 7th, and 10th grade boys and girls and that would discriminate between students having high and low self-concepts. The construction of the scale consequently reflected what Cronbach (1970) calls the "bandwidth-fidelity dilemma": a test to be used with many grades and purposes might be less effective in measuring specific self-concept areas or it might be less reliable and valid for one of the grades. On the other hand, a separate test for each grade would not measure between-grade changes without elaborate equating procedures. Balancing time and costs against benefits, it was decided to develop the scale according to specifications and to study the results.

METHODOLOGY OF SCALE CONSTRUCTION

Items for this scale were constructed using homogenous methods of scale construction. As a first step toward the construction of this scale, approximately 200 pieces of research were reviewed. Test items were constructed to reflect the results of those studies whose findings differentiated between persons with low and high self-concept. For example, a negative correlation between

Table 7-2

Scale Statistics

Central Tendency and Dispersion Measures	Grade			
	4th	*7th*	*10th*	*Overall*
Long form (88 items)				
Mean	67.90	69.83	72.44	67.66
Standard Deviation	13.15	14.15	13.45	10.01
Skewness	−0.45	−0.71	−1.07	−0.75
Kurtosis	2.41	3.00	4.29	3.71
Short form (34 items)				
Mean	24.39	25.02	26.04	25.08
Standard Deviation	6.19	6.36	5.85	6.17
Skewness	−0.47	−0.70	−1.04	−0.75
Kurtosis	2.31	2.84	3.78	3.14

Table 7-3

The Ten Most Discriminating Items and Overall Phi Coefficients

Item	Phi
7. Generalmente estoy astrasado (a) en mi trabajo. (I am generally behind with my work.)	.57
16. Soy más lento (a) que mis compañeros para hacer los trabajos de la clase. (I am slower than my classmates in doing homework.)	.54
24. Muchas veces me siento completamente inútil. (Many times I feel completely useless.)	.53
26. Muchas veces dejo las cosas sin terminar. (Many times I leave things unfinished.)	.62
33. Generalmente, los maestros me hacen preguntas difíciles de contestar. (Teachers generally ask me difficult questions.)	.53
44. Se me olvida fácilmente lo que aprendo. (I easily forget what I learn.)	.58
53. A menudo me da coraje. (I often get angry.)	.54
55. Si la maestra hace una pregunta tengo miedo de contestar. (I am afraid to answer if a teacher asks a question.)	.59
60. Mis maestros me ponen a hacer cosas tan difíciles, que no puedo hacerlas. (Teachers make me do things that are too difficult for me.)	.57
62. Quisiera ser otra persona. (I would like to be someone else.)	.53

Escala de Autoconcepto, 1980

self-concept and anxiety has been found (Thompson, 1972). Accordingly, some test items measuring anxiety were constructed, such as the following: "Me preocupo mucho por los problemas que puedan surgir" (I worry a lot about problems that may come up). In addition, approximately 30 available self-concept instruments were reviewed. Their methods of approach to the problem and their item analysis results were studied. Items with high indices of discrimination or items that loaded highly on one of the self-concept–related factors were considered for adoption. As a result, 290 test items were constructed in a draft form in Spanish. A dichotomous response format was used, with students indicating whether the item was or was not true most of the time. The Likert-type scale was not used because it had been previously employed in a fourth-grade scale with little success (Whitmore, 1975). Instead, it was decided to use dichotomous items and to include in the final scale a larger number of items than would have otherwise been employed.

A problem of major importance in the construction of this or any other scale in Puerto Rico is the attention that must be paid to the local culture and language. Self-concept, and individual's self-evaluation, has been defined in research according to Anglo standards of achievement and has been used with little change in instrument construction for Chicano children (Muller & Leonetti, 1972). On the other hand, there are no research findings to support the view that it may be defined differently in Puerto Rico, an island that has been under United States control for the past 80 years. A study by Hernandez (1964) lists Puerto Rican adolescent problems and needs very similar to those in the mainland United States. It was therefore hypothesized that self-concept on this island could basically be measured in the same way as on the mainland. Evidence to support this hypothesis was offered in that many items developed on the basis of mainland United States correlates of self-concept had considerable discriminating power (see Table 7-3). The authors, however, recommend tentative use and careful investigation of items whose content has been validated in a culture other than that of intended use.

It was considered important to construct a scale whose language reflected the Spanish spoken by Puerto Rican children. Colloquial Spanish varies from country to country. The authors found a few scales in Spanish, mostly constructed for Mexican American (Chicano) children, but the language in itself was not always usable because constructions frequent among Chicanos are not used by Puerto Ricans. Also, test items could not be directly translated from English because of word frequency problems; the style of many items in scales that were directly translated was disappointing. The language problem was accompanied by the fact that neither author is Puerto Rican: One is a Peruvian who has lived in Puerto Rico for 10 years, and the other is a Greek, very fluent in Spanish, who lived on the island for 6 months. It was decided to enlist the aid of the school districts. Six school personnel members formed a committee that met with the authors several times. The committee reviewed all the items that had been developed and rephrased them, using the expressions Puerto Rican children use. Care was taken not to alter the meaning. With the committee's valuable help, 264 items were developed. The vocabulary used was such that fourth grade students could understand it. Though local expressions were used, no common grammatical errors were included. No item was longer than one and a half lines. Half of the items had negative syntactical constructions.

The 264 items were randomly separated into three forms of 88 in each. Then, the committee members took copies and administered them to small groups of students in their districts noting the time it took fast and slow readers of various grades to complete the forms, the words students did not know, expressions that were not clear, and reactions to the scale. As a result of the small-group administration, several changes were made. It was found that younger students did not respond correctly to the items that contained negative constructions. Therefore, all negative constructions were changed into positive while the negative meaning was kept. The scoring key for the items was prepared according to the findings of the previously conducted literature search. Each item was to be given a score of "1" if answered in the direction that indicated high self-concept. The scale score was to be an unweighted total of items answered in the desirable direction.

METHOD OF DATA COLLECTION

Classes containing a total of 3,134 4th, 7th, and 10th graders in equal numbers were selected at random following a sampling procedure routinely used by the Department of Education, whose main purpose is to include a proportionate number of rural and city students. Only public schools were sampled. The 264 items separated in three forms were administered to the students, who marked their answers on computer-scored sheets. Precise test instructions were prepared and sent to the teachers, who administered the forms to their classes.

The three forms were administered to the students, one each day during 3 consecutive days. This way each student took all three subsets of the item bank. Answer sheets were collected and data were analyzed by the Department of Education computer center. When data were processed, 690 answer sheets had to be eliminated as a result of incorrect or missing student numbers. Therefore, a total of 2,445 returns were used for data analysis.

ITEM ANALYSIS RESULTS

The main purpose of item analysis was to identify items that discriminated between students who scored high and low on the self-concept scale. The analysis was performed on the 264 items and gave difficulty and discrimination indices. The latter were phi coefficients computed for each item between numbers of "right" and "wrong" responses according to the scoring key and number of students whose total score was in the upper and lower 27%. The distribution that resulted was negatively skewed and very leptokurtic. Split-half and Kuder-Richardson reliability coefficients computed for each scale ranged from .83 to .89. The items that had phi coefficients of .4 or higher were selected for each grade separately, and selections for the three grades were compared.

Generally, there was agreement across grades. Thirty-four items had phi coefficients of .4 and above in all three grade levels. Fifty others showed phi coefficients of .4 to .6 for two grades, while in the third, coefficients ranged from .3 to .39. These 84 items were selected for a second analysis. Since the 10th grade was found to share slightly fewer items with phi coefficients of .4 with the other grades, nine more items were added that had coefficients of .3 to .39 at the other levels.

In the second analysis, which included 93 items, the score distribution approached normality much more, and the reliability coefficients rose. They ranged from .89 to .94 (see Table 7-1). Phi coefficients also increased; most items showed phi's of .4 and above in all three grades. The five least discriminating items were eliminated, leaving a scale with a total of 88 items. The 34 best discriminating items in all grade levels were analyzed separately, and it was found that they could provide a short form of the scale (Table 7-3). Kuder-Richardson and split-half reliability coefficients for the short form ranged from .83 and .87 (see Table 7-1).

The 88 selected items were classified on the basis of their content in four categories: (1) school and work (27 items); (2) peer relationships (23 items); (3) self-description (29 items); and (4) parent-student relationships (8 items). Preliminary norms in percentile form were developed for each grade level from existing data.

The scores obtained on the 88 selected items by the 2,445 students were correlated with the students' grade-point average (GPA) of the previous year. A Pearson correlation of .28 was obtained, which is significant at the .0001 level for this sample size. This is lower than the average of .5 reported by Bloom (1976), possibly because the GPA did not reflect current performance and possibly because GPA in Puerto Rico public schools reflects only Spanish, English, and math . . .

DISCUSSION

The scale that was developed seems to have high internal consistency reliability in all three grade levels. Its reliability was highest at the 7th grade level because this grade shared many highly discriminating items with the other two (see Table 7-1).

The method of homogenous scale construction used for item construction provides a basis for the construct validity of the scale. The content of the items is in many respects similar to that of other school-age self-concept scales. The correlation with previous year's grade point average served as an indicator of criterion-related validity.

Mean self-concept scores increased from one grade to the next (see Table 7-2). This is consistent with previous findings (Thompson, 1972). At each grade level the score distribution also became more negatively skewed (−.45, −.71, and −1.07, respectively). Small percentages of students received nearly "perfect" scores (1%, 4%, and 4% in each grade level), but there were no scores approaching zero. This indicates that the scale can successfully be used for the identification of students in all three grade levels who have a low self-concept.

A strong effort was made to balance the numbers of positive and negative items. The most discriminating items, however, tended to be negative. As a result, the 88-item scale contains only 33% positive items. It seems that it is the lack of a negative quality rather than the

existence of a positive quality that characterizes students with high self-concepts in the public schools of Puerto Rico.

The short form of the scale could be used for data collection from groups, particularly if time is very limited, since only a few minutes are necessary for its administration. The 88-item scale can be administered within a 50-minute class period to 4th graders and in much less time (20 to 30 minutes) to upper grades. It is reliable and broad enough in content to permit self-concept assessment of individual students in the Puerto Rico public schools who have third-grade reading skills (see a sample of items in Table 7-3). More statistical work on the scale can produce a set of subscores that will focus on relations with school, peers, and descriptions of self.

Further research is necessary. The divergent validity of the scale regarding reading skills and comprehension must be measured. Test-retest reliability should be established, as well as a correlation with an external criterion of self-concept. If administratively possible, the scores should be correlated with current grade point averages that include all subjects taken. Norms based on the final format of the scale should be established and supplemented with private school data if private schools in Puerto Rico are to use this instrument. It might also be possible to use this scale to assess the self-concept of Puerto Rican children in the continental United States if it is established that they have adequate reading and language skills in Spanish to respond to it.

• •

EXERCISE 37
SCALING THE BOUNDS OF CONSCIOUSNESS

OBJECTIVE

To provide firsthand experience in the scaling of a test.

BACKGROUND

Testtakers are presumed to range in the degree to which they exhibit or possess a characteristic measured by a valid test. In general, the higher or lower the score on the test, the more or less of the characteristic the testtaker is presumed to possess. But how are numbers assigned to responses so that a test score can be calculated?

YOUR TASK

Read the following description of the scaling of the hypothetical "Depth of Hypnosis Scale" (DHS). After you have read it, and with reference to your textbook, write a brief essay on alternative ways the scaling of the DHS could have been approached.

DEPTH OF HYPNOSIS SCALE

Suppose you wish to develop a "Depth of Hypnosis Scale" (DHS) whereby the higher a subject scores on the test, the deeper the subject is presumed to be in a hypnotic trance. You make an arbitrary decision that two of the requirements for this test are that it be brief and easily administered. In the interest of simplicity you make a preliminary decision that there will be 10 items on this test and that possible scores on this test will range from 0 to 10. A score of 0 shall indicate a nonhypnotized state and a score of 10 shall indicate the deepest hypnotic state.

The next step is to assemble an item pool, consisting perhaps of 20 or so possible items from which you will ultimately select the 10 items that you feel measure the construct. One way to assemble this item pool is to enlist the aid of a number of expert hypnotists and instruct each to compose a list of 10 behaviors that, from their experience, represent 10 indicators of depth of hypnosis in ascending order. By examining where there is a consensus between the experts and by resolving discrepancies between the judgments of the experts (by methods such as interviewing the experts or researching the literature), a scale will begin to emerge. You might find that some items on that scale, each scores Yes or No (with one point assigned for each Yes answer), are as follows (in ascending order, as given by the experts):

1. Subject does not obey any commands at all.
2. Subject obeys simple command that his or her eyelids are "stuck together" and, in fact, is unable to open eyes.
5. Subject responds to suggestion of positive hallucination (such as "there is a white elephant in the room").
6. Subject responds to suggestion of negative hallucination (such as "there is no one else in the room but you and me"—when the room is actually filled with people).
10. Suggestion of analgesia (inability to experience pain) is strong enough to sustain patient through major surgery without administration of anesthesia.

Some points about the DHS and the method used to derive it are useful in shedding light on scales and scaling methods in general. The DHS is an ordinal scale because the different "depths" are more than merely named, they are ranked. Yet the interval level of measurement is not reached by the DHS, since it is not necessarily the case that equal intervals exist between points on the scale. Ordinal scales such as the DHS can be obtained by numerous methods, such as through the use of *sorting techniques* whereby the people doing the ranking (usually referred to as the "judges" or "raters") sort a pile of cards with respect to the degree to which they believe a particular trait is reflected.

Sorting techniques can also be used to obtain nominal scales. For this purpose, subjects would be instructed to sort the cards (or objects or whatever) into mutually exclusive categories, each category then being assigned a number and/or a name. Sorting tasks may even be used to obtain interval scales—or scales that are at least presumed to be equal (Thurstone, 1929).

EXERCISE 38
GUTTMAN SCALING

OBJECTIVE

To provide firsthand experience in the creation of a Guttman scale.

BACKGROUND

A Guttman scale lists items that range sequentially from weaker to stronger expressions of the attitude, belief, or feeling being measured. A feature of Guttman scales is that they are designed so that all respondents who agree with the stronger statements of the attitude will also agree with milder statements. Here is a sample:

Directions: Circle the letter of the statement with which you agree.

Item 1

A. If the woman in a mature, responsible, financially secure, loving married couple is infertile, then the couple should have the right to contract with a surrogate mother to bear the father's child.
B. If a mature, responsible, financially secure, loving married couple is infertile, then they have a right to adopt a child.
C. If a mature, responsible, financially secure, loving married couple is having difficulty conceiving a child, then they have the right to seek medical intervention.
D. All mature, responsible, financially secure, loving married couples have a right to have children.

If this were a perfect Guttman scale, all respondents who agree with item A (the most extreme position) should also agree with items B, C, and D, which appear to represent progressively less extreme positions. All respondents who do not agree with A but who do agree with B should also agree with C and D, and so forth.

YOUR TASK

Using Guttman scaling, write one test item on any topic you wish.

EXERCISE 39
ITEM ANALYSIS:
QUANTITATIVE METHODS

OBJECTIVE

To enhance understanding of, and provide firsthand experience with, various methods of quantitative item analysis.

BACKGROUND

Which items within a pool of possible items represent the best items? Which items need to be modified or eliminated in order to make the test a better test? These are typical questions asked by many test developers (as well as test users) and the process of answering them typically entails item analysis. *Item analysis* refers to a test item evaluation process involving quantitative and/or qualitative methods. In this exercise we focus on *quantitative* methods designed to yield information regarding characteristics of test items such as level of difficulty and power of discrimination. In Exercise 40 we focus on *qualitative* methods of item analysis designed to yield information regarding characteristics of test items such as ambiguity and social desirability.

Exactly which of the many available quantitative item analytic techniques will be employed will vary as a function of variables related to (a) the nature of the test and (b) the item analyzer's definition of "best items." For example, while computation of indices of both item difficulty and item discrimination would be appropriate when analyzing an achievement test (or any test where there are right or wrong answers), only the computation of one of these indices—the index of item discrimination—would be appropriate with respect to a personality test (or any test where there are no right or wrong answers). In cases where the correlation of items with some external criterion (such as a personality trait or some other factor) is deemed essential, other quantitative techniques such as factor analysis may be an integral component of the item analysis process. Factor analysis may also be used to learn about the internal consistency of a test as might other methods designed to yield indices of item reliability. An item-validity index (a measure of the validity of individual items) is yet another measure that may be derived quantitatively to answer the question "Which items are the best?"

YOUR TASK

In Part 1 of this exercise, your task is to calculate and interpret an item-difficulty index and an item-discrimination index. Part 2 is comprised of a series of short-answer problems related to item analysis.

In preparation for Part 1, your *instructor's* task is to make up a list of 10 words to be administered in the form of an impromptu spelling test. The list should contain a mix of words estimated to be of low, middle, and high level of difficulty for college-age testtakers. The instructor reads each of the ten words aloud as each student writes it out. At the conclusion of the test, students find a partner to exchange papers with and all papers are scored. Still holding on to their partner's test paper, all students will individually report the performance of the testtaker of the paper they are holding as the instructor tallies the information at the board. The objective here will be to work together as a class to obtain an item-difficulty index and an item-discrimination index for each of the ten items (words) on the test.

Part 1

1. *Calculating and interpreting an item-difficulty index.* What proportion of the examinees got the item right? An index of item difficulty provides the answer to this question and it can be found by using the following formula:

$$p_1 = \frac{\text{number of examinees who got the item correct}}{\text{number of people who attempted to answer the item}}$$

where p_1 stands for "item difficulty index for item 1."

In the process of calculating an item-difficulty index for each of the 10 items on the test, you will discover firsthand the paradoxical meaning of the term *item-difficulty index.* More specifically, you will find that the *higher* the index of item difficulty, the *easier* the item. You will also find the reverse to be true: the lower the index of item difficulty, the more difficult the item.

Items on tests where the objective is maximum discrimination across the entire range should contain an assortment of items ranging in difficulty level from about .40 to about .70. However, occasions do arise—particularly in very selective screening situations—where the test user might find a test containing items with an average difficulty of .1. But for the test we've been working with in this exercise the .40 to .70 range will do just fine; now, which items on the spelling test would you recommend for elimination (or modification)? Which items would you recommend for inclusion in a revised form of the test (assuming a revised form of the test was planned)?

2. *Calculating and interpreting an item-discrimination index.* "Are testtakers who are thought to be higher in the ability measured by the test more likely to get the item right than testtakers who are thought to be lower in the ability measured by the test?" "Are testtakers who are thought to possess more of a personality trait measured by a specific personality test more likely than other testtakers to respond to a personality test item in a predicted direction?" These are the kinds of questions that a discrimination index is designed to shed light on.

Symbolized by *d*, an *item-discrimination index* is a measure of the difference between the proportion of high scorers answering an item correctly and the proportion of low scorers answering the item correctly; the higher the value of *d*, the greater the number of high scorers answering the item correctly.[1] The group of high and low scorers may be comprised of test-takers who respectively achieved the top and bottom 25% to 33% of the scores. A negative value of *d* is indicative of a situation where low-scoring examinees are more likely to answer the item correctly than high-scoring examinees—a situation that calls for action such as revision or elimination of the item.

While there exist many methods of measuring item discrimination, the one you will be using to obtain *d* for each item in your spelling test is simple and straightforward. Here are the steps you'll be following as a class:

Step 1

Sort all of the test papers into one of three groups on the basis of the test score. The three groups that papers will be sorted into will be the high scorers (Group H), the medium scorers (Group M), and the low scorers (Group L). Based on the number of papers in the class, use the most convenient figure between 25% and 33% as the cutoff point. For example, if there are 12 students in the class, you may wish to use the 33% figure as a cutoff point—this so that there will be 4 papers in each of the three groups.

Step 2

Focusing solely on the papers in Group H, ask "How many members of this group got the item correct?" for each item.[2] For each item, express the answer to this question as a proportion with *N* (the total number of test takers in Group H) as the denominator.

Step 3

Focusing solely on the papers in Group L, ask "How many members of this group got the item correct?" for each item. For each item, express the answer to this question as a proportion with *N* (the total number of testtakers in Group L) as the denominator.

Step 4

For each item, solve for d *by subtracting the proportion you obtained for* L *from the proportion you obtained for* H.

Three questions that may come up as you calculate and then attempt to interpret item-discrimination indices for each of the 10 items in the spelling test are as follows:

- What value of *d* is an acceptable cut-off? At what point can I be assured I have an item good enough to be included in my revised test?
- Why was the data from "Group M" not used in the calculation of *d*?
- How should one proceed if the test results are not amenable to a clear separation of high-, middle-, and low-scoring papers?

There are no hard and fast rules regarding what constitutes an acceptable cut-off point for an index of discrimination. There are many ways to calculate such an index and each of these may yield different values. In practice, the setting of an acceptable level of item discrimination—like the setting of an appropriate level of item difficulty—will depend on the nature of the test and the use of the test data. As a rule of thumb for the purposes of this exercise, let's arbitrarily set .40 as an acceptable level of item discrimination; any item with a *d* value of .40 or better (higher) will be eligible for inclusion in the revised form of the test.

The data from the middle range of scores on the test, Group M, were not used in order to clearly separate respondents in terms of ability—in the present instance, spelling ability. The presumption is that the high scorers on this test are more able spellers than are the low scorers on the test. But what can be said about the examinees who scored in the middle range? These respondents could be either good spellers who, due to error in the psychometric sense, did not exhibit their "true" ability on the test or, alternatively, relatively

[1] "Translating" this explanation with reference to personality testing and the measurement of a specific personality trait, *d* is a measure of the difference between the proportion of testtakers who scored high on the particular personality trait being measured and the proportion of testtakers who scored low on the particular personality trait being measured.

[2] "Translating" to the language of testing where there are no right or wrong answers—such as in personality testing—this question might be rephrased, "How many members of this group responded to this particular item in the way that indicated that they did possess the trait in question?" More specifically, on a test of introversion where Group H was composed of people whose overall score on the test was high, the relevant question would be "How many members of Group H responded to this particular item in the way that we would expect introverts to respond?"

poor spellers who, due to error in the psychometric sense, did much better on this particular test than might have been expected based on their "true" ability. You may then ask, "Why not more precisely discriminate between the extreme (upper/lower) groups by using only the top and bottom 5% or 10% of scorers?" The answer here is that if the sample is large enough, such a practice would be feasible. In most applications, however, employing only the top and bottom 5% of respondents would yield too few cases with which to work.[3]

In attempting to calculate *d* with respect to your instructor's spelling test items (or with any other application) you may find that your data are not amenable to clear separation into high-, medium-, and low-scoring groups. You would like to keep the number of cases in Group H and Group L equal and to do so may mean that Group M contains a different number of cases (or precious few cases or no cases at all). Sometimes in this effort to balance the two extreme groups (H and L) an excess of scores of one or another value occurs in one or the other groups. The operative term in eliminating these excess scores is *do it randomly*. One simple way for eliminating data is to use a coin; flip it saying, "Heads you stay, tails you go." Up one notch in sophistication from that technique is reference to a table of random numbers (found in most introductory statistics texts); with all test papers coded by number, simply eliminate those test papers with a code number that corresponds to the number(s) in the random numbers table that appear(s) first.

Part 2

If Part 1 of this exercise has left you craving for more experience with the concept and practice of item analysis, assume now that you are the author of a 100-item (draft) test for a ninth-grade-level American history test (AHT) and that your objective is to have this test distributed by a commercial test publisher. You envision the final version of the AHT as containing only 50 items and plan to use item analysis as a tool in helping you to eliminate 50 items while retaining the "best" remaining items. You recently administered the test to 100 ninth-graders and those data are waiting to be analyzed.

1. Using your textbook as well as any other relevant books as a resource, briefly describe how you would (or would not) use the following indices in your

---

[3] We note in passing that some computerized item-discrimination programs are sophisticated and elegant enough to incorporate the middle range of scores in the computation of an item-discrimination index. For our pencil-and-paper purposes, however, use of the extreme (upper/lower) groups will suit us just fine.

efforts to narrow the field of 100 AHT items to the best 50 items:

- item-difficulty index
- item-validity index
- item-reliability index
- item-discrimination index

2. What follows are two sample items from your AHT:

AHT ITEM #1

Who was Vice President of the United States under President Jimmy Carter?

(a) Gerald Ford
(b) George Bush
(c) Walter Mondale
(d) Bob Dole

AHT ITEM #2

What was the name of the first communication satellite launched by the United States?

(a) Sputnik
(b) Telstar
(c) Comtrex
(d) Orbitron

Like the items above, each AHT item contains four possible answers. What is the probability of guessing correctly on this (or any single item) on the basis of chance alone?

3. What is the optimal level of item difficulty for any AHT item?

4. If 60 of the 100 examinees were correct in their response to Item 47, what is the item-difficulty index for Item 47?

5. If 69 of the 100 examinees were correct in their response to Item 93, what is the item-difficulty index for Item 93?

6. Which item was the more difficult, Item 93 or Item 47?

7. Calculate the item-score standard deviation of Item 93 and Item 47.

8. Item 16 has an item-score standard deviation of .40. The point-biserial correlation between the item score and the total test score is .75. What is the item-reliability index of Item 16?

9. From all of the test papers for the 100 students who took the AHT you form two groups—Group *H*, which consists of the upper-scoring 27% of the papers, and Group *L*, which consists of the lower-scoring (*L*) 27% of the papers. You put aside for the moment all of the test papers that fall into the middle range (46% of the papers). There are a total of 27 papers in Group *H* and a total of 27 papers in Group *L*. The table below illustrates the number of test takers in each group who responded correctly to each of the two items listed below:

Item	H	L
1	25	8
2	9	14

Determine the item-discrimination index (d_i) for each of the these items. Which item is the better of the two? Why?

10. After looking at the data for Item 2 (below), decide whether or not you believe this item to be a good item or not. Provide a brief rationale for your opinion based on (a) the overall contrast in performance with respect to the *H* and *L* groups and (b) the performance of the distractor choices. How might you go about revising this item if indeed you find it to be in need of revision?

Item 2

	Alternatives (*answer keyed as correct)			
Group	a	b*	c	d
H	15	9	2	1
L	3	14	4	6

11. Now look at the data for response to Item 1. What can you conclude from it?

Item 1

	Alternatives			
Group	a	b	c*	d
H	2	0	25	0
L	18	0	8	0

EXERCISE 40
ITEM ANALYSIS: QUALITATIVE METHODS

OBJECTIVE

To enhance understanding of, and provide firsthand experience with, various methods of qualitative item analysis.

BACKGROUND

In addition to methods of item analysis that utilize numbers, statistics, graphs, formulas and the like—quantitative methods—there exists another class of methods that may be used to analyze and evaluate test items. This latter group of techniques, referred to as *qualitative* in nature, relies instead on techniques such as one-on-one interviews and group discussion. In what we will refer to as the "Think Aloud" method, an examinee verbalizes thoughts as they come to mind in the process of having the test individually administered. Another method, the Small Group Discussion method of qualitative item analysis, is just that—a group discussion of reactions to each of the items on the test as each item is administered.

YOUR TASK

As a class, you will conduct a qualitative item analysis using a combination of the Think Aloud and Small Group Discussion techniques. The stimulus for this analysis will be the MPPI (see Appendix A).

The instructor (or student) interviewer/moderator will read each item aloud and class members—each playing the role of a testtaker—will respond with some of their impressions regarding various aspects of the time. In order to better understand each item and the process by which testtakers might mentally arrive at an answer to it, the moderator should encourage testtakers to think aloud as they arrive at an answer. Additionally, information regarding the perceived ambiguity, offensiveness, inappropriateness, or foolishness of each item will be important when conducting a qualitative item analysis. And if the test being analyzed were a veritable personality test—as opposed to a mock personality test—other variables to watch for in the analysis would include the extent to which an item is perceived as an invasion of privacy, the *transparency* of an item, and the *social desirability* of an item.

Transparency refers to the extent to which examinees can "see right through" an item and unless there is some specific reason to the contrary, the less transparent an item is, the better. Consider, for example, a test examining the personality variable of locus of control. An item such as "I usually wear seat belts in a car" is better—at least with respect to transparency—than an item such as "I feel that I have little control over my life." While both items tap perceived locus of control—the extent to which people feel that they are the master of their own fate—the seat belt item does it in a more subtle (and preferable) way.

Social desirability is another factor that may bias a test taker's response to an item on a personality test; the term refers to a tendency to respond to personality test items in a way that will place the respondent in the most favorable light (regardless of what the true response to the item might be). Look at the two personality test items that follow and ask yourself which answer, True or False, is the socially desirable response:

1. I hope to be able to take care of my parents in their old age.	True | |	False | |
2. I tend to betray my friends.	True | |	False | |

For Item 1, the socially desirable response is True and for Item 2 the socially desirable response is False. For obvious reasons many testtakers—especially those taking a personality test as part of a hiring, promotion, or some other selection process—may strive to make all of their responses fall in the socially desirable range. Personality test developers have attempted to counter this tendency in a number of ways such as (1) motivating testtakers to respond candidly by persuading them that it is in their best interest to do so; (2) building faking detection scales (such as the MMPI Lie Scale) into the test; and (3) structuring the test so that the testtaker must respond to one or more alternatives that are equally undesirable. The latter technique entails writing what are called *forced-choice* types of items such as the following:

Which is true (or more true than the other)—*a* or *b*?

a. I tend to betray my friends.
b. I tend to double-deal my business associates.

While you may not find transparency or social desirability response bias to be major factors influencing responses to the MPPI, in practice these (as well as related) factors may be quite problematic to test developers and test users.

EXERCISE 41
WRITING "GOOD" ITEMS

OBJECTIVE

To enhance understanding of, and obtain firsthand experience with, test-item writing.

BACKGROUND

"What range of content should my test items cover?" "Which of the many different types of item formats should be employed?" These are but two of the many questions that must be answered by the creator of a test— be it a test to be nationally standardized or a test to be used for a one-time classroom administration.

YOUR TASK

1. Develop a five-item test on the following subject: "American History from 1940 to 1980." All five of the items should be of the same item format. (For the sake of this test construction exercise, let's limit the choice of item formats to the following three: multiple-choice, true/false, or essay.)
2. Provide a brief rationale for (a) the range of content your test covers and (b) your choice of item format.
3. Checking against the discussion of the criteria for "good" items found in your textbook, "trouble-shoot"

the items you've written; are they indeed "good" items? Why or why not?
4. Now rewrite all five items into a different one of the three item formats (multiple-choice, true/false, or essay); are the rewritten items also "good" items (according to the criteria set forth in your text)? Why or why not?
5. Discuss some of the feelings and/or questions you had in completing the four exercises above. What did you feel good or confident about? What did you lack confidence or felt you wished to know more about? What do you think it takes to be a good item writer and test developer?

REFERENCES

Abadzi, H. & Florez, S. (1981). Constructing the Puerto Rico Self-Concept Scale. *Applied Psychological Measurement, 5,* 237–243.

Bloom, B. *Human characteristics and school learning.* New York: McGraw-Hill, 1976.

Bock, R. D. & Jones, L. V. (1968). *The measurement and prediction of judgment and choice.* San Francisco: Holden-Day.

Brookover, W. B., Patterson, A., & Thomas, S. *Self-concept of ability and school achievement.* East Lansing, MI: U.S. Office of Education, Cooperative Research Project No. 845, East Lansing Office of Research & Publications, Michigan State University, 1962.

Campbell, P. B. School and self-concept. *Educational Leadership.* 1967, *24,* 510–515.

Cohen, R. J., Swerdlik, M. E., & Smith, D. K. (1992). *Psychological testing and assessment: An introduction to tests & measurement,* 2nd ed. Mountain View, CA: Mayfield

Coppersmith, S. *The antecedents of self-esteem.* San Francisco: W. H. Freeman & Company, 1967.

Cronbach, L. *Essentials of psychological testing* (3rd ed.). New York: Harper & Row, 1970.

Fink, M. B. Self-concept as it relates to academic achievement. *California Journal of Education Research,* 1962, *13,* 57–62.

Fitts, W. H. The self-concept and human behavior. *Mental Health-Center Research Bulletin.* 1965, 1, 1–78. (Monograph)

Gill, M. P. *Patterns of achievement as related to the perceived self.* Paper presented at the annual meeting of the American Educational Research Association, Los Angeles, CA, April 1969.

Gordon, I. J. *Studying the child in the school.* New York: John Wiley & Sons, 1966.

Hernández, M. *Necesidades y problemas de los estudiantes adolescentes de escuela superior en Puerto Rico.* Hato Rey, Puerto Rico: Departamento de Instrucción Pública, Oficina de Evaluación, 1964.

Jackson, D. N. (1970). A sequential system for personality scale development. In C. D. Spielberger (Ed.), *Current topics in clinical and community psychology.* Vol 2. New York: Academic Press.

Muller, D. G., & Leonetti, R. *Primary Self-Concept Scale: Test Manual.* Ft. Worth, TX.: National Council for Bilingual Education, 1972 (ERIC Document Reproduction Service, No. ED 062847).

Puerto Rico Departamento de Instrucción Pública, Centro de Evaluación. *Escala de autoconcepto.* Hato Rey, Puerto Rico: Author, 1980.

Purkey, W. W. *Self-concept and school achievement.* Englewood Cliffs, NJ: Prentice-Hall, 1970.

Richmond, B. O., & White, D. F. Sociometric predictors of the self-concept among fifth- and sixth-grade children. *Journal of Educational Research,* 1971, *64,* 425–429.

Stanwyck, D. J., & Felker, D. W. *Measuring the self-concept: A factor analytic study.* Paper presented at the annual meeting of the National Council of Measurement in Education, New York, April 1971 (ERIC Document Reproduction Service, No. ED 053161).

Thompson, W. *Correlates of the self concept* (Monograph No. 6). Nashville, TN: Dede Wallace Center, 1972.

Thurstone, L. L. (1927). A law of comparative judgment. *Psychological Review, 34,* 273–286.

Thurstone, L. L. (1959). *The measurement of values.* Chicago: University of Chicago Press.

Thurstone, L. L. & Chave, E. J. (1929). *The measurement of attitude.* Chicago: University of Chicago Press.

Whitmore, J. R. *Thinking about my school, TAMS: The development of an inventory to measure pupil perception of the elementary school environment* (R & D Memorandum No. 125). Palo Alto, CA: Stanford University, Stanford Center for Research and Development in Testing, 1975 (ERIC Document Reproduction Service, No. ED 100998).

4-QUESTION CHALLENGE

1. Scaling may be defined as
   (a) the assignment of numbers according to rules.
   (b) the process of setting rules for assigning numbers in measurement.
   (c) a method for estimating the strength of a particular trait in testtakers.
   (d) the shrinkage of item validities that occurs after cross-validation.

2. Guttman scales yield this level of measurement:
   (a) nominal
   (b) ordinal
   (c) interval
   (d) ratio

3. An index of an item's difficulty is obtained by calculating the proportion of
   (a) the total number of testtakers who got the item right.
   (b) the total number of testtakers who reported the item to be difficult.
   (c) the total number of testtakers who got the item right compared to a matched sample of testtakers.
   (d) None of the above

4. An item characteristic curve is a graphic representation of
   (a) testtaker responses to correct versus distractor alternatives.
   (b) characteristics of performance on orally administered versus paper-and-pencil tests.
   (c) characteristics of performance on written versus computer-administered tests.
   (d) testtaker ability plotted by probability of correct response.

THE ASSESSMENT
OF INTELLIGENCE

Chapter 8

Intelligence and Its Measurement: An Overview

On the Relativity of "Intelligence"

In the now classic film Saturday Night Fever, *paint store clerk/disco dancer Tony Manero (John Travolta) attempts to win over Stephanie (Karen Lynn Gorney), a fellow resident of Bay Ridge, Brooklyn, who aspires to the life of a sophisticated Manhattanite. In a scene shortly after the two rehearse for an upcoming disco dance contest, Tony—perhaps feeling inadequate—asks Stephanie if she thinks that he's intelligent. Stephanie responds with a laugh and some indecision but ultimately concludes, "Yeah, maybe. Maybe intelligent." Among other things, the scene is a lesson in the relativity of the attribution of intelligence and the importance of keeping in mind not only the object of the assessment but also the frame of reference of the assessor.*

Outline for Chapter 8 of Cohen et al. (1996)
INTELLIGENCE AND ITS MEASUREMENT: AN OVERVIEW

What Is Intelligence?
The 1921 Symposium
Francis Galton
Alfred Binet
David Wechsler
Jean Piaget
The Factor Analysts
The Information-Processing View
The 1921 Symposium Revisited

Measuring Intelligence
Measuring Intelligence in Infancy
Measuring the Intelligence of Children
Measuring the Intelligence of Adults
Measuring the Intelligence of Special Populations
   People with disabilities
   People with psychological disorders
   The gifted

Issues in the Measurement of Intelligence
Nature versus Nurture
   Inheritance and interactionism
The stability of intelligence
   The rise and fall of IQ
Other Issues
   The process of measurement
   Personality factors
   Gender
   Family environment
   Culture

A Perspective on Intelligence

CLOSE-UP:
   Culture-Fair/Culture-Loaded

EVERYDAY PSYCHOMETRICS:
   The Bell Curve Controversy

EXERCISE 42
THE CONCEPT OF INTELLIGENCE

OBJECTIVE

To enhance understanding of and provide firsthand experience with the development of a definition of intelligence.

BACKGROUND

Widely differing views as to the meaning of "intelligence" exist among psychologists, educators, and lay people. Studies conducted by Robert Sternberg (1982) with lay people, for example, have yielded definitions as diverse as "displays common sense" to "reads with high comprehension." Among professionals, the view that intelligence is a kind of evolving biological adaptation to the outside world, and the view that "intelligence is whatever intelligence tests measure," are only some of the many beliefs that have been expressed regarding the concept of intelligence.

YOUR TASK

This is a two-part task that entails (1) developing your own conception of intelligence, and (2) comparing it to some of the existing definitions. Let's do it in stepwise fashion:

Step 1

List 10 things—they could be single words or terms—that you believe are characteristic of "adult intelligence."

1. _____
2. _____
3. _____
4. _____
5. _____
6. _____
7. _____
8. _____
9. _____
10. _____

Step 2

List 10 things that you believe to be characteristic of the construct "unintelligence" (again confining your observations to the adult age range).

1. _____
2. _____
3. _____
4. _____
5. _____
6. _____
7. _____
8. _____
9. _____
10. _____

Step 3

On the basis of the characteristics you cited above, write a paragraph or two that sets forth what you conceive intelligence in adults to be.

Step 4

Compare and contrast the definition of intelligence you derived with "intelligence" as it has been conceived of and defined by

(a) Francis Galton,
(b) Alfred Binet,
(c) David Wechsler,
(d) Charles Spearman, and
(e) E. G. Boring.

EXERCISE 43
INTERPRETING IQ SCORES

OBJECTIVE

To enhance understanding of the types of interpretation that can legitimately be made—as well as the types of interpretation that *cannot* legitimately be made—on the basis of intelligence test data.

BACKGROUND

IQ data is used in school systems as well as other settings for the purpose of making determinations as to students' level of learning ability and academic performance. Learning difficulties may be diagnosed on the basis of an intelligence test and such data may serve as a guide to an assignment of special educational opportunities. Yet as Professor John R. Hills of Florida State University has asked, ". . . can IQ scores do all these things for us?"

YOUR TASK

To help better understand the information that IQ scores can and cannot provide, Hills provides the following 10 questions. Mark each item True or False while noting any questions or comments to be raised in class.

THE INTERPRETING IQ SCORES TEST*

Tests that provide IQ scores are widely used in schools. A score that tells how "bright" a student is, or how readily he or she will learn in school, would be a handy bit of information, and it might be essential as a trustworthy and reliable guide for diagnosing learning difficulties, for providing students with special educational opportunities, or for predicting future educational performance. But can IQ scores do all these things for us? Try the following questions about scores from intelligence tests. Indicate whether the stated interpretation of the IQ score is sound. Circle either T or F for each question. Mark a response for each question; there is no penalty for guessing. This is an untimed test.

ANSWER	ITEM	QUESTIONS/COMMENTS
T F	1. Manny got an IQ score of 115. This score means that Manny's innate ability to do things that require brains or intelligence is about one standard deviation above the mean or at about the 84th percentile.	
T F	2. Manny's IQ score came from a recent revision of a widely used intelligence test with a long and honored history. One can be confident that the score was derived by finding Manny's Mental Age on the basis of his answers to the test questions, dividing that by his Chronological Age, and multiplying by 100, as in (MA/CA) $\times$ 100 = IQ.	
T F	3. If Manny had been given a different IQ test, one that was used as widely and with an equally long and illustrious history, the resulting IQ score would be about the same level (within 2 or 3 points either way).	
T F	4. If Manny received the IQ score of 115 when he was in the sixth grade, we know that he was old enough that the score will remain stable, neither increase nor decrease appreciably, for many years.	
T F	5. Manny happens to be black. Knowing this, we can estimate that Manny's score is lower than it should be because IQ tests are biased against minority groups.	
T F	6. The test that Manny took had two scores, one for Verbal skills and one for Performance or Nonverbal skills. The difference between the Verbal and Nonverbal IQs was 15 points. A skilled clinician can use that information by itself to make	

*By John R. Hills, "Interpreting IQ Scores." From *Hills Handy Hints,* reprinted by permission of the publisher, the National Council on Measurement in Education, Washington, D.C.

ANSWER		ITEM	QUESTIONS/COMMENTS
		a useful diagnosis of emotional disturbance or organic brain injury.	
T	F	7. Manny's brother, Sherman, took the same IQ test and got a score of 102. Because his score is below 110, there is little chance that he could be admitted to a college.	
T	F	8. The IQ test that Manny and Sherman took was an established and highly respected test, but the publisher still may not have checked to see whether the IQ scores are useful for predicting performance in school and may not have published relevant results in the test manual.	
T	F	9. Although Manny's teacher needs to know Manny's score, and it should be posted in the school records, Manny should not be allowed to know what his IQ score is.	
T	F	10. If someone had taken Manny aside and showed him how to do some of the kinds of items on the IQ test and let him practice on those kinds of items a bit, his score might have been noticeably higher.	

EXERCISE 44
"MENTAL AGE"

OBJECTIVE

To impart an historical and conceptual understanding of the now seldom used concept of "mental age."

BACKGROUND

For many years after intelligence tests were first introduced, the concept of a mental age played a critical role in the computation of an intelligence quotient (IQ).

YOUR TASK

After reading the essay that follows, answer these questions:

1. Describe how mental age was once used in the calculation of an IQ.
2. Describe the intuitive appeal of the mental age concept.
3. Describe the drawbacks of using the mental age concept when describing test results.

"MENTAL AGE" AND IQ

Have you ever found yourself telling someone something like, "You're acting like a 2-year-old?" Such statements reflect the great intuitive appeal the concept of "mental age" holds—the idea that someone can behave in a way that is more typical of a person who is either younger or older. Perhaps the first reference to "mental age" in the scholarly literature was made by Esquirol (1838), who observed that an idiot—one diagnostic classification of mental retardation of the day—was incapable of learning at the same rate as other people of the same age. Duncan and Millard (1866) and Down (1987) were referring to mental age when they suggested that to increase one's understanding of mentally retarded children, it would be helpful to compare their behavior and abilities to younger children—a practice that has continued long after such a recommendation was first made (Goodman, 1978). Another early reference to the concept of mental age came when a psychiatrist, Hall (1848), testified during a murder trial that it was his professional opinion that the defendant in the trial had the knowledge of a 3-year-old.

The first use of the mental-age concept in a test was in 1877 when S. E. Chaille published an infant test in the *New Orleans Medical and Surgical Journal*. This infant test included items arranged according to age level. The assignment of particular age levels was made by determining the levels at which the tests were commonly passed. It was Alfred Binet, however, who refined the mental-age concept—first referring to it as "mental level"—made it more concrete in definition, and popularized it. Terman and Merrill (1960, p. 5) remind us that "One of Binet's basic assumptions of the original scale was that a person is thought of as normal if he can do the things persons of his age normally do, retarded if his test performance corresponds to the performance of persons younger than himself, and accelerated if his performance exceeds that of persons his own age." The mental-age concept brought to Binet's test a readily comprehensible "yardstick" by which the examinee's intellectual functioning could be gauged, a yardstick that no doubt also served to stir professional—as well as popular—interest in the test.

Similar to the infant tests that had been developed by Chaille, the placement of items in the 1916 revision of the Binet-Simon scale (Terman) at various age levels had been determined by calculating the age level at which the majority of normal children in the standardization sample passed the particular item. The first step in the calculation of an individual's mental age entailed finding the sum of the total number of mental age credits assigned to test items passed (including all items that were below the established basal age but presumed to be passed). The "mental age" for a testtaker was the "ceiling" (or highest) age level passed by the examinee. A conversion table in the manual indicated what a mental age was equivalent to in terms of an intelligence quotient (IQ). But what is an "IQ"?

Soon after Binet's death in 1911, Stern (1914) introduced the notion of a "mental quotient," suggesting that the index of intellectual functioning derived from the Binet-Simon test could be expressed as the ratio of the testtaker's mental age to his or her chronological age—and then multiplied by 100 for the sake of convenience and to eliminate decimals:

$$\text{mental quotient} = \frac{\text{mental age}}{\text{chronological age}} \times 100$$

Thus, if a child earned a mental-age equivalent exactly equal to his or her chronological age, his or her mental quotient would be equal to 100.

The concepts of mental age and ratio IQ were not without their critics. For example, L. L. Thurstone (1926) attacked the mental-age concept as ambiguous, and he urged test users as well as test developers to abandon its usage. In place of the concept of mental age, Thurstone advocated percentile scores or standard scores based on the mean and standard deviation of raw scores of the normative group within each level.

David Wechsler was among those psychometrists who agreed with Thurstone. In the intelligence tests that Wechsler developed, the concept of mental age was completely abandoned. Wechsler argued that the intelligence level of, say, an 18-year-old retarded adult with a calculated mental age of 9 was qualitatively quite different from that of a 7-year-old with a calculated mental age of 9—yet both would be described in mental age terminology as "9 years." Wechsler also pointed to conceptual difficulties inherent in the ratio IQ concept. For example, a 5-year-old with a mental age of 6 and a 10-year-old with a mental age of 12 would both have an IQ calculated to be 120, yet one child would be two years advanced in mental age whereas the other would only be one year advanced in mental age. Wechsler further observed that the concept of mental age has little utility in describing adult functioning, as "mental age" ceases to be very meaningful beyond certain ages; is a 28-year-old apt to have more intellectual ability than a 29-year-old, for example? A test developer would be hard put to develop an intelligence test where mean scores on the test would increase with age at the ages, for example, of 20, 25, 30, 35, and 40. Because growth in intellectual abilities is disproportionately rapid in the first few years of life and through early childhood, it would appear to be a mistake to equate the 16-year-old with a calculated mental age of 14 to the 4-year-old with a calculated mental age of 2; although both individuals' calculated mental ages are exactly two years behind their chronological ages, the degree of overall impairment is probably much greater in the 4-year-old.

As an alternative to the ratio IQ, Wechsler proposed what he called a "deviation IQ"—a measure to describe how much an individual's intellectual ability deviates from the average performance of others of approximately the same chronological age. Initially devising a test to measure adult intelligence, Wechsler (1939) culled the standardization sample's data and constructed tables so that the person who scored just at the average level for his or her age group (for example, 20 to 24 years of age) would receive an IQ of 100. The standard deviation was set at 15 points, meaning, for example, that IQs ranging from 85 to 115 would also be considered to be within the normal range of Wechsler tests. With the development of Wechsler's tests for children, IQs were obtained by comparing the child's performance to the average performance of those of his or her age.

In contrast to previous editions of the Stanford-Binet, the third (1960) edition of this test no longer expressed testtakers' performance in terms of a ratio IQ but, like the Wechsler scales, expressed performance in terms of a deviation IQ. Terman and Merrill (1960) noted that the deviation IQs avoided the inadequacies of the ratio IQs in that,

(a) a given IQ now indicates the same relative ability at different ages, (b) a subject's IQ score, ignoring errors of measurement, remains the same from one age to another unless there is a change in ability level, and (c) a given change in IQ indicates the same amount of change in relative standing regardless of the ability level of the subject. (pp. 27–28)

Although the 1960 revision of the Stanford-Binet yielded a deviation IQ, it remained an age scale with the "guiding principle . . . [having been] to secure an arrangement of tests that makes the average mental age that the scale gives agree closely with chronological age" (Terman & Merrill, 1960, p. 25). By 1986 and the publication of the fourth edition of the Stanford-Binet, the concept of mental age had essentially become a term of historic interest rather than practical value.

EXERCISE 45
SUCCESSIVE AND SIMULTANEOUS PROCESSING

OBJECTIVE

To enhance understanding of two types of information processing: successive and simultaneous.

BACKGROUND

Successive and simultaneous processing are two different, sometimes complementary, styles of information processing. In successive processing, also referred to as sequential processing, each bit of information is individually processed in a logical, sequential fashion. By contrast, in simultaneous processing, also referred to as parallel processing, information is integrated and synthesized at once and as a whole.

Examples of stimuli likely to be processed in successive and simultaneous fashion are presented in Figure 8-1. Contrast course outline "A" (likely to be processed in simultaneous fashion) with course outline "B" (likely to be processed in successive fashion).

YOUR TASK

Create two forms of some other stimulus and explain why one is more likely to be processed in successive fashion, while the other is more likely to be processed in simultaneous fashion.

EXERCISE 46
RATING THE GIFTED

OBJECTIVE

To provide firsthand experience in the development of a rating scale.

BACKGROUND

In the discussion of the gifted, your textbook provides an example of a half-dozen items used to rate emotional development (see page 276 in Cohen et al., 1996).

YOUR TASK

Using the above-referenced rating scale for emotional development as a model, develop a half-dozen items of your own to measure *social* development. To answer this question, you will have to think about all possible factors that contribute to people becoming social in nature.

EXERCISE 47
GRAPPLING WITH SOME MEASUREMENT ISSUES

OBJECTIVE

To enhance understanding of and obtain firsthand experience with some of the issues attendant to the measurement of intelligence.

BACKGROUND

Ever since people have attempted to define and measure intelligence, numerous differences and issues have arisen regarding the nature of such definitions and measurements. Is intelligence "encoded" and does it merely "unfold" with age? Alternatively, is an individual born with a mind like a *tabula rasa* (blank slate) and does it remain for environmental influences to entirely influence the course of its development? As people and groups of people differ systematically in terms of physical characteristics, so do they differ in terms of intellectual (as well as personality-related) characteristics as well? These are some of the many questions that have been raised regarding the nature and measurement of intelligence.

Figure 8-1   on your test

Successive and Simultaneous Processing. Successive and simultaneous processing are two different, sometimes complementary, styles of information processing; each is represented below. In which form would you prefer to receive the seminar outline? Why?

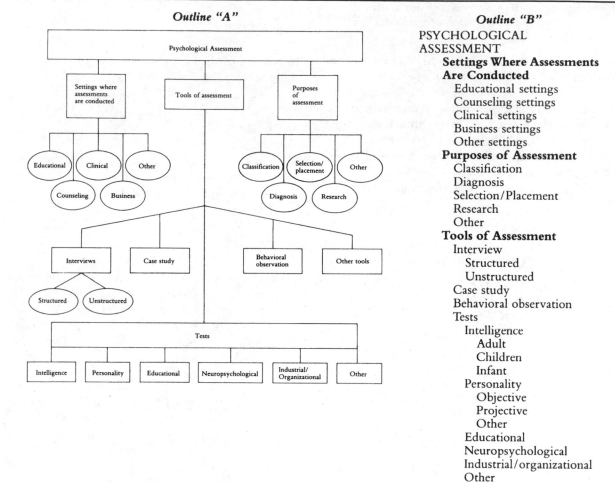

Outline "A"

Outline "B"
PSYCHOLOGICAL
ASSESSMENT
   Settings Where Assessments Are Conducted
      Educational settings
      Counseling settings
      Clinical settings
      Business settings
      Other settings
   Purposes of Assessment
      Classification
      Diagnosis
      Selection/Placement
      Research
      Other
   Tools of Assessment
      Interview
         Structured
         Unstructured
      Case study
      Behavioral observation
      Tests
         Intelligence
            Adult
            Children
            Infant
         Personality
            Objective
            Projective
            Other
         Educational
         Neuropsychological
         Industrial/organizational
         Other
      Other tools of assessment

YOUR TASK

Expand on the definition of intelligence you developed by imagining that a test based on your conception of intelligence (YCI) has been developed.

1. How is intelligence as you have defined it acquired? Is it solely the product of heredity? Of learning? Of an interaction between the two? Explain.
2. How might factors such as personality and gender influence measure intelligence?
3. According to your definition and test of intelligence, would you expect to find systematic differences between groups of people with respect to observed performance on it? Explain with reference to different groups of people such as people of different cultural or racial groups.
4. According to your definition and test of intelligence, how stable would you predict measurements of intelligence to be over time?

5. Is your test "culture loaded"? How might you decrease such culture-loading? What if you wished to *increase* the culture-loading of the test; what might you do?
6. A critic of your conception of intelligence as well as your test charges that you have improperly defined intelligence and that your test is limited to measuring intelligence only as you have defined it. Explain how you would respond to this critic noting where you would agree or not with the view expressed.
7. An organization called GEPDEF (Green-Eyed People's Defense Emergency Fund) files a lawsuit claiming that your test unfairly discriminates against green-eyed people; on the basis of preliminary research by GEPDEF, it's been found that people with green eyes tend to score lower on your test than people with any other eye color. Your attorney has asked you to draft a brief response indicating (a) why the charge of bias is unfounded, and (b) how the preliminary research by GEPDEF may have been experimentally flawed. What might you say?

EXERCISE 48
MORE ISSUES, MORE GRAPPLING

OBJECTIVE

To grapple with some of the issues and questions inherent in the definition and measurement of intelligence that were not tackled in Exercise 47.

YOUR TASK

Answer each of the following five questions in detail sufficient enough to provide evidence of your own thoughts on each of the topics:

1. Shockley (1971, p. 375) has argued that "nature has color coded groups of individuals so that statistically reliable predictions of their adaptability to intellectually rewarding and effective lives can easily be made and profitably used by the pragmatic man-in-the-street." Do you agree with Shockley? Why or why not? What are your own thoughts regarding Shockley's statement?

2. Arthur Jensen (1980, pp. 737–738) has written that differences in measured intelligence between the races,

> should not be permitted to influence the treatment accorded to *individuals* of any race—in education, employment, legal justice, and political and civil rights. . . . Those who would accord any treatment to *individuals* solely by virtue of their race will find no rational support in any of the scientific findings from psychological testing or present day theories of differential psychology.

Do you agree? Why or why not? What are your own thoughts regarding this statement by Jensen?

3. In "Thinking about Human Abilities," Horn (1988, p. 645) raises a thought-provoking question:

> When one looks for a studied moment at the myriad of abilities that humans display, it's as if one were to look into the heavens on a clear night and become stirred by the ceaseless drift of the clouds of the Milky Way. On such a night one might be dimly aware that there is order and system in the celestial white. But where among the drifting haze might one draw dimensions to represent this order? At first there is no answer to this question, only befuddlement. The same is true for human abilities. They appear as freefloating swarms emerging from spaces of unknown many dimensions. Is there genuine order in this throng, or can one at least impose an order that will not do great injustice to the complexity and still enable one to organize thinking and talking about it?

What is *your* answer to this question? By the way, in thinking about your answer, you may wish to consult Horn's (1988) article or some of his other writing on the subject (for example, Horn 1986a, 1986b, 1985).

4. Eric Heiden's ability in speedskating earned him an unprecedented five gold medals in the XIIIth Winter Olympics, with Olympic records shattered in each of the competitions. Would Heiden have accomplished this feat had he been born in the Bronx? Appalachia? Cairo? Had he been born in 1935? Had he been born to royalty? Do you think that the place, time, and other such circumstances enter into the extent to which innate ability is or is not cultivated?

5. "Tests of intelligence should be culture-specific." Make an argument for the statement above.

6. "Tests of intelligence should be culture-free." Make an argument for the statement above.

REFERENCES

Duncan, P. M., & Millard, W. (1866). *A manual for the classification, training, and education of the feeble-minded, imbecile, and idiotic.* London: Longmans, Green.

Esquirol, J. E. D. (1838). *Des malades mentales considerees sous les rapports medical, hygienique et medicolegal.* Paris: Balliere.

Goodman, J. F. (1978). Wanted: Restoration of the mental age in the 1972 revised Stanford-Binet. *Journal of Special Education, 12,* 45–49.

Hall, B. F. (1848). The trial of William Freeman. *American Journal of Insanity, 5*(2), 34–60.

Horn, J. L. (1985). Remodeling old models of intelligence: Gf-Gc theory. In B. B. Wolman (Ed.), *Handbook of intelligence.* New York: Wiley.

Horn, J. L. (1986). Intellectual ability concepts. In R. J. Sternberg (Ed.), *Advances in the psychology of human intelligence.* Hillsdale, NJ: Erlbaum. (a)

Horn, J. L. (1986). Some thoughts about intelligence. In R. J. Sternberg & D. K. Detterman (Eds.), *What is Intelligence? Contemporary viewpoints on its nature and definition.* Norwood, NJ: Ablex. (b)

Horn, J. L. (1988). Thinking about human abilities. In J. R. Nesselroade & R. B. Cattell (Eds.), *Handbook of multivariate psychology.* New York: Plenum.

Jensen, A. R. (1980). *Bias in mental testing.* New York: The Free Press.

Shockley, W. (1971). Models, mathematics, and the moral obligation to diagnose the origin of Negro IQ deficits. *Review of Educational Research, 41,* 369–377.

Stern, W. (1914). *The psychological method of testing intelligence.* Baltimore: Warwick & York.

Sternberg, R. J. (1982, April). Who's intelligent? *Psychology Today,* pp. 30–33, 38–39.

Terman, L. M. (1916). *The measurement of intelligence.* Boston: Houghton Mifflin.

Terman, L. M., & Merrill, M. A. (1960). *Stanford-Binet Intelligence Scale Manual for the Third Revision: Form L-M.* Boston: Houghton Mifflin.

Thurstone, L. L. (1926). The mental age concept. *Psychological Review, 33,* 268–278.

Wechsler, D. (1939). *The measurement of adult intelligence.* Baltimore, MD: Williams & Wilkins.

THE 4-QUESTION CHALLENGE

1. Which is true regarding the 1921 Symposium on Intelligence?
   (a) No two psychologists agreed on a definition.
   (b) Edwin Boring's definition won widespread acceptance.
   (c) Ways of measuring intelligence were standardized.
   (d) Carl Spearman's definition won widespread acceptance.
2. A major theme running through the theories of intelligence of Binet, Wechsler, and Piaget is
   (a) assimilation.
   (b) accommodation.
   (c) interactionism.
   (d) pluralism.

3. According to Cattell's two-factor theory of intelligence, the factor that is being tapped by a memory-for-digits test item is
   (a) successive processing.
   (b) simultaneous processing.
   (c) crystallized intelligence.
   (d) fluid intelligence.
4. Which is most associated with culture-loaded assessment?
   (a) power tests
   (b) speed tests
   (c) performance tests
   (d) nonverbal content

Chapter 9

Tests of Intelligence

Putting the Pieces Together

Cliff Robertson attempts to "get it together" in the title role of the film Charly. *By the way, the task he is engaged in is quite similar to a Wechsler-type subtest. Which subtest is it? What aspect of intelligence is tapped by this subtest?*

Outline for Chapter 9 of Cohen et al. (1996)
TESTS OF INTELLIGENCE

The Stanford-Binet: Fourth Edition
The Standardization Sample
Psychometric Properties
Test Administration
Scoring and Interpretation
An Evaluation

The Wechsler Tests
The Wechsler Adult Intelligence Scale-Revised (WAIS-R)
  The standardization sample
  Psychometric properties
  An evaluation
The Wechsler Intelligence Scale for Children-Third Edition (WISC-III)
  The standardization sample
  Psychometric properties
  An evaluation
The Wechsler Preschool and Primary Scale of Intelligence-Revised (WPPSI-R)
  The standardization sample
  Psychometric properties
  An evaluation
The Wechsler Tests in Perspective

Other Tests of Intelligence
The Slosson Intelligence Test-Revised/(SIR-R)
Figure Drawings as Measures of Intelligence
Group Intelligence Tests
  Group intelligence tests in the schools
  Group intelligence tests in the military

Measures of Specific Intellectual Abilities
Measures of Creativity
Other Measures

CLOSE-UP:
Short Forms: Do They Work?

EVERYDAY PSYCHOMETRICS:
Construct Validity, Factor Analysis, and the WISC-III

EXERCISE 49
TESTS OF INTELLIGENCE

OBJECTIVE

To enhance understanding of and obtain firsthand experience with tests of intelligence.

BACKGROUND

Binet's test of intelligence was the forerunner of generations of intelligence tests to come. The Wechsler tests, originally developed by David Wechsler, include the Wechsler Adult Intelligence Scale-Revised (WAIS-R), the Wechsler Intelligence Scale for Children-III (WISC-III), and the Wechsler Preschool & Primary Scale of Intelligence-Revised (WPPSI-R). Each of these three tests was devised to assess an individual's "overall capacity to understand and cope with the world around him" (Wechsler, 1974, p. 5). Because the tests share a common theoretical foundation, they are also similar in structure.

As the Wechsler tests are based on "intelligence" as conceived by David Wechsler, so tests such as The Ordinal Scales of Psychological Development and The Concept Assessment Kit-Conservation are based on "intelligence" as conceived by the Swiss psychologist Jean Piaget. Such tests were designed to shed light on aspects of the developmental stage the testtaker is in with reference to Piaget's theory of cognitive development.

Some of the many other tests of intelligence available for use with people of different ages include the Slosson Intelligence Test (a particularly quick and easy-to-administer test), the Bayley Scales of Infant Development (designed for use with infants ranging in age from 2 months to $2\frac{1}{2}$ years), the Gesell Developmental Schedules (useful in the evaluation of children from 4 weeks of age to 6 years), and the Otis-Lennon School Ability Test (a paper-and-pencil, group-administered test). And as we will emphasize in the exercise that follows, many other tests exist to measure special intellectual abilities and talents which are not typically subsumed under the heading "intelligence."

YOUR TASK

In the previous chapter you were asked to develop your own definition of intelligence and to imagine that a test based on that definition (the YCT test) had been developed. Now it is time to develop that test. Using everything you know about the different types of tasks used to measure intelligence and related abilities, outline a plan for a test of intelligence that is consistent with your own conceptualization. To add some, but not a lot of, structure and uniformity to this task, we will again limit our focus

to adult intelligence. Let's also say that the total number of subtests included in your test of intelligence will be 10. Now, briefly answer each of the following 10 questions:

1. Name and describe each of the 10 subtests.
2. Provide a rationale for including each of these 10 subtests.
3. Does your test contain both verbal and nonverbal (performance) subtests? Why or why not?
4. How would you develop the actual items to be used in each of these subtests?
5. Describe the process by which your test would be normed.
6. Describe the process by which you would establish the psychometric soundness of your test.
7. Describe how each of the subtests should be administered; if, for example, your test contains both verbal and nonverbal subtests, will such tests be administered in alternating fashion? Why?
8. Briefly describe the scoring and interpretation of each of the subtests.
9. Will the scoring on each of the subtests in some way contribute to some global measure of intelligence (such as an IQ)? Why or why not?
10. For what purposes would you recommend that your test be used? In what circumstances or under what conditions would you advise against its use?

EXERCISE 50
TAILORING WITHOUT NEEDLES OR THREAD

OBJECTIVE

To impart firsthand experience in the creation of items to be used in an adaptive testing format.

BACKGROUND

Adaptive testing refers to testing that is individually tailored to the testtaker. Other terms used to refer to adaptive testing include tailored testing, sequential testing, branched testing, and response contingent testing. As typically employed in tests of ability, adaptive testing might pose to a testtaker a question in the middle range of difficulty. If the testtaker responds correctly to the item, an item of greater difficulty is posed next. If the testtaker responds incorrectly to the item, an item of lesser difficulty is posed.

YOUR TASK

Create three test items, each of a different level of difficulty, to tap a student's knowledge of the material in Chapter 9 of Cohen et al. (1996). The items should be suitable for placement in an adaptive testing format. Item 1 should be designed to be of an intermediate difficulty level. If the testtaker failed to respond correctly to Item 1, the testtaker would be administered Item 2, an item that is less difficult than Item 1. If the testtaker responded to Item 1 correctly, the testtaker would be administered Item 3, an item that is more difficult than Item 1.

EXERCISE 51
FACTOR ANALYSIS AND TESTS OF INTELLIGENCE

OBJECTIVE

To enhance understanding of how factor analysis can be used in the development of intelligence tests, and the measurement of the construct validity of an intelligence test.

BACKGROUND

As discussed in the Chapter 9 *Close-up,* different intelligence tests define intelligence in different ways. Accordingly, we would expect factor analysis of test items for various construct valid intelligence tests to vary in predictable ways.

YOUR TASK

Conduct an "eyeball" analysis of Figure 9-1, which shows sample items from the Otis-Lennon School Ability Test (OLSAT). Based on this sample, and without conducting a formal factor analysis, what factors would you say this test appears to be measuring? Why? From the theories of intelligence you are aware of, which one do you think is closest to the theory that guided the development of the OLSAT?

EXERCISE 52
MUCH ADO ABOUT MENSA

OBJECTIVE

To encourage independent thought about the nature of intelligence and in particular some social implications of this concept.

BACKGROUND

Mensa is a club in which the key requirement for membership is being in the top 2% of measured intelligence. The notion of such a club smacks of elitism to some people, although it is quite appealing to others.

YOUR TASK

Read the following material on Mensa, then write an essay expressing your own thoughts on the organization, as well as the test items employed to screen for membership.

MENSA

You may belong to a social, professional, or religious fraternity or sorority in which you engage in a wide variety of activities such as athletics, discussion groups, museum trips, speaker presentations, and parties. There is one social organization that is like these groups in all respects except that the requirement for membership is proof of high intelligence. That organization is called Mensa and it has more than 70,000 members worldwide, with chapters not only throughout the United States but also in Europe, South America, Australia, India, Israel, and Japan. Members include cab drivers, physicians, homemakers—in short, a wide variety of people in a wide variety of occupations.

Mensa was founded in England by two attorneys as a kind of roundtable discussion club for a group of intellectual equals; in fact, the word *Mensa* is derived from the Latin word for "table." The group was founded shortly after World War II, its primary agenda then to discuss and arrive at ways of preserving world peace. Today, the objectives of the organization would not appear quite so ambitious; the group is a social club that also fosters scientific pursuits through an educational and research foundation and through a research journal. The group also awards scholarships to postsecondary students to encourage them to fulfill their intellectual potential; some chapters have a group to aid in the rehabilitation of high-IQ prison inmates. Special-interest groups existing within Mensa cover different kinds of activities ranging from astronomy to motorcycles to Zen.

According to Mensa, each year about 30,000 people attempt to qualify for membership; but since only people whose measured IQs fall within the top 2 percent in intelligence qualify, only about 2 of every 50 people who apply are admitted. Are you interested in joining Mensa? If so, contact the local chapter and request a membership application. They will send you a list of intelligence tests that you may have taken at one time or another in your life; and if you can document that your score on any of the tests meets the club's cutoff point, you pay your dues and you're in. If you are unable to document your IQ to the club's satisfaction, it's going to take a bit more effort on your part. For a nominal fee, the club will send you a take-home IQ test with questions similar to those in Table 9-1. If you pass the take-home test, you then will

Figure 9-1

Sample OLSAT Items.

- Verbal Analogy items assess the ability to infer the relationship between a pair of words and to select a word that bears the same relationship to a given stimulus word.

  Bird is to **nest** as **bee** is to —
  f hive   g flower   h buzz   j sting   k wasp

- Verbal Classification items assess the ability to determine which word in a set does not belong, according to some principle operative within the set.

  Which word does *not* go with the other four?
  a tall   b big   c small   d short   e loud

- Sentence Completion items assess the ability to determine logical relationships among words in a sentence in order to supply a missing word.

  Choose the word that *best* completes this sentence:
  We will not begin the meeting _____ everybody is here.
  a because   b until   c if   d when   e after

- Sentence Arrangement items assess the ability to integrate a group of words into a meaningful sentence.

  If the words below were arranged to make the *best* sentence, with which letter would the <u>last</u> word of the sentence <u>begin</u>?

  | streets | the | caused | to | rain | heavy | flood |

  a s   b f   c h   d r   e c

- Numeric Inference items assess the ability to evaluate the relationship among pairs or trios of numbers and to select a number that is related to a stimulus number in the same way.

  The numbers in each box go together by following the *same* rule. Decide what the rule is, and then find the number that goes where you see the question mark (?) in the last box.

  | 10, 5 | | 6, 3 | | 16, ? |

  a 2   b 4   c 8   d 11   e 13

- Quantitative Reasoning is dependent on the ability to evaluate groups of numbers in order to infer relationships among them and to infer and apply computational rules.

- Figural Analogy items assess the ability to infer the relationship between a pair of geometric shapes and to apply that relationship in selecting a shape that is related to a stimulus shape in the same way.

- Series Completion items assess the ability to predict the next step in a geometric series in which each element changes according to a given rule.

  The drawings in the first part of the row go together to form a series. In the next part of the row, find the drawing that goes where you see the question mark (?) in the series.

Table 9-1

Try these typical IQ-test questions.

1. What word means the same as (p-a-y) in one sense and the same as (b-o-t-t-o-m) in another sense?
2. Which of the following sentences best describes the meaning of the old bromide "The used key is always bright"?
   (a) Keep on the scene in order to stay with it.
   (b) If you use a test key, you will appear bright.
   (c) New devices often don't work well.
   (d) Old ideas are the best.
3. Which one of the following games does not belong in the group?
   (a) Chess   (d) Mah-jongg
   (b) Bridge   (e) Backgammon
   (c) Go
4. The word procure is the opposite of which of the following words?
   (a) Retain   (d) Appropriate
   (b) Abscond   (e) Purchase
   (c) Forfeit
5. Complete the following analogy: Green is to yellow as orange is to _____ ?
   (a) Blue   (d) Yellow
   (b) Purple   (e) White
   (c) Brown
6. The word aggravate means the same as which of the following words?
   (a) Burden   (d) Intensify
   (b) Enrage   (e) Complain
   (c) Infect
7. Which of the following words are most opposite in meaning?
   (a) Intense   (d) Extreme
   (b) Extensive   (e) Diffuse
   (c) Majority
8. Which one of the following words does not belong in the group?
   (a) Stone   (d) Pontoon
   (b) Brick   (e) Oar
   (c) Canoe
9. Which two of the following words have the most similar meanings?
   (a) Divulge   (c) Reveal
   (b) Divert   (d) Revert
10. Complete the following analogy: Mountain is to land as whirlpool is to _____ ?
    (a) Fluid   (d) Sky
    (b) Wet   (e) Shower
    (c) Sea
11. The old saying "Don't trade horses when crossing a stream" most nearly means which of the following?
    (a) You might fall off and get wet.
    (b) Don't attempt something until you are fully prepared.
    (c) Decide what you are going to do before you do it.
    (d) Don't change plans when something is half completed.
12. If a house is 36 feet long and 27 feet wide, how wide would a house of the same proportions be if it were 72 feet long?
13. Which number, when multiplied by 4, is equal to $\frac{3}{4}$ of 112?
14. What word means the same as (h-i-r-e) in one sense and the same as (b-e-t-r-o-t-h) in another sense?
15. Which word does not belong in the following group?
    (a) Car   (d) Happy
    (b) Moon   (e) Belief
    (c) Fish
16. If seven belly dancers can lose 20 pounds altogether in eight hours of dancing, how many additional belly dancers would be needed to lose that same 20 pounds in only four hours of dancing, providing the new dancers shed weight only half as fast as the original seven dancers?
    (a) 7   (d) 14
    (b) 21   (e) 12
    (c) 27
17. Which two of the following words are the most similar in meaning?
    (a) Autonomy   (c) Oligarchy
    (b) Autocracy   (d) Dictatorship
18. What number comes next in the following series? 2, 3, 5, 9, 17 _____
19. Some Mensa members are geniuses. All geniuses have some human virtue as redeeming qualities. Using these two facts, which of the following conclusions is most correct?
    (a) Mensa members all have some virtues.
    (b) All geniuses are quality Mensa members.
    (c) Some Mensa members have redeeming qualities.

Table 9-1 (*continued*)

20. The old saying "The good is the enemy of the best" most nearly means which of the following?
    (*a*) If you are good, you will best your enemy.
    (*b*) Be good to your best enemy.
    (*c*) Don't accept less than your best.
    (*d*) The good struggle against the best.

Mensa Quiz Answers

1. (Foot). 2. (a). 3. (b). 4. (c). 5. (d). 6. (d). 7. (a & e). 8. (a). 9. (a & c). 10. (c). 11. (d). 12. (54 feet). 13. (21). 14. (engage). 15. (d). 16. (d). 17. (b & d). 18. (33). 19. (c). 20. (c).

Scoring Scale

Give yourself one point for each correct answer. You receive an additional four points if you completed the test in less than 10 minutes; three points if you completed it in less than 15 minutes; two points if you completed it in less than 20 minutes; and one point if you completed it in less than 25 minutes.

The authors of this text note that the original article contained a score interpretation guide indicating that a score of 20–24 qualified you as a "perfect candidate" for Mensa; 15–19 and you were still a candidate; 10–14 and "you might want to try the Mensa test"; and fewer than 10—"forget about joining." Of course, how much faith you place in a test interpretation guide should at least in part be a function of your evaluation of the psychometric soundness of the test. With no evidence as to reliability or validity of this test, we would advise that regardless of your test score, should you desire to join—go for it!

Source: Grosswirth (1980)

---

be invited to take, for a nominal fee, a proctored test. If you then score high enough to pass Mensa muster on the proctored test, you're invited to join. Needless to say, there are some people—many of whom might qualify for membership—who do not view such an organization in positive terms but who instead see it as elitist and snobbish.

EXERCISE 53
CREATE AN ALTERNATIVE MEASURE OF INTELLECTUAL ABILITY

OBJECTIVE

To enhance understanding of and obtain firsthand experience with alternative measures of intelligence.

BACKGROUND

Professionals who study intelligence appreciate that traditional tests of intelligence provide only a sample of an individual's intellectual ability. Intellectual skills and abilities such as critical thinking and artistic talent, for example, may not be tapped in traditional measures of intelligence.

YOUR TASK

Using any popular song—and let's define "popular" as a song that is among the top 20 in sales as listed in the current issue of *Billboard Magazine*—develop a "Music Appreciation and Listening Skills" (MALS) test. The administration instructions for the MALS will be as follows:

I am going to play a tape of a song. After you hear the song, you are going to be asked some questions about

it. Please listen to the song carefully so that you will be prepared to answer the questions. I will play the song only once. Ready?

Using a portable cassette recorder (or whatever equipment is available in the setting where the test is being conducted), the examiner then plays the song. After the song has been played in its entirety, the examiner hands the respondent a sheet with the MALS test questions—questions that you have prepared about the song. The questions may be in any format—true/false, short answer, essay, or whatever. Along with the questions, devise a corresponding answer key. Once having devised this test, answer each of the following:

1. Describe the process of norming this test.
2. How would the psychometric soundness of this test be established?
3. What problems do you foresee in administering, scoring, and interpreting this test? How might these problems be dealt with?
4. Describe why you think your test taps some aspect of intelligence not tapped by traditional measures of intelligence.
5. How might your test be used in everyday practice?
6. How might cultural factors influence scores on your test?
7. How might you make this test less culture-bound?

EXERCISE 54
ADMINISTERING THE MALS

OBJECTIVE

To obtain firsthand experience in administering a would-be alternative measure of intelligence.

BACKGROUND

In the previous exercise, you developed a test of Music Appreciation and Listening Skills (MALS). In this exercise, you administer the MALS test to a friend or neighbor and obtain their reaction.

YOUR TASK

Ask a friend or neighbor to serve as a subject and take the MALS test. Explain to that person that the MALS is not a real psychological test, but one made up by you as part of an exercise in developing alternative measures of intellectual ability. After the testtaker has taken it, discuss with him or her how the test would be scored and interpreted. Obtain and record feedback about the test administration, scoring, and interpretation process from the point of view of the subject. What are the subject's thoughts about the test? Does he or she believe it to be, on its face, a valid alternative measure of intelligence? What "bugs" need to be worked out on the basis of this pilot administration, scoring, and interpretation of your test? How might you revise the test and these procedures before administering it again?

EXERCISE 55
PICK-A-TEST: TESTS OF INTELLIGENCE

OBJECTIVE

To learn more about individual and group tests of intelligence not reviewed in the textbook.

BACKGROUND

The approach in your textbook is to highlight only a few of the many tests that exist in any given area. For every test covered in your textbook there may well be dozens of other tests designed to measure the same attribute(s). The Pick-A-Test exercise represents an opportunity to learn more about a particular test not covered in your textbook.

YOUR TASK

A list of individual and group tests of intelligence along with a brief description of each follows below in Table 9-2. From this list, select one test that you think you would like to know more about. Then, use all of the resources at your disposal to answer the following:

1. Describe what the test measures.
2. Who would be most apt to use this test? Why? Include in your answer sample questions the test user might hope to answer through the use of this test.
3. Who would be most apt to take this test? Why?
4. Describe the full range of people to whom it would be appropriate to administer this test, and include comments about who would not be appropriate. If the test may be group-administered, describe how this test lends itself to group administration.
5. Describe what is known about the test's reliability.
6. Describe what is known about the test's validity.
7. Imagining that you are a measurement consultant, would you recommend this test to clients who are test users? Why or why not?

REFERENCES

Grosswirth, M. (1980). Mensa: It's a state of mind—but a mind finely tuned. *Science Digest, 87,* 74–79.

Wechsler, D. (1974). *Manual for the Wechsler Intelligence Scale for Children—Revised.* New York: Psychological Corporation.

THE 4-QUESTION CHALLENGE

1. A primary use of group tests of ability or intelligence is
   (a) screening large numbers of people.
   (b) measuring reading ability.
   (c) gauging applicants' ability by means of a power test.
   (d) All of the above
2. Which statement is true?
   (a) Validity sets a limit on a test's reliability.
   (b) Validity sets a limit only on a test's inter-rater reliability.
   (c) The validity of a test is limited only by the test's inter-rater reliability.
   (d) The validity of a test is limited by its reliability.
3. Which test is used by the United States Department of Defense as a means of screening candidates and determining most suitable job positions?
   (a) WAIS-R
   (b) ASVAB
   (c) OLSAT
   (d) SB:FE
4. "Paper Folding and Cutting" is a subtest on
   (a) the WISC-III.
   (b) the WPPSI-R.
   (c) the SB:FE.
   (d) the Slosson.

Table 9-2

Some Tests of Intelligence

Individual Tests	
Test	*Description*
Cattell Infant Intelligence Scale	For ages 3 to 30 months, this test is in large part a downward extension of the Stanford-Binet Intelligence Scale.
McCarthy Scales of Children's Abilities	For ages 2.6 to 8.6 years, this is a test that measures cognitive and motor development using toylike and gamelike materials.
McCarthy Screening Test	For ages 4 through 6.6 years and based in part on the McCarthy Scales for Children, this test is designed to screen for children who may be at risk for learning problems.
Test of Word Knowledge	For ages 5 through 17 years, this test is designed to evaluate receptive and expressive vocabulary and may have application in the assessment of the gifted and talented.
Raven's Progressive Matrices	This series of three nonverbal ability tests has a total age span that ranges from 5 through 80 years old. It was designed to measure the nonverbal component of Spearman's *g*, and more specifically the abilities to perceive and think clearly, among others.
Mill Hill Vocabulary Scale	This series of two tests has a total age span that ranges from 11 years to adult. The test was designed to measure acquired verbal knowledge, and as a complement to Raven's Progressive Matrices.
Columbia Mental Maturity Scale	For ages 3.5 through 10 years, this is a mental ability test that requires no verbal response from the testtaker and only a minimum of motor-responding. Most typically, it is used with able or disabled children entering pre-school, or disabled children in school.

Group Tests	
Test	*Description*
Silver Drawing Test of Cognitive Skills and Adjustment	For ages 6 and over, this test is designed to assess knowledge of sequential and spatial concepts, as well as other aspects of cognition. Another component of the test screens for depression.
Screening Assessment for Gifted Elementary Students	For ages 7 to 12, this test is designed to help in the identification of gifted children with measures of aptitude, achievement, and creativity.
Gifted and Talented Scale	For grades 4 to 6, this is another test designed to assist in the identification of gifted and talented children.
Shipley Institute of Living Scale	For ages 14 and above, this test yields a general measure of intelligence and cognitive impairment.
Ennis-Weir Critical Thinking Essay Test	For high school and college students, this test focuses on the aspect of intelligence related to critical thinking, specifically focusing on one's ability to formulate a response to a particular argument.
AH6 Group Tests of High Level Intelligence	For age 16 and up, this test is designed to measure reasoning ability in groups known to be of high ability.
Schaie-Thurstone Adult Mental Abilities Test	For ages 22 to 84, this test yields a general measure of mental ability.
Wonderlic Personnel Test	For adults, this test yields a measure of intellectual ability specifically designed for use as an instrument in the selection and placement of employees in business and industry.

Chapter 10

Preschool and Educational Assessment

Among other things, the pre-school period is a time for increasing socialization experiences, and a shedding of confusion between fantasy and reality. Arnold Schwarzenegger attempts to help matters along in the film Kindergarten Cop.

Outline for Chapter 10 of Cohen et al. (1996)
PRESCHOOL AND EDUCATIONAL ASSESSMENT

Preschool Assessment
  Preschool Tests

Achievement Tests
  Measures of General Achievement
  Measures of Achievement in Specific Subject Areas

Tests of Aptitude
  The Elementary School Level
    The Metropolitan Readiness Tests (MRT)
  The Secondary School Level
    The Scholastic Aptitude Test (SAT)
  The College Level and Beyond

Diagnostic Tests
  Reading Tests
    The Woodcock Reading Mastery Tests-Revised
  Math Tests
  Other Diagnostic Tests
  Learning Disabilities Assessment

Psychoeducational Test Batteries
  Kaufman Assessment Battery for Children (K-ABC)
    The standardization sample
    Psychometric properties
    Administering the test
    Scoring and interpreting the test
    An evaluation

Other Tests Used in Educational Settings
  The Peabody Picture Vocabulary Test-Revised (PPVT-R)
  Peer Appraisal Techniques
  Performance, Portfolio, and Authentic Assessment
  Study Habits, Interests, and Attitudes

CLOSE-UP:
  Tests of Minimum Competency

EVERYDAY PSYCHOMETRICS:
  Adapting to Adaptive Testing: The Case of the GRE

EXERCISE 56
PRESCHOOL ASSESSMENT: PHYSICAL DEVELOPMENT

OBJECTIVE

To obtain firsthand experience in assessing aspects of the physical development of preschool children.

BACKGROUND

You and your classmates have been selected to make a presentation at the "Annual Conference on the Experience of Being a Preschool Child." The exact date—and length—of this annual conference will be determined by your instructor, and the location will be your classroom. Each participant must come prepared with fascinating observations about the experience of being a preschooler—observations gleaned from firsthand assessment of a preschooler with any or all of the tests in this chapter. If all three exercises in this chapter are assigned, it is suggested that they be executed over the course of two sessions: one session for Exercises 56 and 57, and a second session for Exercise 58. Make certain to note the child's age (including date of birth for reference) on all assessment reports.

YOUR TASK

For this as well as the remaining two exercises in this chapter, you are going to need access to a preschool child (age 4 give or take a year or so) and the consent of the child's parent (or guardian) to conduct the exercises. If you do not have your own child to work with, a child that belongs to a friend, a neighbor, a relative—even a complete stranger in married student housing—will do. Explain to the parent the purpose of the assessment—that it is a requirement for a course designed to help provide experience with testing preschoolers. Describe in advance all of the "tests" that will be administered. Additionally, inform the adult(s) who grant permission that while you will be pleased to share your "findings," (1) you are using training materials, and not any valid psychological test, (2) that for the purposes of this exercise you are making your best judgments regarding your observations but that you are not a trained or expert observer, and (3) that no norms exist for these tests and it is therefore impossible for you to gauge how typical or "normal" the child's performance is. It is suggested that the parent not only be present during the assessment but be an active participant in it as well, acting as the examiner; you will then be free to devote your complete energy and attention to the task of observation and evaluation.

The only material needed for this first exercise is a ball that is more or less baseball size and as weightless (such as the plastic versions that are available) as possible.

1. The Walking Test
   The child is instructed by the parent to walk from one end of a room to the other. Any difficulties noted?
2. The Skipping Test
   The child is now instructed to skip from one end of a room to the other. Any difficulties noted?
3. The Hopping Test
   The child is instructed to hop on his or her right foot from one end of the room to the other. Afterward, the child is instructed to return hopping on her or his left foot. Any difficulties noted?
4. The Circle Walk/Skip/Hop Test
   As a means of further assessing gross motor development, repeat Tests 1, 2, and 3, this time by having the child walk, skip, and hop around a circle (3-foot diameter or so) that has been defined in this room by an imaginary line. Any difficulties noted?
5. The Shoe-and-Sock Test
   As a means of helping you to assess fine motor coordination, the parent asks the child to remove his or her shoes and socks and then put them back on. Any difficulties noted?
6. The Ball-Catch Test
   The child's task here is to catch a ball that is (1) rolled on the floor to her, (2) lobbed directly to her, and (3) thrown up in the air so that it must be caught like a fly ball. Your task is to observe and report on the child's performance with respect to such factors as ability to visually track the ball and to coordinate muscular movements in order to successfully catch the ball. The parent repeats each mode of presenting the ball to the child three times before moving on to the next.

EXERCISE 57
PRESCHOOL ASSESSMENT: COGNITIVE DEVELOPMENT

OBJECTIVE

To obtain firsthand experience in assessing aspects of the cognitive development of preschool children.

BACKGROUND

It is during the preschool years that the child develops the ability to mentally represent objects and events—in Piagetian terms, there is a shift from the sensorimotor to a preoperational level of development. The exercises in this section are based in part on the work of Piaget (1969; see also Ginsburg & Opper, 1988) as well as others (Gelman & Gallistel, 1986). For each of these, the only materials needed are a clean table and a dozen or so napkins of each of two colors. It does not matter what the two different colors of the napkins are, but they must be distinctly different in color. For the purposes of this example, let's say that one stack is white and the other is red.

YOUR TASK

With the parent acting as examiner and you as the observer, the following three tests are administered to the child.

1. The Dinner Guest Test

   Seated at the kitchen or dining room table, the parent is instructed to hold up a stack of napkins (one color only) and say to the child: "There will be four people having dinner here tonight, and each person will get their own napkin. Would you count out four napkins and place them on the table?"

   If the child does this correctly, the parent praises his or her performance and says, "Good. Now there are four napkins on the table." Make sure the napkins are spread out as if for four place settings before going to the second test in this series.

   If the child does not do this correctly, he or she is given the opportunity to correct the number of napkins placed with a prompt from the parent such as, "No, that's not right; I said four people are coming, and each one will get their own napkin. So place four napkins on the table." Napkins placed on the table are replaced in the stack and handed to the child. If the child does not place the correct number of napkins this time, the parent places four napkins on the table, spread out as if for four place settings and says, "Now there are four napkins on the table."

2. The Conservation Test

   With only the four napkins on the table, and with the child watching, the parent now stacks the four napkins into one pile and asks the child, "Are there still four napkins on the table now?" The answer to this question will depend, at least in part, on whether or not the child demonstrates the Piagetian concept of conservation —that is, an understanding that the rearrangement of objects or of a mass still contains the same amount of that object or mass. Again, the child is praised for a correct answer. If the child gives an incorrect answer, she or he is given an explanation, complete with a demonstration, that there are indeed four napkins on the table. At the end of the exercise all of the napkins are collected and replaced into the stack of napkins of the same color.

3. The Classification Test

   (A) The parent now places the original stack of napkins, along with an approximately equal-size stack of napkins of a different color, at about the center of the table. Handing one of the red napkins to the child, the parent says, "This is a red napkin. Place it with the other red napkins." The child is praised for a correct response, and given a second chance if the response is incorrect. The child is shown the correct response if the second response is also incorrect.

   (B) Now handing one of the white napkins to the child, the parent says, "This is a white napkin. Place it with the other white napkins." Again, the child is praised for a correct response, and given a second chance if the response is incorrect. The child is shown the correct response if the second response is also incorrect. If the child "fails" both parts A and B of this test, discontinue the Classification Test. If the child responds correctly to at least one part of this test, continue with Part C.

   (C) The parent says, "We're going to set the table for four people, and each person is going to get his or her own napkin. There will be two boys coming, and the two boys will get red napkins. There will be two girls coming, and the two girls will get white napkins. So now, set the table for the two boys with two red napkins, and for the two girls with two white napkins."

   Part C of this test may prove difficult for many preschoolers, especially those at the younger end of the preschool age range. Still, the task may prove informative to the observant examiner in terms of how the child deals with the task and questions asked. The child who does not respond correctly at first is given another explanation, and one additional chance to put out two red and two white napkins before the test is terminated. So that the "test session" ends on a successful note, it is suggested that if the child fails this last task, the parent ask an additional question that the child is sure to succeed on (such as "Let me hear you count to five").

EXERCISE 58
PRESCHOOL ASSESSMENT: LANGUAGE AND SOCIAL DEVELOPMENT

OBJECTIVE

To obtain firsthand experience in assessing aspects of the language and social development of preschool children.

BACKGROUND

Unlike the short and incomplete sentences of the toddler, the language of the preschooler sounds very much like

English—that is, after you discount the fabricated words. Development of social skills is also proceeding; however, as with language skills, such skills have not reached the level of the school-age child. For example, the pre-schooler is able to have fun playing with friends while not being able to take cognitively their point of view; this type of situation may result in pain or injury to an unsuspecting playmate who is perceived as an obstacle to enjoyment or pleasure.

YOUR TASK

Observe the child interacting with other children and make a report of your findings. Make an appointment with the parent and child to observe the child for a 2-hour period. A morning, afternoon, or early evening time period will do, but it must be some period of time wherein the child can be observed interacting with other children. As you observe the child, listen to the language that is used; how many new words have the pre-schoolers coined during your period of observation? How would you characterize the quality of the communication between the youngsters? What can you say about the level of socialization you observe? What kind of efforts are made, if any, by one child to help another? When does adult assistance seem to be required to maintain smooth social interaction?

EXERCISE 59
ASSESSMENT IN THE SCHOOLS

OBJECTIVE

To enhance understanding of the process of psychological assessment in the schools.

BACKGROUND

Tests of intelligence, achievement (both general and specific), and aptitude (both general and specific), are but a few of the types of tests regularly administered in educational settings—you know that not only from your reading but also from your own personal experience. The three brief articles that follow will hopefully expand on that knowledge base. And after you've read each of them, incorporate what you've learned into your written response to the scenario that follows.

YOUR TASK

You are the principal of a new, private elementary school called the "Progressive and Enlightened School" (PES)—a school that caters to a bright, enlightened, and upwardly mobile clientele of parents. You are writing a letter to the parents of the 100 or so pupils enrolled in the school to explain to them the role psychological tests will play in their child's education. Write a draft of your letter beginning with "Dear Parent:" and proceed to discuss the following:

- why tests of school ability (as well as related abilities) are (or are not) necessary in a school setting;
- the role tests will (and will not) play at PES;
- how any tests used at PES will be selected; and
- how parents will be informed of findings with respect to readiness, achievement and ability.

In writing this letter you may wish to draw on your textbook, your own knowledge and experience, and any of the four Psychological Corporation articles reprinted below as sources.

• •

Assessing School Ability

Ruth Wilson

The principal task of the school is to facilitate cognitive learning in children. There are, of course, many other goals: to contribute to self-understanding and character development, to foster and encourage artistic abilities and manual skills, and to develop social qualities and physical health, to name a few. Yet, important as they may be, other goals can never be viewed as alternatives to cognitive learning.

Different children show different degrees of the ability to learn in school, and in order to achieve equality of educational opportunity, such variations must be taken into account. To bring a child to maximum functioning level, it is necessary to start where he or she is at the time. Each child's strengths and weaknesses must be assessed so that educational plans may be realistic and effective.

Every teacher realizes that it is unreasonable to expect the same level and speed of attainment, or the same quality of understanding and learning, from all pupils. For the teacher to meet responsibly his or her duties, instruction must be tempered to the needs and qualifications of each learner, insofar as this is possible. Decisions concerning what instructional methods and materials to use will necessarily involve prediction.

The process of making predictions goes on constantly. Explicitly or implicitly, judgments are made about how well each pupil is going to perform. Observation is essential to decision making; but in the absence of reliable test scores, such important functions as the assigning or placing of pupils, adapting instruction to their needs, discovering their talents, and evaluating their progress become more difficult and less objective. A school ability test is designed to give important, objective evidence concerning the general ability that underlies each pupil's performance in all areas of academic learning. It is an efficient and dependable means of obtaining *some* of the information necessary for sound decision making and for predicting future scholastic attainment.

PURPOSE AND CONTENT OF A SCHOOL ABILITY TEST

What skills and abilities are necessary for learning new things in school? Children must be able to perceive accurately, to recognize and recall what has been perceived, to think logically, to perceive relationships, to abstract from a set of particulars, and to apply a generalization or abstraction to a new and different context.

These mental operations lend themselves to objective measurements through performance on such tasks as detecting likenesses and differences, recalling words and numbers, recognizing absurdities, defining words, following directions, classifying, establishing sequence, and solving arithmetic and analogy problems. Tasks of this type (associative and relatively abstract in character) are less subject to the effect of previous in-school learning than is the material found on achievement test batteries or tests covering one specific curricular area. Yet they are clearly school-related and indicative of potential for future school success.

Tests of general school ability, which assess current status by measuring performance on tasks such as the above, have as one of their chief purposes the prediction of rate of learning in school. Although such tests are quite comprehensive, they make no attempt to assess the totality of the pupil's intellectual functioning, nor do they constitute an indexing of the whole of an individual's intellectual ability. For this reason, the term "school ability" is a more accurate and precise description of that which is measured than the more general terms "intelligence" and "mental ability."

Scores on any test of this nature are the result of complex and interacting influences, including environmental and experiential elements. They should never be taken in a deterministic sense, but should be perceived as descriptive of the *pupil at a given time*. However, numerous studies testify to the fact that, as predictors of future scholastic attainment, they are very useful.

USES OF TEST RESULTS

How can the results of a school ability test be helpful to teachers and administrators? Knowledge of each pupil's general ability, since it underlies performance in all domains of learning, provides valuable insights into the following areas of concern.

1. How does this pupil's present capacity for scholastic work compare with what he or she is actually achieving in each area? In what areas is he or she doing less well than might be expected in view of overall learning ability?

2. Are the goals that have been set challenging enough in view of this pupil's ability to learn? Does this test's score support observations of the pupil's performance made in the classroom? What chance does this pupil have for succeeding in accelerated or enriched programs?

3. Are the instructional goals that have been set too high for this pupil? In what curricular areas does this pupil need further diagnostic evaluation and perhaps remediation? In view of all available evidence, should the pupil be referred to the school counselor or psychologist for further evaluation?

Teachers and administrators, faced with these concerns, must make decisions using whatever information is available to them. By yielding an objective measure of potential for learning, the school ability test is a valuable complement to teacher judgment and informal appraisal. Properly used and interpreted, results from this type of test become a positive factor in ensuring that all pupils— from all backgrounds—are assisted in gaining as much as possible from their educational experience.

Three general uses of the school ability test are implicit in the questions posed above. These are

a. Identification of the Gifted and Talented

One of the notable things about ability tests is that they unearth talent that might be and frequently is overlooked in the absence of such tests. Classroom instruction is most often geared to the needs and interests of pupils of average ability, while the needs of low-ability pupils are so obvious that they demand the teacher's special attention. Consequently, the gifted children are the most often neglected; many of them "languish in idleness." Contrary to widespread belief, these children frequently cannot grow toward their potential without special assistance. Placed in unchallenging educational environments, which sometimes are even hostile to their behavior, they tend to conceal their extraordinary abilities and even bury them in underachievement. In fact, in the absence of test scores, gifted children are frequently identified as behavior problems. "Prevented from moving ahead by the rigidity of normal school procedures, . . . the gifted youngster typically takes one of three tacks: (1) he drifts into a state of lethargy and complete apathy; (2) he conceals his ability, anxious not to embarrass others or draw their ridicule by superior performance; or (3) not understanding his frustration, he becomes a discipline problem."[1]

Talent is available in all quarters, on all levels, but it is the culturally different child who poses the most difficult identification problem. In the absence of a good testing program, minority children and children from a low socioeconomic level often stand little chance of

---

[1] Excerpted by special permission from "The Other Minority," by Harold C. Lyon, Jr., *Learning: The Magazine for Creative Teaching*, Vol. 2, No. 5 (January 1974), p. 65, © by Education Today Co., Inc.

being correctly identified as gifted and given an appropriate education.

Historically, standardized ability tests first opened up many of the top colleges in America to bright youths from lower-class backgrounds who had previously been passed over by traditional methods of selection.[2] With the passage of the Gifted and Talented Children's Educational Assistance Act in 1974 (ESEA Title IV Amendment), the United States Government has mandated that special educational opportunities be afforded to all school children evidencing outstanding ability. Here again, the school ability test has a critical role to play.

b. Preliminary Screening of Pupils Requiring Special Educational Treatment

Where ability scores indicate that the instructional goals of a particular classroom exceed the capacity of some of the pupils, it is incumbent upon teachers and administrators to make the necessary adjustments so that these pupils, also, can get the most from their educational experiences. Teachers, unfortunately, sometimes use low ability scores to explain why some pupils do not learn, rather than to help all pupils learn more. Too little attention is paid to the fact that whatever the level of ability, the range of potential achievement associated with it is large. By providing an appropriate environment for learning, pacing instruction to the varied learning rates of pupils, and adapting instructional strategies to respond to their needs, teachers can foster the achievement of the so-called "slow learner."

The data obtained from school ability testing should be supplemented by other information before any important decisions are made concerning these low-scoring pupils. Group tests provide little opportunity for direct observation of the pupil's behavior or for identifying the cause of poor performance; rather, they indicate the need for further testing and careful screening so that appropriate instructional intervention may be planned. Public Law 94-142, the Education for All Handicapped Children Act, establishes sound guidelines for use in such cases. It requires that, in making placement decisions, a school district draw upon information from a variety of sources, including aptitude tests, but it prohibits placement in programs solely on the basis of test scores or on psychometric input viewed in isolation (PL 94-142, Sections 121a.531, 121a.533). The regulations ensure that the identification and placement process is a multi-disciplinary activity, with decisions based on a variety of sources of information which, taken together, give a comprehensive view of the "total child."

In this regard, special attention should be given to children of minority groups. School ability tests are measures of learned or developed abilities in the broadest

sense, and implicit in any comparison of scores is the assumption that all examinees have had an equal opportunity to learn the types of things included in the tests. Studies show that middle- and upper-class children are generally encouraged by their parents to develop verbal and reasoning abilities, while such home training is less common among other groups. Background factors can contribute to the creation of handicaps to learning, and test scores may indicate the need for special instructional programs and strategies to overcome this disadvantage.

It is important to remember that *predictive validity* of the test as regards the pupil's ability to cope with school-related material is not called into question for low scorers. It is the *use* made of the information that calls for a special degree of discernment and sensitivity.

c. Comparison of School Ability with Actual Achievement

For the majority of pupils, the most important use of a school ability test is to provide a basis for comparison between their potential for learning and their actual performance. For this group, comparison with others is relatively unimportant; the concern of teachers and administrators is to evaluate the relationship between each pupil's measured achievement and what could reasonably be expected, based on his or her school ability score.

Data of this kind are best obtained through comparing scores attained on a school ability test with those derived from a standardized achievement test. The significance of such a comparison rests in the distinction between *what is tested* on these two types of tests.

Achievement tests assess highly specific types of behaviors that are taught in school, behaviors that represent important outcomes of instructional programs. In order to obtain dependable information concerning instructional outcomes, separate tests are given for each of the instructional domains, such as reading, mathematics, science, social studies, etc. Typically, achievement tests also yield a total battery score, but this score is not the basis of potential/achievement comparisons. Pupils do not learn "in general" as a result of instruction in school; they learn to spell, to read, to compute, to use language correctly, and to function in other specific ways. The purpose of these comparisons is to determine whether pupils read as well as their ability indicates they are able, or whether they compute as well, etc.

School ability tests, on the other hand, are not constructed in accordance with curricular objectives or goals of instruction. They are made up of tasks designed to measure generalized cognitive traits and abilities. Many of these tasks involve verbal and numerical symbols, yet the content is usually quite different from that in a reading or mathematics test. Most general ability tests administered to pupils in Grade 3 and below require no

---

[2] *Report of the Commission on Tests: I. Righting the Balance* (New York: College Entrance Examination Board, 1970), pp. 11–32.

reading at all by the pupils, while tests at the upper levels are so constructed that reading ability itself is not a major source of variance in test scores. For example, the readability level of a school ability test administered to fifth grade pupils might be substantially lower than that of fifth grade reading materials. Likewise, with the test items requiring arithmetic skills, the difficulty of the item is centered on the conceptual process or problem analysis, not on arithmetic or computational abilities.

Performance on a school ability test reflects the cumulative influence of a great many experiences encountered both in and out of school. In contrast, achievement tests measure the effect of the school's instructional program. By comparing scores received on these two types of tests, a teacher can judge the effectiveness of classroom instruction as regards each individual pupil and can establish appropriate educational goals, methods, and paces for each pupil to make optimal progress.

TESTING THE CULTURALLY DIFFERENT CHILD

School ability tests are designed to predict the performance of pupils in the present school system; their norms supply useful information concerning the probability that a particular child will succeed, *as a pupil,* in the traditional American school. Typically, public education has functioned to blur cultural distinctions. Most instruction is in English, and the curricular content focuses on Anglo-American institutions, history, and literature. The values that the schools strive to cultivate are themselves culturally saturated.

For children and adults alike, cultural differences may become cultural handicaps when individuals move out of the culture in which they have been reared and endeavor to function, compete, or succeed within another culture. In planning instructional programs, it is essential to consider the extent to which a child's background affects his or her ability to learn.

The skills and knowledge measured in ability tests are precisely those required for success in school. Though they may be culturally influenced, these are the criteria for assessing a pupil's likelihood of succeeding in learning what is being taught in school. In fact, no device captures those consequences of cultural differences that are *important to schooling* as efficiently as the general ability test.

The attempt to estimate *general mental ability* from such a test, however, is based on the assumption that all pupils have had substantially equal opportunity to learn the types of things included in the test and that all pupils are equally motivated to do their best on the test. Although absolute equality in these regards is impossible, the majority of school children meet these qualifications, and for these children, a school ability test may yield an appropriate assessment of general ability; however, for some minority groups within the general population, these assumptions cannot be made.

The common characteristic of these minority groups is membership in a culture other than the dominant one in American society. Racial and ethnic backgrounds are factors, as is economic status.

For many pupils within these minority groups, the assumption that they have had the opportunity to learn the types of things included on ability tests is open to question. For such pupils, the significance of ability test scores should be limited to the prediction of success in school—to measuring *school ability*. Any interpretation of scores as being indicative of *general mental ability* must be tempered by considerations of the cultural background of the examinees.

The classroom teacher involved in the education of culturally different children should recognize that the educational difficulties displayed by these pupils may represent a difference in background, rather than a special kind of intellectual difficulty, and should concentrate on getting the children to transfer skills they already possess to the tasks they encounter in the classroom.

The assumption of equal motivation to do well on a test is also brought into question with this group of children. Among the relevant conditions differing from culture to culture are interest in the test content, the desire to surpass others or to do well on a test, rapport with the examiner, and past habits of solving problems individually or cooperatively.

A teacher must be extremely careful when testing children of races and cultures other than his or her own and should be alert to any nuances in their behavior that suggest their test performance might be invalid. Cultural differences can create communication problems that affect not only the rapport but the child's ability to understand and respond to the test questions. Every attempt should be made to elicit the child's best performance, without, in the process, compromising standard procedures.

By far the most important consideration in the testing of culturally diverse groups pertains to the use made of the scores. In using tests to evaluate minority children's performance, special efforts must be made to study and learn about their cultural patterns. Care must be taken that no inferences are drawn about some presumed inherited, immutable capacity. The task of a conscientious teacher is to ponder what lies behind the test scores and use them to the educational advantage of the children.

To the evaluation of the teacher, which will always be subjective and may also be unduly influenced by personal biases and prejudices, school ability tests add an objective standard of learning potential, which, properly understood, works to the advantage of minority children. Such objectivity is necessary if programs are to be evaluated accurately, decisions on curriculum are to be based on evidence, and educational opportunities are not to be denied due to bias and discrimination.

CONCLUSION

For all groups and at all levels within the educational system, the need exists for the identification of talent, for better diagnosis and understanding of the nature of learning disabilities, for setting realistic instructional goals and establishing appropriate paces. These needs must be met if all pupils are to profit from their educational experience. No single piece of information is adequate to the task, but when considered in conjunction with other available data, scores on a school ability test make a unique contribution. Properly used and interpreted, this type of test can be a useful tool in channeling individual aptitudes and talents into those avenues of endeavor that will be most rewarding to the individual.

• •

Selection and Provision of Testing Materials

Roger T. Lennon, *Test Department*

The educational historian who comes to write the story of American education during the 1950's and since can hardly fail to note, as one of its distinctive features, the pervasive use of the standardized test, at every level and for a variety of purposes. The best available estimate indicates that some 200,000,000 standardized tests are administered annually in the schools of this country—and the trend, which has been steadily in the direction of greater use of such tests, shows no sign of abating.

The majority of the standardized tests used—perhaps two-thirds of them—are so-called "achievement" tests, seeking to measure attainment of specified instructional goals. Second largest category are general or special ability—aptitude—tests, seeking to measure learner characteristics, for improved guidance or educational diagnosis. The sheer volume of standardized testing, to say nothing of the profound impact such testing has on so many phases of the educational enterprise, calls for the most thoughtful attention to selection and provision of the best testing materials.

STANDARDIZED TESTS AND THE INSTRUCTIONAL PROCESS

Standardized tests are indeed essential "instructional" materials. Let us consider for a moment some of the functions that standardized tests most commonly serve, the better to appreciate how inextricably bound up they are with the instructional process.

1. *Tests provide measures of status* in particular skills or content areas for a pupil, a class, or a school. They reveal where the learner or group is at a given time, and thus provide a clue to the level at which instruc-

tion must be pitched. If we are to adapt instruction to the particular needs of individual pupils, it follows that we need dependable information as to precisely how they differ in their attainment or mastery—and such information is most easily come by through the use of standardized tests.

2. *Tests provide measures of growth, development, or progress* toward desirable educational goals. Measurement of growth presupposes repeated administrations of tests; from these repeated measurements we may infer the extent to which the learner is in fact making progress toward instructional goals and whether his rate of progress compares favorably with what is typical for his peers, or with what may reasonably be expected of him in light of his ability.

3. *Tests provide measures of differential status,* revealing areas of relative strength and weakness that are of significance for guidance purposes.

4. *Tests provide analytical or diagnostic information,* which permits sharper definition of learning difficulties, and enables instruction to be brought to bear more forcefully on points where it is most needed.

5. *Tests provide inventories of skills,* which serve both as checks on progress and as guides to further instruction.

6. *Tests are one source of data essential for continuing evaluation* of the adequacy of the total instructional program.

It is axiomatic that evaluation is an integral part of the instructional process. Education without evaluation, as someone has put it, is target practice in the dark; without knowledge of the efficacy of our efforts, improvement is impossible. Standardized tests are by no means the whole of evaluation, but they are a rich source of the kind of data on which sound evaluation must depend.

In a word, tests are fact-finding devices; they do nothing but develop in an economical, reliable manner information that helps the teacher, the supervisor, and the administrator to discharge more effectively their instructional responsibilities. Standardized tests are means, not ends; they are a necessary first step in understanding the learner, in keying instruction to his needs, and in evaluation. The prominence that they have come to enjoy in American education is perhaps the best witness to their status as true instructional aids.

In the light of what has been said about the role of tests as instructional materials, let us turn to the proper selection and provision of tests. Perhaps the most fruitful way to approach this topic is to place it in the larger context of planning a testing program, for testing is most effective when carried on as part of a comprehensive, continuous program, rather than on a sporadic, *ad hoc* basis to meet particular or transient needs. I should like to consider briefly several aspects of planning a testing program: the "who," the "what," the "when," and the "how" of such planning.

THE TESTING PROGRAM: WHOSE RESPONSIBILITY?

Almost every member of a school's staff who is charged in any way with responsibility for the instructional program is vitally concerned with test data. Rare is the supervisor, the administrator, the counselor, the psychologist, or the director of research who feels no need of such data as a basis for carrying on his work. Since each has a stake in the application and interpretation of test results, the planning of testing and selection of tests will be done best if it takes account of their respective needs for test data. Their interests are sometimes common, sometimes diverse.

The device that many school systems have found effective in giving voice to these varied elements is the testing committee, a standing committee with membership representative of the several elements, charged with responsibility for planning the system's testing program, and keeping it under continuing review. The chairman of this committee may be a director of testing or research, a director of instruction, a psychologist, the superintendent himself, or some other staff member, according to local organizational practice; the important thing is to insure a broadly based concept of testing throughout the entire system.

A testing committee, like any committee, will be successful only to the extent to which it perceives its mission with clarity. As a first duty, the committee needs to formulate an explicit statement of the purposes to be served by testing—a definition of the particular goals sought by the testing program—in effect, a policy statement on testing for the system. The committee needs, moreover, to bring to its task, or develop as it goes, certain special knowledges and skills that will enable it to make proper choices among available tests and sound judgments as to the conduct of a program, use of results, etc. Not every member of a testing committee need be a test expert, nor would this ordinarily be either feasible or desirable. Every member, however, ought to realize or be informed about the importance of such features as reliability, adequacy of standardization, equivalence of forms, and the like, so that all can appreciate the need for giving some weight to those factors in making their choices.

At the same time, test selection should not be made altogether on purely statistical considerations. In the selection of achievement tests, particularly, major weight should be given to what we term the "content validity" of the test—the extent to which the skills or knowledge measured by the test are in accord with, and sample reasonably from, the body of skills and knowledge established as the goals of instruction in the local program. And it may be noted in passing that appraisal of this type of validity is not always best made by the psychologist or test expert, but by the teacher or the supervisor, who is closer to the curriculum and the content of instruction.

Responsibility for testing, therefore, is shared by many in the school system. The various persons or groups contribute to the selection of instruments on the basis of their special knowledges or interests. A testing committee will best discharge its planning and selection responsibilities when it is systematically trained for this task, informed about the criteria that should prevail in the selection of tests, and alert to the varied uses to which test data will be put.

THE TESTING PROGRAM: ITS SCOPE

If we accept the essential relation between instruction and evaluation, then it follows that the scope, or "what," of an evaluation program is as broad as the range of instructional goals. A testing committee—perhaps better an "evaluation" committee—should concern itself with evidence as to the attainment of *all* the instructional goals of the system. Many of them, to be sure, will not lend themselves to assessment through standardized tests, but in planning a comprehensive testing program, the committee should at least canvass the possibilities of finding and using suitable test instruments for all outcomes.

To speak of a testing "program" implies comprehensiveness, continuity, regularity, and medium- or long-range planning of testing activities, with corollary implications for the scope of the testing committee's work. The committee should be aware of the advantages inherent in the use of a single battery of tests that covers a wide range of grades; only through such a battery can comparisons across subjects and over the range of grades be made most dependably. There are merits in continued use of a given test or battery over a period of years, if meaningful longitudinal studies of pupils are to be made. At the same time, achievement tests, like textbooks, do become obsolete and should be replaced by more current editions or by newer testing instruments. Weighing the pros and cons of changing tests is a good example of the type of judgment the committee needs to exercise.

The testing committee will need to consider the frequency with which tests should be administered, the establishment of priorities among testing needs, the choice of appropriate grades in which to administer various types of tests, the time of year at which the various tests should be administered, arrangements for scoring, types of reporting systems, and the dissemination of test results in the most expeditious manner to all those having need of them. It has, of course, the crucial task of selecting, or at least of recommending the selection of, the tests to be used.

THE TESTING PROGRAM: WHEN TO PLAN

A testing committee's work should be viewed as continuous and its deliberations should look to the future as well as to planning for more or less immediate testing needs. A testing program should be planned between six months and a year in advance of the time when it is actually to take place, depending somewhat on whether it is a spring or a fall program, on local budgeting practices, on the size of the system and consequent communications and training problems, and similar factors. When a major program is being contemplated, one that covers many subjects at many grade levels with a single battery, it will ordinarily be desirable to think in terms of establishing a program that will be maintained for several years. In giving thought to this type of program, it is well to have in mind such matters as the availability of alternate forms, and the possibility that revised editions of the test in question will be appearing over the period of the proposed program.

THE "HOW" OF TEST SELECTION

Let us assume that a school system, through its testing committee, has defined its testing needs, has planned a program to the extent of knowing what kinds of tests are to be given, at what grade levels, at what time of year, and is now ready to choose the tests most appropriate for the purposes. How does it go about making a selection from among the many available tests?

The first requisite, of course, is that the committee know what tests are available. Just as with textbooks, it finds this out from study of the catalogs of the various test publishers. There are about ten publishers of tests for school use, whose publications probably account for more than 90 percent of all standardized tests used in schools. The catalogs of these publishers describe their respective offerings in various areas, and the committee can readily determine which tests it ought to consider or examine in given fields. Tests should never be selected on the basis of titles alone, or catalog descriptions; there is no substitute for actual examination of a test prior to selection. Publishers will be glad to send examination copies of their tests to committees considering test selection.

In making a selection, there should, most importantly, be an assessment of content validity, in the case of achievement tests, of "predictive" validity, for aptitude tests. There should be evaluation of the technical attributes of the test—reliability, adequacy of norms, appropriateness of difficulty level, etc. There should be consideration of the mechanics of the instrument—its ease of administration, its scoring, etc. And increasingly, consideration is being given to the availability of services: can arrangement be made for outside scoring, analysis, preparation of pupil reports, etc.?

There are resources available to the committee to help with the task of test evaluation. Among these should be mentioned the *Standards for Educational and Psychological Tests and Manuals* developed by a joint committee of the American Psychological Association, the American Educational Research Association, and the National Council on Measurement in Education. These *Standards*[1] describe desirable practices in the reporting of information about tests and serve in effect as a guide or check list for appraising tests. *Mental Measurements Yearbook*,[2] a compilation of critical reviews of published tests issued periodically, is a rich source of helpful information.

PROVISION OF TEST MATERIALS

Since we are concerned not only with the selection but with the *provision* of tests, it is appropriate to say a few words about the ordering of test materials and about provision for them in the budget. As with any supplies, you are likely to get what you want if you order well in advance and if you are careful, in placing the order, to give complete information. An astonishing number of test orders cannot be filled without correspondence because schools fail to indicate such essential information as level, form, or edition. You will get better service from test publishers if you will familiarize yourself with the information on ordering that is a part of practically every test catalog. Moreover, because testing is seasonal and so many school systems want tests at about the same time, it is helpful to place orders well in advance so that they will not be subject to the delays that are incidental to peak seasons.

It is important, too, to give thought to budgetary provision for test materials. While the amounts required for even a very comprehensive program of standardized tests are negligible in relation to the total outlay per pupil for instructional services, they should, nevertheless, be definitely and specifically provided for in a budget for such materials. At the elementary level an expenditure of approximately 50¢ per pupil per year will, on the average, provide adequate test materials to cover the major subject-matter areas; at the secondary level an expenditure of $1.25 per student per year will provide not only achievement test materials, but also mental ability and special aptitude tests for a comprehensive guidance program. Increasingly, schools are seeking to have scoring and other services accomplished for them on a service basis, and these additional services, if desired, should also be provided for in the budget. Costs for scoring an achievement battery begin at about 30¢ per pupil and range upward to as much as $1.25, or even more, depending upon the complexity of the test battery involved, the amount of statistical analysis called for, the variety and scope of reports, etc.

---

[1] Available in pamphlet form from the American Psychological Association, 1200 Seventeenth St., N.W., Washington, D.C. 20036
[2] O. K. Buros, Editor, The Gryphon Press, Highland Park, N.J.

SUMMARY

Selection and provision of adequate standardized test material may be viewed as a continuing responsibility of several different elements in the school system—teachers, supervisors, guidance counselors, psychologists, administrators—whose varying needs and views on testing should be given voice through a permanent committee on testing. Like selection of textbooks, selection of tests calls for sophistication and understanding as to the characteristics that differentiate one instrument from another, as to the appropriateness of given materials in a given school system, and as to the ease with which given materials may be handled by the personnel in a given school system.

Selection of tests should be based primarily on the suitability of the chosen instruments for the purposes to which they are to be put: where the primary emphasis is on the improvement of instruction, then the greatest weight in test selection ought to be given to the content validity of the materials.

There should be specific provision in the budget for standardized test materials. Planning should be sufficiently in advance of the intended use of the materials to permit ordering and local distribution of the materials in ample time for testing. As with any instructional materials, the ultimate criterion is the extent to which the information provided by standardized tests makes a genuine contribution to improved instruction of pupils.

• •

Some Things Parents Should Know About Testing

A Series of Questions and Answers

Q. Why do the schools test our children?

A. It is no news to parents that children differ. Even within a single family, some children learn to walk or to talk sooner than others. One child may be a good reader; another may excel in sports. When children come into school, the teacher needs to know as much as possible about how they differ in order to be able to match the classroom teaching to the specific needs of the children. The school administration also needs to be able to plan for the long-term education of the pupils.

Q. Why do teachers need to use published tests?

A. Commercially published tests give the teacher much important information about the pupils, information which the teacher cannot obtain himself. Of course, teachers get a great deal of information about their pupils by observing their day-to-day work in class and by testing their progress with teacher-made tests. Commercially published tests are written by people who are experts in writing test questions. These people are also curriculum specialists who know what is being taught in schools all across the country. Most commercially published tests cover a wide range of skills in one test, whereas teacher-made tests usually cover only a single unit of work. But perhaps the most important reason for using commercially published tests is that the school can use the results obtained from them to compare a pupil's school progress with the school progress of other children throughout the country. These comparisons can be made because the tests are *norm-referenced* and *standardized* on a *national population*.

Q. What do you mean by *norm-referenced*?

A. Knowing that a pupil got 40 questions right on a test doesn't give you enough information by itself. How many questions were there? Were they easy or hard? Is 40 a "good," "average," or "poor" score? Often, what we really want to know is how this score compares with the scores of other pupils of the same age or in the same grade. Is it high, medium, or low *in relation to* the scores of pupils in some large group? This way of describing performance is called *norm-referenced* and the numbers that are used to give meaning to a pupil's performance are called *norms,* or *norm-referenced scores.*

Q. What does *standardized* mean?

A. The test publisher develops the *norms* or norm-referenced scores by a process called *standardization*. In order to find out what scores are high, medium, or low, he must give the test to a large number of schoolchildren across the country. The pupils who will be in this *national population sample* will be carefully chosen. They cannot all live in one area; they cannot all go to big schools; they cannot all be of one race or socio-economic group. The publisher will use government census data and his own experience and knowledge to help him select a group of several thousand pupils so that their scores on the test will represent the scores that would have been gotten if all the millions of children in the country had been tested.

Once the test has been written and the standardization group has been selected, the test publisher must make sure that the test's directions are so clear and so specific that the test can always be presented in the same way to all pupils. This is done so that all children have the same chance to know what they are supposed to do on the test. A test which has been written in this way and given to a carefully selected group of pupils in a controlled manner is said to be a *standardized test.*

Q. How do you get norms from standardization?

A. The norms are a way of summarizing how the pupils in the standardization group did on the test. In this sense, the pupils make the norms, not the test-maker. After the test has been given, the test publisher has something that looks like this:

120 third graders correctly answered 29 questions
180 third graders correctly answered 28 questions
215 third graders correctly answered 27 questions

and so on for each grade and each possible score. In order to make this information easier to understand, the test-publisher summarizes it. One way of doing this is by reporting, for each test, the average score in each grade. These are called grade equivalent norms. Another way is to report what percentage of the pupils in a grade scored at or below a certain score. These are called percentile rank norms. A third type of norm describes how far a pupil's performance is above or below the average performance for that grade. These are called standard scores. (The most common standard score is a stanine.) All of these methods of expressing a score are simply ways of indicating where a particular score fits into the *pattern* of all the scores earned by the pupils in the norm group.

Q.   What do you mean by the pattern of scores?

A.   For practically any characteristic you can name, there are differences among individuals. There is an average (or medium, or typical) weight, or height, or shoe size, or reading test score. But there is also wide variation in both directions from that average. The weights, heights, or reading scores of most people tend to bunch up close to an average weight, or height, or reading ability. And there are fewer people at the extremes; i.e., there are fewer adults who are six inches taller or shorter than the average than there are those who are only one inch taller or shorter than the average. The average and the pattern of scores for any characteristic can be determined, and one individual's score can always be described in terms of the whole pattern. For most characteristics measured by educational tests, the pattern of scores looks something like this:

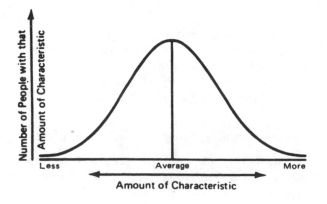

Q.   You say norms can be expressed in several ways. What is a *percentile rank?*

A.   A percentile rank tells you what percent of the pupils in the norm group got the same score or a lower score on the test. For example, if a score of 25 correct answers on a certain test for fourth graders has a percentile rank of 52, it means that 52 percent of the pupils in the norm group scored 25 or lower on the test. Since the norm group was representative of all fourth graders in the nation, it is estimated that a pupil scoring 25 on the test is performing at a level equal to or above 52% of all the fourth graders in the nation. For most standardized achievement tests, percentile ranks are developed separately for each grade and for a particular time of the year. A score of 25, for example, may have a percentile rank of 52 for a fourth grader in the fall of fourth grade and a percentile rank of 47 in the spring of fourth grade. A percentile rank is not in any sense a "percent correct." It is *not* the percent of questions the pupil answered correctly, but rather the percent of pupils in the norm group who scored at or below that score.

Q.   What is a *stanine?*

A.   A stanine is a score on a nine-unit scale from 1 to 9, where a score of 5 describes average performance. The highest stanine is 9; the lowest is 1. Stanines are based on the pattern of scores described earlier. Except for 1 and 9, they divide the baseline into equal amounts of the characteristic being measured. Stanine 8 is as far above average (5) as stanine 2 is below average. As is shown in the figure below, most pupils score in the middle three stanines; 54 percent will score in stanines 4, 5, and 6. On the other hand, very few (4 percent) will score a stanine of 1 or a stanine of 9. The relationship of stanines and percentile ranks can also be seen in this figure.

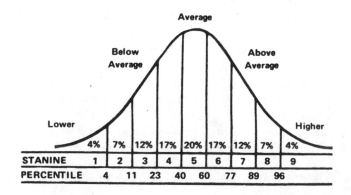

Teachers may use stanines to describe a pupil's performance to his parents during a parent-teacher conference. They may also be used to group pupils for special instruction. Since there are only 9 stanines, students, parents, and teachers are not likely to give too much weight to small differences among scores. Sometimes stanines are combined into more general classifications with verbal descriptions. Stanine 9 describes higher performance; stanines 7 and 8, above average; stanines 4, 5, and 6, average; stanines 2 and 3, below average; and stanine 1 describes lower performance, *in relation to the norm group's performance*. Remember, stanines, like all other norms, describe comparative, not absolute, performance.

Q. But we usually hear about *grade equivalents*. What are they?

A. A grade equivalent indicates the grade level, in years and months, for which a given score was the average or middle score in the standardization sample. For example, a score of 25 with the grade equivalent of 4.6 means that, in the norm group, 25 was the average score of pupils in the sixth month of the fourth grade. If, after the test has been standardized, another pupil in the sixth month of the fourth grade were to take the same fourth-grade test and score 25 correct, his performance would be "at grade level" or average for his grade placement. If he were to get 30 right or a grade equivalent of 5.3, he would have done as well as the typical fifth grader in the third month *on that test*. This does not mean that the fourth grader can do all fifth grade work. There are many things a fifth grader has learned that are not measured on a fourth-grade test. Similarly, a 3.3 grade equivalent for a fourth grader would mean that he is performing, on the fourth-grade test, the way the average pupil in the third month of third grade would perform on that same test. It does *not* suggest that he has learned only third grade material.

Although grade equivalents may sound like a simple idea, they can be easily misunderstood. For this reason, schools are increasingly coming to rely on percentile ranks and stanines as more useful ways to interpret scores in relation to a norm group. In fact, some publishers recommend that grade equivalents *not* be used to report to teachers, parents, pupils, or the general public.

Q. Newspapers sometimes write about "scoring at or above the norm." What does scoring *at the norm* mean?

A. Whereas the word *norms* is used to describe the full range of scores the norm group obtained, the term *the norm* refers only to the mid-point in that range. People sometimes refer to *the norm* as the acceptable or desirable score. This is inaccurate. On a norm-referenced test, *the norm* is the average score obtained by the pupils who took the test during its standardization. *The norm* only indicates what is average; it does *not* describe how good that performance is in absolute terms. Suppose a reading test were given to a large, representative, national norm group and the average score for the group was 25. *The norm* for that group, then, is 25. It must be remembered, however, that of all the pupils in the national norm group, *half scored above 25 and half scored at or below 25!*

When the norm is expressed as a grade equivalent, it is still describing the middle score in the norm group. If the norm group was tested in the sixth month of grade 4, the average score for the group would convert to the grade equivalent of 4.6. But note that even in that norm group, fully half of all pupils actually in the sixth month of the fourth grade scored at or below that norm or "grade level." If the same test is then given to another group, it would not be surprising to find many pupils scoring "below the norm." Remember, half of the norm group itself scored at or below the norm; that's the meaning of the word.

Q. But if a child's reading is "below the norm," that means he is a poor reader, doesn't it?

A. Not necessarily. It probably means he is not reading as well as the *average* American child in his grade, assuming that the test was well standardized. But it doesn't tell you how well the average child reads. If most of the children in the norm group read "well," *the norm* or average represents good reading. If most children read poorly, *the norm* would represent "poor" reading. Whether the norm group reads well or poorly is a judgment the test cannot make. Such decisions must be made by schools and parents.

Q. But wouldn't it be worthwhile to try to teach all children to read at or above the norm?

A. Suppose that to score *at the norm* on a fourth-grade test, a pupil most answer 25 questions out of 40 correctly. Then, suppose we improve the teaching of reading so that all fourth-grade children in the nation score at least 25 and many score much higher than 25. Now all children are reading "at or above the norm," right? Wrong! As the scores have changed, so has their average—*the norm*. If you were to standardize the test again, you might find that the middle or average score for the national norm group is now 31 out of 40. So, *the norm* now is 31, not 25, and half the pupils are still reading at or below the norm and half are reading above the norm. In other words, if everybody is above average, it's not the *average* anymore! This is the reason that *the norm* is not an absolute goal for everyone to attain. It is simply a statement of fact about the *average* of a group. If they *all* read better, then the norm moves higher. You've done something worthwhile, indeed, but it didn't bring everyone "up to the norm"! (The norm for a test which was standardized in the 1950's is no longer *the norm,* since more than half the pupils now read better than that. This is one of the reasons new tests must be standardized by the publishers every few years.)

Q. Some parents and teachers claim that most published standardized tests are unfair to minority group and inner-city children. Is that true?

A. There are really two questions involved here. The first has to do with the knowledge area being measured. Is it "fair," for example, to test a pupil's knowledge of addition? If this skill is considered important, and is part of the school's curriculum, then it is "fair" to test a child's mastery of this skill. It is important that parents and the school know how well each child performs on each skill. Of course, very few people would consider that mastery of addition was *not* a necessary skill. Test publishers try to concentrate on areas that most people consider important. However, if a test measures many areas that a community does *not* consider important, then the test should not be used in that community.

Assuming that it *is* important to measure particular areas, a second question must still be answered. Does the test measure the areas "fairly"? Have some test questions been stated in a way that will give certain children an "unfair" advantage? Will some questions "turn off" some children so that they will not do their best? Test publishers have been giving increasing attention to the question of the fairness of their tests. Many writers and editors from different backgrounds are involved in test-making. Questions are reviewed by members of several ethnic groups to correct for unintentional, built-in biases. In addition, the topics in most reading tests are chosen to be unfamiliar to almost all students. This helps to ensure that scores are based on reading skill and not on familiarity with the subject matter of the particular passage.

Q. Are national norms valid for all children?

A. Yes, national norms *do* have meaning and significance for all school systems. National norms represent one reality—they represent the pattern of performance of *all the nation's schoolchildren*. All kinds of schools in all parts of the country are represented in that total pattern. The pattern of scores in any *one* area, even in a large city, is not likely to match the total pattern exactly. Differences are to be expected and should be explained to parents and the general public.

However, our children are growing up in a rapidly changing, competitive, and highly mobile society. After attending school in one community, they may, in later years, have to compete in the job market with others from all over the country. Thus, it is valuable for parents and school personnel to be able to evaluate local school performance in relation to the nation as a whole.

Q. But aren't there other useful comparisons to be made?

A. Of course! And there are other kinds of norm groups besides the national norm group. The group chosen for comparison should depend on what information the school needs. It is quite possible and often advisable to compare individual pupils with pupils in a district or city, with other pupils in similar communities nearby, with all pupils in the state, and so on. These regional or local norms are developed in a way similar to that for national norms. However, they describe the pattern of performance for some more narrowly defined group.

Q. Why don't you have tests that tell you whether or not a pupil has learned a skill, regardless of what other pupils know?

A. Such tests do exist; they are called *objective-referenced* or *criterion-referenced tests*. In fact, the tests teachers use in their own classrooms are more like this kind of test than they are like norm-referenced tests. Suppose a teacher has given the class ten words to learn how to spell. At the end of the week, a teacher-made spelling test is given to see whether or not each pupil has learned to spell those ten words. The teacher is not interested in what percent of pupils nationally can spell those words; the question is, rather, "Can John spell these words or not?" An objective-referenced or criterion-referenced test is, then, a test which is used to determine whether or not an individual pupil has met an objective or a criterion of performance. An objective may be stated something like this: "The pupil can add two two-digit numbers requiring regrouping." Important questions arise, however, when you begin to plan an objective-referenced test. How many correct answers are needed to show that the pupil has achieved the objective? At what grade level should we expect him to meet the objective? Should every pupil be expected to meet every objective? These are not easy questions to answer. Who will make the decisions? Other questions arise when a child does achieve the objective. Is it typical for a fourth grader to achieve this objective? Do most fourth graders know how to perform this task? Answering these questions brings us back to a comparison among individuals—or to a norm-referenced interpretation of test scores.

Of course, it is not necessary to choose between these two kinds of tests or ways of interpreting test results. Each way of looking at a pupil's performance provides useful information about what the schools are teaching and about what pupils are learning. In the future, more tests will probably be designed to offer both kinds of interpretation.

Q. Where can I get more information about testing?

A. You might first contact the testing coordinator or guidance director in your local school system. If there is a college or university nearby, you might seek information from the professor who teaches courses in tests and measurements. The testing of children is an important responsibility. We feel it is also part of our responsibility, as test publishers, to help you understand why and how testing is done. The staff of the Test Department at Harcourt Brace Jovanovich, Inc. will be glad to be of service. Write to one of our offices listed at the end of this notebook if you would like more help from us.

On Telling Parents about Test Results

In recent years and in various parts of the country, concerned parents have brought law suits against the schools, charging them with negligence for failure to supply adequate information about the progress of their children. Regardless of the legal merits of such cases, it is easy to understand and sympathize with the irate parents who, in some cases, have discovered only after their children have graduated from high school that they have some serious learning problem. A ruling by the courts is not necessary in order that a judgment may be made; the lack of adequate communication between the school and the parents can, and often does, pose a serious problem.

Two interdependent principles provide a sound basis for communicating with parents. First, parents have the right to know whatever the school knows about the abilities, the performance, and the problems of their children; and second, the school has the obligation to communicate understandable and usable knowledge.

The parent's right to know is indisputable. But to know what? What type of communication is required of the schools in order that they may meet their obligation to supply understandable and usable information? The school grades which are periodically sent home on the children's report cards are sometimes misinterpreted by the parents. This is particularly true where homogeneous grouping is practiced in the school with grading based on performance within the group. A slow learner placed in a low section may stand well in that group and thus earn good grades, while still performing below level for the grade as a whole. Testing across the entire grade level is necessary to reveal these discrepancies. In fact, it is difficult to get a complete and accurate idea of a child's performance without comparing it with the performance of other children of the same age and educational background. Such a comparison is best made through the use of a standardized test. Results obtained from standardized tests are by no means the only element needed to evaluate the child's progress, but they are a major element, contributing information important to both the school and the parent.

However, the same statistical data which make standardized tests useful to administrators and teachers can be the source of confusion and misunderstanding to parents unless they are put in the proper context. Before interpreting individual results for parents, it is important that they understand what standardized tests are like and what can and cannot be expected of them. Many schools adopt the policy of sending home a brief introductory statement on testing in general as a preparation for teacher conferences with individual parents.*

At the elementary level, the most advantageous way of telling parents about their children's standing in school is the parent-teacher conference. Ideally, both parents should be present, although in many cases, a discussion with one parent or a brief conference during a parents' day or night might suffice. Written communications mailed to the home or comments included with report cards are not desirable substitutes for a face-to-face discussion.

It is both reasonable and practical for the teacher to assume the responsibility of talking with the parents. The teacher is in contact with the child each school day and is most intimately aware of his or her behavior. It is the teacher who is identified in the minds of the parents as the person who is guiding and directing their child and is in all other ways responsible for the child's school learning. Moreover, the teacher is often in the best position to judge how much and what kinds of information should be communicated to individual parents.

No single reporting procedure can be appropriate for every kind of parent. To well-adjusted or well-educated parents, a numerical report of test scores may enhance their understanding of their child's status and of what the school has to give. To somewhat insecure and less knowledgeable parents, the identical information may result in misunderstanding that will be damaging to the child. Whenever test scores are given to parents, it is important to point out both their value and their weaknesses. The teacher should be prepared to explain why a particular test was chosen, the relevancy of its norms to the immediate situation, and the uses that are to be made of the test results. Since norms are expressed in numbers, parents may assume that they are infallible measures. In fact, they represent a range of values, not an absolute value. Also, they are subject to variation, part of which is due to the test itself while a larger part is due to the constantly changing conditions of the child.

Test Service Notebook No. 34, "Some Things Parents Should Know About Testing," could serve this purpose. Copies are available from The Psychological Corporation.

Most parents will be best able to use and understand test scores when they are reported qualitatively, that is, when they are carefully explained in terms of what the child can and cannot do in the various subject areas. Added to the parents' wholesome desire to know how their child compares with other children is the desire to be of assistance in the improvement of the child's achievement. The parent-teacher conference gives the opportunity for exploring this possibility in practical and concrete terms.

REPORTING ON READINESS

Test results should never be reported to parents in a way that might give the erroneous impression that the child's educational future can be determined by the scores. This is particularly true in reporting on readiness. Readiness tests, which assess the skills and abilities that must be present before instruction in such fundamentals as reading and mathematics can be effective, are generally the first standardized tests given to the child. Tests in basic concepts determine whether the child has the necessary foundation for organizing his or her own experience, understanding the teacher, and communicating with others. Other types of readiness tests measure performance in those language, listening, and numerical skills that are important for early school success. They supply teachers and parents with valuable information concerning the *present* status of the child.

At this level, numerical scores can be particularly misleading. Children who are just beginning school are in a critical stage of development. Natural growth processes, planned activities, and normal experiences at home and at school can lead to rapid changes in the child's responses. Test results are best reported to parents in non-numerical, descriptive terms. A performance rating of *high, average,* or *low* is sufficient for all practical purposes; this should be accompanied by concrete examples of those specific skills and abilities in which the child needs help.

Many parents are in a position to give this help, and a good parent-teacher conference will include a description of activities that can easily be carried out at home. The *Metropolitan Readiness Test,* for example, offers a four-page Parent-Teacher Conference Report. This, in addition to describing the test and reporting the child's rating, gives a list of ways in which parents can help in skill development. The teacher is encouraged to use the report as the basis of discussion with the parents, but it is *not* recommended that it be mailed to the home. It is intended to facilitate joint teacher-parent planning for meeting the child's instructional needs.

However, test results and their applications are not the only components of a good report. It is the total child, with all the complexities and uniqueness of an individual personality, that is the concern of the parents. Social adjustment, behavioral patterns, emotional response, and general health are but a few of the other factors that contribute to an understanding of growth and development. When this type of information is coupled with an analysis of test results, the parents are in a better position to understand and benefit from the teacher's communication.

As an example of the type of information that might be given as the result of readiness testing, the following sample report might be helpful: "Your child, Alice, has good auditory and visual skills but is below average in language skills and lacks some of the basic concepts necessary to understand directions and communicate with others. Here are some of the things you can do to help her.

1. Read and look at books with her. Ask her to tell you about the pictures and stories.
2. Make up stories and ask her to end them.
3. Play word games in which you say a word and Alice says a word that means the opposite. Use words like 'above-below'; 'over-under'; 'inside-outside'; 'near-far.' Help her to understand these concepts by simple demonstrations.
4. Ask your child to sort objects according to size, type and use. Get her to explain what she has done.

Alice shows an eagerness to learn, but it is obvious that her lack of language skills makes communication difficult. She enters willingly into those activities that don't require speech, but is shy and withdrawn during discussions or story-telling activities. She is receiving special help in class, but you can make learning easier for her by the help you give at home."

Another possible report on readiness, and one which unfortunately is often overlooked by teachers, might contain the following considerations: "Your child, Stephen, is ready to learn to read. Children with his skills have nothing to gain from our kindergarten readiness program and are likely to become bored with school if they are not allowed to progress at their own rate. It is when Stephen is not interested in what the class is doing that he becomes restless and disruptive. Let's discuss the advantages of having him join a reading group in Ms X's class where the children are just at his level."

All information should be presented in a positive manner that will result in maximum benefit for the individual child, but the back bone of the report must be a truthful analysis of the pupil's present status.

Perhaps, the most difficult report to make to parents is the type that must include the following considerations: "The results of Eric's posttest in readiness confirm the conclusions I have already reached regarding his progress. As you know, his initial scores were very low. I feel that, over the past months, you and I have worked as a well-integrated team in our efforts to help him. However, he has continued to fall farther and farther behind the children in his group. It is painful to watch, since he is very sensitive and well aware of his own difficulties. I would like to refer him to our school psychologist for further testing. There is a great deal that can be done through specialized instruction once the child's particular learning difficulty is identified."

REPORTING ON ACHIEVEMENT

Children's achievement in school can be reported to parents in two ways: by comparison with their peers and by comparison with their own past performance. The first type of report answers the question, "Is my child doing as well as other children of the same age and grade?" The second addresses the question, "How is my child progressing? Do the test scores indicate normal growth and development?" Both types of information can be readily obtained through analysis of the results of a standardized achievement test.

National and local norms provide the basis for comparisons across grade levels. National norms are based on a carefully selected sample representative of the nation's entire school population. They represent one important reality about the child's performance, but since no local community corresponds completely with a national cross section, norms based on the school system or district can also contribute to an accurate assessment.

Through the use of norms, the raw scores obtained by a pupil are converted into several different types of derived scores, each of which has usefulness to teachers and administrators. However, they are not all equally appropriate for reporting to parents. In this respect, the different kinds of scores vary considerably in the problems they pose.

Grade equivalents and *standard scores* of various kinds may substitute the illusion of precise, scientific communication for real communication. Standard scores have no more meaning for parents than raw scores, unless there is an opportunity for extensive explanation. Grade equivalents *seem* simple and straightforward, but serious misunderstandings may result from their use. For example, on a test given in the sixth month of the fifth year, the pupil with a grade equivalent of 5.6 would be performing "at grade level." A classmate with a grade equivalent of 7.3 would have done as well as the typical seventh grader in the third month—*on that fifth grade test.* However, this does not mean that the fifth grader can do seventh grade work, since there are many things a seventh grader has learned that are not measured on a fifth grade test. In the same way, a 3.3 grade equivalent for a fifth grader does *not* suggest that only third grade material has been learned, but that performance on the fifth grade test was what might be expected of the average student in the third month of the third grade, given a fifth grade test. Because they can so easily be misunderstood, grade equivalents are not recommended for reporting to parents.

If *percentile ranks* are to be used as part of the content of a report, their two essential characteristics must be made clear: (1) that they refer not to the percent of questions answered correctly but to the percent of children whose performance the pupil has equalled or surpassed, and (2) who, specifically, are the children with whom the pupil is being compared. The second point, a definite description of the comparison or norm group, is especially important in making the meaning of test results clear. Percentile ranks are specific to the particular group on which they are based and are not comparable from one subject to another. Parents may be misled if they learn of the standing of their child in one group and assume that this can be directly compared with the standing in another group.

Probably the best statistical data to give to parents are those produced through *stanine* groupings. Although they differentiate sufficiently for most reporting purposes, these broad categories prevent overinterpretation of small differences. Stanines may be based on the national standardization sample or on local community and school system distributions. They have the advantages of being comparable from one level to another up and down the scale. This simple nine-point scale is an easy concept to explain and illustrate and supplies sufficient information to tell parents where their child stands in relation to the peer group, both nationally and locally.

Stanines are defined descriptively as follows:

9 Very superior
8 Superior
7 Considerably above average
6 Slightly above average
5 Average
4 Slightly below average
3 Considerably below average
2 Poor
1 Very poor

Using these designations as a basis, the teacher can prepare reports that are qualitatively descriptive and which give an overall picture of the pupil's adjustment, not merely an isolated piece of information concerning how he or she scored on a particular test.

For example, users of *Stanford Achievement Test* might use stanines to construct reports on three individual pupils as follows:

Stanford Test	Stanine		
	Pupil TM Gr 4	Pupil HD Gr 5	Pupil NR Gr 6
Vocabulary	6	6	5
Reading Comp.	3	8	6
Word Study Skills	3	3	7
Math. Conc.	6	5	9
Math. Comp.	6	4	7
Math. Appl.	7	5	5
Spelling	4	4	7
Language	3	5	6
Social Science	5	7	6
Science	3	7	7
Listening Comp.	6	9	5
OLMAT	5	6	5

Combining these data with work in the classroom and the teacher's own observations, a report to the parents for each of these pupils might contain the following remarks:

Pupil TM: "Tommy's best work is in mathematics in which his achievement is above average. His Vocabulary and Listening Comprehension scores are also above average. These require no reading. Tommy's greatest need is to improve in reading. He is being given special instructions in phonics and is being encouraged to read more. If you will get easy, interesting books for him to read at home, the practice should be beneficial."

Pupil HD: "Helen is above average in Comprehension, both Reading and Listening. This ability is also reflected in her scores in Science and Social Studies. She has contributed a great deal to our class by developing and caring for our science table. She seems particularly interested in biology and has reported on some very interesting things. Her Word Study Skills are below average, and this could account for her Spelling scores which are also slightly below average. I would also like to see her improve in Math. I will be sending home worksheets in Computation and Word Parts; you can help her by seeing that she does this homework and by giving her any assistance she needs."

Pupil NR: "Nancy's work is on or above average in all her subjects. She is a hard worker and seems to need approval. I hope you will be satisfied, as I am, with the quality of her work and will not try to push her to excel. She is a nervous child who seems to have difficulty making friends. I would like to see her entering into our games and play activities with the same enthusiasm she brings to her school work."

Stanine scores may also be used to supply the parents with information concerning the ongoing progress of their child. A cumulative pupil profile, including test scores for several years, can express in graphic form the consistencies and inconsistencies of both strengths and weaknesses. If a pupil has been losing ground in some subject area or is not performing at the level indicated by his or her achievement in previous years, a comparison of stanines on a graph or chart will afford a rapid, visual appraisal. Parents easily grasp the concepts involved in such profiling and welcome a frank explanation of accumulated test information.

The example that follows is for the *Metropolitan Achievement Tests* and shows the pupil's accumulated scores during the period from first to fourth grade. Each subtest has been plotted each year on the graph, and the record has been transmitted from one teacher to the next as the child advanced through school.

In discussing Louis' record with his parents, the fourth grade teacher might note the following:

"There have been no unusual changes in Louis' progress from year to year. His reading skills are very good and have remained higher than his mathematics skills. Although a difference of one stanine is not usually considered significant, it appears that Louis is losing

METROPOLITAN ACHIEVEMENT TESTS Cumulative Record

Name: *Martin, Louis*

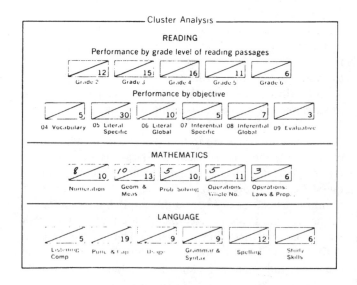

ground in mathematics. Failure to master very basic skills in the first or second grade may have put him at a disadvantage. Even though his current achievement is at an average level, I felt diagnostic testing was needed. Our test showed that Louis' skills in subtraction are poor. Since he is able to finish reading assignments before the rest of the class, I am using this time to help him with his math."

Most achievement tests furnish the teacher with detailed information which would help to support the conclusions reached regarding Louis' progress in mathematics. A cluster analysis will show the number right out of the number possible for all the mathematics objectives covered by the test. In the following example, Louis' low scores in problem solving and operations are indicative

Cluster Analysis

READING
Performance by grade level of reading passages

12	15	16	11	6
Grade 2	Grade 3	Grade 4	Grade 5	Grade 6

Performance by objective

5	30	10	5	7	3
04 Vocabulary	05 Literal Specific	06 Literal Global	07 Inferential Specific	08 Inferential Global	09 Evaluative

MATHEMATICS

8/10	10/13	5/10	5/11	3/6
Numeration	Geom & Meas	Prob Solving	Operations Whole No.	Operations Laws & Prop.

LANGUAGE

5	19	9	9	12	6
Listening Comp	Punc & Cap	Usage	Grammar & Syntax	Spelling	Study Skills

of the nature of his difficulty. This type of analysis by instructional objective is a useful method of reporting in detail on a child's particular strengths and weaknesses.

REPORTING ON ABILITY

The use of stanines also makes possible the construction of expectancy charts containing usable and readily understood information. These charts enable a teacher to interpret a pupil's obtained score on an achievement test by comparison with the score that would be expected for children of the same grade and level of scholastic aptitude. Of course, these "expectancies" must be based upon actual data obtained through the administration of specific achievement and school ability tests to the *same student population*. The resulting bivariate charts afford a general classification as follows: (1) low achiever—low achievement in relation to measured ability, (2) within the expected range—school ability and achievement well related, and (3) high achiever—high achievement in relation to measured ability.

The following chart shows the relationship between a school ability test and an achievement test in mathematics computation for a fourth grade class of twenty-five pupils:

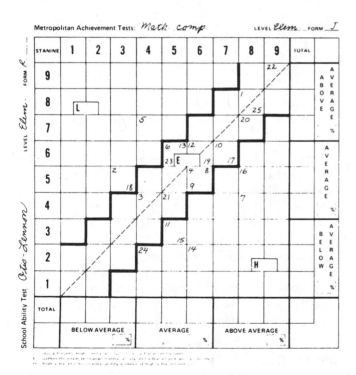

Where norms for a school ability test and an achievement battery have been based on the same population, it is possible to establish the predicted achievement range for each pupil in each of the learning areas covered by the achievement battery. Based on standardization data, each score obtained on the ability test is equated to a limited range of scores in the domains of reading, mathematics, science, etc. By comparing these established ranges with the actual score achieved by each pupil in these domains, it is possible to determine whether individual achievement is comparable with what can reasonably be expected.

For example, when the 5th Edition of the *Metropolitan Achievement Tests* is given in combination with the *Otis-Lennon School Ability Test,* achievement and ability can be compared by means of the Individual Report shown below.

Although Joseph's achievement scores are average, his School Ability Index indicates that he is not performing as well as might be expected. This is particularly true in Language and Science where he falls well below the predicted range. A report to his parents might include the following observations: "Joseph is much more interested in sports than he is in classroom activities. Although he has no difficulty keeping up with his lessons, his scores are somewhat disappointing. He is often disruptive in class, distracting the other children and neglecting his work. He says he wants to be a physician, and probably he has the necessary ability. I hope you can help me convince him that the study habits he forms now will help him later on and that our classroom work in science is a good preparation for more advanced studies. Frankly, his low score in Language surprises me. I feel he was just being careless when taking the test."

This type of comparison, between the pupil's own ability and present achievement, is the most important use of a school ability test for the vast majority of pupils. Other uses exist, such as screening for learning disabilities and identifying the gifted. However, no constructive purpose can be served by reporting the results of an ability test, *in isolation,* to parents. Although these tests give useful and reliable information regarding the pupil's likelihood of success in school-related subjects, the results obtained are subject to serious misunderstanding by those who do not recognize their limitations and their

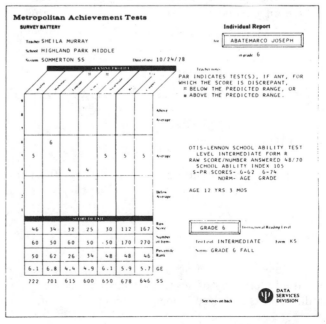

focus. Too often, school ability scores are regarded as measuring a fixed characteristic of the child tested and are used as a basis for a final conclusion rather than as a piece of information useful in further planning. Teachers should be aware of the potential danger of indiscriminately reporting these test scores to parents.

SUMMARY

The examples of possible reports given here are intended to increase the teacher's awareness of the many ways that test scores can be combined with classroom work and teacher observations to give parents an understandable and usable assessment of their child's status and progress. Without the firm statistical basis made possible by the administration of a standardized test, an objective standard, essential to a true understanding of a child's school work, is missing. Parent-teacher conferences may fail by being too subjective, by stressing behavior at the expense of achievement, or by the inclusion of such ambiguous (though true) statements as "he is doing his best." Statistical data presented without adequate explanation can be misleading and useless. Test scores should be evaluated by the teacher in the light of other information about the pupil such as performance in class, attitude, motivation, etc. Mere numbers, no matter how accurate or comprehensive, can never take the place of good judgment based on personal experience.

Reports to parents may have far-reaching effects. Parental hopes and plans for their child's future will be largely based on the information they receive from the school. If these plans are unrealistically high, they have the right to know, even though the knowledge may be disappointing. On the other hand, parents should be alerted to the exceptional talents of their children in time to make long-term plans for an adequate educational future. Test scores form a basis upon which cooperation between parents and the school can be built toward the common goal of achieving the best possible education for our children.

EXERCISE 60
STANDARDIZED ACHIEVEMENT TESTS

OBJECTIVE

To enhance understanding of and provide firsthand experience with standardized achievement tests.

BACKGROUND

Achievement tests measure accomplishment and may be classified along any of several dimensions such as standardized/unstandardized, general/specific, and evaluative/

diagnostic.[1] But how is a standardized achievement test developed? And how should the results of an administration of a standardized achievement be reported to the community? After you've read the two Psychological Corporation articles that follow, you'll be better prepared to answer these questions, and those that follow below.

YOUR TASK

You wish to create a standardized achievement test to evaluate mastery of the material in the chapter on educational assessment in your textbook.

1. In broad terms, state how you might go about developing such a standardized achievement test. Include a half-dozen or so sample items.
2. Discuss your plan for reporting the results to the community.

• •
How a Standardized Achievement Test Is Built

Lois E. Burrill, *Test Department*

* * * * *

There is no one, "hard-and-fast" set of rules for building a standardized achievement test series. Each step described in this notebook is typical of the way tests are built by many of the major test publishers, but there are many variations possible in technique. In general, the text which follows describes the development of standardized achievement tests at Harcourt Brace Jovanovich, Inc.

* * * * *

Let us assume a test publisher has decided to build a new series of achievement tests for use in elementary schools. Achievement tests are designed to measure the extent to which pupils have "achieved" or mastered the skills and knowledge which are the goals of the school's instructional program. The school should then be able to use the test results in planning an instructional program to meet the needs of each pupil. Since achievement tests are so closely related to curriculum, the publisher will build his tests to reflect what is typically being taught in classrooms around the country.

DEVELOPMENT OF EXPERIMENTAL FORMS

An essential prelude, then, to determining what the content of the test will be is the identification of what is being taught country-wide: in other words, an analysis

---

[1] This dimension refers to the ultimate use of the achievement test data: Will the data be used primarily to make an overall evaluation of mastery or to uncover diagnostic information about the examinee's strengths and weaknesses with respect to the subject matter?

Figure 1

Part of a Topical Analysis of 5th Grade Mathematics Texts. A, B, C, etc. refer to various well-known textbook series. The number entries are the percent of total pages devoted to the topic. Taken from Curricular Analysis for Metropolitan Achievement Tests, *1970 Edition.*

Topic / Text	A	B	C	D	E
Fractions	23.4	29.0	26.4	23.4	19.4
Geometry	11.5	19.0	10.3	11.5	5.9
Rates & Ratios	13.2	2.0	2.6	12.3	2.5
Decimals	5.8	1.3	3.9	5.8	8.4
Graphs & Scale Drawings	2.7	4.0	4.8	2.7	4.4
Place Value	1.5	—	2.3	1.5	3.4
Measures	1.2	—	2.6	1.2	1.6
Other Number Bases	—	—	1.3	—	2.8

of the curriculum. Curricular analysis for a major achievement series is a long and arduous task. It requires the detailed summarizing of published textbook series, syllabuses, outlines of objectives, and other current curricular material from across the country. (See Figure 1.) In addition to analyses of current texts and course outlines, curriculum experts in each of the skills and subject matter areas to be tested are consulted for suggestions as to what trends the curriculum might be taking in the future. Since curricular analysis and prepublication research typically extend over a period of several years, it is essential for the test publisher to make an evaluation of future curriculum trends. (The transition from "traditional" to "modern" mathematics during the sixties is an example of the type of curricular change the test developer must anticipate in his determination of what content should be included.)

The end result of this process is a set of content outlines specifying behavioral objectives in each subject and skill area. The relative emphasis given to each objective is also analyzed so as to provide an indication of the percent of the test questions which should be developed to measure each one. The test developer will use this information as a blueprint in planning the building of the test. Often, these blueprints will be sent to curriculum experts for their review and comment.

The next step in the process is the actual writing of the test questions or items. Questions may be written by test authors, by teachers whom they employ to write questions, and/or by members of the publisher's staff. Item writing is not a simple process. The question, or stem, must state clearly what is being asked; the correct answer must be clear and unambiguous, and the incorrect choices (distractors) must be both attractive (to the examinee who *does not* know the answer) and clearly incorrect (to the examinee who *does* know the answer). Before ever being tried out, each test question may go through several cycles of editing, rewriting, and review by different experts. Curriculum specialists will study the questions to check that they measure objectives being

Figure 2

Item Card showing Data from the Item Analysis Research Program. 63.1 percent of the pupils in Grade 3 answered this question correctly. Of the top 27 percent group, 90.1 percent got the correct answer; 25.6 percent of the bottom group also answered correctly. 9.3 percent of the total group marked "Don't Know," and 5 percent omitted the item. (Note the total percent correct for each grade 2–5, the grade progression of these percents correct, and the discrimination values for each grade. This is a pretty good item.)

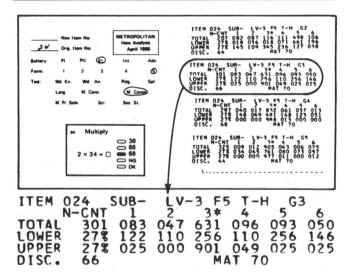

```
ITEM  024   SUB-    LV-3  F5  T-H    G3
        N-CNT   1     2    3*   4     5     6
TOTAL   301   083   047  631  096   093   050
LOWER   27%   122   110  256  110   256   146
UPPER   27%   025   000  901  049   025   025
DISC.   66                      MAT 70
```

taught in the classroom. Test construction experts will review them to be sure questions conform to rules of good item-writing. Other experts will review questions to determine that the context of the question does not bias its validity for any particular subgroup of the population and to make sure they will not psychologically or emotionally "turn off" a youngster. Any drawings to be used in test questions must be planned, executed, and (particularly at the lower grade levels) carefully edited and reviewed right along with the test questions to be certain that all the objectives of the question are being met.

All questions in a standardized test will be "tried out" before being included in the final version of the test. Test publishers know from past experience that, no matter how thorough the reviewing process, a number of proposed questions will have to be discarded at that time for any of a number of reasons which will be discussed below. At HBJ, editors also want to have a surplus of usable questions so that they can choose the best ones from among them. The total number of questions written, therefore, maybe as many as three to four times the number of questions needed for the final versions of the test.

Many other details are discussed at this time. For example, decisions are made concerning the directions to the teacher and to the pupil. Sample questions will be written to acquaint the pupil with the task he will be asked to perform. Methods of indicating responses, types of answer documents, size of type, format of booklets, and such topics will be discussed.

After the many questions have been written and edited, they are assembled into experimental test forms for "tryout" and subsequent analysis. Typically, each of these experimental forms looks like a final test form and meets the specifications set up for the test in the blueprint. Often, however, each form has more items per objective than the final form is planned to have, and some or all forms may include sets of questions experimenting with a new "item type" or a new set of directions. In page size, layout, typography, directions for administration, etc., these forms will, however, be virtually identical with those planned for the final edition, since all these aspects of the test must also be "tried out" along with the items before final decisions are made.

TRYOUT: NATIONAL ITEM ANALYSIS PROGRAM

Tryout administration of these experimental forms is called an "item analysis" program. A publisher such as HBJ plans a research program in order to get a variety of information about the questions that have been developed for the test:

1. the difficulty level of each question—that is, what percent of the pupils in the total tryout group answer the question correctly.
2. the discrimination of each question—that is, how well the answering of this question correctly distinguishes between students who score high (within the top 27% of the sample) on the total test and those who score low (within the bottom 27% of the sample).
3. the grade progression in difficulty—that is, if a question is used in tests for several successive grades, do a progressively greater percent of pupils answer the question correctly at successively higher grades?

In addition to the statistical characteristics of individual questions, other types of information are obtained during the course of a good item analysis program. For example, teachers administering the experimental forms are requested to complete questionnaires asking their judgment concerning the appropriateness of content for their own classroom, the clarity of directions and questions, and other pertinent matters regarding the test.

The schools participating in an item analysis program are carefully chosen to be representative of the population for whom the test is designed. The communities are typically selected on the basis of such factors as size, geographical location, and socioeconomic level (as indicated by adult level of income and education, previous test results for pupils, etc.). A test of scholastic aptitude or mental ability is often administered as part of this achievement test tryout program in order to check on the ability levels represented by the participating schools, and to provide a basis for matching the groups taking the various experimental forms.

Wherever possible, classroom teachers themselves administer the tests so that the administration situation will correspond as closely as possible with that in which the final published tests will be used. However, in a tryout administration, the tests are typically administered without time limits so as to give each pupil ample opportunity to attempt all items on the experimental form. Teachers record the time required for their classes so that final time limits can be determined in such a way as to make certain that every pupil will be able to finish the test in the allotted time. Experimental forms are also often administered in the grade just above and the one just below those for which the questions are ultimately intended, in order to secure further data on the questions.

DEVELOPMENT OF FINAL FORMS

The selection of test items for the final forms of the tests is begun only after the results of the item analysis program have been carefully studied and interpreted by the team of authors and editors. (See Figure 2.) The final selection of these questions depends jointly on content specifications and statistical requirements. A number of general statistical guidelines for selection are usually set up for use in all tests in the series. The following set of guidelines was used for a recently-published achievement series:

1. average difficulty level—the median difficulty level for the questions in the final test should be .55 for the target grade level (an average of 55% of pupils answering an item correctly).
2. range of difficulty values—the various questions in the final form should range in difficulty from .90 to .20 for the pupils in the grade for which the test is intended.
3. item discrimination—except for very easy or very difficult questions, the items in the final form must distinguish clearly between high- and low-scoring pupils.
4. grade progression—the difficulty level of each question for each grade in which it was tested should indicate an increasingly larger percent correct, grade by grade.

The questions which have survived the tryout administration phase are again reviewed by outside experts who are familiar with the needs and styles of pupils from a variety of minority backgrounds in an attempt to make sure that no questions are inappropriate or offensive to such children. Then the selected items are divided into the various final forms in such a way as to make each form match both the content and statistical specifications previously agreed upon. Both careful development of content specifications and tryout of all proposed questions are vital to the building of a test that will be worth standardizing.

The procedure described above could be applied, with some modifications, to many test-building tasks, whether or not norms were to be developed for the instrument. However, in order to complete the development of a *standardized* test, several further steps must be taken.

Part of a typical definition of a standardized test would read something like ". . . and interpreted in reference to certain normative information." The development of those norm data is the next step in the building of a standardized test.

NORMING: THE NATIONAL STANDARDIZATION PROGRAM

Norms provide the means for comparing the performance of one pupil or group of pupils with that of some particular reference group. There are many types of reference groups which might be used. Norms may be developed by age or sex, for particular geographical areas, for private schools, for suburban areas, or for other distinct groups. To develop a norm, however, the norm group must be carefully defined.

Let us suppose that our hypothetical test publisher has determined that the group for which his test is being developed is the total elementary school population. Therefore, the most important norm data he must collect is for that reference group. He has already collected preliminary data from one sample of the national school population in his item analysis. Now, by a process called standardization, he will develop national normative information for the final forms of the test. This research program will yield data on the performance of a sample of pupils selected to represent the total population of pupils. When the sample has been well-chosen, one can assert with reasonable confidence that the norms developed from these data truly reflect the performance of the national school population in all its variety. The quality of the job the test developer does in selecting this sample population and in describing it to the user will, therefore, have tremendous long-range effects on the confidence with which test users can apply the norms.

Many variables are used to select these "reference group" samples, and later to describe them. They include characteristics of pupils themselves (chronological age, sex, mental ability scores, etc.), characteristics of school systems (public-private, teachers' salaries, time spent teaching various subjects and skills, etc.), and characteristics of the communities which the schools serve (geographical area, size of city, level of adult schooling and income, etc.). Clearly, the characteristics that are used as criteria in sampling should be those which have been shown to be related to test performance, and on which information is reasonably accessible, both to test developer and to test user. For example, Harcourt Brace Jovanovich, Inc., in selecting school systems for its standardization samples, uses the following community variables:

1. size of community
2. geographic region
3. socioeconomic index (the community's median family income and median years of schooling for persons over 24 years, combined and classified in some manner)

Using national census data for each of these variables, the test developer will draw up a model to indicate how many sample cases from communities of various types should be included in the total so as to reflect the makeup of the total national school population. School systems, chosen randomly from a list of all schools, are classified with respect to each of these variables and assigned to a cell. Certain school systems then are invited to participate in the standardization. These systems are selected in such a way as to produce a representative sample of all school systems in the nation. Other similarly classified school systems are selected as alternates to fill needed slots whenever a chosen system is unable or unwilling to participate. Schools agreeing to inclusion in the sample will be asked to provide many other pieces of information which will be useful in describing the sample population. Included in such questionnaires may be items regarding teachers' salaries and experience, promotion and grouping policies, length of school year, entrance age, availability of kindergarten experience, textbooks in use, tests used in the system, etc.

The test developer may also set up criteria for his norm group in terms of individual pupil characteristics— usually chronological age and mental ability, as measured by some standardized instrument. Although he cannot get more than a rough indication of these attributes before his actual testing begins, he will adjust his sample afterwards, as is illustrated in the following example. Frequently, a criterion for the norm group is that the mental ability of the pupils match the mental ability of the national population, both in average ability and the spread above and below average. This is usually checked by administering, along with the achievement test being standardized, an already-standardized mental ability test. The data thus collected will be analyzed to determine the median mental ability, as well as the variability of ability scores for the sample. Some adjustments may have to be made, either by eliminating cases or by weighting the results of various school systems in order to correct any errors in the original selection of the sample and to make sure that the total national school population is in fact accurately represented in this standardization sample. If the original design was well planned, little adjustment will be necessary.

The development of the norms themselves is one of the most important aspects of standardized test construction. From the scores of the pupils in the norm sample, distributions of raw scores on each level or "battery" of the tests are made. To give meaning to these scores and to provide national bench-marks, various kinds of national norms may be developed. For elementary achievement tests, the types most often developed include grade equivalents (GEs), percentile ranks (PRs), and stanines (Ss). The Harcourt Brace Jovanovich Test Department usually provides all three types of national norms for its new tests. The following sections briefly describe each type of norm and the way in which it is developed.

The development of grade-equivalent norms is quite complicated and several steps are required. First, in order to be able to translate raw scores from several different batteries or levels of the test into a single scale of grade equivalents, the raw scores on each level of the test must be related to the raw scores on the other levels. To accomplish this, pairs of tests are given to special, experimental groups and the equivalent raw scores from one test to the next are determined. In this way, raw scores on all levels can be translated into a single set of numbers. These numbers are then marked along the vertical axis of a graph, with the school years marked along the horizontal axis in months (1.0–9.9). Next, the median (middle) scores from each grade level of the standardization sample are plotted on the graph and the straight lines connecting each pair of points are smoothed out into a curved line. (See Figure 3.) From this norm line, then, the grade equivalent scores for each possible test score can be read and tabled. It must be remembered, however, that the only grade equivalents which are actually derived from the standardization testing are those for the one time of year at which the test was standardized: i.e., 3.2, 4.2, 5.2, etc. The other grade equivalents are estimates, taken from the smoothed curve between the obtained grade equivalents. This "interpolation" of the in-between grade equivalents involves the assumption that growth is evenly spread throughout the school year.

This explanation of how the grade equivalent norms are developed may also help explain the meaning of the grade equivalent. It is a way of expressing how the raw score of a pupil taking one test compares with the scores obtained by the *average pupils at each grade level* in the standardization administration of all levels of the test. If a pupil achieves a raw score equal to a grade equivalent of 5.8, that means his *score* was similar to that of the average 5th grader in the 8th month of the 5th grade. From the explanation given above, however, it also can be seen that a 3rd grader, taking the test designed for the 3rd grade, may have answered a quite different set of questions from the set answered by the 5th grader taking a 5th grade set of questions, although both achieve the same grade equivalent score.

Percentile rank norms provide quite a different interpretation of test scores. Instead of comparing a pupil with average pupils over a whole range of grade levels, his score is compared only with those of others at his own approximate grade placement. A percentile rank for a given raw score indicates the percent of pupils at a particular grade placement in the norm group who received scores equal to or lower than the given raw score. Developing percentile rank norms for the time of year the test was standardized is a relatively simple matter. The distribution of raw scores for the grade is plotted on a normal percentile chart, a smooth curve is fitted to the points, and the PR for each raw score is read off. (See Figure 4.) Our test developer could let it go at that and provide percentile rank norms only for the time of year the test was standardized. However, he will probably want to provide at least two, perhaps three, sets of norms for various times of the school year (beginning, middle, and end-of-year, for example). Unless he standardizes his test at all of these times and with very carefully matched groups, he will have to "interpolate" norms for times of the year other than those at which he actually standardized. This is not complicated, but it involves again the assumption that growth proceeds at a constant rate throughout the school year. (See Figure 5.)

Stanine norms make use of a nine-point scale of standard scores, with a mean of 5 and a standard deviation of 2. For a normal distribution of scores such as those obtained in a national standardization, the correspondence between percentile ranks and stanines is fixed. For such

Figure 3

Schematic Illustration of Grade Equivalent Norm Line for One Subtest, Grades 2.2–9.2

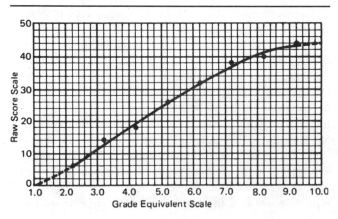

Figure 4

Schematic Illustration of Percentile Rank Norm Lines for One Subtest, Grades 5.1 and 6.1

R.S.	Percentile		1	5 10 20 30 50 70 80 90 95	99
	5th	6th			
30-31		100			
28-29	100	98			
26-27	99.7	95		Grade 6	
24-25	99	89			
22-23	98	82			
20-21	95	73			
18-19	91	64			
16-17	84	53			
14-15	75	43			
12-13	63	33		Grade 5	
10-11	50	24			
8-9	35	15			
6-7	20	8.3			
4-5	8.3	3.2			
2-3	2.1	.7			
0-1	.2	.1			
			1	5 10 20 30 50 70 80 90 95	99
				Percentile Scale	

Figure 5

Schematic Illustration of Percentile Rank Norm Lines for Beginning, Middle, and End of Year

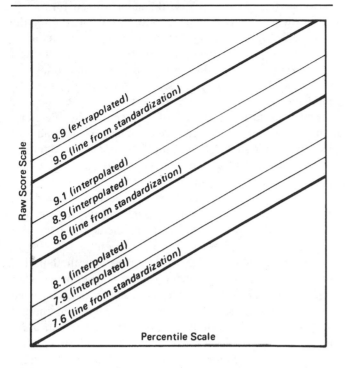

Figure 6

Schematic Illustration of a Normal Distribution of Scores, Showing the Relationship Between Percentile Ranks and Stanines

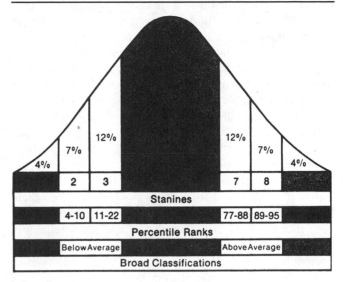

distributions, the development of stanines is automatic, once percentile ranks are available. For example, the range of percentile ranks 40 through 59 becomes stanine 5. (See Figure 6.)

National norms, as described above, have meaning for all school systems, regardless of the ways in which a system's pupils may be different from the national population as a whole. This is true because national norms describe one reality, i.e., the typical performance of the nation's schoolchildren. In this respect they are an important frame of reference. However, our test publisher may choose to provide other sets of norms for certain subgroups of the population. Thus, he may develop distributions of raw scores for pupils in large cities or for suburban areas, for geographical regions or for types of schools (Catholic school norms, for example). From these distributions, the publisher may develop percentile rank or stanine norms. It should be noted, however, that grade equivalent norms are never developed for any norm group other than the national school population.

THE MANUAL: INFORMATION FOR THE TEST USER

In selecting a standardized test series to fill his own testing needs, the prospective test user should look for assurances that the test is appropriate for his system and that, in fact, the norm sample population is "representative"

of the total national school population. The test developer, in his manual for the test, will usually take care to describe the way in which the norm or standardization group was chosen and, as well, to describe that sample in terms of other criteria related to school performance. The test user should, moreover, look for evidence that the test itself is good of the purposes for which he intends to use it, since even "beautiful norms" are worthless if they are for a test with no value in his specific situation. The test publisher will probably collect the pertinent information and data into a manual for the test. Much of what the test user needs to evaluate the true worth of the test itself will typically be presented in sections labeled *validity* and *reliability*.

Validity may be described as the degree to which a test serves the purpose for which it is used; that is, how close it comes to doing what you want it to do. Since validity is specific to the purposes of the test, different kinds of validity evidence are appropriate to different kinds of tests. Most survey achievement tests are intended to assess current status in the subject areas being tested. They are in this sense, then, a sample set of items which are representative of a universe of information. The type of validity information most needed by the user is the blueprint or set of specifications on which the test was built and which has been described earlier. Test publishers will typically include some such content outline information in the manual. The user himself will then make his own determination of *content validity:* that is, the degree to which the test's specifications match his school's own objectives and curriculum. Included in the manual as well may be a discussion of the way in which the blueprint was developed, by whom, and other pertinent data.

The test developer cannot present statistical data to support a claim of content validity, since such validity must be specific to each school. Publishers may, however, present correlations of test scores with some other criterion (perhaps another well-known achievement test) as evidence of the validity or usefulness of the new test.

One of the most fundamental requirements of any measurement is that it be reliable; in other words, the obtained scores should be dependable. Test *reliability* may be described as the extent to which a test is consistent or stable in its measurement of whatever it is measuring. As with other measuring instruments, however, no test is perfectly accurate. The degree of accuracy possible depends in part on the fineness of the distinctions the test is expected to make. The greater the spread of scores the pupils have obtained, the more reliably the test will be able to distinguish among them. Since there is no one reliability figure for a test, the figures the test publisher presents are estimates of the test's reliability under typical circumstances. The publisher will also present, along with the reliability estimates, estimates of the "measurement error." In this way, the user may take into account the lack of perfect accuracy of the test when he interprets the scores obtained.

We noted, in the section describing the item analysis, the attention given to the degree to which questions distinguished between high- and low-scoring pupils. The total of the discrimination indices for questions chosen for final forms gives a crude indication of reliability and, thus, a preliminary assurance the standardized test will be fairly reliable.

At the time of standardization, several statistical procedures will be employed in analyzing the data and the results will be reported as evidence of the test's reliability. One statistic frequently reported is the "split-half" reliability coefficient which is obtained when the two halves of the test are correlated to provide an answer to the question, "How consistently is the test measuring the same thing throughout?" Another type of reliability statistic which may be presented is the "test-retest" or "alternate-form" reliability coefficient which is an indication of the correspondence between results on alternate forms and thus a measure of their reliability.

Since no test score is ever completely reliable, the test's developer may include data in his manual estimating the possible magnitude of error in the obtained scores of individuals. These data are called standard errors of measurement and are usually given for each test at each grade. He may also present data concerning the heterogeneity of his norm sample by giving the standard deviations of test scores of his norm groups, as well as their mean and median scores. When more than one form of a test is published, the test developer may provide evidence in the test manual that the alternate forms are comparable. As we have seen, the final forms are built to be as alike as possible in terms of item analysis data. However, the standardization program will probably either standardize each form directly or include a supplementary experimental program in which alternate forms will be administered to matched groups in order to relate scores on other forms to scores on the standardized form.

The test developer may include data concerning the intercorrelations among subtest scores in his achievement battery, the correlation of the achievement test scores with mental ability test scores, data concerning sex differences in test scores, and so on. Finally, the test publisher will usually give the test user suggestions for the interpretation and use of test scores by teachers, curriculum specialists, guidance counselors, and administrative personnel. These should be considered "must" reading for any test user who wishes to get the greatest possible benefit from his use of the test.

When all of these procedures have been completed and the results analyzed and interpreted and written up in a way the test user will find meaningful, the new standardized achievement test is ready for publication.

The paragraphs above have described only the building of a standardized achievement test. Of course, many other types of test instruments may be built and standardized by a test publisher, including tests of general mental ability or school learning potential, prognostic and diagnostic tests of various types, tests of specific aptitudes, interest and personality measures, etc. Many of the steps in developing these other types of tests are similar to those described above; in other ways, however, they may be quite different. In choosing the questions for a standardized scholastic aptitude test, for instance, emphasis would be placed, not on the content of the curriculum, but rather on skills or tasks which are found to be predictive of success in academic programs. In such cases, too, the type of validity sought is predictive, rather than content validity, and the estimates of reliability will be concerned more with stability over time than are those used in estimating the reliability of achievement measures.

Standardized tests are an important tool for evaluation of the educational process but they are not the only type of test which publishers build. The essence of a standardized test is in the use of a norm-reference: that is, that scores on the test are described in terms of a comparison with the scores others have made on the same test. The other major category of test instruments is those which use a criterion-reference rather than a norm-reference. Scores on criterion-referenced tests are described, not in terms of a comparison with what others have done, but in terms of the degree of attainment of some specific criterion or standard of achievement.

Because criterion-referenced and norm-referenced tests are built for different purposes and used in different ways, the techniques used to build them are also somewhat different. The present publication deals only with norm-referenced tests. A later publication will take up the question of how a criterion-referenced test is built.

The development of a good test instrument, of whatever type, is a time-consuming and demanding task. At

Harcourt Brace Jovanovich, Inc., several years of research and development go into the publication of a major standardized test series. The painstaking care with which a published test has been developed, however, will help to assure that the resulting instrument will be of value to all those involved in the educational process.

• •

Reporting Standardized Achievement Test Results to the Community

Lois E. Burrill

A recent development in the field of education has been the emergence of the notion of "accountability." There has been growing public concern about the quality of our educational system and about the effectiveness of the money being spent for education, both locally and at the federal level. There is nothing especially new in the concept of educational responsibility. Implicit in local supervision of the educational process is the requirement that school personnel keep the public informed concerning educational matters. However, the demand for "hard data," for facts and figures, for scientific quantification of the educational process has been growing steadily.

In the past, many school administrators have been extremely reluctant to publicize test results because they recognized the possibility of misunderstanding and the dangers of misinterpretation. A disgruntled school board member has been quoted as saying, "The school officials seem to assume that the public cannot understand (the meaning of test scores) if results are announced."

How can these opposing viewpoints be reconciled? There are two principles which we believe should govern decisions regarding the reporting of test score information to the community. They are:

1) Specific score units, such as grade equivalents, percentile ranks, stanines, and standard scores, are not self-interpreting. Consequently, they may become sources of error and confusion within the school system itself as well as in the public press. Most measurement specialists are aware that test scores by themselves represent incomplete information about school achievement. Certainly, the nonspecialist cannot be expected to interpret isolated test scores correctly.

2) On the other hand, in our tradition of tax-supported, community-controlled public education, the public *has* the "right to know." In fact, if an educational system is to operate at all, the public should be in possession of *all* the pertinent information upon which educational decisions are to be made. Since testing is a legitimate educational activity, part and parcel of the total instructional program, parents, school board members, and the entire tax-paying public must be fully informed about this aspect of the school's instructional program.

These two principles, taken together, indicate that the school must be ready to report test results (as well as all other kinds of information about the functioning of the school) to its constituency as a matter of course. To communicate effectively, schools must report enough information and in such a way as to make it meaningful and useful to the general public. The key phrase is *effective communication*. The highly technical statistical summaries prepared by testing professionals should be avoided.

The community to which this discussion refers is more inclusive than that of the system's pupils and their parents; it extends to all residents of the community. In a broad sense, of course, effective communication is necessary with several "communities," i.e., the pupils themselves, their parents, and the school staff. Further discussion regarding the reporting of individual or group test results to these communities is, however, beyond the scope of this discussion. We have also chosen to limit the discussion to the reporting of results on standardized achievement tests. This should not be taken to mean that effective communication does not include the reporting of information concerning other parts of the testing program—far from it. But while many school systems have differing policies with regard to both the administration and the reporting of aptitude, mental ability, interest and/or personality tests, the majority of school systems do have survey achievement testing programs. Furthermore, the public is probably most interested in knowing about students' achievement in the skills and knowledges that are the goals of the instructional program.

PLANNING A PROGRAM OF EFFECTIVE COMMUNICATION

Although the focus of this presentation is on the reporting of test results to the public, the test results are really only one aspect of the total testing program of the school. The whole program may be considered to have three major phases: a) designing and planning the program, b) administration of the tests, and c) interpreting and using the results. Effective communication between school and community should be planned for and included in each of these phases.

Effective Communication Before Testing Begins

The first steps toward reporting test information should be taken well in advance of the actual testing dates for the current year. There are a number of topics that may be presented to the community at the time the testing program is planned. Effective communication at this time will help to prepare the way for better understanding of both the uses and the limitations of standardized test data. The following paragraphs include examples of this type of reporting.

I. The nature of the testing program
a. Why are you testing? School personnel may recognize the role of measurement in the teaching-learning process,

but it is helpful to develop a clear statement for the public. Every effort should be made to clarify the rationale behind survey achievement testing and to help the public become aware of the usefulness of test results in the ongoing planning of the school. At the same time, it must be made quite clear that survey tests do not answer all the questions that need to be asked, and that the total evaluation process of the school includes many additional techniques.

b. What are you testing? The public should be informed about what testing is being done; that is, what tests are being used, at what grades, and in what skills or content subject matter areas. The school's report might well include the publisher's description of what each test or subtest is designed to measure. A time schedule for testing might also be included here.

c. What real use will be made of the results? This question is part of the larger one involving the school's reasons for testing in the first place, but some specific information is in order here. Will results be used in decisions regarding remedial reading staffing? in the evaluation of a new math program? in a longitudinal study of some aspect of the instructional program? The public should be informed of these special uses of test results in decision making, as well as about the ongoing evaluation of strengths and weaknesses in the instructional program.

d. What is a standardized test anyway? What is a grade equivalent? What are norms? Test publishers and users are so accustomed to their own jargon that it is sometimes difficult to remember that it is not well understood by others. There are a number of concepts that are important for the public to understand. It would be well to describe how a standardized test differs from a teacher-made classroom test, how national norms are derived and what they mean, and so on. Descriptive definitions of testing terms may prove useful to the school staff charged with writing releases concerning the school's testing program and may also serve as a quick reference for news media personnel. A publication containing a narrative description of such terms is available upon request from Information and Advisory Services, The Psychological Corporation.

II. The uses and limitations of standard achievement tests

It is advisable to emphasize, *before testing begins,* that standardized test scores, valuable as they may be, are only part of the school's total evaluation program. They cannot "tell all." Many goals of the school's program cannot be measured by a paper-and-pencil test. Attitudes, interests, and many other areas must be evaluated in other ways. The public should also be cautioned that scores from even the best available tests lack precision. When information is expressed in numbers, we are all prone to assume a degree of exactness that test scores do not merit. It is important to point out that our instruments for measuring a child's height or weight or eyesight are more precise than those we have for measuring his reading comprehension or his potential to master a foreign language. The public should be cautioned that test results are estimates based on observations and that, as with all observations, there are inherent limitations to their use. These comments need to be made *before* testing begins, although they bear repeating when test results are reported. Waiting until after the results are in to point out the shortcomings of testing may appear to the public as an avoidance of responsibility. On the other hand, mention of the limitations of standardized tests should not be allowed to overshadow the fact that test scores are usable and useful; that they can be, in fact, tremendously valuable as part of the total evaluation process.

III. Nonschool factors related to achievement

It is a common misconception that the average achievement test scores can be interpreted, by themselves, as a direct index of the effectiveness of school instruction. Too often, tests are taken to be an accurate yardstick for measuring the quality of teaching—even of education in general. If the scores surpass the national norms, there is a strong temptation to consider them as "proof" of the superiority of a school's teachers, methods, and/or materials. If the scores are lower than norm, there is a tendency to blame the school and even individual teachers or administrators.

It is all too easy to forget that many other factors are involved in the determination of a group's average performance. Characteristics of the pupil population, their parents, and the community as a whole may influence the relative achievement of the pupils to a considerable degree. Every pupil's achievement pattern is the result of a highly complex combination of factors that have been interacting for many years, both prior to and during school attendance. The quality of the instruction received is, naturally, vitally important, but it is far from being the only factor influencing achievement. Some of the factors considered to be most crucial are discussed briefly in the following paragraphs. The list is by no means complete, but the characteristics discussed may be those the school will wish to include in pretesting releases.

It should be noted that several variables known to correlate with school achievement are *not* mentioned in these paragraphs, among them the racial mix of the school population, socioeconomic status of parents, and educational level of parents. The omission is intentional. Although it is known that these factors are statistically related to achievement at the present time, the nature of the relationship is by no means clear. And it is likely that the reason these variables *seem* to predict achievement is that they form a rough index to the more general characteristics described below, especially those relating to the nature of the community. While it is far easier to quantify "years of education of adults" than it is to quantify "value placed on education," the more critical variable is almost certainly the latter. We would urge, therefore, that any discussion of the nonschool factors related to achievement stress these affective characteristics rather than the census-type data.

Discussion of the factors influencing achievement is difficult at best, and unless it is well done, the resulting story may appear to "whitewash" the school of any responsibility for student achievement, when in fact the instructional program should attempt to compensate for any influences that may handicap learning.

A. Characteristics of the individual pupil

Potential for academic learning—In school-learning aptitude, as with most other human characteristics, there is a wide range of individual differences. Pupils differ greatly in their ability to demonstrate mastery of the skills and knowledges that are the goals of our instructional system.

Personal characteristics—Although it is difficult to assess the extent of their influence, it is inevitable that a pupil's health, personality traits, social adjustment, and interests affect, to some extent, both a pupil's achievement and the ability to demonstrate that achievement on a standardized achievement test. Desire to learn, interest in school, and willingness to put forth maximum effort are also contributing factors.

Activities outside of school—The way in which a child spends his or her time outside of school hours may either stimulate or tend to retard progress in school.

Previous attendance and achievement pattern—Pupils who move frequently from school to school, or who are absent from school a considerable proportion of the time, may be handicapped in their ability to profit from classroom instruction. School learning is a sequential process, with each day's achievement and each year's performance building on competencies already developed. Pupils who have not mastered the basic skills will experience increasing difficulty over the years, not only in those skills, but also in other content areas that utilize those skills, e.g., reading skills in social studies, mathematics skills in physics. Previous experiences of "success" and "failure" in school, as perceived by the pupil, may also affect confidence and the motivation to do well.

B. Characteristics of pupils' homes and of the community at large

The value placed on education—A pupil's perception of school, its importance, and its value, is influenced most strongly by family attitudes. But to a considerable extent, the community as a whole also plays a role in providing an atmosphere where formal learning is either valued and sought after or considered as something from which to escape.

The degree of school-home and school-community cooperation—In many instances, the effectiveness with which the school communicates both with parents and with the total community has a marked influence on the attitude and performance of pupils within the school. In

like manner, the degree to which parents and community are involved in the school's goals and activities may profoundly affect the pupil performance level in the school.

The opportunities provided by home and community for augmenting school learning—The average pupil is under the direct influence of a teacher about 30 hours a week during the nine or ten months of the school "year." It is, therefore, likely that some of the learning measured in an achievement test takes place *outside* the classroom. The degree to which *outside* learning experiences reinforce and enrich classroom instruction may have considerable influence on measured achievement.

IV. School-related factors influencing achievement

If the school wishes to do so, some of these factors may also be discussed in releases made prior to testing. Factors that may be mentioned include per-pupil expenditure, classroom size, special staff available, teacher experience and training, and staff mobility or turnover. We would also include here the school's preparedness to instruct pupils whose native language is not English. In other words, the factor critically affecting the achievement of non-English-speaking children is not their native language, but the ability of the school to plan an appropriate instructional program for them.

Effective Communication at the Time of Testing

The school's survey testing program itself typically extends over a period of several weeks. During this period, the communication emphasis is directed primarily towards teachers, parents, and pupils, rather than towards the community at large. To get the most from the testing program, school administrators should make every effort to ensure that the entire school staff supports the program; that they understand why the testing is being done, how the results are to be used, and the role each of them plays in the program's success. Truly effective communication with teachers and other school personnel would include pretest workshops, used to demonstrate techniques of test administration and to explain how the information obtained will be useful to them in their daily classroom work.

In turn, teachers and other school staff need to be able to communicate effectively with pupils and their parents. The anticipation as well as the actual experience of taking a test is sometimes an upsetting experience for children. The notion of testing may be anxiety-producing for parents as well. We talk about testing as being fundamentally for the good of the pupils, but how well is this fact communicated to them and to their parents? If teachers themselves are persuaded of the value of the testing, they may be able to talk with their pupils, explaining why the test is being given and how a better understanding of their own strengths and weaknesses can be helpful to them. Most importantly, pupils and their parents need to be reassured that the testing is being done *for* them, not *to* them, and that its purpose is not to label or judge individuals but to enable the school to plan for their continued learning. To create this climate for a successful testing program is not easy, but the degree to which it is achieved will have real significance for the value of the test results.

Effective Communication After Testing Is Completed

Reporting test results is the most difficult phase of effective communication between school and community. The task of making numerical data meaningful to the school staff and especially to the general public is critical to the success of the entire testing venture. Since the ways in which these data are reported and interpreted are extremely important, appropriate personnel within the system must give careful thought to two questions: *What* should be reported to *whom?* and *How* should the information be presented? No data should be released to the news media, or any other group, until it has been carefully analyzed and put into a format that will make it comprehensible to the audience to whom it is being reported. It is important, however, that this process be completed as soon as possible after the test results are available. A "leak" that leads to the publication of the data out of its appropriate context and without meaningful interpretation can be painfully counterproductive.

The following steps, taken prior to the release of test data to the news media or the general public, have proved helpful in a number of communities. First, the appropriate school administrators should be informed regarding test results for the system in general and for their individual districts or buildings in particular. Giving them this information before it is released to the public is not merely a courtesy. These administrators, at the local district or building level, will carry much of the burden of later explanation and interpretation of results, and it is critical that they be prepared to answer any questions that may arise. In a number of large school districts, principals and other administrative personnel are called together, and presented with the test results, along with explanations of their import. They are given an opportunity to comment on or question the data and the interpretation placed on these data. In some school districts, administrators are also given a kit of materials containing a suggested agenda for a local level meeting, capsule information on the testing program of the school system, good down-to-earth layman's definitions of test terms, and information regarding types of test scores and what they mean. Some of these materials could be made into visual aids to be used in reporting to parents and other concerned citizens.

In many school systems, posttest workshops are held for teachers and other school staff to inform them of the results for their own classrooms, buildings, and districts, both in relation to local or national normative data and in relation to results of past years' testing programs. Appropriate subjects for these workshops are: reporting test information to pupils and parents, the teachers' use of the test score information in improving and individualizing instruction, and the implications of test results for restructuring the curriculum.

A third procedure that has been found helpful in many areas is a carefully planned presentation of test results to the local school board. Such a presentation might parallel that described above for the school's administrative personnel. It is most important that lay school board members be given an adequate interpretation of what the results mean (and what *cannot* be inferred as well). Often this information is presented to the board in a formal report incorporating charts, graphs, and other descriptive information.

Once a formal report has been made to the school board, the document becomes public information. In the past, many school districts have been content to let the report "speak for itself." However, many school districts find it advisable to hold a press "briefing" or background session for representatives of the local press, radio, and television. At such a session, conducted by appropriate school personnel, information regarding the how and why of the testing program may be added to data in the written report. Explanations of the nature of standardized tests, types of scores, the meaning of "norms," and factors that influence achievement might also be included in such a session. The news coverage of the testing program is more likely to contain accurate interpretations of the test data if reporters have had an opportunity to become informed about tests and testing in general as well as about the specific results. Reporters must also be given ample opportunity to ask questions and to challenge the school staff's interpretation of the data. The school's representative must be prepared to answer difficult questions.

One further comment should be made. Distortion in the reporting of test results is sometimes an inevitable result of political or factional controversy within the community. More often, however, misrepresentation of the test results is not deliberate but is due to a lack of understanding on the part of the writer, reporter, or graphic artist who attempts to interpret a table of figures provided by the school system. Some common misunderstandings will be discussed below, but in general, the more complete the information supplied by the school system, the more likely it is that the published accounts will accurately report the results of the testing program.

GUIDELINES FOR PREPARING REPORTS OF ACHIEVEMENT TEST RESULTS

Determining what achievement test results should be reported to the community is, in the final analysis, an administrative policy decision that must be made at the local level. It should be understood, therefore, that the following discussion includes suggestions that we believe merit thoughtful consideration.

1. Do not use grade equivalents in reporting test results to the community.

Grade equivalents *seem* simple and straightforward, but serious misunderstandings may result from their use. For example, a score of 5.2 on a third grade test does not mean that the pupil is capable of doing fifth grade work; it simply means that the third grader did as well *on that third grade test* as the average fifth grader would be expected to do on the same test. Likewise, a score of 1.2 would not mean that the third grader could do only first grade work. It would mean that, on that test, the average first grader would probably achieve the same score.

2. In reporting average scores for groups of pupils, do not use **mean** scores *unless your test provides norms for group averages. Do not use individual pupil norms to interpret mean group performance.*

Most recently published standardized achievement batteries (including the Metropolitan and Stanford) provide group norms as well as individual pupil norms. Group norms describe the distribution of group averages within the standardization; the more familiar individual norms describe the distribution of individual pupils' scores. It is not hard to see that individuals vary much more than do groups; therefore, to use the wrong benchmark may be very misleading to the public.

For example, let's suppose that a particular score on a fifth grade reading test converted to a percentile rank of 54 and a stanine of 5 for an individual pupil. However, to have a group—say all fifth graders in a system—have that same score as an *average* (mean) would place that group much higher in the distribution of group averages—perhaps as high as stanine 7 or 8.

3. If the test you are using does not provide norms for group averages, then report the score corresponding to the local median or 50th percentile point, rather than the mean.

The median of a group of scores describes the achievement level of the typical pupil and may be more appropriately interpreted in terms of individual norms than may a mean. The mean is influenced by any extreme scores at either the high or low end of the score scale. For example, in a group of five scores—7, 6, 5, 5, 4—the median score is 5; the mean is 5.4. If, however, the highest score was 10, instead of 7, the median would remain 5, but the mean (arithmetic average) would be 6, in spite of the fact that only one score was *above* 6. For such a group of scores (10, 6, 5, 5, 4), the median of 5

is more descriptive of "average" or "typical" performance than is the mean of 6.

If only a single score is reported for a group, it becomes particularly important to point out that, in any large group, there is a *range* or spread of scores. Even where the middle score is low, there *are* many individuals performing at higher levels. To demonstrate again, in the set of scores 10, 6, 5, 5, 4, although median performance is 5, one score in the set is far above the median score.

In presenting this kind of material in a report of scores, the school administrator might wish to point out that the "national norm" is, in fact, the *median* for the national standardization group and to emphasize that where a score is identified as the "national norm," fully one half of the national sample were in fact scoring at or below that "norm," while half were scoring above the norm. It should be pointed out that a "norm" in this sense is simply a description of median or typical performance as it has been measured by the test instrument, and is not in any way to be construed as a standard of excellence.

Some communities insist on having test results reported in terms of the "percent of pupils scoring below the norm." If the report shows that 60 percent of its 4th graders are reading "below the norm," it should clearly state that, in the national population, *50 percent of the* pupils are reading "below the norm." It is also wise to point out that 40 percent of the local group are, in fact, performing above the norm.

4. If possible, report scores representing several points in the total score distribution.

A single reported score may give some useful information about the typical performance of a group of pupils, but it cannot be expected to give the full picture of that group's performance. It is useful to know how far above the median the top pupils are, and how far below the typical pupil the poorer pupils are. School administrators may choose to report the extremes of the score range (the highest and lowest scores obtained by the group), or they may prefer to report scores in terms of stanine ranges. The most widely used method, however, is to report the scores corresponding to the midpoints of the upper and lower halves of the score distribution. These two points represent the 75th and 25th percentiles, respectively. Together with the median, they divide the full range of scores into quarters at quartile points Q_3, Q_2, and Q_1.

Compare two groups with the *same* median or typical score of 50, on a test with scores from 1 to 100.

Points in the Score Range	Scores for Group A	Scores for Group B
75th percentile (Q_3)	90	60
50th percentile (median)	50	50
25th percentile (Q_1)	40	20

For each group, we have reported the three scores that divide the group into four subgroups, each including one fourth of the pupils of the group. Although both groups have the same median, more of the pupils in Group A are obtaining very high scores than in Group B, and fewer are obtaining extremely low scores. These additional pieces of information indicating the spread of achievement *within the group* have considerable implication for the instructional decision maker, and such data, when added to the median results, make the scores far more meaningful.

The reporting of scores for other points of the distribution can be carried further. Scores may be reported for the 10th and 90th percentile points in addition to those for the 25th, 50th, and 75th, but as a rule, beyond a certain point, reporting on more numbers increases the chance of public confusion.

5. Wherever appropriate, report test results in terms of more than one norm group or frame of reference.

For most standardized tests, national norm data are available as a benchmark or reference point to use in evaluating local test performance. By using national norms as a basis of comparison, the local school system can describe the performance of its pupils in terms of a group representative of pupils in the entire United States. National norms, since they are a representative sample of all the wide variations found in the United States, present a composite picture of national performance. However, there are very few individual communities in the entire nation that match that composite picture across all comparisons. In some communities, the discrepancies between local characteristics and those represented as the typical (by the national norm) are so great that the comparison may seem worthless, irrelevant, or even dangerous. Nevertheless, national norms do have meaning and importance for all school systems, regardless of the ways in which individual systems may differ from "norm," since they do describe the typical performance of the nation's schoolchildren. They form one frame of reference, a point of departure for decision making. In interpreting a school district's test results in relation to the national norm, school administrators may wish to point out the differences between their communities and the national norm group by making reference to the factors influencing achievement, mentioned above.

The meaningfulness of local test results may be enhanced by comparison of the system's scores with those of appropriate reference groups other than the national norm group. For example, state or regional norms may be used, if such are available; large-city, independent-school, and/or suburban "norms" have been developed by a few test publishers. Many other such "norms" have been or could be developed by school districts cooperating among themselves, or by county or state agencies.

The example below illustrates the possibilities of multiple comparisons.

3rd Grade Reading Comprehension (Standard Scores for March Testing)

Percentile Point	District	State	Nation
75th	52	61	54
50th	32	37	36
25th	11	15	12

From this table, it is easily understood that the typical (median) score for the city's pupils is 32, whereas that of the state is 37 and that of the nation (national norm) is 36. Statements about the 75th and 25th percentile points—25 percent of the city's pupils were above 52, but one fourth of the state's were above 61—are also easy to grasp. This table records test performance at three points in the total distribution for each of three different groups. Of course, when several sets of norms are reported, care must be taken to ensure that they all represent performance on the same measure and at the same time in the school year.

One of the most effective comparisons to be made is that of the school's current performance with its own past performance. A table showing 75th, 50th, and 25th percentile points for this year's score distribution as compared with last year's, or as compared with a local "norm" established using several years' results, can be used very effectively to demonstrate changes in the pattern of local achievement.*

6. Whatever reference or norm groups are used in the report should be carefully defined and described for the reader.

In the last analysis, a "norm" is not simply a table of numbers, but rather a description of the performance of real people at a certain time in their lives. The reader of the report should be informed about who that group of real people were. He must be able to judge how important, relevant, or useful he feels it is for the district's children to be compared with that norm group of children.

We have made previous mention of many intangible factors that seem related to the achievement of schoolchildren. There are, however, other characteristics of school districts and of the communities they serve that have also been shown to have a strong relationship to achievement levels and that *can* be measured and quantified. In selecting a national norm sample, publishers consider a number of such characteristics, many of which are reported in manuals or technical reports. Among the factors considered, perhaps the most commonly reported

---

*Test Service Notebook 133 on the measurement of growth describes how such figures are to be interpreted.

community statistics are the median family income and the median number of years of schooling completed by adults in the community. School characteristics reported include average class size, pupil-teacher ratio, teachers' training and experience, absentee rate, and pupil mobility.

To add further meaning to the test results, some of these variables should be considered in reporting local data. Such information requires careful explanation. The lay public may find it surprising to learn that adult income level, for example, is related to school achievement level. Some further clarification is needed, pointing out that it is not income per se, but the nature of the community that is important. Much of what a community can offer to its children is related to its socioeconomic level, and measures of income (and educational background) are simply indices of more general characteristics. Moreover, it would be erroneous to claim that differences between the local community and the national norm group are the *direct cause* of corresponding differences in obtained test scores. Although researchers have found definite relationships between test results and some of the variables mentioned above, it is not at all certain that they are related in a cause-and-effect pattern. Since many of these factors are closely interrelated, it is often impossible to determine which factors are operating in a given situation. Furthermore, there are other intangible factors at work, influencing relationships one way or another, including those factors listed above. Finally, the report must make every effort to discourage the public from concluding that becomes a relationship is found to exist, it is inevitable and unchangeable. It would be altogether false to permit the public to conclude from such data, "Since our community income level is well below the national average, we cannot hope ever to find our average 4th graders reading at or above the national norm." Communities well below the norm in many characteristics may still have schools whose typical pupils perform at or above the norm.

On the other hand, when a number of community and/or school characteristics are radically different from those of the national norm population, it would not be surprising to find that other characteristics, such as reading achievement scores, are also different. And while these community characteristics cannot be held accountable for the total achievement picture in a school system, they are important. Further, many of these characteristics are beyond the ability of the school to change or control. Important and difficult decisions must be made, at the local level, concerning which factors of this type should be reported and what explanations of them should be made in the accompanying text.

7. Wherever possible, avoid presenting tabular data showing within-community comparisons.

While it is helpful to compare the performance of individuals (or groups) with that of several reference groups of which they are a part, it is not particularly useful to compare any performance with that of some group of which one is *not* a member. In the same way, formal comparisons of one school with another, one area of the district with another, one racial, ethnic, or socioeconomic subgroup with another rarely serve any useful purposes and, indeed, might have many undesirable consequences. It is almost inevitable that the public will tend to "rate" the groups by their test results, since each is likely to vary in its level of median performance, regardless of the fact that the spread of scores among pupils within each subgroup will be even greater than the spread of group medians within the district.

If a school district is obliged to release test information on a school-by-school basis, every effort should be made to give the reader of the report adequate information for drawing appropriate conclusions from the data. Information about each school's characteristics in comparison with those of the district as a whole might be included in a fashion similar to that suggested above for the city and the national norm group.

8. Where possible, report information concerning performance on specific behavioral objectives.

Currently, much attention is being focused on the development, at the local level, of specific curriculum objectives and their expression in terms of observed behavior, and the demand for information about local pupil performance in terms of these objectives is growing. Each item included in a normreferenced survey achievement test *does* measure a specific curriculum objective that could be stated in behavioral terms. Some test publishers issue reports tying the item to the objective. In other cases, an item analysis option is part of the scoring service for the test. In reporting to the community, information concerning performance by specific behavioral objectives should be included, if possible. Parents and other interested adults in the community can easily understand this type of reporting because it describes definite tasks to which they can relate their own experience. Thus, a school district may report that

> By April of grade four, we expect that 60% of all pupils should be able to compute correctly the difference between two four-digit numbers, when the problem is set in the horizontal form. In the standardized test recently administered, 50% of our fourth graders responded correctly to an item measuring this objective.

Many objectives may not be clearly understood without an example of the required behavior. Thus, in the above report, the following sentence might be added: "An example of such a problem might be 9863 − 5429 = ?" However, it should be clearly understood that actual items from the test must *not* be used in such a report and readers should be told that examples used are not from the test itself.

If local item analysis data comes from a testing date roughly equivalent to the time of year at which national normative data were collected, the district may wish to report, along with its local "percent correct" for an item or group of items, the parallel information for the norm group. Thus to the statement above could be added,

> In the national norm group for the test, however, 65 percent of 4th graders were able to respond correctly to this item.

Of course, the district report must not stop with simply reporting these figures. The action to be taken as a result of these findings should also be included in the report. Were the expectations unrealistic? Should the curriculum be changed? The question "What are you going to do about it?" must be approached in the report.

9. Interpret test results in terms of their curricular implications.

Skills such as phonics and mathematics computation, which are fairly closely defined and which are hierarchical in their development, lend themselves best to this type of interpretation. For example, the school might report,

> This year, we have revised and expanded our phonics program in grade 1, as part of our restructuring of the elementary reading curriculum. From analysis of tests given in previous years, we had determined that our

pupils were having more difficulty than the national school population with the matter of reversals, i.e., reading pin for nip, dab for bad, etc. We therefore tried to strengthen our instructional program in this area.

On the test recently administered to our first graders, there were four items measuring this skill at various levels of difficulty. Below are the data on the percent of pupils answering each item correctly on the national norm population and in our own system.

Percent Answering Correctly

	National	Local
a)	70	80
b)	75	85
c)	65	75
d)	50	60

From this information, our reading supervisors are encouraged to feel that difficulty with reversals has been overcome by the revised instructional program. In fact, our pupils are now performing at a level somewhat above the national norm in this particular area. They will, of course, continue to check this periodically.

Of course, due to space limitations, data from only a few items or groups of items can be reported in this way. Yet, a few examples should be given to demonstrate that analysis of achievement test performance on specific content is a valuable tool for instructional planning.

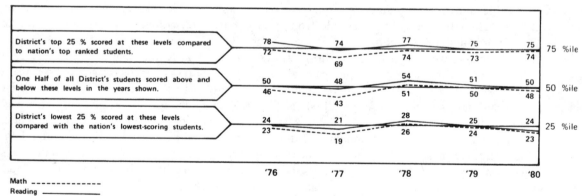

DISTRICTWIDE READING AND MATH 3RD GRADE SCORES

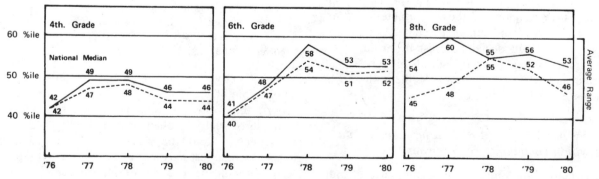

DISTRICTWIDE STANFORD READING AND MATH MEDIAN SCORES

10. Supplement tables with charts, profiles and diagrams.

Effective communication is difficult to achieve with the exclusive use of statistical tables. In order to help parents and the community at large to understand the import and significance of the numbers, materials should be presented graphically as well. Charts, profiles, diagrams, and the like are effective ways of underlining the important summary information, which may otherwise stay buried within the tables of numbers. See examples on previous page.

CONCLUSION

Effective communication requires that the school's report to the community be well planned and well executed. The report must be simple, direct, and easy to understand. Although charts and visuals may help to explain, the most important aspect of the report is the clarity of its textual message. Perhaps most importantly, the school's message about the implications of the test results—what they mean and what actions are to be taken—must be carefully thought out and presented in a straightforward manner that will be clear to all readers: parents, teachers, and the concerned public. After all, test results are only resources for the decision-making process. In order to be useful, they must be well used.

EXERCISE 61
FIRSTHAND PORTFOLIO ASSESSMENT

OBJECTIVE

To impart memorable firsthand experience in the construction of portfolios and the practice of portfolio assessment.

BACKGROUND

Portfolio is synonymous with work sample, and *portfolio assessment* refers to the evaluation of one's work samples. In this definition, "work sample" is defined quite broadly and may refer to anything from a drawing of a tree by a third-grader to the audiotape of a new jingle created by an advertising copywriter. Portfolio assessment in some occupations, such as those related to art, architecture, journalism, and music, has a very long history. Job applicants in such fields have traditionally been evaluated to a large degree not on the basis of test scores, but rather on the basis of past accomplishments as evidenced by a portfolio.

YOUR TASK

Create a portfolio to illustrate all that you have learned about psychological testing and assessment to date. The portfolio should be used to convince your instructor that regardless of grades you have received on any examinations to date, you really should be running an "A" in this course at this time. Submit the portfolio to your instructor. Await feedback.

EXERCISE 62
AUTHENTIC ASSESSMENT . . . REALLY!

OBJECTIVE

To enhance students' understanding of authentic assessment in an educational context.

BACKGROUND

Authentic assessment in educational contexts has been viewed as a tool to gauge performance on meaningful tasks including tasks that are transferable to nonacademic settings. Authentic assessment of students' writing skills would therefore be based on writing samples rather than on responses to multiple-choice tests. Authentic assessment of students' reading would be based on tasks that have to do with reading—preferably "authentic" reading such as an article in a local newspaper as opposed to a piece contrived especially for the purposes of assessment. Students in a college-level psychopathology course might be asked to identify patients' psychiatric diagnoses on the basis of videotaped interviews with the patients.

YOUR TASK

Create a way to assess "authentically" a student's knowledge of Chapter 10 of Cohen et al.'s *Psychological Testing and Assessment: An Introduction to Tests and Measurement.*

EXERCISE 63
PICK-A-TEST:
PRESCHOOL & EDUCATIONAL MEASURES

OBJECTIVE

To learn more about preschool and educational tests not reviewed in the textbook.

Table 10–1

Some Preschool and Educational Tests

Individual

Test	Description
Test of Sensory Functions in Infants	For ages 4 to 18 months, this test is designed to evaluate sensory processing.
Psychoeducational Profile	For preschoolers, this test is designed to assess learning patterns that may be a problem in the classroom.
Miller Assessment for Preschoolers	For 2.9 years through 5.8 years this test is designed to screen for mild to moderate developmental delays.
Boehm Test of Basic Concepts—Preschool Version	For ages 3 to 5 years, this test is designed to measure knowledge of basic relational concepts deemed necessary for achievement in the classroom.
Early Mathematics Diagnostic Kit	For ages 4 to 8 years, this test is designed to diagnose early difficulties with mathematics.
Assessment of Individual Learning Style: The Perceptual Memory Task	For ages 4 years and up, this test gauges perception and various aspects of visual and auditory memory.
Metropolitan Readiness Tests	For prekindergarten to first-grade students, this test is designed to measure the skills that contribute to success in learning.
Learning Behaviors Scale: Research Edition	For kindergarteners, this is a test of learning aptitude.
Wide Range Assessment of Memory and Learning	For ages 5 through 17 years, this is also a test of learning aptitude.
Adolescent and Adult Psychoeducational Profile	This test measures a variety of learning and related skills in autistic as well as developmentally disabled adolescents and adults.
Test of Academic Performance	For kindergarten through grade 12 students, this test assesses achievement in mathematics, spelling, reading, and writing through responses the student must make and not simply identify. This test is also amenable to group administration.

Group

Test	Description
California Diagnostic Mathematics Tests	For grades 1 through 12, this mathematics achievement test is designed for use in instructional planning and program evaluation.
Developing Cognitive Abilities Test: Second Edition	For grades 1 through 12 this test measures aspects of learning deemed essential for academic success.
Basic Economics Test	For grades 4 to 6, this test measures achievement in the area of economics. The results may be used in instructional planning and program evaluation.
Tests of General Educational Development (GED)	For candidates for a high school diploma of any age, this test is designed to assess skills and achievement of a "traditional high school education" for the purpose of granting a secondary school level (GED) diploma.
Descriptive Tests of Mathematics Skills	For beginning college students, this test is designed for use by institutions of higher learning to place students in appropriate entry-level mathematics courses. It may also be used as diagnostic test of mathematics-related deficiencies, and as a measure of outcome upon completion of course work.
College Basic Academic Skills Examination	For college sophomores and juniors, this is a measure of the skills and competencies one would be expected to achieve as a result of the completion of college.

BACKGROUND

The approach in your textbook is to highlight only a few of the many tests that exist in any given area. For every test covered in your textbook there may well be dozens of other tests designed to measure the same attribute(s). The Pick-A-Test exercise represents an opportunity to learn more about a particular test not covered in your textbook.

YOUR TASK

A list of preschool and educational tests along with a brief description of each is shown in Table 10-1. From this list, select one test that you think you would like to know more about. Then use all of the resources at your disposal to answer the following:

1. Describe what the test measures.
2. Who would be most apt to use this test? Why? Include in your answer sample questions the test user might hope to answer through the use of this test.
3. Who would be most apt to take this test? Why?
4. Describe the full range of people who would be appropriate to administer this test to, including comments about who would be inappropriate.
5. Describe what is known about the test's reliability.
6. Describe what is known about the test's validity.
7. Imagining that you are a measurement consultant, would you recommend this test to clients who are test users? Why or why not?

REFERENCES

Gelman, R., & Gallistel, C. R. (1986). *The child's understanding of number.* Cambridge, MA: Harvard University Press.

Ginsburg, H. P., & Opper, S. (1988). *Piaget's theory of intellectual development* (3rd ed.). Englewood Cliffs, NJ: Prentice-Hall.

Piaget, J. (1969). *The child's conception of the world* (J. Tomlinson & A. Tomlinson, Trans.). Totowa, NJ: Littlefield, Adams.

THE 4-QUESTION CHALLENGE

1. The examiner in the photo is administering the PPVT-R. Just from looking at this photo, and knowing nothing else about the PPVT-R, you could surmise that this test uses an easel format for test administration purposes and that it
   (*a*) probably has been proven to be sound psychometrically.
   (*b*) measures one facet of cognitive ability—receptive vocabulary.
   (*c*) may use a double-easel format for test administration.
   (*d*) may not be valid when used with children who have hearing impairments.
2. The acronym BINYL refers to a
   (*a*) test designed to measure English language proficiency.
   (*b*) binary-coded achievement test in an adaptive format.
   (*c*) floor covering used as an alternative to ceramic tile.
   (*d*) None of the above

3. In the years since the SAT was standardized in 1941, SAT scores have tended to
   (*a*) rise.
   (*b*) fall.
   (*c*) stay the same.
   (*d*) alternately rise and fall.
4. You are interviewing videographers for the purpose of finding one to videotape your wedding. The videographers all give you a sample of their work from someone else's wedding. In a sense, the type of assessment you are conducting may best be called
   (*a*) adaptive assessment.
   (*b*) authentic assessment.
   (*c*) portfolio assessment.
   (*d*) video assessment.

PART
4

PERSONALITY ASSESSMENT

Chapter 11

Personality Assessment:
Overview and
Objective Methods

**"How About If I Give You One-Half the 16 PF Today,
and the Other Half Tomorrow?"**

In The Three Faces of Eve, *Joanne Woodward posed a unique problem in personality assessment to her psychiatrist, played by Lee J. Cobb: "which personality to assess today?" In this particular shot, Ms. Woodward seems to be manifesting the "good" Eve, "Eve White"—but that's only one-third of the picture. Parenthetically we will note that from the perspective of Eve's husband (portrayed in the film by actor David Wayne), even the evil side of Eve, "Eve Black," may have had some personality features that could be construed as redeeming. As Gabbard and Gabbard (1987, p. 91) have observed, due to Eve's condition, Eve's husband "realizes the common male fantasy of being married to two women, one for public acceptance and one for sexual adventure."*

Outline for Chapter 11 of Cohen et al. (1996)
PERSONALITY ASSESSMENT: OVERVIEW AND OBJECTIVE METHODS

Defining and Measuring "Personality"
Traits, Types, and States
Personality traits
Personality types
Personality states
Measuring Personality
Methods of personality assessment

Logical or Content Test Construction
The Mooney Problem Checklist

Factor-Analytic Test Construction
The 16 PF
The NEO-PI and the NEO-PI-R

Test Construction by Empirical Criterion Keying
The MMPI
The MMPI-2
The standardization sample
Psychometric properties
An evaluation
The MMPI-A

The Theoretical Approach to Test Construction
The Edwards Personal Preference Schedule (EPPS)

Clinical versus Actuarial Prediction

CLOSE-UP:
Limitations of Self-Report

EVERYDAY PSYCHOMETRICS:
Are Unisex Norms for the MMPI-2 Needed? Would They Work?

EXERCISE 64
"PERSONALITY" AND ITS ASSESSMENT

OBJECTIVE

To enhance understanding of and provide firsthand experience with the concept of "personality"—as well as its assessment.

BACKGROUND

Just as a number of different theories regarding the nature of intelligence have been set forth, so different personality theorists have set forth a variety of definitions of "personality." Many such definitions make reference to constructs such as traits, states, and type. A *trait* has been defined in many ways but for our purposes we may define it, after Guilford (1959, p. 6), as "any distinguishable, relatively enduring way in which one individual varies from another." *State* refers to the transitory exhibition of a personality trait. *Personality* may be defined as a unique constellation of traits and states, and *personality type* may be defined as a constellation of traits and states that is similar in pattern to one identified category of personality within a taxonomy of personalities.

YOUR TASK

1. Using terms such as "traits," "states," and "personality type," develop your own definition of the word *personality;* what does "personality" mean *to you*?
2. Outline a plan for measuring personality based upon the definition you developed. In your outline, be sure to address each of the following questions:

   - What is the purpose of the personality test you've developed? What is it designed to do?
   - Is it to be used to measure traits, types, states, or some combination thereof?
   - Is it to be used to distinguish people on the basis of the healthiness of their personality? Is it to be used to distinguish people on the basis of the suitability of their personalities for a particular kind of work? Is it to be used in general research on personality?
   - What kinds of items will your test contain? How will you decide on the content and wording of these items? Would you, for example, rely on a particular theory of personality in devising these items? Or

would you rely on no particular theory, but rather on your own life experiences?
   - In writing your test items, did you use a true/false format or some other format? Will the items of your test be grouped in any particular order?
   - How might you convincingly demonstrate that your test measures what it purports to measure?

3. Which strategy of test construction do you think you would employ and why?
   (a) logical or content test construction?
   (b) factor analytic test construction?
   (c) test construction by empirical criterion keying? or
   (d) the theoretical approach to test construction?

EXERCISE 65
GEORGE WASHINGTON'S 16 PF

OBJECTIVE

To impart firsthand experience with a computerized, narrative report of personality based on a widely used personality test.

BACKGROUND

Figure 11-1 is a computerized, narrative report for the scoring and reporting of the 16 PF of George Washington (as in "father of our country") at age 44. No, the publishers of the 16 PF were not distributing the test as early as 1776. Rather, several psychologists familiar with the test were asked to study biographical information on Washington and then derive a profile showing how they think he would have scored.

YOUR TASK

Read and comment in writing on George Washington's 16 PF. Knowing George Washington's place in American history, what if anything about this report surprises you? What if anything about this report are you not surprised by?

Now pretend you are a vocational counselor at a large and prestigious vocational counseling firm. Going through the file of a 44-year-old client named George Washington, you find this 16 PF report. Just on the basis of this report, what type of career would you advise Mr. Washington to pursue? Why? Make sure to discuss the role of cultural factors in your decision.

Figure 11-1

George Washington's 16 PF

"Now where am I supposed to get a number 2 pencil?"

```
        N A R R A T I V E    S C O R I N G    R E P O R T
        for The Sixteen Personality Factor Questionnaire— 16 PF


    This report is intended to be used in conjunction with professional
    judgment. The statements it contains should be viewed as hypotheses
    to be validated against other sources of data.   All information in
    this report should be treated confidentially and responsibly.

    NAME-George Washington
                                                        July 4, 1776
                                                        AGE-44; SEX-M

  * * * * * * * * * * * * * VALIDITY SCALES * * * * * * * * * * * * * * *
  *                                                                     *
  *   Validity indicators are within acceptable ranges.                 *
  *      Faking good/MD (sten) score is very low (2).                   *
  *      Faking bad (sten) score is extremely low (1).                  *
  * * * * * * * * * * * * * * * * * * * * * * * * * * * * * * * * * * * *
```

Figure 11-1   *(continued)*

```
      SCORES                             16 PF   PROFILE
   Raw  Sten     LEFT MEANING   1 2 3 4 5 6 7 8 9 10  RIGHT MEANING      %
        U  C                            average
                            ---------------------------
    7   4  4  A    Cool, Reserved      !<---    !      Warm, Easygoing   23
   12  10 10  B Concrete Thinking      !   ---------->  Abstract Thinking 99
   23   9  9  C    Easily Upset        !   -------->   Calm, Stable      96
   15   7  7  E    Not Assertive       !   --->!       Dominant          77
   10   4  4  F   Sober, Serious     . !<---    !      Enthusiastic      23
   17   8  8  G      Expedient         !   ----->      Conscientious     89
   23   9  9  H      Shy, Timid        !   ------->    Venturesome       96
    4   3  3  I    Tough-Minded      <------   !       Sensitive         11
    6   5  5  L      Trusting          !  <-    !       Suspicious       40
   10   4  4  M      Practical        !<---    !       Imaginative       23
    9   6  6  N     Forthright         !   ->  !        Shrewd           60
    6   4  4  O   Self-Assured        !<---    !       Self-Doubting     23
    8   5  5  Q1   Conservative        !  <-   !        Experimenting    40
   16   9  9  Q2  Group-Oriented       !   ------ -->  Self-Sufficient   96
   19   9  9  Q3   Undisciplined       !   ------->    Self-Disciplined  96
    9   5  5  Q4     Relaxed           !  <-   !        Tense, Driven     40
                            ---------------------------
```

Note: "U" indicates uncorrected sten scores. "C" indicates sten scores corrected for distortion (if appropriate). The interpretation will proceed on the basis of corrected scores. This report was processed using
male adult (GP) norms for Form A.

SECOND-ORDER FACTORS

Extraversion..average (4.5)
Anxiety.......low (2.9)
Tough Poise...high (7.8)
Independence..high (7.5)
Control.......very high (8.9)

COMPOSITE SCORES

Neuroticism...below average (3.6)
Leadership....very high (9.4)
Creativity....very high (8.7)

Profile Pattern Code = 2133

PERSONAL COUNSELING OBSERVATIONS

Adequacy of adjustment is above average (7.4).
Rigidity of behavior controls is very high (8.9).

PRIMARY PERSONALITY CHARACTERISTICS OF SPECIAL INTEREST

Capacity for abstract skills is extremely high.
Problems are approached with calm emotional stability and
realism.
Regard for strict moral standards, duty, and conscientious
perseverance is high.
He is venturesome, socially bold and spontaneous, and not
easily inhibited. This tendency is very high.
As a person, he is realistic, tough-minded, and unsentimental.
Being self-sufficient, he prefers tackling things
resourcefully, alone.
He has a definite self-concept and sets out to control himself
to fit what he feels his social reputation requires.

Figure 11-1 *(continued)*

BROAD INFLUENCE PATTERNS

His attention is directed about equally toward the outer environment and toward inner thoughts and feelings. Extraversion is average (4.5).

At the present time, he sees himself as less anxious than most people. His anxiety score is low (2.9).

Tasks and problems are approached with emphasis upon rationality and getting things done. Less attention is paid to emotional relationships. This tendency is high (7.8).

His life style is independent and self-directed leading to active attempts to achieve control of the environment. In this respect, he is high (7.5).

He tends to conform to generally accepted standards of conduct and has probably internalized societal standards as his own. He feels strongly obligated to meet his responsibilities. This tendency is very high (8.9).

VOCATIONAL OBSERVATIONS

At client's own level of abilities, potential for creative functioning is very high (8.7).

Potential for benefit from formal academic training, at client's own level of abilities, is very high (9.4).

In a group of peers, potential for leadership is very high (9.4).

Potential for success in jobs that reward interpersonal, sales, and persuasive skills is very high (8.5).

Potential for success in job areas that reward precision and dependability is high (7.8).

Potential for growth to meet increasing job demands is extremely high (10.0).

The extent to which the client is accident prone is very low (2.1).

OCCUPATIONAL FITNESS PROJECTIONS

In this segment of the report his 16 PF results are compared with various occupational profiles. All projections should be considered with respect to other information about him, particularly his interests and abilities.

1. ARTISTIC PROFESSIONS

   Artist..........................extremely high (10.0)
   Musician........................high (8.1)
   Writer..........................extremely high (10.0)

2. COMMUNITY AND SOCIAL SERVICE

   Employment Counselor...........high (8.2)
   Firefighter....................extremely high (10.0)
   Nurse..........................very high (8.6)
   Physician......................average (6.2)
   Police Officer.................high (8.0)
   Priest (R.C.)..................average (5.3)
   Service Station Dealer.........average (5.9)
   Social Worker..................below average (4.4)

Figure 11-1   *(continued)*

3.   SCIENTIFIC PROFESSIONS

    Biologist....................extremely high (10.0)
    Chemist.....................extremely high (10.0)
    Engineer....................very high (9.4)
    Geologist...................very high (9.4)
    Physicist...................extremely high (10.0)
    Psychologist................extremely high (9.7)

4.   TECHNICAL PERSONNEL

    Accountant..................extremely high (10.0)
    Airline Flight Attendant.......average (6.1)
    Airline Pilot................very high (9.1)
    Computer Programmer..........extremely high (10.0)
    Editorial Worker............extremely high (10.0)
    Electrician.................extremely high (10.0)
    Mechanic....................extremely high (10.0)
    Psychiatric Technician.......extremely high (10.0)
    Time/Motion Study Analyst......high (8.0)

5.   INDUSTRIAL/CLERICAL PERSONNEL

    Janitor.....................very high (8.5)
    Kitchen Worker..............average (5.7)
    Machine Operator............high (8.1)
    Secretary-Clerk.............high (7.8)
    Truck Driver................above average (7.4)

6.   SALES PERSONNEL

    Real Estate Agent...........high (7.9)
    Retail Counter Clerk........above average (6.9)

7.   ADMINISTRATIVE AND SUPERVISORY PERSONNEL

    Bank Manager................very high (8.5)
    Business Executive..........extremely high (9.8)
    Credit Union Manager........high (8.4)
    Middle Level Manager........very high (9.3)
    Personnel Manager...........high (7.6)
    Production Manager..........very high (8.8)
    Plant Foreman...............high (8.2)
    Sales Supervisor............very high (8.5)
    Store Manager...............below average (4.4)

8.   ACADEMIC PROFESSIONS

    Teacher-Elementary Level.......above average (6.5)
    Teacher-Junior High Level......below average (3.5)
    Teacher-Senior High Level......below average (3.7)
    University Professor.........high (7.5)
    School Counselor............above average (7.3)
    School Superintendent.......very high (9.3)
    University Administrator.......extremely high (10.0)

Item Summary

Item responses have not been provided.

EXERCISE 66
EMPIRICAL CRITERION KEYING—CALIFORNIA STYLE

OBJECTIVE

To introduce the California Psychological Inventory (CPI), a personality test that was developed by the method of empirical criterion keying.

BACKGROUND

The CPI has been described as the "kissing cousin" of the MMPI because it was developed by so similar a method. The reading that follows contains more detailed information on the CPI.

YOUR TASK

Read the description of the CPI that follows and then respond in writing to the following two tasks:

1. Describe similarities and differences between the CPI and the MMPI-2.
2. Describe in detail a situation in which you think a counselor might wish to use the CPI with a client, and what the objective of the testing would be.

CALIFORNIA PSYCHOLOGICAL INVENTORY

In contrast to the MMPI, which was developed to assess maladjustment, the CPI was designed for use with normal populations aged 13 and older, and its scales emphasize more positive and socially desirable aspects of personality than do the scales of the MMPI.

The CPI is available from its publisher in its original form (Gough, 1956) or in a revised edition (Gough, 1987). The original edition of the test contains 18 scales, which may be grouped into four categories depending on whether they primarily measure interpersonal effectiveness (including measures of poise, self-assurance, and self-acceptance), intrapersonal controls (including measures of self-control and tolerance), academic orientation (including measures of achievement potential), or general attitudes toward life (including measures of conformity and interests). Eleven of the personality scales were empirically developed based on the responses of subjects known to display certain kinds of behaviors. Factors such as course grades, participation in extracurricular activities, and peer ratings were used in selecting the criterion groups (see Gough, 1956, 1975). Four scales, Social Presence, Self-Acceptance, Self-Control, and Flexibility were developed through internal-consistency item-analysis procedures. Also built

into the inventory were scales designed to detect response sets for faking favorable and bad impressions.

The 1987 revision of the test retained the 18 original scales with only minor changes in content and some rewriting or deletion of items to reduce sexist and/or other bias. Two new scales were added, Independence and Empathy, bringing the total number of scales contained in the 1987 revision of the test to 20. The 20 scales can be organized with reference to three independent themes derived from factor-analytic studies: (1) interpersonal orientation, (2) normative orientation, and (3) realization. Like its predecessor, this edition of the CPI may be hand- or computer-scored. Unlike its predecessor, the 1987 CPI manual provided a theoretical model of personality structure—one subsequently elaborated on in terms of its implications by Gough (1989, 1990) as well as by others (see, for example, Helson & Picano, 1990; Helson & Wink, 1987; Sundberg, Latkin, Littman, & Hagan, 1990).

Normative data for the original version of the CPI were obtained from the testing of 6,000 males and 7,000 females of varying age, socioeconomic status, and place of residence. Test-retest reliability coefficients reported in the CPI manual range from .55 to .75. One meta-analysis of 13 studies assessing the reliability of the CPI estimated test-retest reliability to be .77 and internal consistency to be .72 (Schuerger, Zarrella, & Hotz, 1993). Included in the manual is research concerning the feasibility of making various kinds of predictions with the test scores, predictions ranging from the probability of delinquency or dropping out of school to the probability of success among those in training for various occupations (such as dentists, optometrists, accountants, and so on). An abbreviated form of the original edition of the CPI has been found to correlate in the range of .74 to .91 with the original (Armentrout, 1977).

Like the MMPI, the CPI is a widely used instrument, with published versions of it available in more than two-dozen languages ranging from Arabic to Malaysian to Urdu (Pakistanese) and guides to assist in interpretation (see, for example, McAllister, 1988). Numerous studies reporting on new scales can be found in the professional literature. For example, Gough (1985) reported on the development of a "Word Orientation" (WO) scale for the CPI. The WO scale is composed of 40 items that were found to be correlated with criterion measures such as job performance rating. It was reported that high scorers on WO were dependable, moderate, optimistic, and persevering.

Professionals tend toward extremes when reviewing the CPI—either enthusiastically recommending its use, or not recommending it at all. These extremes were both represented in two reviews published in the *Ninth Mental Measurements Yearbook*. Acknowledging that the then existing edition of the test could be faulted for its lack of an underlying personality theory, the lack of research on profile interpretation, and the fact that the scales correlated with each other, Baucom (1985) went on to commend Gough for "the fruits yielded thus far from the

CPI" (p. 252). Eysenck (1985) criticized Gough for his rationale for the test, which he found to be at best, vague, and at worst, the product of convoluted logic. Eysenck struggled with Gough's assertion that terms used in the CPI such as "dominance" and "sociability" were not traits. Eysenck (1985) also had trouble accepting Gough's rationale for rejecting factor analysis, and ultimately did not recommend use of the test:

> Factor analysis is one important way of imposing some degree of order on this field, and attempting to reach agreed conclusions along methodologies. Gough's refusal to accept this discipline, which he does not attempt even to justify in terms of any kind of acceptable statistical or philosophical argument, leads us straight into a situation where personality models, different inventories, and choice of scales are subject to a kind of Dutch auction, rather than a scientific debate which might result in a universally acceptable conclusion. . . . On the principle that all possible information should be given the test user, the absence in the manual of item intercorrelations and factorial analyses is to be deplored, particularly as no rational argument is advanced to justify it. In the absence of such supporting evidence of internal validity, it is difficult to recommend the test to prospective users. (p. 253)

EXERCISE 67
CLINICAL VERSUS ACTUARIAL PREDICTION

OBJECTIVE

To promote generative thinking regarding the clinical and actuarial approaches to assessment.

BACKGROUND

An actuarial (or statistical) approach to assessment entails evaluation of test and other assessment data according to preset rules, the outcome of which is a statistical formula such as a regression equation—all of this in an effort to make a prediction on the basis of the assessment data. In what has been termed the clinical approach to assessment, interpretation of assessment data is made not on the basis of uniformly applied rules, but on the basis of the evaluating professional's judgment.

YOUR TASK

In what follows, you will read about "Dr. Actu" who subscribes to the actuarial approach to assessment, and "Dr. Clin" who subscribes to the clinical approach. Now pretend you are the head of a worldwide corporation that makes many personnel decisions daily. The workplace is a multicultural environment, and the people who staff the personnel department are committed to keeping it that way. Both Dr. Clin and Dr. Actu apply to head up the personnel department. Who would you select for the position? Why?

CLINICAL VERSUS ACTUARIAL PREDICTION

Suppose that two psychologists, one who subscribes to the actuarial approach, "Dr. Actu," and one who subscribes to the clinical approach, "Dr. Clin," were called on to make a recommendation concerning whether a "Mr. T. Taker" should be hired as an executive with a large corporation. Both clinicians are given identical files on Mr. Taker, containing scores on various standardized tests, case-history data, projective-test data, and interview material. Both clinicians are aware that the corporation wants to hire executives with superior abilities in the areas of leadership, decision making, organizing and planning, interpersonal skills, and creativity.

Dr. Actu might approach his task by going through all of the available data on Mr. Taker and then applying certain preset rules (for example, some equation to combine the data for each variable) to come up with a score on each of the five variables to be judged. If the scores on, say, three out of five of these variables exceed a certain preset cutoff score, Dr. Actu would recommend that Mr. Taker be hired. Dr. Clin may or may not arrive at the same recommendation on the basis of his analysis of the same data. The process employed by Dr. Clin is more freewheeling and less replicable than that employed by Dr. Actu. Something—virtually anything—in the data on Mr. Taker is capable of influencing Dr. Clin's judgment as to whether this applicant has executive potential. For example, Dr. Clin may have noticed that the written physical description of Taker included the fact that he wore one gold earring to the interview. On the basis of this fact alone, Dr. Clin might recommend that Taker not be hired; having interviewed hundreds of executives and prospective executives for this firm, Dr. Clin has mentally formulated an image of what the successful male executive looks like—and there is no provision for one gold earring in that picture.

The sample situation we describe is exaggerated for the purposes of illustration, for the clinical approach is characterized by careful scrutiny of all available data; and conclusions are typically drawn on the basis of a constellation of factors, not just one (such as preference for wearing earrings). Still, our summary is useful in highlighting the nature of clinical as opposed to actuarial judgments. Dr. Clin may have rejected Taker solely on the basis of an element of his attire. Taker might also have "lost points" with Dr. Actu for this manner of dress as well, but only if "manner of dress" were one of the preset criteria to be rated in the assessment equation; exactly what importance, weight, or relevance the earring would be given in the hiring equation would have to have been placed into the selection equation before the selection procedure had begun. The actuarial approach, in contrast to the clinical one, is strictly empirical in nature. If a large body of existing data indicates that males who wear one earring to employment interviews (or, stated more broadly, persons who dress in a manner inconsistent with the "image" of a particular corporation) turn out to be poor executives, such persons will lose points in their evaluation. With respect to the clinical approach, the body of data being used as a reference is the information, knowledge, and experience of the clinician making the judgment.

A difference between the two approaches that must be emphasized concerns the *meaning* assigned to certain data. Because the actuarial approach is so empirical in nature, meaning of responses and behaviors is deemphasized in favor of how such responses and behaviors correlate with a certain criterion. If successful male executives for the company in question do not tend to sport earrings, that will be sufficient for Dr. Actu to reject the applicant. Alternatively, Dr. Clin might overlook and "see beyond" the earring, noting that other data suggest Taker to be a highly creative, artistic, and independent individual who would do well in a particular executive slot that the corporation needs to fill. Clin's report to the corporation might recommend Taker be offered the executive position, conditional on his removal of the earring. If Taker was hired, consented to removing the earring, and did very well in the position, the corporation might then seek to recruit other applicants who fit a similar profile.

Since there is a finite set of data available to the clinician, it would be nice if there was one best way to interpret that data. An architect of the actuarial approach, Meehl (1984) likened the clinical approach to leaving a supermarket and saying, "Well, it looks like I spent about 17 bucks worth" instead of consulting the cash register receipt to know what was actually spent. Citing reasons why the actuarial approach has failed to achieve widespread adoption, Meehl's list included the following factors: (1) the ubiquity of irrationality in the conduct of human affairs, (2) sheer ignorance, (3) the threat of technological unemployment, (4) strong theoretical identifications on the part of some clinicians, (5) claims that actuarial techniques are "dehumanizing," (6) mistaken concepts of ethics, and (7) computer phobia.

Einhorn (1984) has asked how we can presume to make predictions about the course of human life if we can't even do it for interest or mortgage rates. Einhorn argued that clinicians must accept the reality that there will always be error in prediction. Since clinicians have more limited information-processing than computers, there would appear to be more room for error in the clinical approach.

Others have added that the process of making predictions clinically may be tedious whereas computers may make the same or better decisions within seconds. And others have argued that computers compute and can at best show low levels of relations; in essence, they yield regression equations with neither understanding, compassion, nor the ability to anticipate unforeseen and unanticipated (that is, nonprogrammed) events. With respect to the latter point, no computer ever predicted that there would be a national oil shortage in this country in the early 1970s. The shortage arose as a result of an Arab fuel boycott, which arose in part as a consequence of the support of the United States for Israel in the *Yom Kippur* war. Thus while there was no shortage of computer printouts indicating rates of fossil fuel consumption and production in this country and throughout the world, no computer could have forecasted the unlikely chain of events that resulted in not only the oil shortage but also a number of related consequences (such as gas-station lines, federal energy usage restrictions and incentives, and the imposition of a national speed limit of 55 miles per hour).

Clearly, both the clinical and the actuarial approach have much to be said for them. The actuarial approach tends to be much more efficient than the clinical one in terms of making predictions in a variety of situations, especially those in which many predictions must be made and a large data base for making those predictions exists (Meehl, 1954, 1959, 1965). Owing to its rigor, the actuarial approach lends itself well to research; volumes have been written, for example, concerning descriptions of persons with particular MMPI patterns. Being less subject to empiricism and to rules, the clinical approach has as its chief advantage flexibility and the potential for using the novel combination of data ("programmed" as well as "unprogrammed") to arrive at decisions, descriptions, predictions, and hypotheses.

In summary, the difference between the clinical and the actuarial approach to assessment is in some ways similar to the difference between a courtroom trial that will result in a ruling by either a judge or a computer. Both the computer and the judge will take in all of the evidence and weigh it. Each will arrive at a verdict on the basis of the weight of the evidence and the applicable standard ("guilty beyond a reasonable doubt" in a criminal proceeding and "preponderance of the evidence" in a civil proceeding). The computer will weigh the evidence according to preprogrammed rules and arrive at a verdict. The judge will also weigh it according to ("preprogrammed") rules but with more openness to nuances of information that might not be in the "rulebook." Whereas the computer's decision can be expected to conform to the letter of the law, the judge's decision can be expected to conform with not only the letter of the law but its spirit as well.

EXERCISE 68
PERSONALITY TEST SCALES

OBJECTIVE

To enhance understanding of and provide firsthand experience with personality test scales.

BACKGROUND

A personality test may contain numerous scales—some designed to assess traits or attributes associated with personality (such as the clinical scales of the MMPI-2) and some designed to measure other aspects of performance on the test. As an example of the latter, consider the three validity scales of the MMPI-2 discussed below.

The "L" scale of the MMPI-2, sometimes referred to as the "Lie" scale, contains items that are somewhat negative but that apply to most people—for example, "I gossip a little at times" (Dahlstrom et al., 1972, p. 109). The willingness of testtakers to reveal *anything* negative about themselves will be called into question if the score on the L scale does not fall within certain limits. The F scale ("f" referring to frequency/infrequency) is composed of items that are infrequently endorsed by normal test-takers; an example is "It would be better if almost all laws were thrown away" (Dahlstrom et al., 1972, p. 115). Because a testtaker's endorsement of items on the F scale may not fit into any known pattern of deviance, an elevated F scale may suggest that the testtaker did not take the test seriously, responded at random to the questions, misinterpreted some of the questions, and/or was trying to "fake bad" on the test. The K ("Correction") scale is composed of items reflective of an overwilling-ness or underwillingness to admit to deviancy, and scores on it may be used to statistically correct scores on some of the clinical scales.

YOUR TASK

1. Create a nine-item Credibility (CR) Scale to be used in the scoring of the Mid-Pawling Personality Inventory (MPPI; see Appendix A). The test was written with nine items that belong on this scale. For some of the items, a "True" response will earn a point on the CR scale. For other items, a "False" response will earn a point on the CR scale. The higher one's CR scale, the greater the possibility that the respondent was either not taking the test seriously, lying, or responding randomly. In the space below, list your candidates for the nine-item CR scale, indicating whether it is a "True" or a "False" response that earns the respondent a point on it.

Items Scored on the CR Scale of the MPPI

Item Number	Response to be Scored (True or False)
——	——
——	——
——	——
——	——
——	——
——	——
——	——
——	——
——	——

Now, to put your CR Scale to use, award one point for each incredible response your subject made on the MPPI. The total CR score of your subject may there-fore range from 0 (if there were no incredible responses) to 4. In consultation with your classmates, determine what the mean, median, and modal CR score was for all of the people who took the MPPI. How did your subject compare to other testtakers with respect to her or his CR score?

2. Another type of scale that could be used as an aid in determining whether an individual is responding randomly is one which focuses on the consistency of the testtaker's response. On the MPPI, for example, we could evaluate whether the testtaker answered different pairs of items in a way that makes sense. Consider in this context the following pair of items:

16. I enjoy watching soap operas.
61. I do not enjoy soap operas.

Was consistency or inconsistency evident in the response to each of these two items? Items 16 and 61 comprise one item pair that could be used to devise what we will call an Inconsistency (IN) Scale for the MPPI. In addition to this item pair, there are four other item pairs that could be used in our IN Scale. Find them, and check whether your subject responded consistently or inconsistently to each of them. Obtain an IN score by summing the number of inconsistent responses. In consultation with your classmates, deter-mine what the mean, median, and modal IN score was for all of the people who took the MPPI. How did your subject compare to other testtakers with respect to her or his IN score? How does your subject's IN score compare to your subject's CR score? Are both scores higher or lower than average? What might you conclude from these scores?

Item Pairs on the MPPI IN Scale (List item numbers)	Consistent or Inconsistent Response (Check one)	
	Consistent	Inconsistent
Item #16 and Item #61	_____	_____
Item #__ and Item #__	_____	_____
Item #__ and Item #__	_____	_____
Item #__ and Item #__	_____	_____
Item #__ and Item #__	_____	_____
Total number of inconsistent responses = _____		

3. Do groups of people who take the MPPI tend to differ in any significant way on the test as a whole or on any particular grouping of items? For example, do males differ from females with respect to their response on any group of items? To explore the hypothesis that a difference does exist between the responses of male and female testtakers, you are now going to create your own Masculinity/Femininity (M/F) Scale. Keeping in mind that there aren't any right or wrong answers here, select five items on the test that you believe will best differentiate females from males—that is, items on which you believe males and females might respond differently. For example, if you believe that females might respond differently than males to item #27 ("I love shopping for shoes"), include item #27 on your list. List the five items on your M/F Scale below, as well as whether you would predict males or females to respond with a "True" or "False" response to each of the items.

The MPPI M/F Scale

Item Number	Males would respond . . . (Circle one)	Females would respond . . . (Circle the other one)
_____	True or False	True or False
_____	True or False	True or False
_____	True or False	True or False
_____	True or False	True or False
_____	True or False	True or False

How does the M/F Scale you've created compare to the M/F Scale created by your classmates; do you share many of the same items? Now, looking at the class data only from testtakers whose CR and IN scores were 0, determine if there were any items on the entire test that did indeed differentiate male from female respondents. How many such items were there? How many of them had you selected for your M/F Scale?

4. Let's return to the question posed above, "Do groups of people who take the MPPI tend to differ in any significant way on the test as a whole or on any particular grouping of items?" Perhaps groups of people—depressed versus nondepressed people, students versus business people, members of serpent-handling religious cults versus nonmembers, and so on—do differ in their responses to clusters of items on the MPPI. In collaboration with your classmates as a project, and using the data you've already collected as a kind of "pilot study," create your own MPPI Scale consisting of any number of items you deem necessary. What is the name of the scale you've created? What particular group of people do you think can be identified using this scale? Why? What purpose might such a scale serve? How might you go about setting cutoff scores in identifying membership in the group you've identified? If feasible, conduct a study under your instructor's supervision to determine if the scale you created does differentiate members of the target population from nonmembers.

5. With items sometimes overlapping with the MPPI's CR scale, we can identify another type of response. We will call this scale the "Unusual Response scale" or "UN-scale." All of these are responses that would not be expected from most people. Like the CR scale, responses scored on the UN-scale may be indicative of an inability to take the test seriously or of random responding. And if this were a valid personality test—which we emphasize it is not—responses scored on the UN-scale might be indicative of severe psychopathology. Thirteen items qualify for placement on this UN-scale. Identify ten of them below.

Items Scored on the UN-Scale of the MPPI	
Item Number	Response to Be Scored (True or False)
_____	_____
_____	_____
_____	_____
_____	_____
_____	_____
_____	_____
_____	_____
_____	_____
_____	_____
_____	_____

6. Some people taking a test of personality, for their own reasons, either "fake good" (attempt to present themselves in as favorable a light as possible) or "fake bad" (attempt to present themselves in as negative a light as possible). Let's devise a scale on the MPPI designed to measure the degree to which a testtaker is attempting to fake good or bad. We'll call the scale the "FA" (or Faking) scale, and it will be comprised of two subscales designated as "FA+" for faking good, and "FA−" for faking bad. On the FA+ scale are five

items disclosing something that is somewhat negative, but still something that most people nonetheless would admit to. Testtakers who have a high FA+ may either be trying to fake good, or simply trying to present themselves in a way that is socially desirable. On the FA− scale are five items that in essence say something very negative about the testtaker. A high FA− score may be indicative of someone who is trying to fake bad, as might be the case for an individual attempting to be committed to a mental institution or be excused from a crime on the basis of an insanity plea. Identify the five items on each of the scales below.

FA+ Scale
MPPI Item Number   *(True or False)*

——————   ——————
——————   ——————
——————   ——————
——————   ——————
——————   ——————

FA− Scale
MPPI Item Number   *(True or False)*

——————   ——————
——————   ——————
——————   ——————
——————   ——————

EXERCISE 69
"JUST YOUR TYPE"

OBJECTIVE

To encourage critical thinking regarding a theory of personality linked to body type, to provide additional practice in scale development.

BACKGROUND

William Sheldon and his associates (Sheldon & Stevens, 1942; Sheldon, Dupertuis, & McDermott, 1954) proposed a personality typology based on body build. A description of this theory is presented in Figure 11-2.

YOUR TASK

After the description of Sheldon's somatotype typology that follows, respond to these two items.

1. Which body type would best describe you, and how accurate would the personality description be that characterizes that type? What about other people you

know; what body types best describe them, and how applicable would Sheldon's descriptions be to them? What types of studies would Sheldon have to conduct if he wanted to validate this theory? Which tools of assessment would be particularly useful in such research? What problems would you expect Sheldon to encounter in trying to conduct such research?

2. Develop a "Sheldon Scale" for the MPPI consisting of three subscales to measure endomorphy, ectomorphy, and mesomorphy. Explain whether the response to the item would be "True" or "False" to be scored on the scale. Each of these three subscales should have two items on it.

The Sheldon Scale of the MPPI

Endomorphy
MPPI Item #   *True or False*

——————   ——————
——————   ——————

Ectomorphy
MPPI Item #   *True or False*

——————   ——————
——————   ——————

Mesomorphy
MPPI Item #   *True or False*

——————   ——————
——————   ——————

EXERCISE 70
PICK-A-TEST: PERSONALITY TESTS

OBJECTIVE

To learn more about a personality test not reviewed in the textbook.

BACKGROUND

The approach in your textbook is to highlight only a few of the many tests that exist in any given area. For every test covered in your textbook there may well be dozens of other tests designed to measure the same attribute(s). The Pick-A-Test exercise represents an opportunity to learn more about a particular test not covered in your textbook.

YOUR TASK

A list of personality tests along with a brief description of each follows in Table 11-1, page 185. From this list,

Figure 11-2

Sheldon's Typology. William Sheldon and his associates believed that the body betrayed a great deal about the mind. More specifically, they believed that a person's body type told a great deal about the person's personality. To explore this theory scientifically, Sheldon developed a typology of body types. To be classified according to these body types, measurements of body mass had to be taken, and various ratios had to be calculated. On the basis of such data, people were classified with regard to three basic body types: the endomorph, the mesomorph, and the ectomorph. Associated with each of these body types are specific predispositions and temperaments. The endomorph, for example, was said to have a "viscerotonic" disposition, which implied, among other things, a love of good food and good company and general eventemperedness. The mesomorph is "somatotonic": action-oriented, adventuresome, and dominating, among other things. The ectomorph is "cerebrotonic": physically and emotionally restrained, future-oriented, and introverted.

For Sheldon, the task of assessment was one of classifying persons with respect to three dimensions of physique. Each individual was rated on a scale from 1 to 7 according to the amount of endomorphy, mesomorphy, and ectomorphy that was deemed to be present. An individual who was the epitome of an endomorph would thus be rated a "7-1-1"; 7 for endomorphy (the highest possible rating), 1 for mesomorphy, and 1 for ectomorphy (the lowest possible rating). An individual who was high on mesomorphy, medium on endomorphy, and low on ectomorphy would be rated 3-7-1; presumably such as individual would also have a temperament that corresponded to this particular "somatotype" (or "body type").

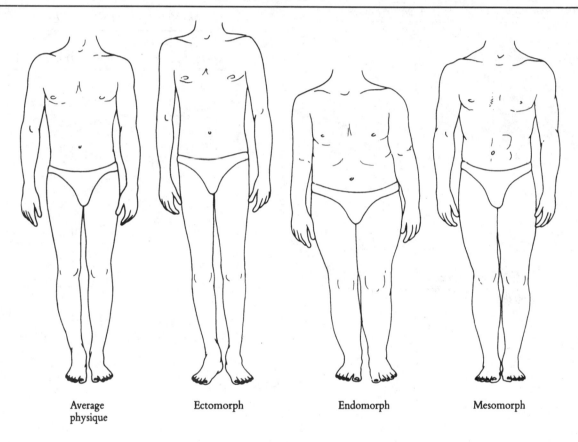

Average physique   Ectomorph   Endomorph   Mesomorph

select one test that you would like to know more about. Then use all of the resources at your disposal to answer the following:

1. Describe what the test measures.
2. Who would be most apt to use this test? Why? Include in your answer sample questions the test user might hope to answer through the use of this test.
3. Who would be most apt to take this test? Why?
4. Describe the full range of people who would be appropriate to administer this test to, including comments about who would be inappropriate.
5. Describe what is known about the test's reliability.
6. Describe what is known about the test's validity.
7. Imagining that you are a measurement consultant, would you recommend this test to clients who are test users? Why or why not?

REFERENCES

Armentrout, J. A. (1977). Comparison of the standard and short form score of Canadian adults on the California Psychological Inventory. *Perceptual & Motor Skills, 45*(3, Pt. 2), 1088.

Table 11-1

Some Tests of Personality

Test	Description
Children's Personality Questionnaire	Designed to evaluate children's behavior with regard to 14 personality factors, this test may have application in the evaluation of children with emotional and conduct disorders.
High School Personality Questionnaire	Designed to assist in the diagnosis of behavior problems in adolescents, this test, like the Children's Personality Questionnaire, focuses on 14 personality factors for interpretation.
Gordon Personal Profile Inventory	This test consists of two companion instruments (the Gordon Personal Profile and the Gordon Personal Inventory) and is designed for use in personal and vocational counseling, as well as occupational selection and placement.
Basic Psychological Inventory	Designed to measure personality and selected aspects of psychopathology, this test requires a fifth-grade reading ability and has separate norms for adolescents and adults.
California Life Goals Evaluation Schedules	Designed to identify personality types relative to various recreational and occupational activities, the manual includes average responses of people in different occupational groups.
Multidimensional Personality Questionnaire	Designed to measure various dimensions of personality, some of which bear resemblance to the "big five."
Personality Assessment Inventory	Designed to measure various symptoms of psychopathology, this test can be computer scored and interpreted and is available in a Spanish language edition.
Psychological Screening Inventory	Designed to screen for psychopathology, administration time can be as brief as 15 minutes while scoring can be accomplished in as little as 3 minutes.

Baucom, J. (1985). Review of the California Psychological Inventory. In J. V. Mitchell (Ed.), *The ninth mental measurements yearbook.* Lincoln: University of Nebraska Press.

Dahlstrom, W. G., Welsh, G. S., & Dahlstrom, L. E. (1972). *An MMPI handbook: A guide to use in clinical practice and research.* Minneapolis: University of Minnesota Press.

Einhorn, H. J. (1984). *Accepting error to make less error in prediction.* Paper presented at the 92nd annual meeting of the American Psychological Association, Toronto, Ontario, Canada.

Eysenck, H. J. (1985). Review of the California Psychological Inventory. In J. V. Mitchell (Ed.), *The ninth mental measurements yearbook.* Lincoln: University of Nebraska Press.

Gabbard, K., & Gabbard, G. O. (1987). *Psychiatry and the cinema.* Chicago: University of Chicago Press.

Gough, H. G. (1956). *California psychological inventory.* Palo Alto, CA: Consulting Psychologists Press.

Gough, H. G. (1957). *California psychological inventory manual* (Revised 1964). Palo Alto, CA: Consulting Psychologists Press.

Gough, H. G. (1975). *California psychological inventory manual* (Revised). Palo Alto, CA: Consulting Psychologists Press.

Gough, H. G. (1985). A work orientation scale for the California psychological inventory. *Journal of Applied Psychology, 70,* 505–513.

Gough, H. G. (1987). *California psychological inventory* (Revised 1987). Palo Alto, CA: Consulting Psychologists Press.

Guilford, J. P. (1959). *Personality.* New York: McGraw-Hill.

Helson, R., & Picano, J. (1990). Is the traditional role bad for women? *Journal of Personality and Social Psychology, 59,* 311–320.

Helson, R., & Wink, P. (1987). Two conceptions of maturity examined in the findings of a longitudinal study. *Journal of Personality and Social Psychology, 53,* 531–541.

McAllister, L. W. (1988). *A practical guide to CPI interpretation* (2nd ed.). Palo Alto, CA: Consulting Psychologists Press.

Meehl, P. E. (1954). *Clinical versus statistical prediction: A theoretical analysis and a review of the evidence.* Minneapolis: University of Minnesota Press.

Meehl, P. E. (1959). A comparison of clinicians with five statistical methods of identifying psychotic MMPI profiles. *Journal of Consulting Psychology, 6,* 102–109.

Meehl, P. E. (1965). Seer over sign: The first good example. *Journal of Experimental Research in Personality, 1,* 27–32.

Schuerger, J. M., Zarrella, K. L., & Hotz, A. S. (1993). Factors that influence the temporal stability of personality by questionnaire. *Journal of Personality and Social Psychology, 56,* 777–783.

Sheldon, W. H., Dupertuis, C. W., & McDermott, E. (1954). *Atlas of men: A guide for somatotyping the adult male of all ages.* New York: Harper & Row.

Sheldon, W. H., & Stevens, S. S. (1942). *The varieties of temperament: A psychology of constitutional differences.* New York: Harper.

Sundberg, N. D., Latkin, C. A., Littman, R. A., & Hagan, R. A. (1990). Personality in a religious commune: CPIs in Rajneeshpuram. *Journal of Personality Assessment, 55,* 7–17.

THE 4-QUESTION CHALLENGE

1. In their writings about personality, Adler and Hippocrates seemed to have much in common with regard to the topic of
   (a) psychological traits.
   (b) psychological states.
   (c) psychological types.
   (d) the Oedipal conflict.

2. A senior instructor at the Air Force Academy insists that his "personnel test" for officer candidate school need only consist of one question: "Did you ever fly a model airplane that you built yourself?" If this one-item test was actually used to select officer candidates, we could assume that the test
   (a) would be unreliable and invalid.
   (b) would be based on logical test construction.
   (c) would be based on empirical criterion keying.
   (d) would be based on the MMPI-2 content scales.

3. In the language of psychometrics, a "cookbook" is
   (a) a collection of MMPI profiles.
   (b) a test validation strategy.
   (c) a "recipe" for reliability.
   (d) a listing of raw scores for Julia Child on the Mooney Problem Checklist.

4. Personality tests that have multiple scales and that are scored in ipsative fashion are most amenable for comparisons of the testtaker's performance to
   (a) the testtaker's performance as compared to a norm group.
   (b) the testtaker's performance as compared to a hypothetically ideal profile.
   (c) the testtaker's performance as compared to test-

Chapter 12

Projective Methods

While viewing such films that take a poke at the Rorschach we may laugh at the humor inherent in responses such as the one provided by Allen. Yet in the role of a test administrator, laughter in the course of test administration would be inappropriate, regardless how bizarre the response. And as you will learn in your study of the Rorschach, any response given during a real administration of this test would be analyzed not only with respect to its content, but also with respect to other categories as well. What are some of those other categories? What do some of these other categories tell us, if anything, about the testtaker's personality or the way the testtaker sees the world?

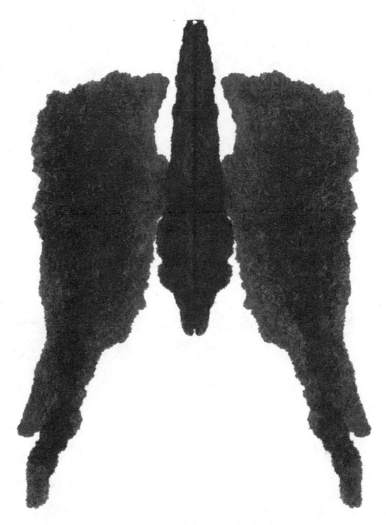

What Might This Be?

In Take the Money and Run, *Woody Allen as confirmed sociopath Virgil Starkwell is tested with a Rorschach-like inkblot and provides the following response: "It looks like two elephants making love to a men's glee club."*

Outline for Chapter 12 of Cohen et al. (1996)
PROJECTIVE METHODS

Inkblots as Projective Stimuli
    The Rorschach
        Psychometric properties
        Exner's comprehensive system

Pictures as Projective Stimuli
    The Thematic Apperception Test (TAT)
        Reliability
        Validity
    Other Picture-Story Tests

Words as Projective Stimuli
    Word Association Tests
        The Kent-Rosanoff Free Association Test
    Sentence Completion Tests

Figure Drawings as a Projective Technique
    Machover's Draw-A-Person Test
    Other Figure-Drawings Tests

A Perspective

CLOSE-UP:
    The DAP Screening Procedure for Emotional Disturbance

EVERYDAY PSYCHOMETRICS:
    Some Basic Concerns about Projective Methods

EXERCISE 71
UNDERSTANDING AND USING PROJECTIVE TECHNIQUES

OBJECTIVE

To enhance understanding of and provide firsthand experience with projective techniques of personality assessment.

BACKGROUND

Projective techniques are personality assessment methods designed for use in the evaluation of the unique way an individual projects onto an ambiguous stimulus (such as an inkblot, a picture, or something else) "his way of seeing life, his meanings, significances, patterns, and especially his feelings" (Frank, 1939, p. 403).

YOUR TASK

Your task in this exercise is threefold in nature:

1. Create a projective test battery.
2. Administer the battery to a subject.
3. Interpret the resulting data.

Creating a projective test battery.   The projective methods you will be using in this exercise will all be of your own creation. The battery will include the following five components:

1. *One monochromatic Rorschach-like inkblot.* All you'll need to create your very own inkblot is some black ink and a blank sheet of paper. Spill some ink on the page, fold and *voilá*—you're ready to begin testing as soon as the ink dries.
2. *One TAT-like picture.* You may have one you can use for this exercise hanging on your wall. Alternatively, you may cut out a picture from a magazine or even use a photograph from your own photo album if appropriate.
3. *One word association test consisting of a list of 10 words.* Write down 10 words that you suspect might provide useful personality-related information if administered to subjects in the context of a word association task.
4. *One sentence completion test consisting of 10 sentence completion stems.* Create 10 sentence completion stems that you suspect might provide useful personality-related information.
5. *One picture frustration item similar to the items found in the Rosenzweig Picture Frustration Study.* If you can draw, you can probably create one of these items complete with at least two figures, one filled-in "balloon" and one balloon to be completed by the examinee. If you feel like you can't even draw an acceptable stick figure, you might also use a picture from a magazine, newspaper or other source for this item; simply draw in the two balloons (filling in one and leaving the other blank).

Administering the battery.   Pair off with another student in the class and in turn, administer to one another your freshly prepared projective test batteries. In the interest of obtaining some firsthand experience in projective test administration—even if your subject is fully aware that the task is only an academic exercise—orient your subject as follows:

"The tests you are about to take are of the type designed to help psychologists learn about personality. There are no right or wrong answers to any of these tests so please feel free to respond with your first and most immediate response; your first response is your best response. Are there any questions?"

If there are no questions begin by placing the inkblot in front of the testtaker and ask, "What might this be?" Respond to any questions the testtaker might ask by again indicating that you wish a response to the inkblot. Allow the testtaker to point out as many things as he or she sees in the inkblot and write down the responses verbatim.

Remove the inkblot and place down in front of the subject your TAT-like stimulus saying: "I'd like you to make up a story about this picture. Your story should have a beginning, a middle, and an end. Tell me what the people [if there are people in the picture] are thinking and feeling. Tell me what is going to happen." Again, write down the subject's responses verbatim. If the subject provides only a beginning or a beginning and a middle to the story, probe with "What is going to happen?"

After the subject has responded to this TAT-like task it is time to administer your Word Association Test. Prepare for administering this test by (1) making certain that no potentially distracting stimuli are in the room, (2) having your list of 10 words in front of you, and (3) having pen and paper in front of you to record the subject's responses. We will note that the professional administering this test might also have a stopwatch going throughout the administration; this is to note response times to each of the words (though for our purposes the stopwatch is not necessary). Instruct the subject as follows: "I'm going to read you a list of words, one word at a time. As soon as you hear each word, please tell me the very first thing that comes into your mind. In order for you to fully concentrate on the words, I will ask you to close your eyes and listen very carefully." Now, read the lists of words, writing down verbatim the subject's responses.

Your neatly typed sentence completion test complete with stems followed by a sufficiently long line to enter a response is placed on a desk before the subject for self-administration along with a pencil and the following instructions: "Here are some incomplete sentences which you are to finish with the first thoughts that come to mind. Work quickly and remember that your first response is your best response."

The administration of your homemade projective test battery is concluded after the subject responds—again in self-administered fashion—to the picture frustration item. Present this task to the subject with the following instructions: "Look at this picture and after you have read the words in one 'balloon,' fill in the second balloon with the first thoughts that come to mind."

After the subject has responded to this final item you may wish to conclude the test session in a way that will elicit some feedback with respect to the testtaker's feeling and attitudes about the session, the test materials, and/or you as an examiner. A simple statement and question such as "That concludes this test session . . . how did you like it?" may be all that is necessary in this context.

Interpreting the resulting data. Interpret the projective test battery protocol according to the guidelines for interpretation of such material presented in your text. Keep in mind, however, the following two points: (1) no one expects you to be expert at test interpretation; the exercise was designed to help you better understand such tests as well as to provide some firsthand experience in administering them, and (2) any interpretations you do make must be thought of strictly as the products of an academic exercise—and invalid as a basis of veritable personality assessment. Since the psychometric soundness of the homemade test battery you employed was not researched in any way, such instruments—as well as any interpretations made on the basis of data deriving from their use—must be presumed to be unreliable, invalid, and groundless from a professional perspective. This test session, like each of the others described in this book, is *not* designed to be of benefit to your volunteer subject; it is an educational exercise designed to be of benefit to you, the student, by providing firsthand experience in the administration of testlike materials.

EXERCISE 72
THE HOLTZMAN INKBLOT TECHNIQUE

OBJECTIVE

To introduce students to an inkblot technique designed to be more psychometrically rigorous than the Rorschach.

BACKGROUND

The Holtzman Inkblot Technique (HIT) was designed to be a more psychometrically sound version of

the Rorschach. The piece that follows explains how and why.

YOUR TASK

Read the material on the HIT that follows. Then pretend you are an invited speaker at the centennial meeting of "The International Rorschach Society." You will address a very large group of people who live to administer, score, and interpret Rorschach inkblots. The title of your talk will be "A Call for More Research on the HIT." Write a five-minute speech designed to compel the society members to devote more time to exploiting the full potential of the Holtzman Inkblot Technique.

THE HOLTZMAN INKBLOT TECHNIQUE (HIT)

Based on the same underlying premise as the Rorschach, the HIT was constructed to be a psychometrically sound projective instrument. The test consists of two parallel forms (A and B), each composed of 45 inkblots with two additional trial blots identical in both test forms. Included are inkblots that are achromatic and chromatic. Unlike the Rorschach, which consists of symmetrical blots (similar on both sides), asymmetrical blots were also included in the HIT. *Inkblot Perception and Personality* (Holtzman, Thorpe, Swartz, & Herron, 1961) serves as a manual and a scoring guide for the test. The inkblots are presented one at a time to the subject, and (unlike the Rorschach) subjects are instructed to produce only one response per blot. A brief inquiry follows immediately, wherein the examiner seeks to determine where the percept was seen and the qualities of the blot that contributed to the forming of the percept.

Responses on the HIT are scored according to 22 variables, some (such as "reaction time") quite familiar to Rorschach users, with others (such as "penetration") less familiar. For the record, "penetration" refers to that which "might be symbolic of an individual's feeling that his body exterior is of little protective value and can be easily penetrated" (Holtzman, 1975, p. 247). Factor analysis of the different scoring categories has resulted in the establishment of six clusters or dimensions that reflect interrelationships among the variables. Some of these interrelationships are listed in Table 12-1. A computer-based interpretive scoring system has been developed for the HIT.

Psychometric properties. The HIT was standardized on over 1,400 normal, schizophrenic, depressed, and retarded individuals who ranged in age from 5 years through adulthood. Percentile norms based on these groups were developed. Several differences in test construction between the HIT and the Rorschach result in the HIT being more adaptable to psychometric analyses. The

Table 12-1

Key Variables on the Holtzman Inkblot Test (HIT)

Factor Number	Variables
I	Movement
	Integration
	Human
	Barrier
	Popular
II	Color
	Shading
	Form definiteness (reversed)
III	Pathognomic verbalization
	Anxiety
	Hostility
	Movement
IV	Form appropriateness
	Location
V	Reaction time
	Rejection
	Animal (reversed)
VI	Penetration
	Anatomy
	Sex

limitation of only one response per inkblot eliminates the problem of variability in productivity that may sometimes complicate statistical analyses of the Rorschach (that is, since there is no restriction on the number of responses a subject may give to each Rorschach card, responses may theoretically range from 0 to however many the examiner will sit for before stopping the respondent—a situation that makes for difficulty when trying to compare protocols from different people). The availability of two forms of the instrument constructed concurrently during test development and "carefully paired on both stimulus and response characteristics to enhance the equivalence" (Holtzman, 1975, p. 244) enables test-retest and alternate form-reliability procedures to be conducted. Additionally, the order of presentation of "achromatic and chromatic blots is sufficiently random to minimize undesirable sequential effects" (Holtzman, 1975, p. 245), enabling split-half reliability procedures to be conducted.

Internal consistency measures based on 50 samples and employing split-half (odd-even blots) procedures resulted in median reliability coefficients mostly in the .70s and .80s, with some being above .90. Inter-scorer reliability with respect to the HIT system was found to be exceptionally high, with reliability coefficients above .95 on all but two scoring categories. Test-retest reliability estimates using alternate forms of the test and extending over intervals from one week to one year were found to range from .36 to .81 for the standardization sample. In one cross-cultural longitudinal study of test-retest reliability, Holtzman (1975) used alternate forms of the test with a population of American and Mexican children. Over a six-year period, children were tested at 6 years 8 months, 9 years 8 months, and 12 years 8 months. Retesting intervals varied from one to five years. Test-

retest reliability was found to be highest at the older age levels. In addition, as the length of time of the testing interval increased, the reliability decreased. Test-retest reliability estimates were found to be the highest for the Location scoring category (reliability coefficients falling mostly in the .80s), followed by estimates for the Movement, Human, and Form Definiteness categories.

Validity investigations have compared HIT findings with data obtained from other assessment instruments. For example, a study comparing HIT scores with scales on the Personality Research Form (PRF) resulted in significant correlations between high color scores on the HIT and high scores on the PRF scales of Impulsiveness, Exhibitionism, and Nurturance. These findings appear to be consistent with Rorschach theory, which holds that "the ways . . . color is handled in responding to the blots are believed to cast light upon the overt emotional reactions of the subject to the impact of his social environment" (Klopfer, Ainsworth, Klopfer, & Holt, 1954, p. 278). Also found to be positively correlated as the HIT score of Integration and the PRF scale of Understanding, both of which reflect intellectual abilities.

Information concerning intergroup differences in performance on the HIT was illustrated in data obtained from the standardization sample, where the performance of "normals" was compared with such groups as depressives, chronic schizophrenics, and retardates. Mosely's (1963) reanalysis of Holtzman's standardization sample data resulted in differentiation of normals from schizophrenics, depressives from schizophrenics, and depressives from normals. Computer analysis of over five thousand cases of individuals, including depressives, neurotics, schizophrenics, the brain-damaged, and alcoholic groups, from the United States and 16 other countries have led to the development of additional normative data (Gorham, Mosely, & Holtzman, 1968). Mittenberg and Petersen (1984) explored the validity of the HIT measure of anxiety in a study that employed biofeedback measures and concluded that their findings supported the validity of the HIT as a measure of anxiety (though they weren't sure whether the anxiety was state or trait in nature).

A standardized edition of the HIT designed for group administration by means of projection of slides has also been developed. The reliability of the group technique using split-half and test-retest procedures has been found to approximate that of individual administrations. However, certain scoring categories, such as Location, Color, or Space, were found to receive higher scores during group administration, suggesting that when viewed from a distance, these qualities of the inkblots become more prominent. In addition, higher variance on the variable of anxiety was found to occur in group administration of the HIT, possibly substantiating the premise that the interpersonal relationship between examiner/examinee is of consequence in testtaking.

In spite of what many view as the superior qualities of the HIT from a purely psychometric standpoint, the

Table 12-2

The Rorschach and the HIT Compared

Rorschach	HIT
Intended for individual administration	May be administered individually or in groups
One form of the test	Two forms of the test
Comprises 10 inkblots	45 inkblots in each form
No trial blots	Two trial blots
Inkblots are bilaterally symmetrical	Both symmetrical and asymmetrical inkblots are included
Both achromatic and chromatic cards are included	Both achromatic and chromatic cards are included
No limit on the number of responses a subject may give	Only one response per card is allowed
Inquiry follows presentation of *all* the cards and allows for additional responses	Inquiry follows immediately after each response
Traditional methods for assessing reliability have not proved easily adaptable	Test construction results in its being conducive to assessment of reliability
Computer scoring and interpretation available	Computer scoring and interpretation available

Rorschach has prevailed as the dominant projective inkblot method (see Table 12-2). We may speculate as to the possible reasons: (1) for many years the Rorschach was the only technique available, and clinicians interested in projective techniques would be routinely trained in its use—familiarly with the Rorschach, lack of familiarity with the HIT, and sheer inertia may therefore be factors; (2) the Rorschach is viewed as supplying more clinical content since there is no limit on the number of responses obtainable and the procedure allows for extensive inquiry; and (3) some users of projective techniques may place their clinical intuition above any touted benefits of superiority with respect to psychometric qualities. At the very least, the HIT does seem to have been of value in stimulating thought and investigation with respect to the use of inkblots as a projective technique.

EXERCISE 73
THE SZONDI TEST

OBJECTIVE

To acquaint the student with a projective-type test that is very much an oddity in the history of psychological testing.

BACKGROUND

In the world of news reporting, there are "hard" news stories (such as the legislature passing a bill into law), and "soft" news or feature stories (such as a story on how a chef developed a particular recipe). In a course in psychological testing and assessment, there are some tests that you really do need to know about (such as the

MMPI-2 and the Rorschach) and some tests that are more of a curiosity than anything else. The Szondi Test clearly falls into the latter category.

YOUR TASK

Read the text that follows on the Szondi Test. Afterward, imagine a turn-of-the-century (that is, the turn of the twenty-first century) debate between Lipot Szondi and a member of the editorial board of *Psychometrica* (a journal devoted to the scholarly study of psychometrics). Write position statements for both parties. From the perspective of Dr. Szondi, argue for the merit of the test and the research that needs to be done to prove its psychometric worth. From the perspective of the *Psychometrica* editor, argue the case that Dr. Szondi's test is an anachronism in the year 2000. Oh, and when writing from the perspective of the *Psychometrica* editor, please refrain from the use of Greek letters.

THE SZONDI TEST

Developed by Lipot Szondi (1947, 1948) and popularized in the United States by his student Susan K. Deri (1949a), the Szondi test was designed to be an aid to therapy. Only in the context of *Schicksalanalysis* (a confrontational therapy) would the test findings have diagnostic meaning (Webb, 1987). The test materials consist of 6 sets of 2-inch by 3-inch photographs, with each set containing 8 photographs, a total of 48 in all. Each of the photographs of a set is of a different person who had been diagnosed into one of the following then-existing psychodiagnostic categories: (1) homosexual, (2) sadistic, (3) epileptic, (4) hysteric, (5) catatonic, (6) paranoid, (7) depressive, and (8) manic (see Figure 12-1). According to Deri (1949b):

Figure 12-1

Some Sample Photographs from the Szondi Test. The diagnostic categories for the patients pictured in the top row, from left to right are: homosexual, sadist, epileptic, and hysteric. For the bottom row, left to right, catatonic, paranoid, depressive, and manic.

The eight types of mental disorders in the test are those which Szondi believes follow Mendelian laws of inheritance. That is why these pictures were used and not others. Szondi's basic hypothesis is that we respond to these pictures in the basis of inner promptings originating in our own genetic structure. (p. 448)

Set 1 of 8 photographs is laid out before the testtaker in a manner prescribed in the test manual and the examiner asks, "Now look at all these faces and pick out first the two you like most and then the two you dislike most. Don't think long, just do it spontaneously (or quickly); you don't have to give any reason for your choice." After the two liked and disliked pictures have been selected and put aside, all of the remaining photographs in Set I are put back into the test kit and the procedure is repeated, one set at a time with the remaining five sets of photographs. At the conclusion of the sorting of Set VI, the examiner now places the accumulated total of 12 "liked" cards before the testtaker and asks which 4 were liked the most. The administration of the test is completed with the selection of the 4 most disliked cards from the pile of 12 disliked cards previously chosen, though an optional addition to the test administration could be a story-telling component where the respondent would use the Szondi pictures much like TAT cards. Deri (1949a, p. 14) advised that "The administration of the test has to be repeated at least six, preferably ten, times, with at least one day intervals between administrations, to be able to give a valid clinical interpretation of the personality." When repeated, it would be important to make the testtaker understand that the purpose of the readministration was not to check on consistency, but rather to see "how he feels today in regard to these pictures" (Deri, 1949a, p. 15).

The testtaker's responses are scored and interpreted according to an elaborate scoring system that has some theoretical basis in the work of Kurt Lewin (1935), particularly with respect to Lewinian concepts pertaining to organismic needs and drives. The eight types of Szondi pictures were designed to correspond to eight types of psychological needs "which to some degree exist in everybody. . . . Depending on the degree of (or intensity of) the state of tension in each of the eight need-systems, the pictures representing the corresponding needs will assume valence character in various proportions . . . the subject *chooses* pictures from the factor corresponding to his own need in tension. . . . Relatively great numbers of choices (four or more) from one category means that the corresponding need is in a state of strong tension . . . lack of choices in a certain category means that the corresponding need is *not* in state of tension" (Deri, 1949a, pp. 26–27). Deri (1949a) discussed at length the psychological needs associated with each of the eight psychodiagnostic categories included in the test. Thus, for example, the focus in her discussion of the diagnostic category of homosexuality was not sexual preference, but rather the feminine, "tender, more yielding part of sexuality" (p. 67) and the desire "to be loved by somebody the way they were loved by their mother" (p. 68).

Research has not supported the assumptions on which the Szondi Test is based (Guertin, 1951; Gordon, 1953; Lubin & Malby, 1951; Prelinger, 1950, 1952; Mussen & Krauss, 1952; Wiegersma, 1950); and, except as the subject of a dissertation once every great while, one seldom reads of any research being conducted with it. Still, this test holds a place of fascination in the annals of psychological testing, perhaps because of the age-old fascination and intuitive appeal of being able to tell something about people from their face.

EXERCISE 74
THE PSYCHOMETRIC SOUNDNESS OF PROJECTIVE METHODS

OBJECTIVE

To enhance understanding of and provide firsthand experience with the process of establishing the reliability and validity of a projective instrument.

BACKGROUND

A hypothetical psychologist by the name of Williams has developed a hypothetical projective instrument called the Williams Inkblot Projective Method (WIPM). Williams believes that the test (which consists of 10 monochromatic inkblots administered in much the same fashion as the Rorschach) can be of great value in identifying sadists. Williams calls upon you as an expert consultant in the area of tests and measurement—which immediately tells you something about Williams's judgment—to advise him how he might design a study to research the reliability and validity of the test.

YOUR TASK

Write a letter to Williams asking any questions you might have while explaining (a) the problems inherent in conducting such research with a Rorschach-like test, and (b) how he might proceed.

EXERCISE 75
PICK-A-TEST:
PROJECTIVE PERSONALITY MEASURES

OBJECTIVE

To learn more about a projective personality test not reviewed in the textbook.

BACKGROUND

The approach in your textbook is to highlight only a few of the many tests that exist in any given area. For every test covered in your textbook there may well be dozens of other tests designed to measure the same attribute(s). The Pick-A-Test exercise represents an opportunity to learn more about a particular test not covered in your textbook.

YOUR TASK

A list of projective personality measures along with a brief description of each follows below in Table 12-3. From this list, select one test that you think you would like to know more about. Then use all of the resources at your disposal to answer the following:

1. Describe what the test measures.
2. Who would be most apt to use this test? Why? Include in your answer sample questions the test user might hope to answer through the use of this test.
3. Who would be most apt to take this test? Why?
4. Describe the full range of people it would be appropriate to administer this test to, including comments about who would be inappropriate.
5. Describe what is known about the test's reliability.
6. Describe what is known about the test's validity.
7. Imagining that you are a measurement consultant, would you recommend this test to clients who are test users? Why or why not?

REFERENCES

Deri, S. (1949a). *Introduction to the Szondi Test.* New York: Grune & Stratton.

Deri, S. K. (1949b). The Szondi Test. *The American Journal of Orthopsychiatry, 19,* 447–454.

Frank, L. K. (1939). Projective methods for the study of personality. *Journal of Psychology, 8,* 389–413.

Gordon, L. V. (1953). A factor analysis of the 48 Szondi pictures. *Journal of Psychology, 36,* 387–392.

Gorham, D. R., Mosely, E. C., & Holtzman, W. H. (1968). Norms for the computer scored Holtzman Inkblot Technique. *Perceptual & Motor Skills Monograph Supplement, 26,* 1279–1305.

Guertin, W. H. (1951). A factor analysis of some Szondi pictures. *Journal of Clinical Psychology, 7,* 232–235.

Holtzman, W. H. (1975). New development in Holtzman Inkblot Technique. In P. McReynolds (Ed.), *Advances in psychological assessment* (Vol. 3).

Holtzman, W. H., Thorpe, J. S., Swartz, J. D., & Herron, E. W. (1961). *Inkblot perception and personality: Holtzman Inkblot Technique.* Austin, TX: University of Texas Press.

Table 12-3

Some Projective Measures of Personality

Test	Description
Children's Apperception Test	Designed for ages 3 through 10, this is essentially a downward extension of the TAT that features drawings of animals in social situations.
Joseph Pre-School & Primary Self-Concept Screening Test	Designed for ages $3\frac{1}{2}$ through 9, this semi-projective test requires children to draw their own face and then answer a series of questions about it that are objectively scored.
Tell-Me-A-Story	Designed for ages 5 to 18 years, this is a picture-story test that features full-color pictures in two forms, one for minority testtakers and one for nonminority testtakers.
House-Tree-Person Projective Drawing Technique	Designed for ages 3 and up, the subject draws a house, a tree, and a person and is given the opportunity to describe, define, and interpret the drawings.
Draw-A-Story	Designed for ages 5 years and up, this test features blank pages for drawing and writing stories. It is marketed as a screening tool for depression.
Family Apperception Test	Designed for ages 6 to 15, this picture-story test features common family activities and situations. Stories are scored with regard to variables such as obvious conflict, conflict resolution, and quality of relationships.
Adolescent Apperception Cards	Designed for use with adolescents in two versions (one for white testtakers, the other for black testtakers), this test is marketed as being particularly sensitive to issues of abuse and neglect.
Make A Picture Story	For use with adolescents and adults, this test features "cut-out" figures (women, men, police, etc.) that may be set against different background scenes. The subject selects figures and the backdrop and then explains the choices.
Kinetic Person Drawing Task	Designed for use predicting the ability of psychiatrically impaired adults to participate in activities of daily living.
Rotter Incomplete Sentences Blank, Second Edition	Designed for use with high school and college students as well as adults, this sentence completion test features norms and cut-off scores based on adjusted and nonadjusted samples.
Miner Sentence Completion Test	A sentence completion test that was designed to help in the prediction of managerial success and the motivation to manage.

Lubin, A., & Malby, M. (1951). An empirical test of some assumptions underlying the Szondi Test. *Journal of Abnormal and Social Psychology, 46,* 480–484.

Mittenberg, W., & Petersen, J. D. (1984). Validation of the Holtzman Anxiety Scale by vasomotor biofeedback. *Journal of Personality Assessment, 48,* 360–364.

Mosely, E. C. (1963). Psychodiagnosis on the basis of the Holtzman Inkblot Technique. *Journal of Projective Techniques and Personality Assessment, 27,* 86–91.

Mussen, P. H., & Krauss, S. R. (1952). An investigation of the diagnostic value of the Szondi Test. *Journal of Abnormal and Social Psychology, 47,* 399–405.

Prelinger, E. (1950). On the reliability of the Szondi Test. *Psychological Service Center Journal* (Brooklyn College), *3,* 227–330.

Prelinger, E. (1952). Kleine studie uber die verlasslichkeit des Szonditests (A note on the validity of the Szondi Test). *Psychological Abstracts, 26,* No. 5625.

Szondi, L. (1947). *Experimentelle triebdiagnostik.* Bern: Hans Huber.

Szondi, L. (1948). *Schicksalanalyse.* Basel: Bruno Schwabe.

Webb, M. W. (1987). Lipot Szondi (1893–1986). *American Psychologist, 42,* 600.

Wiegersma, S. (1950). Een onderzoek naar de gelddigheid van de Szonditest voor de psychologische praktijk. [Investigation of the validity of the Szondi Test for psychological practice]. *Psychological Abstracts, 25,* No. 372.

THE 4-QUESTION CHALLENGE
---

1. The procedure of "testing the limits" in a Rorschach administration refers to
   (a) presenting the cards out of the usual sequence.
   (b) holding a card upside-down to test the response.
   (c) asking specific questions about the cards.
   (d) None of the above

2. Which would be least likely to be one of the raw materials used by a clinician to draw conclusions about a college student examined with the TAT?
   (a) notes regarding the assessee's manner of storytelling
   (b) notes regarding the assessee's extra-test behavior
   (c) a transcript of the assessee's stories
   (d) a transcript of the assessee's grades

3. In traditional interpretations of figure drawings, the rendering of large eyes has been associated with
   (a) compensatory tendencies.
   (b) suspiciousness.
   (c) fear of nearsightedness.
   (d) dependency.

4. Which is an example of a projective instrument that employs a story completion method?
   (a) Rosenzweig
   (b) Hand Test
   (c) Blacky Test
   (d) Kinetic Family Drawing

Chapter 13

Other Personality
and Behavioral Measures

Terminating Therapy
Obviously a practitioner of unorthodox and ethically questionable methods, the psychiatrist in Halloween, *Dr. Loomis (Donald Pleasance), evidences little interest in using any other tools of personality assessment.*

Outline for Chapter 13 of Cohen et al. (1996)
OTHER PERSONALITY AND BEHAVIORAL MEASURES

Self-Report/Self-Rating Methods
  Self-Concept Measures
    The Beck Self-Concept Test
    Piers-Harris Children's Self-Concept Scale
    Q-sort Techniques
    Adjective Checklists
    Self-Concept Differentiation
  Locus of Control
  Learning Styles

Situational Performance Measures
  The Character Education Inquiry
  Leaderless-Group Situations
  Situational Stress Tests

Measures of Cognitive Style
  Field Dependence and Independence
    The Group Embedded Figures Test
  Reflective versus Impulsive Cognitive Styles
  Leveling versus Sharpening

Behavioral Assessment
  An Overview
  The Who, What, When, Where, and How of It
  Behavioral Observation and Behavior Rating Scales
    The Social Skills Rating System
    The Self-Injury Trauma (SIT) Scale
  Analogue Studies
  Self-Monitoring
  Role Play
  Unobtrusive Measures
  Issues in Behavioral Assessment

Psychophysiological Assessment
  Biofeedback
  The Polygraph
  Plethysmography
  Pupillary Responses

Ratings of Personality and Behavior by Others
  The Personality Inventory for Children
  Potential Limitations of Rating Scales
    The rater
    The instrument
    The context of evaluation

CLOSE-UP:
Confessions of a Behavior Rater

EVERYDAY PSYCHOMETRICS:
Classical versus Generalizability Theory in Psychometric Evaluation

EXERCISE 76
THE Q-SORT AND THE CONCEPT OF SELF

OBJECTIVE

To enhance understanding of and provide firsthand experience with the assessment tools other than personality inventories and projective techniques—such as the Q-sort.

BACKGROUND

In addition to personality inventories and projective techniques, there exist numerous other kinds of personality assessment instruments; included are measures of interest, attitude, cognitive style, and situational performance. One technique useful in measuring self-concept is the Q-sort. This technique may take many forms but with specific reference to personality assessment typically entails the sorting of cards with different trait terms printed on them; the individual doing the sorting may be instructed to "Place the cards in an order that you deem to be most characteristic of yourself." After that sorting has been completed and the order recorded the sorter may next be instructed, "Now place the cards into an order that you deem to be your 'ideal self'—the way you'd ideally like to be." In a counseling or therapy situation, the nature of the self versus ideal self discrepancy may provide useful information in terms of areas that will require intervention.

YOUR TASK

Many of the previous exercises have required you to enlist the aid of volunteer subjects to serve as testtakers. However, for this exercise, you will be the test developer, test administrator, test interpreter, and testtaker. Your task is fourfold in nature:

1. Create a Q-sort by writing any 10 trait terms on 10 index cards, one to a card. Note that if you have difficulty in thinking of trait terms you should feel free to glance through the personality assessment chapters in your text and pay particular attention to the tables and figures describing the contents of many of the instruments. In the unlikely event that you still have difficulty coming up with 10 trait terms, consult Allport and Odbert (1936).
2. Sort the cards according to how you see yourself today with the first card in your sorting being most characteristic of yourself and the last card in the sorting being least characteristic of yourself. Make a record of your sorting and then shuffle the deck.

3. Sort the cards according to how you would ideally like to be. Here again, the first card in your sorting should reflect the most prominent characteristic of your ideal self and card number 10 in your sorting should reflect the least prominent characteristic of your ideal self. Make a record of your sorting.
4. Write an interpretation of your findings which includes, at a minimum, (a) an explanation of any observed self/ideal-self discrepancies and (b) an "action plan" for reducing any such observed discrepancies over the course of the next few years. At the end of your interpretation of your findings add the following disclaimer: "The foregoing was based on a homemade self-concept test of unproven reliability and validity which was administered in the context of an academic exercise (and not as part of a veritable personality assessment)."

EXERCISE 77
SITUATIONAL PERFORMANCE MEASURES

OBJECTIVE

To enhance understanding of and provide firsthand experience with situational performance measures.

BACKGROUND

A *situational performance measure* is a procedure that allows for observation and evaluation of an individual under a standard set of circumstances; it typically involves performance of some specific task under actual or simulated conditions.

YOUR TASK

In this exercise, you and your classmates role-play participants at a town meeting of the own that your school is located in. All of you are town council members except for four of you who have volunteered—or "been volunteered"—to play the role of one of the following town commissioners:

- the Police Commissioner
- the Fire Commissioner
- the Sanitation Commissioner, or
- the Commissioner of Education.

The scenario for this situational performance measure is as follows: the town mayor (role-played by none other than your instructor) informs all assembled of the necessity for a 20% budget cut in the upcoming year. The

20% budget cut could be taken entirely from the police, fire, sanitation, or education budget, or it could be divided in any which way between each of these town agencies.

The four commissioners are each asked to make their case against any budget-cutting of their respective departments in an impromptu speech lasting no longer than five minutes; each speech, made before the entire town council, should make as strong a case as possible for exemption from any budget cuts. Town council members, all keen listeners and behavioral observers, take notes on points made by each of the commissioners and prepare to make recommendations to the mayor as to the apportionment of the budget cuts. After all four commissioners have been given the opportunity to plead their case, the mayor calls upon each one of the town council members for their opinions as to how the upcoming budget cuts should be apportioned (and why).

After the last town council member has "voted" regarding apportionment of the budget cuts, and after the mayor has properly thanked each of the commissioners for their efforts, all town council members (as well as all commissioners and the mayor) resume their more mundane roles in the classroom and list and discuss the skills and abilities that a "town meeting"-type situational performance measure can potentially tap. How might the personnel manager of a large corporation employ this type of task to screen and/or select applicants for executive positions? Are there any other types of applications for which you could envision the use of a measure such as this?

EXERCISE 78
BEHAVIORAL OBSERVATION

OBJECTIVE

To obtain firsthand experience in behavioral assessment.

BACKGROUND

In some situations, behavioral observation may provide a most efficient means for evaluating deficiencies in behavior, and what is needed for constructive change.

YOUR TASK

For the purpose of obtaining firsthand experience with behavioral assessment, devise a behavioral observation task designed to assess some aspect of an individual's social skills. For example, your task might call for the gathering of a half-dozen or so students who will play the roles of invitees to a social gathering of singles. One participant will play the role of assessor, another the role

of assessee, and the other invitees to the party. The assessee seeks a self-introduction to someone the assessee is attracted to at a cocktail party. The participants role-play the interaction, and the assessor provides constructive feedback.

EXERCISE 79
PICK-A-TEST:
MEASURES OF SPECIFIC
ASPECTS OF PERSONALITY

OBJECTIVE

To learn more about a personality test designed to measure a specific aspect of personality.

BACKGROUND

The approach in your textbook is to highlight only a few of the many tests that exist in any given area. For every test covered in your textbook there may well be dozens of other tests designed to measure the same attribute(s). The Pick-A-Test exercise represents an opportunity to learn more about a particular test not covered in your textbook.

YOUR TASK

A list of personality tests focused on a particular aspect of personality follows below in Table 13-1. From this list, select one test that you think you would like to know more about. Then use all of the resources at your disposal to answer the following:

1. Describe what the test measures.
2. Who would be most apt to use this test? Why? Include in your answer sample questions the test user might hope to answer through the use of this test.
3. Who would be most apt to take this test? Why?
4. Describe the full range of people to whom it would be appropriate to administer this test, including comments about those who would be inappropriate.
5. Describe what is known about the test's reliability.
6. Describe what is known about the test's validity.
7. Imagining that you are a measurement consultant, would you recommend this test to clients who are test users? Why or why not?

REFERENCE

Allport, G. W., & Odbert, H. S. (1936). Trait-names; A psycholexical study. *Psychological Monographs, 47* (Whole No. 211).

Table 13-1

Measures of Specific Aspects of Personality

Test	Description
Self-Perception Profile for Children	For use with children in kindergarten through grade 2, this test measures various aspects of a child's self-concept including those related to physical appearance, social acceptance, and competence.
Social Anxiety Scale for Children	For use with children in grade school, this test was designed to measure aspects of anxiety including fear of negative evaluation and social avoidance.
Children's Loneliness Scale	For use with children in grades 3 through 6, this test is designed to gauge loneliness and social dissatisfaction.
Tennessee Self-Concept Scale	For use with persons age 12 and up, this test is designed to profile various aspects of one's self-concept including the physical self, the family self, the social self.
Emotional-Social Loneliness Inventory	For use with persons in high school and older, this test is designed to measure various aspects of loneliness including emotional isolation and social isolation.
Life Orientation Test	For use with college students and adults in general, this test is designed to explore the degree to which the testtaker is generally optimistic or pessimistic.
Personal Evaluation Inventory	For use with college students, this test taps various aspects of self-confidence.
The Body-Esteem Scale	For use with college students, test explores various feelings regarding one's body, appearance, and related areas.
Shyness Scale	For use with college students, this test is designed to measure various aspects of social anxiety and inhibition of behavior.
Mental Health Locus of Origin Scale	For use with college students, this test is designed to measure the extent to which different factors are presumed to influence the onset and maintenance of psychopathology.
Mental Health Locus of Control Scale	For use with college students, this test is designed to measure the extent to which different parties to a therapeutic endeavor actually control the changes made.
The Weight Locus of Control Scale	For use with adults, this test is designed to assess the testtaker's beliefs about how weight is gained and lost.
Multidimensional Health Locus of Control	For use with adults, this test measures beliefs regarding the control of one's health.
Self-Estrangement	For use with adults, this test measures the degree to which one negatively evaluates oneself and the degree to which one may be "detached" from the self.
Cultural Estrangement	For use with adults, this test measures the degree to which the testtaker's ideas and opinions are congruent with those of people in the cultural groups with whom the testtaker identifies.
Affectometer 2	For use with adults, this test attempts to measure "general happiness" by, in essence, subtracting negative feelings from positive feelings and analyzing the difference.
The PSYCHAP Inventory	Another measure of general happiness for use with adults, including measures of "happy personality" and "happiness lifestyle."

━━━━━━━━━━━━ **THE 4-QUESTION CHALLENGE** ━━━━━━━━━━━━

1. Carl Rogers used Q-sort techniques to
   (a) estimate inter-rater reliability in self-concept.
   (b) estimate degree of field dependence in students.
   (c) measure self-concept in preschool children.
   (d) estimate self-ideal discrepancy in testtakers.
2. If you regularly buckle your seatbelt, the chances are good that you would score
   (a) high on a measure of sharpening.
   (b) low on a measure of reflective cognitive style.
   (c) high on a measure of locus of control.
   (d) low on a situational stress test.

3. The Personality Inventory for Children is designed to be completed by
   (a) the child.
   (b) the child's parent.
   (c) the child's teacher.
   (d) the child and the parent.
4. The behavioral approach to assessment, in contrast to more traditional approaches, tends to treat personality constructs as
   (a) summaries of specific behavior patterns.
   (b) reflections of enduring, underlying traits or states.
   (c) behaviors that may be targeted for change.
   (d) All of the above

PART

5

TESTING AND ASSESSMENT IN ACTION

Chapter 14

Clinical and Counseling Assessment

Wild in the Consulting Room

It's point-counterpoint and transference/countertransference as analyst Hope Lange and analysand Elvis Presley are Wild in the Country.

Outline for Chapter 14 of Cohen et al. (1996)
CLINICAL AND COUNSELING ASSESSMENT

An Overview

The Interview
The Mental Status Examination
Other Specialized Interviews

The Case History

Psychological Tests
The Psychological Test Battery
Diagnostic Tests
The Millon tests
Measures of Depression
Beck Depression Inventory
Children's Depression Inventory
Other measures of depression
Measures of Values
The Study of Values
The Rokeach Value Survey
The Work Values Inventory
Other tests

Special Applications of Clinical Measures
Forensic Psychological Assessment
Competency to stand trial
Criminal responsibility
Readiness for parole or probation
Custody Evaluations
Evaluation of the parent
Evaluation of the child
Child Abuse and Neglect
Physical signs of abuse and neglect
Emotional and behavioral signs of abuse and neglect
Risk assessment
Assessment in Health Psychology

The Psychological Report
Writing the Clinical Report
The Barnum Effect

CLOSE-UP:
Marital and Family Assessment

EVERYDAY PSYCHOMETRICS:
Psychometric Aspects of the Interview

EXERCISE 80
THE INTERVIEW AS A TOOL OF ASSESSMENT

OBJECTIVE

To enhance understanding of and provide firsthand experience with selected tools of clinical and counseling assessment.

BACKGROUND

Clinical psychology is that branch of psychology that has as its primary focus the prevention, diagnosis, and treatment of abnormal behavior. Like clinical psychology, *counseling psychology* is a branch of psychology that is also concerned with the prevention, diagnosis, and treatment of abnormal behavior, but its province tends to be the less severe behavior disorders and the "everyday problems in living" (such as marital and family communication problems, career decisions, and difficulties with school study habits). Three tools of assessment commonly employed by both clinical and counseling psychologists (as well as other psychologists) are the interview, the case study, behavioral observation, and tests. Here we focus on the clinical interview. In Exercise 81 we focus on the case study, and the subject of Exercise 82 is behavioral observation.

One special type of interview is a *mental status examination*—the parallel to the general physical examination conducted by a physician. A mental status examination is used to screen for intellectual, emotional, and neurological deficits.

YOUR TASK

One student will play the role of "depressed oil heir/heiress" while one other student will play the role of clinician/interviewer. The rest of the class is the attentive, note-taking audience. The scene is that the last family-owned oil well has just run dry and the imminent fear is that he or she may actually have to go out and work for a living. Other problems—which the role-player can invent—add to the depressed state of mind. The clinician will conduct an entire mental status interview as outlined by Cohen et al. (1996). Included will be questioning or observation with respect to each of the areas listed in Table 14-1.

The action begins with the depressed patient knocking on the door outside of the room where the interview will be conducted. The interviewer (as well as the audience of vicarious interviewers) should be aware that the mental status examination begins from the first moment the

Table 14-1

Areas Covered by a Mental Status Examination

- *Appearance.* Is the patient's dress and general appearance appropriate?
- *Behavior.* Is anything remarkably strange about the patient's speech or general behavior during the interview? Does the patient exhibit facial tics, involuntary movements, difficulties in coordination or gait?
- *Orientation.* Is the patient oriented to person; that is, does he know who he is? Is the patient oriented to place; that is, does she know where she is? Is the patient oriented to time; does he or she know the year, the month, and the day?
- *Memory.* How is the patient's memory for recent and long-past events?
- *Sensorium.* Are there any problems related to the five senses?
- *Psychomotor activity.* Does there appear to be any abnormal retardation or quickening of motor activity?
- *State of consciousness.* Does consciousness appear to be clear, or is the patient bewildered, confused, or stuporous?
- *Affect.* Is the patient's emotional expression appropriate? For example, does the patient (inappropriately) laugh while discussing the death of an immediate family member?
- *Mood.* Throughout the interview, has the patient generally been angry? depressed? anxious? apprehensive? What?
- *Personality.* In what terms can the patient best be described? Sensitive? Stubborn? Apprehensive? What?
- *Thought content.* Is the patient hallucinating—seeing, hearing, or otherwise experiencing things that aren't really there? Is the patient delusional—expressing untrue, unfounded beliefs (such as the delusion that someone follows him or her everywhere)? Does the patient appear to be obsessive—does the patient appear to think the same thoughts over and over again?
- *Thought processes.* Is there under- or over-productivity of ideas? Do ideas seem to come to the patient abnormally slow or fast? Is there evidence of loosening of associations? Are the patient's verbal productions rambling or disconnected?
- *Intellectual resources.* What is the estimated intelligence of the interviewee?
- *Insight.* Does the patient realistically appreciate his or her situation and the necessity for professional assistance if such assistance is necessary?
- *Judgment.* How appropriate has the patient's decision making been with regard to past events and future plans?

Source: Cohen et al., 1996.

interviewee enters the room; the examiner takes note of the examinee's appearance, gait, and so forth.

In clinically interviewing patients with different presenting problems, there are unique considerations that the trained clinician/interviewer is—or should be—aware of. For example, in interviewing a severely depressed individual, it is advisable for the interviewer to cover the topics listed below:

- *Changes in eating behavior.* Depression may bring with it disturbances in eating—either an increase or a diminution of food intake.

- *Changes in sleeping habits.* Depression typically brings with it a desire to sleep more than usual and a reluctance to get out of bed in the morning. If the depression is accompanied by severe anxiety, sleep patterns may be disrupted by a shortening of the amount of restful sleep the patient is able to obtain.
- *Changes in sexual behavior and desire.* Depression may bring with it disturbances in sexual behavior or a decrease in usual sexual desire. Alternatively, an increase in interest in sexual activity may be the consequence of the use of such activity as a kind of "anti-depressant."
- *Leisure pursuits and hobbies.* Decreased interest in hobbies and previously favored past-times may be an accompaniment of depression. The decreased interest in such activities may be symptomatic of decreased interest in life in general.
- *Depersonalization.* In very severe cases of depression, aspects of the patient's identity that should readily be familiar to the patient seem alien to him or her. Has the patient lost sight of his greatest personal assets? Does the patient experience an emptiness where there once was a sense of fulfillment? These may be signs of depersonalization.
- *Preoccupation with the past.* Is there an overabundance of thought content that is tied to sorrowful past events? This is yet another area to explore with the severely depressed patient.
- *Slowness in body movements.* The vim, vigor, and pep of the spirited cheerleader is the antithesis of the stereotypical, very slow moving, depressed individual. It is an effort for the depressed patient to do simple things such as stand up from a seated position, and it may take a depressed person several minutes to perform a simple task such as buttoning a shirt.
- *Physical complaints.* In assessing the depressed individual, it is important to also probe for physical complaints such as aches and pains, gastrointestinal disorders such as diarrhea, and dryness or unpleasant taste in the mouth.
- *Social withdrawal.* While in the early stages of depression, social contacts might be sought, as the depression deepens social withdrawal becomes more the rule. Sometimes this withdrawal is accompanied by the conception of oneself as a burden to others.
- *Sense of loss.* Sometimes a precipitating factor in an acute—as opposed to a chronic—depression is a sense of loss. The loss may have been of virtually anything ranging from a love object (such as a family member or friend) to an element of one's own self-concept (such as a loss of power, position, and/or self-esteem).
- *Suicidal ideation.* It is incumbent upon the assessor of a severely depressed individual to be attuned to communications both overt and symbolic, and both verbal and nonverbal, that may be indicative of suicidal ideation. Is the option of suicide perceived as a viable one to regain control over one's fate? Is the option of

suicide perceived as the only way to control extreme anger toward someone else (and a desire to commit homicide)? Is the option of suicide seen as "the only way out" of a situation that is perceived as dreadful? Does the depressed individual have a realistic plan for how the suicide would actually be committed? Is there a history of suicidal gestures? These are but a few of the relevant questions to be asked of the depressed patient in this context.

The *manner* in which the depressed individual is interviewed is also important. On an initial interview especially, it is very important that the interviewer be serious yet sympathetic and inquisitive regarding many of the patient's complaints; patients must perceive that a safe environment exists for discussing their feelings and that the interviewer is "with them." Humor on the part of the interviewer or even a misplaced smile during the initial interviews may be perceived as a sign that the interviewer does not understand, refuses to accept, or will not tolerate the severity of the situation as the patient sees it.[1]

Just prior to terminating the mental status interview, the student conducting the interview should ask for questions directed to the patient from the floor. Audience members will then have the opportunity to direct any questions they wish to the patient. All such questions should be designed to either (1) cover territory in a mental status examination that was not covered during the interview proper, or (2) clarify an answer to a question that was not quite clarified during the interview.

After all questions have been entertained by the patient, it's time to write up the findings. Each class member (including the student who played the patient) will write his or her report describing the mental status of the depressed patient character.

EXERCISE 81
THE CASE STUDY

OBJECTIVE

To enhance understanding of and provide firsthand experience with the case study as a tool in clinical and counseling assessment.

---

[1] Humor may well have a place in an interview with a depressed patient whom the interviewer/therapist has developed a good rapport with over the course of several months or years. In this context the author recalls a therapy patient of longstanding (who had not originally sought treatment for depression) becoming acutely depressed over a career-related setback. In one session, the patient tearfully confided that she had seriously thought of throwing herself in the path of an oncoming subway train. My response: "Then I think we should think about clearing up your bill." The patient laughed heartily—the first time she had done so in weeks. This comment, made to this particular patient under those conditions, was therapeutic.

BACKGROUND

The case study or case history is a widely used tool in the field of psychological testing. A *case history* or *case study* (we will use the terms synonymously) is a compilation of data on a single individual; the data may be culled from interviews, institutional or other records, biographical or autobiographical materials, and related sources. Case history data may be very useful to the clinician or counselor attempting to understand a presenting problem in the context of the subject's previous (as well as current) life circumstances.

YOUR TASK

One controversial case study published in the *Journal of Consulting and Clinical Psychology* explored the possibility of exposure to Christian Science as a contributory factor in the etiology of one woman's obsessive disorder. "Socially Reinforced Obsessing: Etiology of a Disorder in a Christian Scientist" (Cohen & Smith, 1976) is reprinted in the pages that follow along with two replies (Cohen, 1977; Cohen, 1979, pp. 76–83) to the many published comments on this case study.[2]

Harrison (1979) prefaced her reprinting of the Cohen and Smith (1976) case study with the following:

Part of the report deals with events the authors observed directly, such as what the patient said or did in their presence. Some of the material couldn't have been observed by the authors but must have been reconstructed from what the client told them, such as what happened when she was 15. And some of the comments are clearly interpretations by the authors. . . . As you read this case study, try to distinguish these three kinds of comments. (p. 9)

The exercise suggested by Harrison (1979) above—that of distinguishing direct behavioral observation, reconstructions, and interpretations—seems useful and one that is now your task. Additionally, as you read the following materials, jot down any alternative diagnostic interpretations or any alternative courses of therapeutic action that come to mind.

CASE STUDY

Socially Reinforced Obsessing: Etiology of a Disorder in a Christian Scientist

A 28-year-old mother and housewife was referred for treatment for a variety of complaints, the keystone of

which was her obsession with disease. As an adolescent she was introduced to Christian Science. During the next decade she had a number of experiences that either reinforced or challenged her beliefs in the efficacy of prayer and the validity of "thought cures." As crises mounted in her life she began thinking about disease to an obsessive degree. In spite of the fact that she recognized these thoughts to be unrealistic and much of her associated behavior to be irrational, she was incapable of resisting either the thinking or the overt behavior. Individual psychotherapy, employing a variety of modes, was quite effective in dealing with her difficulties.

There is no provision for any form of physical therapy or psychotherapy within the framework of Christian Science because it is this group's belief that

drugs are stupid substitutes for Divine Mind; they have no power in themselves; they operate by the "law of a general belief", . . . a disease, in the terminology of the sect, is a "belief", or a "claim", and the proper treatment is to "deny" it, or to "demonstrate" over it. (Podmore, 1963, p. 284)

Ambivalence with respect to the efficacy of Christian Science treatment is not tolerated because "persistence in the face of alarming physical evidence to the contrary may be what is needed to bring about a healing" (Christian Science Publishing Company, 1966, p. 239). In the present study, the case of a former Christian Scientist who exhibited pronounced obsessive behavior and fears is reviewed and examined in the context of her theological training. It is suggested that the client's faith and subsequent conflict regarding her religious beliefs were instrumental in the initiation of obsessive behavior.

PRESENTING PROBLEM[1]

Mary, an attractive, 28-year-old mother of two, was referred to an outpatient mental health center for treatment by a hospital psychiatrist who interviewed her when she came to the emergency room at 3:00 A.M. asking that her 4-year-old son be treated for rabies. He had been knocked to the ground by a stray dog the previous afternoon. Although she knew that it was impossible for him to contract rabies from the dog's paws, she said that thinking about the incident disturbed her so much that she felt impelled to wake her son and bring him to the hospital in the middle of the night. The next day, in the initial interview conducted at the center by the second author, Mary complained of being "afraid of everything." A partial list of things that she said were anxiety arousing included dogs, cats, rabies, botulism, "childhood diseases," and tetanus. Mary said she sought help because the fears began

[2] See for example London (1976), Halleck (1976), Stokes (1976), Coyne (1976), and McLemore & Court (1977). Note that many of these comments focused on the issue of informed consent to treatment—an issue important in its own right, but of only tangential relevance for the present purposes. Cohen, R. J., & Smith, F. J., Socially reinforced obsessing, *Journal of Consulting and Clinical Psychology,* 1976, *44,* 14, 142–144.

[1] Details of the client's history not directly or readily relevant to the focus of the study have been omitted.

dominating her daily thoughts and consequently her behavior. Her fear of botulism led to her adopting a severely restricted and costly diet for her family in which only fresh meat and vegetables were prepared; jars were held suspect, and all canned food was outlawed. An additional consequence of her fear of botulism was that her children were prohibited from eating at friends' houses, and it was only with a substantial degree of anxiety that she allowed them to purchase school lunches. So great was her fear of contracting tetanus, she would rush to her doctor's office demanding a tetanus shot if she as much as pinpricked a finger. Mary also reported sleeping difficulties which she attributed to her concern over her fears. Overconcern for the welfare of her children prompted her to quit a full-time job she had held for over 1 year.

FAITH, AMBIVALENCE, AND THE ETIOLOGY OF THE OBSESSIVE BEHAVIOR

Mary was introduced to Christian Science at the age of 15 by Paul, the man she later married. Mary was raised as a Methodist (though religion was not emphasized in her home) but began attending weekly Christian Science services to please Paul. She described her attendance as 80% for the first 2 years and noted that her faith in Christian Science principles grew over this period to the extent that at age 17 when she was 8 months pregnant with her first child she refused medical consultation in favor of treatment by a Christian Science practitioner. When she went to the hospital to deliver the child she did so convinced, as the practitioner had taught her, that it would be painless. However, she experienced an extremely painful labor. Because the pain did not yield to the practitioner's ministrations and because she wished to "do the best thing for the child," she sought the help of a physician.

This childbirth, as well as subsequent experiences, served to disillusion Mary with respect to the power of Christian Science. One such event occurred during a conversation with a friend who was a Christian Science practitioner. Following the death of a mutually known devout Scientist who had sought treatment at a Christian Science sanitarium, the practitioner made the remark that "it never should have been allowed to happen," implying to her that some form of traditional medical intervention should have been attempted. The suggestion that medical help should be sought when Christian Science appears to be failing borders on heresy and perhaps particularly so when the suggestion is made by a Christian Science practitioner. Understandably, Mary's questioning of the efficacy of Christian Science healing was increasing but not without a concomitant

increase in guilt. According to her, part of her guilt arose from a conflict within herself regarding the nature of God. She struggled to reconcile teachings concerning the basic goodness of God with the evils she saw in the world. She gave considerable thought to questions like, Is God good or is He only half good? Did God make a good earth or is He sadistic? If I'm any kind of a human being, why don't I believe in God?

Harshly disillusioned, Mary disavowed Christian Science teachings and for a period of approximately 10 years did not attend services. However, just prior to the onset of the severely maladaptive obsessive behavior which brought her to the clinic, Mary suffered a miscarriage. In addition, she reported three experiences that occurred during her pregnancy that served to reawaken her Christian Science beliefs. The first incident involved a friend who had suddenly become stricken with multiple sclerosis. Mary said that "besides just feeling sorry for her," she found that she could give comfort to her friend by offering prayer. Dissonance theorists, as well as self-perception theorists, might well argue that Mary's calling upon and verbalizing her previously acquired Christian Science skills may in some way have reinforced her belief in the efficacy of the procedures.

Second, during this same period of time, Mary's $3\frac{1}{2}$-year-old son John was complaining of pains in his feet at night. The pain was extreme enough to awaken the boy. Fresh from the experience of having had a close friend contract a major disease, Mary was afraid to even consult a medical doctor concerning her son's condition. Instead, Mary called a practitioner and asked the practitioner to pray for her son. Though the practitioner never saw the child, there was a complete cessation of his symptoms after the second treatment (prayer). This relief at the hands of the practitioner served to rekindle and reinforce Mary's faith in Christian Science teachings.

The third and most crucial event was the miscarriage itself. Mary cited at least two reasons for feeling guilty over the loss of the baby. First, during the pregnancy the family was involved in moving and, in order to economize, Mary helped with the moving of furniture. It is possible that this heavy labor precipitated the miscarriage. Second, and more crucial to the present analysis, neither Mary nor her husband wanted her to become pregnant, and they both openly expressed this. Mary even reported casually "wishing that she was not pregnant." When informed by the doctor of the miscarriage, it occurred to her that the baby may have actually been "killed by thought."

It seems reasonable to infer that events surrounding Mary's third and most recent pregnancy served to renew her interest in previously disavowed Christian Science belief. The traumatic experience of losing the baby linked to the notion that the child may actually have been done away with by thought made the power of thought more salient and served to make Mary acutely cognizant of, and cautious with, her own thoughts. In her own words, Mary began "tuning in on disaster." For example, whereas another mother would not become overly concerned if her child complained of a cold, such a complaint would elicit in Mary a variety of thoughts such as, "God never created a cold, so how could it exist; How can God's perfect child have anything not harmonious in him?" Indeed, consistent with Christian Science beliefs, disease and pain do not exist and, therefore, should be denied:

> Bodily conditions they view as effect rather than cause—the outward expression of conscious and unconscious thoughts. On this premise what needs to be healed is always a false concept of being, not a material condition. (Christian Science Publishing Company, 1966)
>
> You say a boil is painful; but that is impossible for matter without mind is not painful. The boil simply manifests, through inflammation and swelling, a belief in pain; and this belief is called a boil. Now administer mentally to your patient a high attention of truth and it will soon cure the boil. The fact that pain cannot exist where there is no mortal mind to feel it is a proof that this so-called mind makes its own—that is, its own belief in pain. (Eddy, 1875, p. 284)

Imbedded in Mary's past were reports of several experiences where this philosophy had apparently been validated. One such event occurred when Mary decided to use the techniques she had been taught in order to quit smoking. She had been smoking up to three packs a day for 3 years. One day before boarding an interstate bus she resolved to use thought to cure herself of her habit. Mary reported that by the time she was ready to get off the bus, she felt as if she had never smoked at all. She has not smoked since. But although the power of concentration has long been known to be instrumental in bringing about positive behavioral consequences (Bain, 1928), a religious reliance on the use of such techniques may be psychologically harmful. As in this case, previously minor concerns such as pinpricks or reports of botulism poisoning in the news media may have inadvertently and paradoxically been made more salient to a person who devotes her energies to denying all but spiritual entities. Actively trying to deny the existence of something may actually increase the amount of time one spends thinking about it; as Mary once so aptly put it, "when all you think about is dieting, all you see is food."

As time went by, Mary became locked into a spiral of ever increasing ambivalence. If, for example, her son was running a high temperature, her initial reaction would be to deny the existence of sickness. But in spending the day and night trying to mentally treat the problem, her guilt feelings for depriving her son of medical attention increased. Additionally, she would imagine grave consequences (e.g., blindness, paralysis) that might result from her failure to medically treat the problem. The net result of the constellation of factors that appeared to be operating was that the slightest provocation (e.g., the dog knocking her son down with his paws) became a stimulus for panic and frantic seeking of medical attention.

NOTE ON TREATMENT

The primary focus of the present study has been the etiology of an obsessive disorder, and only cursory attention will be given to the treatment procedure undertaken. Mary was seen weekly for a total of 24 sessions. Approximately the first half of the total number of sessions was taken up with a discussion and clarification of her various problems in living, and no attempt was made to deal directly with her relatively stable pattern of obsessiveness. Around the 15th session, Mary reluctantly brought up her involvement with Christian Science (which she had previously avoided mentioning), and a probable basis for her obsessive behavior became clear. The therapist (the first author), wishing to remain neutral with respect to resolution of Mary's division of loyalty, neither encouraged her to continue therapy nor discouraged her from adhering to the tenets of the Christian Science philosophy. Mary elected to continue therapy and was given relaxation training to help reduce anxiety during the day and to help her sleep at night. In addition, she was taught a thought-stopping procedure (described by Lazarus, 1971) to deal with the obsessions directly. From about the 16th session to the termination of treatment there occurred an increasing disavowal of the efficacy of Christian Science procedures and a concomitant decrease in Mary's report of obsessive thinking. At the time of termination of treatment, Mary was manifesting none of the urgent and irrational fears that she had experienced when referred for therapy. Additionally, she once again sought and obtained employment. Three months later, she spontaneously called to say that she was continuing to do quite well.

Socially Reinforced Obsessing: A Reply*

This comment reviews the comments of London, Halleck, Coyne, and Stokes on "Socially Reinforced Obsessing: Etiology of a Disorder in a Christian Scientist." In their haste to address a hypothetical ethical issue, London, Halleck, and Coyne overlooked

---

*Cohen, R. J. (1977). Socially reinforced obsessing—A reply. *Journal of Consulting and Clinical Psychology, 45,* 1166–1171.

temporal aspects of the case study. Additionally, London confused the arbitrariness-of-psychopathology issue with the main issue, Halleck misinterpreted the concept of "therapist neutrality," and Coyne's restatement of Halleck compounded previously made errors. A counterargument to the views presented by a representative of the Christian Science church is also made.

"Socially Reinforced Obsessing: Etiology of a Disorder in a Christian Scientist" was presented by Cohen and Smith (1976) as an interesting case study of the development of one individual's obsessive thought disorder. It was not subtitled "Treatment of a Disorder . . ." because the focus of the study was clearly on etiology; only one paragraph dealt with treatment, and that paragraph was included more to provide the reader with a sense of closure than anything else. Of course, the treatment or methodology of any published case study or experiment—even those primarily concerned with etiology—are automatically subject to discussion of possible ethical questions raised. This is so because what is done and the way in which it is done is as much a matter of professional concern as the outcome and/or findings. It is argued here that the appropriateness of Cohen and Smith as a point of departure from which to discuss "psychotherapy for religious neuroses" (London, 1976) or to debate the issue, "Did the treatment of a highly religious person succeed at the expense of her abandoning her religious convictions?" (Halleck, 1976, p. 146) is questionable.

The first time I saw London's and Halleck's comments was in February of 1976 when they appeared following our case study (Cohen & Smith, 1976). Although I noted that Halleck had made the questionable assumption that the patient was "highly religious" and that both discussants had overlooked the crucially important fact that the patient (Mary) had first broached the subject of her religious beliefs 15 weeks after therapy began, I did not reply to the comments because the *Journal* had not requested rebuttal or solicited any further information and I was confident that clinicians carefully reading the adjacent articles would detect the errors. However, the need for reply became pressing when a restatement and compounding of the errors appeared in December (Coyne, 1976). In using Cohen and Smith (1976) as a point of departure from which to discuss "the place of informed consent in ethical dilemmas," Coyne has pushed simple lack of thoroughness one step further. In essence, Coyne demanded that therapists be mystics capable of foretelling before therapy begins the most remote revelations to follow 15 weeks hence.

LONDON'S COMMENT

The three most important questions that arose for Perry London (1976) were:

First, is it true that "religion can make you crazy?" Second, does this case demonstrate that thesis? Third, if it is true, what are the ethical implications of sticking one's therapeutic thumb into the ecclesiastical pie? (p. 145)

To abstract from the case study that the essence of what we were saying is that "religion can make you crazy" or that religious belief fosters "religious neuroses" is as illogical as it is unfair. If one were to accept London's interpretations, one would be forced to conclude that *all* Christian Scientists must be suffering from obsessive disorders and that all forms of worship must appear psychopathological to "not very religious" therapists. London's exposition of this first point confuses the arbitrariness-of-psychopathology issue with the etiological question at hand. Academic debate over whether religious zeal is or is not psychopathological is to be encouraged. However, the usefulness and relevance of such discussions with regard to Mary's case is questionable and tenuous at best. The presence of psychopathology and marked behavioral impairment that severely compromised the adaptive functioning of Mary (and consequently that of her children) is evident or should be evident from even a cursory reading of the case study. In fact, it seems fair to say that failure to intervene at such a patient's request could be ethically questioned. But returning to the question of etiology . . .

London (1976) reviewed the data presented and concluded that "the correlation suggests no cause" (p. 146). Does London know of *any* case study that proves cause and effect? Indeed, can anyone cite any experimental work in the highly complex area of psychopathology that unambiguously demonstrates cause and effect? As was indicated in Footnote 1 (Cohen & Smith, 1976, p. 142), an attempt was made to shear the case study of the mounds of subjective impressions that accumulated during an extended course of therapy. Only those behavioral vignettes immediately relevant to our point of view were abstracted for presentation. Even though London complained that the reader was presented with "data shortage" and that he found the material wanting for data on "psychosexual stages" (1976, p. 146), I am satisfied that a compelling case for the etiology of an obsessive disorder was made on the basis of the cited events in the patient's learning history. Further, I believe that there is a wide discrepancy in the plausibility of our alternative explanations. But this is a matter for readers to decide for here I am not neutral.

And speaking of neutrality, this is an issue that any discussant addressing the "ethics of religious intervention" (London, 1976, p. 146) must surely be expected

---

[1] Details of the client's history not directly or readily relevant to the focus of the study have been omitted.

to deal with head on. Yet the term *therapeutic neutrality* or any direct reference to it never appears in London's comment. Instead, we are only given analogies of questionable relevance with referents ranging from the Internal Revenue Service to Pandora's Box.

HALLECK'S COMMENT

After reading Halleck's (1976) and the other comments, one might think that the question raised by Cohen and Smith (1976) was whether or not someone with strong religious beliefs should be accepted for treatment in a therapy whose very initiation seems to compromise those beliefs. But in their haste to address this intriguing (albeit hypothetical) issue, all of the discussants ignored the crucial fact that Mary's religious beliefs first came to therapeutic light when she was well into treatment:

> Around the 15th session, Mary reluctantly brought up her involvement with Christian Science (which she had previously avoided mentioning), and a probable basis for her obsessive behavior became clear. The therapist (the first author), wishing to remain neutral with respect to any resolution of Mary's division of loyalty, neither encouraged her to continue therapy nor discouraged her from adhering to the tenets of the Christian Science philosophy. Mary elected to continue therapy. (Cohen & Smith, 1976, p. 144)

Although Halleck objected to Cohen and Smith's "pretense of neutrality" (1976, p. 147), his admonition appears to be based on a misconstrual of one sentence. The myth of therapeutic neutrality has been recognized at least since the days when Rogerians started referring to their treatment as "client centered" as opposed to "nondirective." Halleck (1976) rightly took cognizance of this fact when he pointed out that "to the extent that any troubling behavior is created by socially conditioned responses and beliefs, efforts to change that behavior can never be neutral" (p. 147). From the inception of Mary's therapy, the approach was clearly problem oriented, and no pretense of neutrality was implied. At the time of the Christian Science "revelation," I, "wishing to remain neutral with respect to any resolution of Mary's division of loyalty," let her decide what she wanted to do without overtly applying encouragement or discouragement toward any choice. *Of course* my tacit offer to remain her therapist conveyed my willingness to help her through her disabling obsessions even at the cost of possible infringement on religious beliefs, beliefs that had fostered "a spiral of ever increasing ambivalence" (Cohen & Smith, 1976, p. 144). Fifteen weeks prior to the revelation, the patient had acted decisively to seek out values that she could live with. She had, in effect, greatly minimized the relevance of the principle of neutrality that was alluded to.

Halleck (1976) described my patient as a "highly religious person." However, whether or not Mary could accurately be described as "highly religious" is very much a matter of what that construct means to the individual using it. Mary did describe herself as a Christian Scientist, and there is little doubt that Christian Science teachings influenced her life in many ways (including in the development of an obsessive disorder). But it must also be remembered that Mary was raised as a Methodist in a home in which religion was not emphasized and that she was first introduced to Christian Science at age 15. Even London (1976) recognized that "she arrived late, as a consort aiming to please, not a convert aiming to be saved" (p. 145). After initial disillusionment with Christian Science, she did not attend church services for a period of 10 years. Thus, while faith and ambivalence alternatively were limelighted in this Christian Scientist's life, there is at least a question of whether she could legitimately be described as a highly religious person. One can be a Christian Scientist, a Jew, a Catholic or anything else without being highly religious, a distinction that also eluded James C. Coyne.

COYNE'S COMMENT

The title of Coyne's (1976) paper is misleading, since the article does not even amount to an elaboration of the previously stated advice that "it would seem that the ethical issues could be minimized . . . if the consumer could be adequately forewarned of the possible consequences of treatment" (Halleck, 1976, p. 147). Further, Coyne uses the term *informed consent* as if he and everyone else know what he is talking about. Yet the lone, inappropriate example offered (the question suggested by Hurvitz, 1967) is of little help to the reader. Coyne will be surprised to learn that there is a great deal of controversy over what constitutes the "full information" (Coyne, 1976, p. 1015) and "minimal information" (Coyne, 1976, p. 1016) that he speaks of and that there are special problems in defining informed consent in individual and group therapy as well as in research and psychological testing.

Seemingly oblivious to the patient's ambivalence, the severity of the disorder, and the temporal aspects of treatment, Coyne (1976) stated that

> the case of Mary presented by Cohen and Smith (1976) and the comments by London (1976) and Halleck (1976) are important not only for their elaboration of the complex ethical issues in the treatment of a highly religious person but also for their demonstration of the need to obtain fully informed consent in the conduct of psychotherapy. (p. 1015)

Almost incredibly, Coyne uses Cohen and Smith (1976) as a point of departure from which to discuss the "tacit and often legal expectation that before a surgeon obtains consent to perform even the simplest operation or before a lawyer obtains consent to initiate a civil suit, he must provide the patient or client with full information" (Coyne, 1976, p. 1015). *Would Coyne have wanted the therapist to inform the patient of the possibility of the modification of her religious beliefs 15 weeks before she elected to reveal such beliefs?*

STOKES' COMMENT

Although I was initially surprised and quite eager to read the Christian Science community's comments (Stokes, 1977), I was left disappointed and unenlightened for the effort. As Stokes grappled with the question of whether Cohen and Smith are more ignorant than they are biased or vice versa, he pointed to the church's tolerance of secular medicine with ample quoting from Mary Baker Eddy. Ignoring the inapplicable and somewhat sensational question concerning "mental health professionals using their therapy techniques to change religious belief systems of clients without the knowledge or consent of the client" (Stokes, 1977, p. 1164), the gist of Stokes' comment concerns the typicality of Mary and the relationship between the Christian Science church and science. Although I do not feel qualified to judge whether or not Mary was "thoroughly atypical," as Stokes maintains, it is important to point out that a counterargument can be made.

How typical was Mary? Stokes (1977) cited as the most characteristic feature of Christian Science, "that its healing, far from being a ritual of denials, rests on the acceptance of oneself as the loved child of God" (p. 1164). Mary's problems in this area had been reported by Cohen and Smith (1976) as follows:

> The traumatic experience of losing the baby linked to the notion that the child may actually have been done away with by thought made the power of thought more salient and served to make Mary acutely cognizant of, and cautious with, her own thoughts. In her own words, Mary began "tuning in on disaster." For example, whereas another mother would not become overly concerned if her child complained of a cold, such a complaint would elicit in Mary a variety of thoughts such as, "God never created a cold, so how could it exist; How can God's perfect child have anything not harmonious in him?" (p. 143)
>
> According to her, part of her guilt arose from a conflict within herself regarding the nature of God. She struggled to reconcile teachings concerning the basic goodness of God with the evils she saw in the world. She gave considerable thought to questions like, Is God good or is He only half good? Did God make a good earth or is He sadistic? If I'm any kind of a human being, why don't I believe in God? (p. 143)

Putting aside the question of the source of Mary's difficulties, I would have been most willing to accept (on faith) Stokes' assessment of Mary as a thoroughly atypical Christian Scientist had I not gone to a Christian Science reading room and leafed through some of the offerings. In fact, many of the published testimonies reveal various degrees of ambiguity on the part of the testifiers and more than a fair degree of alternating between medical doctors and Christian Science practitioners for help. For example:

> Five years ago, I had just spent my last dollar on a bottle of medicine for my wife, when an angel of God's presence caused me to tell a friend my tale of woe. He was a student of Christian Science, about which I had never heard. I told him I was about at the end of my row, as I had been spending all I could rake and scrape up for medicine for my wife, and the doctors had said she could not be healed of pellagra, which she had had for years. My friend told me to have no fear, but have my wife read the *Sentinel* which he gave me. Inside of a week or two she was well and out in the field helping me, completely healed.
>
> A few years afterwards my baby boy had infantile paralysis; and nine doctors passed the death sentence. [Note the return to traditional medicine.] Two of the doctors, after taking an X-ray picture, confirmed the sentence. I had help from a Christian Scientist practitioner, and the baby was healed at once. When I went to pay the doctor for taking the X-ray picture, he said "I am awfully sorry for you George; I know the child is dead." I told him that Christian Science had healed him, and that he was playing around, happy as a lark.
>
> Since then my wife has had a painless childbirth. We have had many more demonstrations, which cause us to be very grateful to Mrs. Eddy for founding Christian Science to bless the world. (Christian Science, 1966, pp. 95–96)

Another testifier says, in part,

> When I was just a boy, I developed a severe earache. Finally my mother took me to a prominent physician in Brooklyn. He told her that I had a double mastoiditis and both ears would have to be operated on immediately.
>
> We had just begun to study Christian Science and my mother still didn't know too much about it. *She was rather hesitant to depend on it in a case like this,* but she felt impelled to postpone the operation. . . . [italics added here]
>
> On the way home she asked me what *I* wanted—Christian Science treatment or to go to the hospital—and I told her I wanted to be healed in Christian Science. (Christian Science, 1966, p. 113)

One might legitimately question how typical or atypical ambiguity is in *un*published Scientists if such sentiment appears in the most casual perusal of what Stokes (1977) referred to as "a recent authoritative Christian Science work" (p. 1164). Additionally, the Church's indirect recognition of the problem of ambivalence comes in the form of exhortations that "when a Christian Scientist fails to demonstrate the healing power of God in a given situation, he does not question the goodness of God" (Christian Science, 1966, p. 240). The Cohen and Smith (1976) citation that was referred to by Stokes as a "misquotation" can also be construed as an exhortation to "keep the faith": "persistence [in holding to what they call the truth of being] in the face of alarming physical evidence to the contrary may be what is needed to bring about a healing" (p. 142) (bracketed portion inserted from the original text). Although it is unfortunate that in proofreading the manuscript the authors failed to note that the customary three dots (. . .) denoting the omission of the material bracketed above was not included, I think Stokes would agree that the meaning, context, and/or "spirit" of the text had not been violated.

SCIENCE AND CHRISTIAN SCIENCE

The die for the church's somewhat uncharitable view of secular interventions was cast the day that Mary Baker Eddy slipped on the ice in 1866. Though her attending physician "saw nothing more to be done" (Christian Science, 1966, p. 3), Mrs. Eddy recovered after reading one of the healings of Jesus in her Bible. Since that time, testimonies expressing anything but gratitude for physicians dot the Christian Science literature. (In this regard the two testimonies presented herein are not atypical.) To date there are thousands of published testimonies attesting to the efficacy of Christian Science in healing maladies as diverse as cancer, alcoholism, business problems, obesity, dental problems, podiatric problems, deafness, arthritis, paralysis, phlebitis, psoriasis, and so on. One testifier's "slight understanding" of Christian Science enabled him to "pasture two thousand sheep on a range infested with poisonous weeds, with no bad results whatever" (Christian Science, 1966, p. 101). But these are all matters of faith neither amenable nor appropriate for scientific inquiry. And unlike Mary Baker Eddy, I am not prepared to assert that it is science or Christian Science that is "pre-eminently scientific" because one is based on "Truth" (cf. Eddy, 1875, pp. 123–124).

To ask whether the most useful healing to be sought "is always of one phase or another of the individual's alienation from God" or "classical Freudian to encounter group and screaming therapy" (Stokes, 1977, p. 1165) is to illegitimately pit religion against science—two dif-ferent systems (each with numerous subsystems) with vastly different sets of rules concerning what constitutes acceptable evidence and proof. And although psychologists have some tentative notions about the kinds of therapy that are most likely to be helpful to some patients under some conditions, we are a long way off from a "universal cure." Generally, psychotherapists try to understand presenting problems by integrating data (e.g., the constructs most salient to the

patient, environmental factors, etc.) into a diagnostic/ therapeutic schema that makes the most sense to them. Stokes confuses Cohen and Smith's attempted understanding of Mary with "reading exactly the same misconception into its religious teachings" and seems not to allow that psychotherapists—like all mortals—can only have a relatively limited acquaintance with the numerous areas that they might want to know more about. Therapists can, however, view the treatment of Christian Scientists, lapsed Catholics, communist FBI agents, and palmist/psychologists as opportunities to learn more about Christian Science, Catholicism, the FBI, and palmistry.

I wish to state as emphatically as possible that I have the utmost respect for pious persons of all faiths who live their lives with exemplary love and regard for their fellow human beings. Although the intermingling of religion with science is not to be encouraged, such enmeshment is bound to occur from time to time. When dilemmas are raised by such overlapping and conflicting interests, I believe that the solution that sides with life, human welfare, and physical/mental well-being must be sought. I fully appreciate that the latter statement may raise more questions than it answers, but it is the best I can do short of a philosophical treatise.

CONCLUDING COMMENT

In clinical psychology today there is heartening interest in the ethics of what we are doing. I encourage such interest and have elsewhere contributed directly and indirectly to discussion of ethics-related matters of both public (Cohen, 1973) and professional (Cohen, 1976a, 1976b, 1976c, Note 1, Note 2; Cohen & DeBetz, 1977) concern. But while I support the enlargement of a literature that has been shamefully underemphasized in the past, I would encourage prospective contributors to address the issues in a manner more focused than the statements (Halleck, 1976; London, 1976) and restatements (Coyne, 1976) discussed herein. With regard to the case study, there was some question as to how religious the patient was; the fact that she offered herself for treatment, came voluntarily week after week, and only revealed that she was a Christian Scientist after 15 weeks of therapy would seem to attest more to her ambivalence and confusion than to her orthodoxy and piety. Had the discussants focused their remarks on the ethics of *continuing* intervention (beyond the 15th session) and had they exhibited some sensitivity to the pain Mary was suffering, their comments may have been relevant to the case study presented by Cohen and Smith (1976). As it was, the distinction between initiating treatment and continuing treatment as well as other important data was lost to discussants whose set it was to debate a hypothetical ethical issue rather than discuss an interesting etiology of a psychopathological state.

Questions concerning Mary's typicality as a Christian Scientist or the relationship between science and Christian Science may well be compelling to segments of the academic community, but they are at best tangential to the case study presented by Cohen and Smith (1976). Similarly, questions concerning the point at which religious zeal should be considered psychopathological may be academically intriguing but of little relevance to the issues at hand. The primary question raised by Cohen and Smith (1976) is certainly not as blanket a question as "Can religion make you crazy?" nor as uninformed a question as "Did the treatment of a highly religious person succeed at the expense of her abandoning her religious convictions?" Rather, the primary question remains, "Was one individual's obsessive disorder created, nurtured, and/ or reinforced by her contact with Christian Science?"

EXERCISE 82
BEHAVIORAL OBSERVATION II

OBJECTIVE

To further enhance understanding of and provide first-hand experience with the assessment technique of behavioral observation.

BACKGROUND

Behavioral observation involves the clinician's own noting of an event in the life of the patient either by personally watching it take place, by having and assistant watch it, or by watching a recording of it. Factors such as behavioral excesses, behavioral deficits, and behavioral assets typically will be noted, as will the consequences and situational antecedents of such actions.

YOUR TASK

This exercise could be subtitled "the brunch exercise" since it entails going to brunch—or breakfast, lunch, or dinner—with a fellow classmate. Students pair off and on two separate occasions go on "field trips" either to the school cafeteria or to a local restaurant. On each occasion, the two students will play the roles of "behavioral observer" and "subject." The behavioral observer is the one with the note pad who dutifully takes notes of

aspects of the subject's brunch behavior including food selection, rate of eating, and activities while eating. Students playing the role of subject being observed have the option of brunching as they normally might, or assuming the role of someone who demonstrates either behavioral excesses or deficits with respect to brunch behavior. Students switch the roles of behavioral observer and subject on the second field trip.

On the basis of your experience as a behavioral observer, write up a brief description of what you observed. If you observed behavioral excesses or deficits in eating behavior, include in your report any implications you believe your findings might have in the treatment of problem eating habits for the character portrayed by your role-playing subject.

EXERCISE 83
P. T. BARNUM AND THE MPPI

OBJECTIVE

To enhance understanding of and provide firsthand experience with the "Barnum effect."

BACKGROUND

Remember that individual to whom you administered the MPPI? It's now time to provide that individual with some feedback . . . well, feedback of a sort.

You may already be aware of a phenomenon referred to in the psychological literature as the "Barnum effect" —the fact that people tend to accept vague and general personality descriptions as uniquely applicable to themselves without realizing that the same description could be applied to just about anyone. But does this effect really work?

YOUR TASK

Contact the person(s) who sat for the MPPI and/or your projective test battery, and request that they read and evaluate a personality description which was derived from those tests; the evaluation is made on the separate form that follows the personality description on the next page. All evaluation forms are brought back to class for discussion. All subjects receive the same "feedback" as to their performance on the MPPI; the feedback is the following general personality description that has been used in a number of studies researching the Barnum effect.

You have a strong need for other people to like you and for them to admire you. You have a tendency to be critical of yourself. You have a great deal of unused capacity that you have not turned to your advantage. While you have some personality weaknesses, you are generally able to compensate for them. Your sexual adjustment has presented some problems for you. Disciplined and controlled on the outside, you tend to be worrisome and insecure inside. At times you have serious doubts about whether you have made the right decision or done the right thing. You prefer a certain amount of change and variety and become dissatisfied when hemmed in by restrictions and limitations. You pride yourself on being an independent thinker and do not accept others' opinions without satisfactory proof. You have found it unwise to be too frank in revealing yourself to others. At times you are extraverted, affable, and sociable, whereas at other times you are introverted, wary, and reserved. Some of your aspirations tend to be pretty unrealistic.

EVALUATION OF PERSONALITY ASSESSMENT INTERPRETATION

Please check one.

I feel that the interpretation was:

_____ Excellent
_____ Good
_____ Average
_____ Poor
_____ Very Poor

After your subject has read and evaluated the personality description above, it's time for a thorough debriefing. Explain to the subject exactly what the Barnum effect is. In this context it may be useful for explanatory purposes to make reference to horoscopes as an analogy. Explain also the value to you in learning about the Barnum effect—the value in avoiding what Meehl (1956) termed "pseudo-successful clinical procedures in which personality descriptions from tests are made to fit the patient largely or wholly by virtue of their triviality."

Debriefing should also take place with respect to the MPPI itself, despite the fact that you initially presented it to your subject as an academic exercise and not a meaningful test. Your explanation of the exercise might briefly make reference to the psychometric concepts of *reliability* and *validity* and how such terms are applied to "real" psychological tests. Explain further that because the test you administered was unresearched and therefore considered to be unreliable and invalid, any results could not be construed to be meaningful in any way. Thank the subject for helping to provide you with firsthand experience in learning about the structure and administration of tests, and ask whether you could answer any questions they might have about the MPPI or about testing in general.

dependence (including alcoholism and drug dependence). The multiple methods were the two tests themselves (the MCMI-II and the MMPI). Table 14-2 lists the four traits studied along with the specific scales of the two instruments used to measure those traits.

McCann (1990) studied the scores of 85 psychiatric inpatients who had completed both the MCMI-II and the MMPI. The scales of interest from the two tests were correlated and entered into a multitrait-multimethod matrix. A portion of the resulting matrix is in Table 14-3. The same variables listed in Table 14-2 are listed across the top and down the side of the matrix in Table 14-3.

YOUR TASK

1. What in the matrix provides you with information about the convergent validity of the two tests?
2. How would you characterize the convergent validity of the two tests?
3. What in the matrix provides you with information about the discriminant validity of the two tests?
4. How would you characterize the discriminant validity of the two tests?

EXERCISE 84
THE MULTITRAIT-MULTIMETHOD MATRIX REVISITED

OBJECTIVE

To review the multitrait-multimethod matrix using an example from the literature in clinical assessment.

BACKGROUND

As you may recall from Chapter 6, a multitrait-multimethod matrix can be used to organize information related to the construct validity of tests. McCann (1990) used this psychometric tool to evaluate the construct validity of the MMPI and the MCMI-II. The multiple traits evaluated were anxiety, depression, psychotic thought, and substance

EXERCISE 85
PICK-A-TEST: CLINICAL MEASURES

OBJECTIVE

To learn more about clinical measures not reviewed in the textbook.

BACKGROUND

The approach in your textbook is to highlight only a few of the many tests that exist in any given area. For every test covered in your textbook there may well be dozens of other tests designed to measure the same attribute(s). The Pick-A-Test exercise represents an opportunity to learn more about a particular test not covered in your textbook.

Table 14-2

Four Traits Evaluated by Means of the MMPI and the MCMI-II

General Construct	MCMI-II Scale	MMPI Scale
Anxiety (Anx)	A: Anxiety	Manifest Anxiety S
Depression (Dep)	D/CC: Dysthymia and Major Depression	Scale 2
Substance Dependence (Sub)	B/T: Alcohol and Drug Dependence	MacAndrew (MAC) Sc
Psychotic Thought (Psy)	SS: Thought Disorder	Scale 9

Table 14-3

*Multitrait-Multimethod Matrix of MCMI-II and MMPI Scales**

| | MCMI-II Scales | | | | MMPI Scales | | |
	Anx	Dep	Sub	Psy	Anx	Dep	Sub
MCMI-II Scale							
Anxiety	—	—	—	—	—	—	—
Depression	.94	—	—	—	—	—	—
Substance Dependence	.53	.56	—	—	—	—	—
Psychotic Thought	.75	.77	.62	—	—	—	—
MMPI Scale							
Anxiety	.84	.86	.51	.78	—	—	—
Depression	.51	.58	.08	.41	.65	—	—
Substance Dependence	−.05	−.05	.40	.13	−.02	−.27	—
Psychotic Thought	.00	.00	.47	.19	.04	−.34	.57

*Note that McCann did not report the reliability of the scales, so dashes appear on the main diagonal in place of reliability coefficients.

YOUR TASK

A list of clinical measures along with a brief description of each follows below in Table 14-4. From this list, select one test that you think you would like to know more about. Then answer the following:

1. Describe what the test measures.
2. Who would be most apt to use this test? Why? Include in your answer sample questions the test user might hope to answer through the use of this test.
3. Who would be most apt to take this test? Why?
4. Describe the full range of people it would be appropriate to administer this test to, including comments about who would be inappropriate.
5. Describe what is known about the test's reliability.
6. Describe what is known about the test's validity.
7. Imagining that you are a measurement consultant, would you recommend this test to clients who are test users? Why or why not?

REFERENCES

Bain, J. A. (1928). *Thought control in everyday life.* New York: Funk & Wagnalls.

Christian Science Publishing Company (1966). *A century of Christian Science healing.* Boston: Christian Science Publishing Company.

Cohen, R. J. (1973). Loyalty or legality in obedience: Note on the Watergate proceedings. *Psychological Reports, 33,* 964.

Cohen, R. J. (1976). Comments on the "cattle-prod controversy." *Perceptual and Motor Skills, 42,* 146. (a)

Cohen, R. J. (1976). Dr. Cohen replies. *American Journal of Psychiatry, 133,* 1348–1349. (b)

Cohen, R. J. (1976). Is dying being worked to death? *American Journal of Psychiatry, 133,* 575–577. (c)

Cohen, R. J. *Clinical psychology: Professional confusion, public chaos, and legal recourse.* Book in preparation, 1977 [Retitled *Professional Psychology and Its Public Image,* under contract with University of Chicago Press.]

Cohen, R. J. *Malpractice: A guide for mental health professionals.* Book in preparation, 1977. [Published 1979 by The Free Press.]

Cohen, R. J. (1977). Socially reinforced obsessing: A reply. *Journal of Consulting and Clinical Psychology, 45,* 1166–1171.

Cohen, R. J. (1979). *Malpractice: A guide for mental health professionals.* New York: The Free Press.

Cohen, R. J., & DeBetz, B. (1977). Responsive supervision of the psychiatric resident and clinical psychology intern. *American Journal of Psychoanalysis, 37,* 51–64.

Cohen, R. J., & Smith, F. J. (1976). Socially reinforced obsessing: Etiology of a disorder in a Christian Scientist. *Journal of Consulting and Clinical Psychology, 44,* 142–144.

Coyne, J. C. (1976). The place of informed consent in ethical dilemmas. *Journal of Consulting and Clinical Psychology, 44,* 1015–1017.

Eddy, M. B. (1875). *Science and health with key to the scripture.* Boston: Trustees under the will of Mary Baker Eddy.

Halleck, S. L. (1976). Discussion of "Socially reinforced obsessing." *Journal of Consulting and Clinical Psychology, 44,* 146–147.

Harrison, N. S. (1979). *Understanding behavioral research.* Belmont, Calif.: Wadsworth.

Hurvitz, N. (1967). Marital problems following psychotherapy with one spouse. *Journal of Consulting and Clinical Psychology, 31,* 38–47.

Lazarus, A. A. (1971). *Behavior therapy and beyond.* New York: McGraw-Hill.

London, P. (1976). Psychotherapy for religious neuroses? Comments on Cohen and Smith. *Journal of Consulting and Clinical Psychology, 44,* 145–147.

McCann, J. T. (1990). A multitrait-multimethod analysis of the MCMI-II clinical syndrome scales. *Journal of Personality Assessment, 55,* 465–476.

Meehl, P. E. (1956). Wanted: A good cookbook. *American Psychologist, 11,* 263–272.

Podmore, F. (1963). *From Mesmer to Christian Science: A short history of mental healing.* New Hyde Park, N.Y.: University Books.

Stokes, J. B. (1977). Comment on "Socially reinforced obsessing: Etiology of a disorder in a Christian Scientist." *Journal of Consulting and Clinical Psychology, 45,* 1164–1165.

Table 14-4

Some Clinical Measures

Test	Description
The Childhood Autism Rating Scale	For ages 2 and up, this observer rating scale is designed to assist in the identification of children with autism and rule out the autism syndrome in children who are otherwise developmentally disabled.
Family Relations Test: Children's Version	For ages 3 to 15, this card sorting test is designed to measure relative importance of different family members and explore emotional relations.
Mental Status Checklist for Children	For ages 5 to 12, this measure employs interview, case study, and behavioral observation methods for the purpose of evaluation and treatment.
North American Depression Inventories for Children and Adults	For ages 7 and up, this self-report measure is designed to evaluate various aspects of depression.
Mental Status Checklist for Adolescents	For ages 13 to 17, this measure employs interview, case study, and behavioral observation methods for the purpose of evaluation and treatment.
Suicidal Ideation Questionnaire	For ages 13 to 18, this is a self-report measure of suicidal ideation.
Beck Hopelessness Scale	For ages 13 to 80, this is a self-report measure that assesses expectations about the future and evaluates risk of suicide.
Whitaker Index of Schizophrenic Thinking	For ages 16 and older, this multiple-choice test gauges the degree to which evidence of schizophrenic thought processes are present.
Student Adaptation to College Questionnaire	For first-year college students, this self-report measure is a measure of adjustment to college life.
Couples' Pre-Counseling Inventory (Revised Edition)	For adults, this measure entails self-report on variables related to a couple's strengths and weaknesses by both members of the couple.
Dyadic Adjustment Scale	For adults, this test is designed to measure adjustment in a cohabiting or marital relationship.
The Custody Quotient	For parents in a custody dispute, this interview followed by an interviewer-completed rating scale is designed to be a measure of parenting skills and other variables relevant to a custody decision.
Personal History Checklist for Adults	Designed to provide a systematic self-report method for history-taking.
Psychiatric Diagnostic Interview (Revised)	For adults, this structured interview is designed to determine the current or past existence of a psychiatric disorder.
S-D Proneness Checklist	For adults, this interviewer-completed checklist is designed to help evaluate suicide proneness and depressive tendencies.

THE 4-QUESTION CHALLENGE

1. When interviewers nod their head or vocalize "um-hmmm" during the course of an interview, the interviewers
   (a) may inadvertently reinforce interviewee verbalizations.
   (b) are most typically conducting a mental status examination.
   (c) are testing the limits of the interviewee's mood and affect.
   (d) None of the above

2. In a mental status examination, the abbreviation "Oriented × 3" is used to convey the information that patients
   (a) can stand up, sit down, and lie down without assistance.
   (b) can accurately point in three directions by a compass.
   (c) know their own name, where they are, and the date.
   (d) None of the above

3. In the jargon of psychological testing and assessment, a *battery* refers to
   (a) a response to a TAT card that keeps going and going.
   (b) an assaultive gesture on the part of the testtaker.
   (c) a testtaker state of heightened achievement motivation.
   (d) None of the above

4. As discussed in the text, competency in the legal sense may refer to all of the following except
   (a) competency to stand trial.
   (b) competency to be executed.
   (c) competency to retain counsel.
   (d) competency to enter into a contract.

Chapter 15

Neuropsychological Assessment

A (neurological) Miracle!
In The Wizard of Oz, *the Scarecrow evidenced remarkable psychomotor coordination for someone* sans *brain.*

Outline for Chapter 15 of Cohen et al. (1996)
NEUROPSYCHOLOGICAL ASSESSMENT

The Nervous System and Behavior
Neurological Damage and the Concept of "Organicity"

The Neuropsychological Examination
The History
The Neuropsychological Mental Status Examination
The Physical Examination

Neuropsychological Tests
Specialized Interviews and Rating Scales
Intellectual Ability Tests in Neuropsychology
Memory Tests
Tests of Cognitive Functioning
Tests of Verbal Functioning
Perceptual, Motor, and Perceptual-Motor Tests
The Bender-Visual Motor Gestalt Test

Neuropsychological Test Batteries
The "Flexible" Battery
The Prepackaged Battery
Halstead-Reitan Neuropsychological Battery
Luria-Nebraska Neuropsychological Battery
Other neuropsychological batteries

A Perspective

CLOSE-UP:
Medical Diagnostic Aids in Neuropsychological Examinations

EVERYDAY PSYCHOMETRICS:
Validity of the LNNB

EXERCISE 86
THE NEUROPSYCHOLOGICAL EXAMINATION

OBJECTIVE

To enhance understanding of and provide firsthand experience with a neurological assessment measure.

BACKGROUND

A neuropsychological examination may be undertaken for any of a number of reasons ranging from general screening purposes to locating the specific site of a neurological lesion. The exact form of the neuropsychological examination (as well as the nature of the tests and measurement procedures employed) will vary as a function of factors such as the purpose of the examination, the thoroughness of the examination, and the neurological intactness of the examinee. In addition to the administration of psychological tests and/or prepackaged test batteries, a history-taking and a physical examination may also be part of the neuropsychological examination. In the two tables below, we have described some of the tests that could be used in a neuropsychological examination; more specifically, these are tests that could be used to evaluate (1) muscle coordination and (2) the intactness of some of the 12 cranial nerves.

YOUR TASK

1. You are a neuropsychologist charged with performing routine neurological screenings on all students in your school who are enrolled in a psychological testing course. Select any three of the four tests described in Table 15-1, and administer these tests to a fellow student in the class.
2. Select any three of the four tests described in Table 15-2, and administer these tests to the same student to whom you had administered the other three tests.
3. Write a brief report of your findings. Include in your report a note about what other tests or prepackaged test batteries you would have also wanted to administer and explain why.
4. Now, trade places—you become the patient and your partner "plays doctor."

Table 15-1

Some Tests Used to Evaluate Muscle Coordination

Walking-running-skipping

If the examiner has not had a chance to watch the patient walk for any distance, he may ask the patient to do so as part of the examination. We tend to take walking for granted; but, neurologically speaking, it is a highly complex activity that involves proper integration of many varied components of the nervous system. Sometimes abnormalities in gait may be due to nonneurological causes; if, for example, a severe case of bunions is suspected as the cause of the difficulty, the examiner may ask the patient to remove his or her shoes and socks so that the feet may be physically inspected. Highly trained examiners are additionally sensitive to subtle abnormalities in, for example, arm movements while the patient walks, runs, or skips.

Standing-still (technically, the Romberg test)

The patient is asked to stand still with feet together, head erect, and eyes open. Whether patients have their arms extended straight out or at their sides and whether or not they are wearing shoes or other clothing will be a matter of the examiner's preference. Patients are next instructed to close their eyes. The critical variable is the amount of sway exhibited by the patient once the eyes are closed. Since normal persons may sway somewhat with their eyes closed, experience and training are required to determine when the amount of sway is indicative of pathology.

Nose-finger-nose

The patient's task here is to touch her nose with the tip of her index finger, then touch the examiner's finger, and then touch her own nose again. The sequence is repeated many times with each hand. This test, as well as many similar ones (such as the toe-finger test, the finger-nose test, the heel-knee test), is designed to assess, among other things, cerebellar functioning.

Finger wiggle

The examiner models finger wiggling (that is, playing an imaginary piano or typing), and then the patient is asked to wiggle his own fingers. Typically, the nondominant hand cannot be wiggled as quickly as the dominant hand, but it takes a trained eye to pick up a significant decrease in rate. The experienced examiner will also be looking for abnormalities in the precision of the movements and the rhythm of the movements, "mirror movements" (uncontrolled similar movements in the other hand when instructed to wiggle only one), and other abnormal involuntary movements. Like the nose-finger test, finger wiggling supplies information concerning the quality of involuntary movement and muscular coordination. A related task involves tongue wiggling.

Table 15-2

Some Tests Used in the Assessment of the Intactness of the 12 Cranial Nerves

Cranial Nerve	Test
I (olfactory nerve)	Closing one nostril with a finger, the examiner places some odiferous substance under the nostril being tested and asks whether the smell is perceived. Subjects who perceive it are next asked to identify it. Failure to perceive an odor when one is presented may be indicative of lesions of the olfactory nerve, a brain tumor, or other medical conditions. Of course, failure may be due to other factors, such as oppositional tendencies on the part of the patient or intranasal disease, and such factors must be ruled out as causal.
II (optic nerve)	Assessment of the intactness of the second cranial nerve is a highly complicated procedure, for this is a sensory nerve with functions related to visual acuity and peripheral vision. A Snellen eye chart will therefore be one of the tools used by the physician in assessing optic nerve function. If the subject at a distance of 20 feet from the chart is able to read the small numbers or letters in the line labeled line "20," then the subject is said to have 20/20 vision in the eye being tested. 20/20 vision is only a standard; and while many persons can read only the larger print at higher numbers on the chart (that is, a person who reads the letters on line "40" of the chart would be said to have a distance vision of 20/40), some persons have better than 20/20 vision. An individual who could read the line labeled "15" on the Snellen eye chart would be said to have 20/15 vision.
V (trigeminal nerve)	The trigeminal nerve supplies sensory information from the face, and it supplies motor information to and from the muscles involved in chewing. Information regarding the functioning of this nerve will be examined by the use of tests for facial pain (pinpricks will be made by the physician), facial sensitivity to different temperatures, and other sensations. Another part of the examination will entail having the subject clamp his jaw shut. The physician will then feel and inspect the facial muscles for weakness and other abnormalities.
VIII (acoustic nerve)	The acoustic nerve has functions related to the sense of hearing and the sense of balance. Hearing may be formally assessed by the use of an apparatus called the audiometer. More frequently, the routine assessment of hearing will involve the use of a so-called "dollar watch." Provided the examination room is quiet, an individual with normal hearing should be able to hear a dollar watch ticking at a distance of about 40 inches from each ear (30 inches if the room is not very quiet). Other quick tests of hearing involve the placement of a vibrating tuning fork on various portions of the skull. Individuals who complain of dizziness, vertigo, disturbances in balance, and so forth may have their vestibular system examined by means of specific tests.

EXERCISE 87
INTERVIEW WITH A NEUROPSYCHOLOGIST

OBJECTIVE

To construct an interview consisting of 10 questions you would like to ask a practicing neuropsychologist, and then conduct the interview.

BACKGROUND

As you read about psychologists in various specialties and the tests and assessment procedures they use in practice, a wealth of questions may arise. Here is your chance to pose any questions you may have about neuropsychological assessment to a practicing neuropsychologist. Your questions may relate to any facet of a neuropsychologist's work—how such work interfaces with medicine, how research is put into practice, and how such a career

has its own unique rewards and drawbacks. Check with your instructor before arranging this interview, as it may prove more feasible to have your instructor arrange a class visit by a neuropsychologist.

YOUR TASK

Write your interview questions, and be prepared to arrange and conduct the interview upon assignment of this exercise by your instructor.

EXERCISE 88
PICK-A-TEST: NEUROPSYCHOLOGICAL TESTS

OBJECTIVE

To learn more about neuropsychological tests not reviewed in the textbook.

BACKGROUND

The approach in your textbook is to highlight only a few of the many tests that exist in any given area. For every test covered in your textbook there may well be dozens of other tests designed to measure the same attribute(s). The Pick-A-Test exercise represents an opportunity to learn more about a particular test not covered in your textbook.

YOUR TASK

A list of neuropsychological tests along with a brief description of each follows below in Table 15-3. From this list, select one test that you think you would like to know more about. Then, use all of the resources at your disposal to answer the following:

1. Describe what the test measures.
2. Who would be most apt to use this test? Why? Include in your answer sample questions the test user might hope to answer through the use of this test.
3. Who would be most apt to take this test? Why?
4. Describe the full range of people to whom it would be appropriate to administer this test, including comments about who would be inappropriate.
5. Describe what is known about the test's reliability.
6. Describe what is known about the test's validity.
7. Imagining that you are a measurement consultant, would you recommend this test to clients who are test users? Why or why not?

Table 15-3

Some Neuropsychological Tests and Test Batteries

Test	Description
Neurobehavioral Assessment of the Preterm Infant	For use with preterm infants ranging in conceptual age from 32 weeks to term, this test assesses the effects of medical as well as other complications (such as maternal substance addiction) on preterm infants.
McCarron-Dial System	For ages 3 and up, this test battery is designed to be of particular utility in meeting the therapy needs of handicapped persons.
Children's Category Test	For ages 5 through 16 years, this test is designed to measure complex intellectual functioning including concept formation and memory.
Portable Tactile Performance Test	For ages 5 and up, this test focuses on the evaluation of tactual performance.
Benton Visual Retention Test	For ages 8 years to adult, this test measures visual perception, memory, and visuoconstructive abilities.
Wisconsin Card Sorting Test Revised	For ages 6.5 through 89 this test is designed to measure several neurological variables including abstract thinking and perseverative thinking.
Behavior Change Inventory	For children and adults, this test focuses on the evaluation of the effects of head injury.
Ross Information Processing Assessment	For adolescents and adults, this test focuses on the evaluation of communication disorder among people with head injuries.
Boston Diagnostic Aphasia Examination	For adults, this test is designed to focus on the nature of deficits in aphasia as well as common clusters of deficit.
Mini Inventory of Right Brain Injury	For ages 18 and up, this test focuses on the evaluation of deficit due to injury of the right hemisphere of the brain.
Stroop Neuropsychological Screening Test	For ages 18 and up, this is a general neuropsychological screening test designed for individual administration.
Bedside Evaluation and Screening Test of Aphasia	For adults, this is a test of language ability for patients who have suffered neurological damage.
Sklar Aphasia Scale	For adults, this test is designed to measure the nature and severity of language disability following neurological damage.
Cognitive Behavior Rating Scales	For adults, and capable of being group-administered, this measure of cognitive impairment and behavioral deficit is completed by informants familiar with the assessee.
Dementia Rating Scale	For adults, this measure is designed to evaluate the cognitive status of an individual with known impairment.
Rivermead Perceptual Assessment Battery	For adults, this test measures nature and degree of visual deficit following stroke or a related injury.

THE 4-QUESTION CHALLENGE

1. A patient with known damage to brain lobes complains of a severely impaired visual field. Which lobes of the brain have the highest probability of having been damaged?
   (a) frontal lobes
   (b) temporal lobes
   (c) occipital lobes
   (d) parietal lobes
2. The term "organicity"
   (a) has been used interchangeably with "brain damage."
   (b) is not synonymous with "brain damage."
   (c) has been used interchangeably with "neurological damage."
   (d) All of the above
3. Which is *not* a test a neuropsychologist would typically administer to routinely evaluate muscle coordination?
   (a) finger wiggle test
   (b) nose wiggle test
   (c) standing still test
   (d) walking-running-skipping test
4. The Bender is a test that entails
   (a) copying designs.
   (b) interpreting proverbs.
   (c) connecting dots.
   (d) All of the above

Chapter 16

The Assessment of People
with Disabling Conditions

Years before the rock opera Tommy *and the hit song from that film "Pinball Wizard," Van Johnson played the blind protagonist in a film called* 23 Paces to Baker Street *(note the hat atop the glass). Such films serve to sensitize viewers to the difficulties that people with disabling conditions may endure in carrying out even routine activities of daily living. Psychological examiners who have occasion to work with members of this population must exhibit sensitivity to their unique needs and strive to create a test environment that will, to the extent that it is possible, fairly assess each examinee's individual deficits and strengths.*

Outline for Chapter 16 of Cohen et al. (1996)
THE ASSESSMENT OF PEOPLE WITH DISABLING CONDITIONS

The Visually Impaired
    Issues in Test Administration and Interpretation
    Available Instruments

The Hearing-Impaired and the Deaf
    Issues in Test Administration and Interpretation
    Available Instruments

The Deaf-Blind

Motor Disabilities
    Issues in Test Administration and Interpretation
    Available Instruments

Cognitive Disabilities
    Developmental Disabilities
    Assessing Adaptive Behavior
        The Vineland Adaptive Behavior Scale
        The AAMD Adaptive Behavior Scale
        Other measures of adaptive behavior

A Perspective

CLOSE-UP:
Attitudes Toward the Disabled

EVERYDAY PSYCHOMETRICS:
Psychometric Evaluation of the Vineland

EXERCISE 89
ADMINISTERING, SCORING, AND INTERPRETING NONSTANDARDIZED PSYCHOLOGICAL TESTS

OBJECTIVE

To enhance understanding of the problems attendant to the administration and interpretation of psychological tests that have been adapted for use with people with disabling conditions.

BACKGROUND

Assessing people with disabling conditions brings with it special problems. For example, in the assessment of people with sensory impairments (such as the visually-impaired and the blind and the hearing-impaired and the deaf), there exists the twofold problem of (1) adapting a given test so that it may be administered to the examinee and (2) interpreting the findings in a meaningful way given the absence of norms that would be useful with respect to the nonstandardized test administration.

YOUR TASK

Review the general description of the types of subtests that appear on the Wechsler scales in your textbook. Next, imagine that you are a psychological consultant to a school district that has inquired about modifying tests to make them amenable for administration to the disabled.

1. Describe the various types of adaptations that might have to be made in each of the subtests in order to adapt the test for administration to (a) a visually-impaired individual *or* (b) a hearing-impaired individual.
2. Advise the school district how to proceed after the modified administration of the test to the individual with a sensory impairment; what guidelines for test scoring and interpretation would you suggest?

EXERCISE 90
ASSESSING ADAPTIVE BEHAVIOR

OBJECTIVE

To enhance understanding of and provide firsthand assessment experience with the concept of adaptive behavior.

BACKGROUND

Many instruments exist for use in assessing the adaptive behavior of examinees. Two such tests, the Adaptive Behavior Scale (ABS) and the Adaptive Behavior Scale, School Edition (ABSSE), are published by the American Association of Mental Deficiency. A partial listing of some of the general types of items that can be found on these two tests can be found in Table 16-1.

YOUR TASK

1. For each type of item listed in Table 16-1, write one item that could be scored "Correct" or "Incorrect" that you believe would measure the adaptive behavior listed. For example, consider Item A: "Eating [(use of utensils, table manners, etc.).]" One item that you might create might read as follows:
   (a) Hand examinee a fork and ask examinee to demonstrate how he or she might eat mashed potatoes. Score "Correct" if fork is held correctly.
2. After you have created your own test of adaptive behavior administer it to someone—anyone—who will take it. If the examinee does not have a cognitive (or other) disability, a "perfect score" will hopefully be obtained. Regardless, on the basis of your (meager) experience, discuss the problems and pitfalls that you can envision one might encounter in (a) devising a test of adaptive behavior, (b) administering such a test, (c) scoring such a test, and (d) interpreting the findings.

Table 16-1

A Partial Listing of Some of the Types of Items Found on the ABS and the ABSSE

I.	INDEPENDENT FUNCTIONING
	A. Eating
	B. Toilet Use
	C. Cleanliness
	D. Appearance
	E. Care of clothing
	F. Dressing/undressing
	G. Travel
	H. Other (such as telephone use)
II.	PHYSICAL DEVELOPMENT
	A. Sensory development
	B. Motor development
III.	ECONOMIC ACTIVITY
	A. Money handling and budgeting
	B. Shopping skills
IV.	LANGUAGE DEVELOPMENT
	A. Expression (such as writing)
	B. Comprehension (including reading)
V.	KNOWLEDGE OF NUMBERS AND TIME
VI.	RESPONSIBILITY
	A. Care of personal belongings
VII.	SOCIALIZATION

As an example of (c) and (d) with reference to the "Eating" question above, the question arises, "What is the correct position for holding a fork? *Is* there a correct position for holding a fork?"

EXERCISE 91
PICK-A-TEST:
THE ASSESSMENT OF PEOPLE WITH DISABLING CONDITIONS

OBJECTIVE

To learn more about a test for people with disabling conditions not reviewed in the textbook.

BACKGROUND

The approach in your textbook is to highlight only a few of the many tests that exist in any given area. For every test covered in your textbook there may well be dozens of other tests designed to measure the same attribute(s).

The Pick-A-Test exercise represents an opportunity to learn more about a particular test not covered in your textbook.

YOUR TASK

A list of tests for persons with disabling conditions along with a brief description of each follows below in Table 16-2. From this list, select one test that you think you would like to know more about. Then, use all of the resources at your disposal to answer the following:

1. Describe what the test measures.
2. Who would be most apt to use this test? Why? Include in your answer sample questions the test user might hope to answer through the use of this test.
3. Who would be most apt to take this test? Why?
4. Describe the full range of people it would be appropriate to administer this test to, including comments about who would be inappropriate.
5. Describe what is known about the test's reliability.
6. Describe what is known about the test's validity.
7. Imagining that you are a measurement consultant, would you recommend this test to clients who are test users? Why or why not?

Table 16-2

Some Tests for People with Disabling Conditions

Test	Description
Assessing Linguistic Behaviors: Assessing Prelinguistic and Early Linguistic Behaviors in Developmentally Young Children	For children from birth through a 2-year-old functional level, this test measures children's performance in various areas of cognitive-social and linguistic development such as language comprehension and communicative intentions.
An Adaptation of the Wechsler Preschool and Primary Scale of Intelligence (WPPSI) for Deaf Children	For ages 4 to $6\frac{1}{2}$ years, this is designed to be a general measure of achievement for deaf and hearing impaired children.
Movement Assessment Battery for Children	For ages 4 through 12, this test is designed to screen and provide management suggestions for children with motor skill disabilities.
Motor Skills Inventory	For children, this is a screening test for impairment in fine and gross motor skills.
CID Phonetic Inventory	For children with hearing impairments, this test evaluates speech ability at the phonetic level.
Living Language	For children, this test is designed to evaluate language skills and impairment.
Behavioral Analysis Language Instrument	For children and adults, this test is designed to identify deficiencies in language.
Employability Maturity Interview	For adult rehabilitation clients, this structured interview was designed to assess readiness for the vocational rehabilitation planning.
Work Personality Profile	For adult rehabilitation clients, this rating scale completed by observers is designed to assess aspects of one's job-related performance deemed to be essential to the achievement and maintenance of employment.
Adaptive Behavior: Street Skills Survival Skills Questionnaire	For developmentally disabled adolescents and adults, this test measures prevocational skills and ability to function independently in the community.

THE 4-QUESTION CHALLENGE

1. Which measure has been widely used with the blind and visually impaired as a measure of intelligence?
   (a) Verbal scale of the Wechsler
   (b) Performance scale of the Wechsler
   (c) Performance scale of the K-ABC
   (d) Vineland Interview Edition

2. Which event was in part responsible for the creation by the United States Congress of Regional Centers for Deaf-Blind Youths?
   (a) the discovery of HIV and AIDS
   (b) the launching of Sputnik by the Soviets
   (c) a nationwide epidemic of rubella
   (d) a nationwide epidemic of hepatitis

3. If there were a need to learn more about the sexual knowledge and attitudes of a developmentally disabled adolescent, which of the following would probably be most helpful?
   (a) Callier-Azusa Scale
   (b) Socio-Sexual Knowledge and Attitudes Test
   (c) Hand Test
   (d) Southern California Sensory Integration Tests

4. Many tests administered to people with various types of disability do not have norms directly applicable to the testtaker. According to the text, the examiner in such a case may have to
   (a) refrain from using the test and use an interview instead.
   (b) improvise somewhat in the test administration and interpretation.
   (c) contact the APA Committee on Testing for an opinion about how to proceed.
   (d) None of the above

Chapter 17

Industrial/Organizational Assessment

Be All You Can Be

If you can bend steel with your bare hands, construction work, plumbing, or even more ambitious undertakings—depending on your other skills and abilities—may be in the offing. In personnel assessment, tests and other assessment procedures are used to pair people with jobs.

Outline for Chapter 17 of Cohen et al. (1996)
INDUSTRIAL/ORGANIZATIONAL ASSESSMENT

Screening, Selection, Classification, and Placement
>   The Resume and Letter of Application
>   The Application Blank
>   Letters of Recommendation
>   Interviews
>   Portfolio Assessment
>   Performance Tests
>   The Assessment Center
>   Physical Tests

Assessment of Ability, Aptitude, Interest, and Personality
>   Measures of Ability and Aptitude
>   The General Aptitude Test Battery
>   Measures of Interest
>   Strong Interest Inventory
>   Personality Measures
>   The Myers-Briggs Type Indicator

Assessment of Productivity, Motivation, and Attitude
>   Productivity
>   Motivation
>   Attitude
>   Job satisfaction
>   Organizational commitment
>   Organizational culture

Other Varieties of I/O Assessment
>   Drug Testing and Tests of Integrity
>   Drug testing and its alternatives
>   Test of integrity
>   Engineering Psychology

A Perspective

CLOSE-UP:
Validity Generalization and the GATB

EVERYDAY PSYCHOMETRICS:
The Use of the Myers-Briggs Type Indicator in Academic and Preemployment Counseling

EXERCISE 92
ASSESSMENT OF PERSONNEL

OBJECTIVE

To enhance understanding of and provide firsthand experience with some of the tools of assessment in personnel psychology.

BACKGROUND

Personnel psychology is that area of industrial/organizational psychology that deals with matters related to the hiring, firing, promotion, and transfer of workers as well as issues of worker productivity, motivation, and job satisfaction. Psychological tests, including measures of interest, aptitude, achievement, intelligence, and personality may all be used in the counseling of prospective employees as well as by psychologists in management charged with tasks such as screening, selection, classification, and placement of personnel.

Screening refers to a relatively superficial selection process based on an evaluation with respect to certain minimal criteria. Perhaps the most widely used tools for employment screening include application blanks, letters of recommendation, autobiographical statements, and the interview. Hiring someone or not and admitting someone or not are examples of *selection*—the case where such a yes/no-type of decision regarding each person (or object in some cases) must be made. Psychological tests (and for some positions physical and situational performance tests as well) are typical elements of the hiring process for many large business or government positions. In contrast to selection, acceptance or rejection is not inherent in *classification*—a term that refers to the categorizing, "pigeon-holing," and/or rating of people (or objects) on the basis of two or more criteria. *Placement* refers to a classification, categorization, or rating made on the basis of one criterion; as an example, the advanced placement test in French you took while in high school was the sole criterion used to determine the level of the French course you would be eligible to take as a college freshman.

YOUR TASK

Picture yourself as a NASA personnel psychologist charged with the responsibility of selecting two astronauts for the first mission to the planet Pluto. It's going to be a long flight—a *very* long flight—so in addition to each astronaut being qualified individually, the two-person crew will have to be highly compatible.

1. Briefly describe the types of tests or measurement procedures that you would employ for the purpose of screening applicants.
2. Briefly describe the types of tests or measurement procedures that you would employ for the purpose of selecting applicants.
3. More specifically, describe the role each of the following variables would (or would not) play in your ultimate selection decision:

   - physical/medical
   - personality
   - intelligence
   - interests
   - cultural factors
   - oral communication skills
   - written communication skills
   - creativity
   - tolerance of ambiguity
   - energy level
   - flexibility
   - decision-making ability
   - ability to delay gratification
   - (insert your own variable here)

4. Beyond the written exercise described above, an in-class exercise would entail one student playing the role of the NASA psychologist screening prospective candidates for the mission (all other class members) by means of a brief interview. All class members then write a paragraph or two on who they felt were the top two choices for the mission and why.
5. Class discussion of each of the above tasks shall take place at the discretion of, and be guided by, "mission control" (the instructor).

EXERCISE 93
TEST PROFILES

OBJECTIVE

To enhance understanding of and provide firsthand experience with test profiles and patterns.

BACKGROUND

In everyday conversation, the word *profile* is synonymous with a side view of something, most typically a side view of a human head. In the language of psychological testing, the word *profile* generally refers to measurements obtained from a test or tests, most typically (though not necessarily) represented in graphic form. The term probably was derived from the shape of the graphic representation of test data when the graph is of the frequency polygon variety—with the connected lines of the frequency polygon forming a shape reminiscent of a person or object in profile. However, *profile* has generalized in meaning and may also be properly used to refer to measurement data displayed in histogram form or data that are simply listed in tabular form.

Test profiles may be derived from virtually any type of psychological test be it an intelligence test, a personality test, and educational test, a measure of interest, a measure of attitude . . . the list goes on. One type of test profile makes reference to the subjects (or, in some instances, raw or scaled scores) of a single test. For example, we might speak of a particular child's WISC-R profile or the profile (or pattern[1]) of test scores obtained by an adult on the WAIS-R. A particular profile of scores (such as one where there are large discrepancies between scores on Verbal and Performance subtests) may be suggestive of neuropsychological impairment. A particular profile or pattern of scores on the MMPI–2 may be suggestive of a particular psychodiagnostic category. And a particular profile of scores on a measure of occupational interest may be suggestive of suitability for one or another profession.

The term profile is also used to refer to a pattern of test results with respect to more than one test. For example, the profile of a day-care-center worker who is convicted of child abuse might include (1) average to below average scores on intelligence tests, (2) scores indicative of maladjustment particularly in the area of social relations, self-esteem, and sexual adjustment on tests of personality, (3) a higher-than-average incidence of self-report of having been abused (themselves) as children.

If a profile is displayed in graphic form, the horizontal axis of the graph will typically list items or subtests or tests while the vertical axis will typically list scores—expressed as numbers (such as in raw or converted form) or expressed with reference to some qualitative category (such as "low/medium/high").

YOUR TASK

1. Table 17-1 gives the data for John D. Doe's scores expressed as percentiles on the 30 subtests of the "Almost Every Conceivable Aptitude Test" (AECAT), a highly reliable and valid (but entirely hypothetical measure) of high school students' aptitude for entry into various occupations and professions. Graph these data in the space provided on the following page as (a) a frequency polygon and (b) a histogram.
2. You are the high school vocational counselor charged with the responsibility of providing vocational guidance to John D. Doe. What advice might you give the test-

[1] The term *pattern* is, in practice, virtually synonymous with *profile*.

Table 17-1

John D. Doe's AECAT Scores

AECAT Aptitude Codes		Percentile Scores for John D. Doe
1.	Domestic engineering	10
2.	Financial planning	30
3.	Clerical	50
4.	Accounting	55
5.	College teaching	60
6.	Food Sciences	65
7.	Computer Sciences	70
8.	Medical Sciences	70
9.	Musical	70
10.	Political	70
11.	Agricultural	75
12.	Mathematics (General)	80
13.	Strategic Planning	95
14.	Military Sciences	99
15.	Dental Sciences	99
16.	Leadership (General)	99
17.	Navigational	80
18.	Physical trainer	90
19.	Verbal (General)	80
20.	Electronics technology	85
21.	Foreign languages	75
22.	Guidance counseling	90
23.	Interpersonal skills	75
24.	Legal	75
25.	Writing (General)	70
26.	Statistical	20
27.	Cosmetology	15
28.	Artistic	15
29.	Pharmaceutical	10
30.	Lighthouse keeper	10

taker—a graduating high school senior—on the basis of these data? What type of career might you suggest that this testtaker learn more about?

3. In the space provided on page 238, draw the AECAT profile of an individual who you predict would be ideally suited to enter the field of psychology and specialize in the area of psychometrics. Then, using additional paper if necessary, briefly explain the profile you constructed.

EXERCISE 94
ANOTHER DAY, ANOTHER PROFILE

OBJECTIVE

To introduce students to the Differential Aptitude Test and provide additional experience with test profiles.

BACKGROUND

The Differential Aptitude Test (DAT) is a vocational aptitude battery that was first published in 1947. It is designed for use with students in grades 7 through 12.

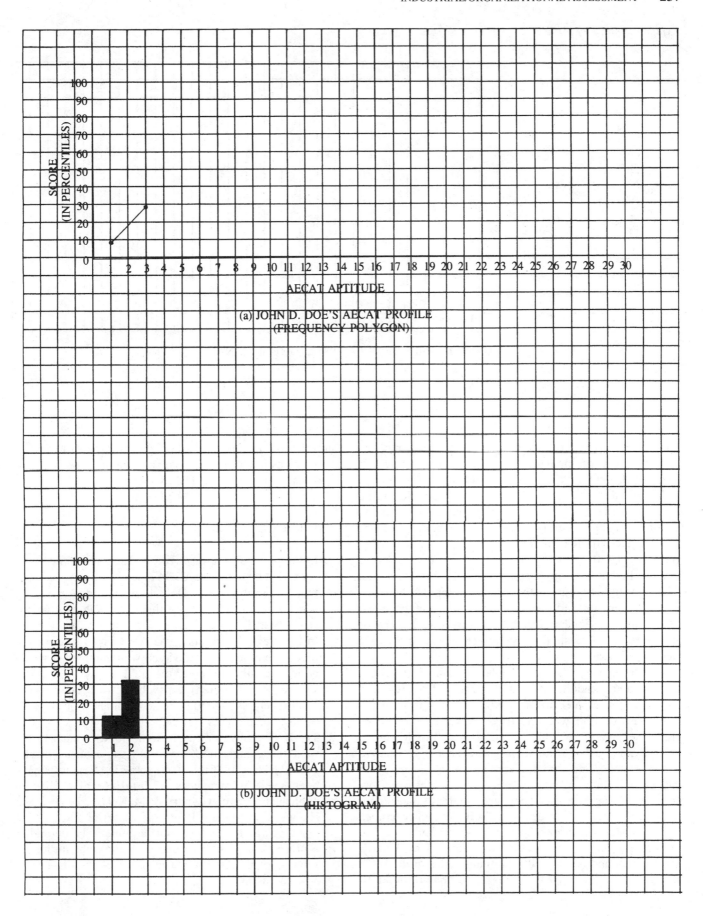

(a) JOHN D. DOE'S AECAT PROFILE
(FREQUENCY POLYGON)

(b) JOHN D. DOE'S AECAT PROFILE
(HISTOGRAM)

Explanation of the Profile

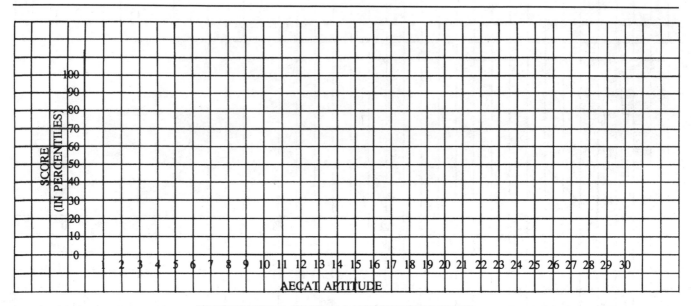

AECAT PROFILE OF "IDEAL PSYCHOMETRICIAN"

The test is based on the idea that people have not one but a variety of measurable vocational aptitudes. It consists of eight subtests, which yield separate scores on eight aptitudes (see Table 17-2). A ninth score, Scholastic Aptitude, is derived from a combination of the scores on Verbal Reasoning and Numerical Reasoning and is designed to provide an indication of academic ability. With the 1990 revision of this test came the Career Interest Inventory, which combines DAT data with data from a supplementary questionnaire tapping interests, educational goals, and preferences. The computerized test report analyzes and discusses the resulting pattern of aptitudes and interests in terms of the appropriateness of various occupational choices.

Approximately 100,000 students from 520 school districts and an additional 22,000 students from research programs participated in the 1990 standardization of the DAT. The sample was stratified on variables such as grade, sex, geographical region, socioeconomic status, ethnicity, and urban/rural/suburban residence. Normative data for males and females are presented separately in the manual. Intercorrelations among the subtests are low enough to suggest that they are, in fact, measuring relatively independent areas. Validity evidence comes from research on workers in specific occupations. For example, a composite scale comprised of the Verbal, Mechanical, and Numerical Reasoning scales of the DAT, along with a visualization task, has been found to correlate acceptably with the actual job performance of apprentices in the trades, such as plumbing, tool making, and machine repair (Hattrup & Schmitt, 1990).

YOUR TASK

1. In the previous exercise, you became acquainted with John D. Doe and his AECAT scores. Based on what you know about Mr. Doe, how would you expect him to score on each of the eight subtests of the DAT? Why?

2. In the previous exercise, you were asked to draw the AECAT profile of an individual who you predict would be ideally suited to enter the field of psychology and specialize in the area of psychometrics. How would you expect this individual to score on each of the eight subtests of the DAT? Why?

3. The DAT seems to measure some abilities that overlap with those measured by intelligence tests (Boyle, 1987; Gakhar, 1986). In fact, some DAT subtests have been used as measures of intellectual ability in published research (Landry & McKelvie, 1985; Lynn, Hampson, & Magee, 1983, 1984). Write a short (one or two paragraphs maximum) argument, taking either a pro or con position, regarding the substitution of subtests of the DAT for a measure of intelligence in a research study.

Table 17-2

The Subtests of the Differential Aptitude Test

Test	Type of Items
Verbal Reasoning	Double-ended analogies designed in part to test ability to abstract. This type of item requires the testtaker to select the pair of words that best completes the beginning and end of a sentence. An example: _____ is to end, as appetizer is to _____ 1. beginning _____ dessert 2. ending _____ appetizing 3. sunset _____ dusk 4. final _____ midterm 5. fruit cup _____ open bar
Numerical Reasoning	Items on this subtest measure computational skills and understanding of numerical relationships.
Abstract Reasoning	The testtaker's task here is to determine which of several alternative figures would logically be next in a series of figures.
Perceptual Speed and Accuracy	Includes tasks resembling those required for clerical jobs (such as filing and coding).
Mechanical Reasoning	Items on this subtest are pictures designed to assess the testtaker's understanding and knowledge of various physical laws and forces affecting activities such as lifting, turning, and pulling.
Space Relations	A two-dimensional picture or pattern is presented, and it is the examinee's task to select which of several alternative pictures or patterns could be produced from the original; this subtest taps the process of visualization—and the ability to mentally rotate objects in space.
Spelling	A word is presented and the testtaker indicates whether the word is or is not spelled correctly.
Language Usage	Basic language skills such as grammar, punctuation, and capitalization are tapped by this subtest.

EXERCISE 95
YOUR PERSONALITY SUITS YOU FOR WORK AS . . .

OBJECTIVE

To introduce students to the Guilford-Zimmerman Temperament Survey.

BACKGROUND

Is a likeable, dominant, persuasive person better suited for work in sales or work on an assembly line? Clearly such an individual, at least with respect to the personality traits described, seems better suited for work in sales. In addition to examining interests and aptitudes, preemployment counseling may also entail the administration of personality tests. Such tests "round out" the vocational assessment by providing additional input. Suppose an individual with an interest in a television news career and a high aptitude for writing is weighing the merits of becoming a television news personality or a television news writer. And suppose further that one of the findings in a personality test was that this individual has a very high need for exhibitionism. The personality test findings, combined with other findings, might lead the consulting psychologist to steer the client toward pursuit of an on-air career. Contrariwise, if the findings from personality tests indicated that this client was low in exhibitionism, had a strong need for independence and autonomy combined with little tolerance for relating to authority figures, the client might be asked to consider the merits of freelance work within the field of television news.

Almost any personality test could conceivably be used within the context of vocational counseling. One such test that has enjoyed widespread usage is the Guilford-Zimmerman Temperament Survey (GZTS). This test is a self-report measure that yields scores on the 10 personality dimensions listed in Table 17-3. The scores on each of these dimensions or factors are derived from responses to 30 statements that may take the form of "yes," "no," or "?" (uncertain). Interpretation is typically not made with respect to any one score but rather on the basis of all the scores—a profile. Thus, for example, consideration of a high score in General Activity alone might lead the interpreter to suspect that the assessee is

Table 17-3

Guilford-Zimmerman Temperament Survey (GZTS) Personality Dimensions

Dimension Name	Description
General Activity (G)	A measure of energy level and the rate at which the individual operates. A high scorer would be a person who moves quickly, works at a rapid rate, and is full of vitality.
Restraint (R)	A measure of self-control, persistence, and deliberate action; to some extent this score provides a measure of responsibility. A person scoring low on this scale would be impulsive, spontaneous, and seemingly carefree.
Ascendance (A)	A measure of the degree to which the individual exhibits leadership, initiative, and assertiveness. A low score on this scale reflects submissiveness.
Sociability (S)	The extent to which the individual seeks and develops social contacts.
Emotional Stability (E)	An indication of evenness or fluctuation of moods, optimism, or pessimism, and whether there are feelings of or freedom from feelings of worry, guilt, or loneliness.
Objectivity (O)	A measure of the degree to which the individual is thick-skinned or sensitive.
Friendliness (F)	A measure of congeniality, respect for others, acceptance, and tolerance.
Thoughtfulness (T)	An indication of observation and reflectiveness of self and others.
Personal Reactions (P)	Acceptance and tolerance of others and faith in social institutions.
Masculinity (M)	A measure of the degree to which the individual is interested in masculine activities and exhibits behavior traditionally associated with masculine roles.

one who works quickly. However, if such a score is coupled with a low score on the Restraint dimension, the interpretation might change from "highly energetic" to "highly impulsive," the latter description being more accurate for someone who acts quickly but with little restraint. In addition to the dimension scales, the GZTS has built into it three verification scales designed to detect response sets, intentional faking, and carelessness.

Normative data for the GZTS are based on a college sample of 523 men and 389 women; profiles of patterns of scores for various high school, college, and adult occupational groups are reported in the test manual (Guilford, Zimmerman, & Guilford, 1976). Reliability estimates obtained on each of the different factors were found to range from .75 to .85. Test-retest reliability based on varying intervals of from one to three years tend to lie in the .50s and .60s range. An overview of the extensive amount of research conducted on this test in the years since its publication is presented in the manual. Included are studies exploring scores on the test as a function of variables such as age, education, gender, occupational group, psychiatric diagnosis, socioeconomic status, ethnic group, and political affiliation.

YOUR TASK

1. Create your own GZTS profile by characterizing yourself as either "low," "medium," or "high" with regard to each of the 10 dimensions described in Table 17-3.
2. On the basis of the GZTS profile of yourself that you have created, what type of work do you think you are best suited for? Why?
3. Create one question that can be answered in a Yes/No format to measure each of the 10 dimensions of the

GZTS. Then describe the process of creating those questions, in terms of its ease or difficulty. What obstacles must be overcome in terms of creating such questions?

**EXERCISE 96
PICK-A-TEST:
INDUSTRIAL/ORGANIZATIONAL
ASSESSMENT**

OBJECTIVE

To learn more about a measure used in industrial/organizational assessment.

BACKGROUND

The approach in your textbook is to highlight only a few of the many tests that exist in any given area. For every test covered in your textbook there may well be dozens of other tests designed to measure the same attribute(s). The Pick-A-Test exercise represents an opportunity to learn more about a particular test not covered in your textbook.

YOUR TASK

A list of measures used in industrial/organizational assessment along with a brief description of each follows below in Table 17-4. From this list, select one test that you think you would like to know more about. Then, use all of the resources at your disposal to answer the following:

Table 17-4

Some Measures Used in Industrial/Organizational Assessment

Test	Description
	Preemployment Measures
How Well Do You Know Your Interests?	For adolescents and adults, this test is a measure of one's liking toward various work-related activities.
How Well Do You Know Yourself?	For adolescents and adults, this is a measure of work-related personality characteristics.
Occupational Personality Questionnaire	For adult workers in business and industry, this is a measure of various work-related personality and motivational characteristics. It is also used by employers to evaluate current employees.
	Personnel Selection Measures
Firefighter Selection Test	For use with applicants for firefighter positions, this multiple-choice test gauges relevant knowledge of firefighting and is designed to predict success on the job.
Human Resource Development Report	For use with candidates for managerial positions, this self-report measure provides information on the applicant's management style.
Inwald Personality Inventory	For use with applicants for police and related security positions, this MMPI-like test is designed to aid in the selection of new officers.
	Work Behavior and Attitudes
Job Attitude Scale	For administration to working employees, this test measures intrinsic and extrinsic aspects of job orientation.
Management Style Inventory	For administration to working managers, this self-report, self-scored measure is designed to provide information about the effect of one's management style on subordinates.
Time Problems Inventory	For administration to working managers and administrators, this self-report measure taps variables related to the wasting of work time.
	Work Environment Measures
Employee Involvement Survey	For current employees in business and industry, this self-report and self-scored test evaluates employees' actual and optimal opportunities for involvement and influence on the job.
Occupational Stress Indicator	Employees' self-report; Cooper, Sloan, and Williams, 1988; "to clarify the nature of stress in organisations by identifying sources of stress, intervening factors, and the effects of stress on employees" (p. 620).
Oliver Organization Description Questionnaire	For administration to current employees, this measure yields a description of the workplace organization along various dimensions.
Survey of Organizational Climate	For administration to current employees, this measure assesses attitudes toward organizational climate on dimensions such as job security and standards of excellence.

1. Describe what the test measures.
2. Who would be most apt to use this test? Why? Include in your answer sample questions the test user might hope to answer through the use of this test.
3. Who would be most apt to take this test? Why?
4. Describe the full range of people it would be appropriate to administer this test to, including comments about who would not be appropriate.
5. Describe what is known about the test's reliability.
6. Describe what is known about the test's validity.
7. Imagining that you are a measurement consultant, would you recommend this test to clients who are test users? Why or why not?

REFERENCES

Boyle, J. P. (1987). Intelligence, reasoning, and language proficiency. *Modern Language Journal, 71,* 277–288.

Gakhar, S. C. (1986). Correctional research-individual differences in intelligence, aptitude, personality, and achievement among science, commerce, and arts students. *Journal of Psychological Researches, 30,* 22–29.

Hattrup, K., & Schmitt, N. (1990). Prediction of trades apprentices' performance on job sample criteria. *Personnel Psychology, 43,* 453–466.

Landry, M., & McKelvie, S. J. (1985). Validity of conventional and unbiased intelligence test items for groups differing in age and education. *Psychological Reports, 57,* 975–981.

Lynn, R., Hampson, S. L., & Magee, M. (1983). Determinants of educational achievement at 16+: Intelligence, personality, home background and school. *Personality and Individual Differences, 4,* 473–481.

Lynn, R., Hampson, S. L., & Magee, M. (1984). Home background, intelligence, personality, and education as predictors of unemployment in young people. *Personality and Individual Differences, 5,* 549–557.

THE 4-QUESTION CHALLENGE

1. In the language of psychometrics, the term "assessment center" refers to
   (a) a place where tests are administered.
   (b) an organizationally standardized procedure.
   (c) the average of a number of assessments.
   (d) None of the above

2. The job-seeking factor found to be most important by Champagne in his study of values with male and female unskilled subjects was
   (a) working with friends and neighbors.
   (b) a job close to home.
   (c) a steady job.
   (d) vacations and holidays with pay.

3. The expectancy theory of motivation is best associated with
   (a) Alderfer.
   (b) Mooney.
   (c) Vroom.
   (d) Vroom-Vroom.

4. An individual who has been denied employment because he or she is HIV positive (has the virus that causes AIDS) may have recourse under
   (a) PL 101-336.
   (b) PL 94-142.
   (c) Title VII of the Civil Rights Act of 1964.
   (d) *Debra P. versus Turlington.*

Chapter 18

Consumer Assessment

Don't Shoot the Sponsor!

In a rather interesting film titled Looker, *a prominent Beverly Hills plastic surgeon (actor Albert Finney, disguised above as a security guard—see the movie, it's too much to explain) is drawn in to intrigue that involves television commercials made in a way so as to subliminally effect compliance with the advertised message.*

In reality, of course, such technology does not exist; and if it did, it would quickly be outlawed. However, consumer psychologists and other professionals may assist advertisers in selling their wares in far less dramatic ways. What are some of those ways?

Outline for Chapter 18 of Cohen et al. (1996)
CONSUMER ASSESSMENT

An Overview
　　The Measurement of Attitudes
　　The Tools of the Consumer Psychologist
　　　　Surveys and polls
　　　　Motivation research methods
　　　　Behavioral observation
　　　　Other methods

Measurement with Surveys and Polls
　　Survey Techniques
　　　　Face-to-face survey research
　　　　Telephone surveys
　　　　Mail surveys
　　Designing Survey Research Questionnaires
　　　　Aggregate scaling methods
　　　　Multidimensional scaling
　　　　The semantic differential technique

Qualitative Assessment
　　One-on-one Interviews
　　Focus Groups
　　Projective Techniques
　　Other Techniques

Psychophysiological Measures
　　Pupillary Response
　　Electrodermal Response
　　Brain-Wave Measurement
　　Other Measures

A Perspective

EVERYDAY PSYCHOMETRICS:
Adaptive Testing, Friends, and Family

CLOSE-UP:
Brand Equity: Smile!

EXERCISE 97
TASTE-TESTS

OBJECTIVE

To obtain firsthand experience with the problems and issues that may arise in conducting a simple consumer experiment such as a taste-test.

BACKGROUND

> "Beer drinkers prefer Brand X to Brand Y by 2 to 1!"
> "Take the challenge and you'll see for yourself why
> the switch is on to Our Cola!"
> "A real butter taste, with no cholesterol!"
> "It tastes identical to sugar, but with no calories!"

Claims involving taste-test data have by now become quite familiar. Often, it seems simple; a group of consumers of a particular beverage—say, carbonated cola soft drinks—taste-test two or more carbonated cola soft drinks and a clear preference emerges. But is it really all that simple?

A wealth of literature attests to the fact that there are a number of relatively complex issues that must be dealt with in terms of taste-test administration, as well as analysis of taste-test data (Brown, Zatkalik, Treumann, Buehner, & Schmidt, 1984; Buchanan & Morrison, 1984; Day, 1965, 1969; Greenhalgh, 1966; Irwin, 1958; Kuehn, 1962; Luce & Suppes, 1965; Morrison, 1981). Additionally, events that may on their face be indicative of taste preferences, may well be due to the operation of other phenomena (Ringold, 1988).

YOUR TASK

1. Simply on the basis of what you know now, design and conduct a taste-test to determine which of two brands of carbonated cola drinks is preferred by 10 people you know. Write a report of your findings. After you have completed your report, consult references in the professional literature (such as those listed at the end of this chapter) to see if there are any issues in taste-discrimination testing that you may have overlooked. Make a list of these overlooked issues, and be prepared to discuss them in class.
2. Gain experience with conducting in-depth interviews by devising a list of questions to "get at the heart" of why different people you know are loyal to different brands of beer. Identify at least six different people who are loyal to three different beers (two subjects for each beer) and administer your interview. Write a brief report of your findings.

EXERCISE 98
PSYCHOGRAPHICS

OBJECTIVE

To acquaint students with the consumer psychology system of "psychographics" and the place of measurement and categorization within that system.

BACKGROUND

Demography is the study of characteristics of human populations in terms of variables such as size, growth, density, height, weight, age, and so forth—all referred to by the plural noun *demographics*. *Psychographics* is a term in marketing, advertising, and consumer psychology (though it may not yet have made it to an English-language dictionary) that refers to the study of psychological characteristics of populations—more specifically, the psychological characteristics of populations of consumers. Why describe groups of consumers in terms of psychological traits? The notion underlying the use of psychographics is that people who share the same or similar personality traits, attitudes, interests, beliefs, and activities will be attracted by the same or similar products and services—and be influenced by the same kinds of advertising and promotion.

Psychographic studies are quantitative studies that tend to employ large numbers of subjects responding to a relatively large number of items. The responses are usually obtained via a format that readily lends itself to quantification (such as Likert scales or semantic differential items), and the data are carefully analyzed in different ways to determine what relationships exist. The object of a typical psychographic study is to identify common psychological and related characteristics of a particular population of people (for example, all people who sent in $400 for a homestudy course in "How to Get Rich Quick in Real Estate," after exposure to a television commercial). Alternatively, a psychographic study might employ as subjects a large, random group of people on whom many psychological measures have been taken and from whom much consumer information has been obtained; from such information psychographic profiles of different "types" of consumers might emerge.

Perhaps the best-known and most widely used typology of consumers, one that is based on psychographic research, is the typology developed by the Stanford Research Institute (SRI). The SRI typology is referred to as VALS (an acronym for an ongoing program of Values and Lifestyles), and in the VALS taxonomy, nine basic types of consumers have been identified: two types of "need-driven" consumers, three types of "outer-directed"

Table 18-1

VALS Lifestyle Segmentation

Percentage of Population	Consumer Type	Values and Lifestyles	Demographics	Buying Patterns	Spending Power
Need-Driven consumers					
6	Survivors	Struggle for survival Distrustful Socially misfitted Ruled by appetites	Poverty-level income Little education Many minority members	Price dominant Focus on basics Buy for immediate needs	$3 billion
10	Sustainers	Concern with safety, security Insecure, compulsive Dependent, following Want law and order	Low income Low education Much unemployment Live in country as well as cities	Price important Want warranty Cautious buyers	$32 billion
Outer-Directed consumers					
32	Belongers	Conforming, conventional Unexperimental, traditional, formal Nostalgic	Low to middle income Low to average education Blue-collar jobs Trend toward noncity living	Family Home Fads Middle and lower market makers	$230 billion
10	Emulators	Ambitious, show-off Status conscious Upwardly mobile Macho, competitive	Good to excellent income Youngish Highly urban Traditionally male, but changing	Conspicuous consumption "In" items Imitative Popular fashion	$120 billion
28	Achievers	Achievement, success, fame Materialism Leadership, efficiency Comfort	Excellent incomes Leaders in business, politics, etc. Good education Suburban and city living	Give evidence of success Top of the line Luxury and gift markets "New and improved" products	$500 billion
Inner-Directed consumers					
3	I-Am-Me	Fiercely individualistic Dramatic, impulsive Experimental Volatile	Young Many single Study or starting job Affluent backgrounds	Display one's taste Experimental fads Source of far-out fads Clique buying	$25 billion
5	Experimental	Drive to direct experience Active, participative Person-centered Artistic	Bimodal incomes Mostly under 40 Many young families Good education	Process over product Vigorous, outdoor "sports" "Making" home pursuits Crafts and introspection	$56 billion
4	Societally Conscious	Societal responsibility Simple living Smallness of scale Inner growth	Bimodal low and high incomes Excellent education Diverse ages and places of residence Largely white	Conservation emphasis Simplicity Frugality Environmental concerns	$50 billion
2	Integrated	Psychological maturity Sense of fittingness Tolerant, self-actualizing World perspective	Good to excellent incomes Bimodal in age Excellent education Diverse jobs and residential patterns	Varied self-expression Ethically oriented Ecologically aware One-of-a-kind items	$28 billion

consumers, and four types of "inner-directed" consumers (see Table 18-1). As you read the description of each, try to decide which of these categories best describes yourself, your siblings, and your parents.

The "Outer-Directed" general category of consumer consists of three distinctive groups that combined represent two-thirds of the U.S. population—and account for almost 78 percent of all purchases. These groups are concerned with appearance and conformity to established social norms. The *Achievers* within this broad category are the leaders of business, professions, and government. They value efficiency, status, materialism, and creature comforts. They have a high medium income and a median age of 42. The *Emulators* are ambitious, upwardly mobile, and status conscious. They are younger than the Achievers, have a lower median income than the Achievers, and aspire to attain the success of the Achievers (some will, but others will fail due to a lack of skills, education, or resources). The *Belongers* are the largest VALS category. They tend to be conservative and traditional, and their lives are focused on the home. They seek to fit in with society rather than stand out.

People who are "Inner-Directed" according to the VALS taxonomy can be characterized by a desire for self-expression and a need to fulfill individual needs. The four groups that make up this category represent about one-fifth of the U.S. population, and they make about 15 percent of the total purchases made in this country. The largest group of Inner-Directeds is the *Socially Conscious* group, a group that places emphasis on simple living, conservation, and environmentalism. The *Experientials* want experience and involvement. They participate in a wide range of activities for the experiences these activities provide. They tend to be hedonistic but often engage in activities such as crafts, building, and do-it-yourself projects because these projects provide opportunities for new experiences. The youngest VALS group is the *I-Am-Me's*. Members of this group are individualistic, impulsive, experimental, and highly energetic. They enjoy faddish items and tend to be innovators, particularly with respect to fashion. Many young adults and students fall into this latter category.

The *Integrated* make up about 2 percent of the population of the United States and spend about $28 billion annually. They are the most highly educated of the groups and have a median age of 40 and a median income of $40,000. This group combines the outward orientation of the outer-directed lifestyle and the sensitivity of the inner-directed. The buying habits of this group revolve around quality, uniqueness, high standards, and ecology. They embrace the values of individualism, tolerance, and a global view.

People who fall into the VALS general category of "Need-Driven" tend to be concerned primarily with security and simply "getting by." Although they represent about 11 percent of the U.S. population they account for only about 4 percent of total annual purchases in the United States. The *Sustainers* include a large number of females, single heads of household, as well as others who are struggling on the verge of poverty. The *Survivors* are typically older and poor. They tend to be cautious, conservative, authoritarian, and removed from mainstream society.

Members of the different VALS groups do exhibit differences in behavior in the marketplace, and a number of firms have found this taxonomy to be useful in defining their markets. Achievers tend to buy luxury cars, belongers tend to buy family-size cars, the socially conscious buy gas-efficient cars, and the need-driven tend to buy used cars (Capeli, 1984). Timex Medical Products Group focuses its marketing activities for digital thermometers, digital blood pressure monitors, and digital scales on the achievers and socially conscious because consumers in these groups tend to be more concerned with staying healthy, are more highly educated, and are more receptive to innovation than are members of the other groups. Belongers are not considered a viable market for these products because their traditional orientation makes them less receptive to high-tech items ("Timex," 1984).

Critics of the psychographic approach have argued that psychographic categories overlap so much as to be virtually meaningless. It has been further argued that when all is said and done, psychographic studies reveal nothing that savvy researchers or practitioners do not already know or could not figure out for themselves. Proponents of psychographics concede that there is overlap in defined lifestyle groups but argue that real differences do exist—marginal as they may be in some instances—and may still be quite useful. Proponents of the psychographic approach would further argue that such studies provide insights that cannot be obtained in any other way. Readers interested in more detailed discussions of various aspects of psychographics are referred to the following sources: Wells (1975); Demby (1974); Veltri & Schiffman (1984); Mitchell (1978); Bearden, Teel, & Durand (1978); Runyon & Stewart (1987); Shim & Bickle (1994).

YOUR TASK

Assuming the role of a consumer psychologist, respond to the following three scenarios with reference to the Stanford Research Institute's VALS taxonomy.

1. A carmaker has developed what it boasts is "the mother of all luxury cars." The car has everything from power ashtrays to bucket seats equipped with

individual heat and massage units. Describe a research study that could help give you insight on how to market this car.

2. A clothing manufacturer seeks your assistance in marketing a paper-thin, extremely inexpensive fabric that provides superior insulation from the cold. The manufacturer is particularly interested in getting jackets and vests of this material into the hands of the homeless living in cold-weather climates. How could you help?

3. A nationally known distributor of dairy products has developed a new food that is something of a cross between frozen yogurt and chocolate mousse. They consult with you in an effort to determine who, if anyone, is the prime consumer of such a product. What do you say?

REFERENCES

Brown, C. E., Zatkalik, N. E., Treumann, A. M., Buehner, T. M., & Schmidt, L. A. (1984). The effect of experimenter bias in a cola taste test. *Psychology & Marketing, 1,* 21–26.

Buchanan, B. S., & Morrison, D. G. (1984). Taste tests: Psychophysical issues in comparative test design. *Psychology & Marketing, 1,* 69–91.

Day, R. L. (1965). Systematic paired comparisons in preference analysis. *Journal of Marketing Research, 2,* 406–412.

Day, R. L. (1969). Position bias in paired product tests. *Journal of Marketing Research, 6,* 98–100.

Greenhalgh, C. (1966). Some techniques and interesting results in discrimination testing. *Journal of the Market Research Society, 8,* 215–235.

Irwin, F. W. (1958). An analysis of concepts of discrimination and preference. *American Journal of Psychology, 11,* 152–163.

Kuehn, A. A. (1962). Consumer brand choice: A learning process? *Journal of Advertising Research, 2,* 10–17.

Luce, R. D., & Suppes, P. (1965). Preference, utility, and subjective probability. In R. D. Luce, R. R. Bush, & E. Galanter (Eds.), *Handbook of mathematical psychology* (Vol. 3). New York: Wiley.

Morrison, D. G. (1981). Triangle taste tests: Are subjects who respond correctly lucky or good? *Journal of Marketing, 45,* 111–119.

Ringold, D. J. (1988). Consumer response to product withdrawal: The reformulation of Coca-Cola. *Psychology & Marketing, 5,* 189–210.

Shim, S., & Bickle, M. C. (1994). Benefit segments of the female apparel market: Psychographics, shopping orientations, and demographics. *Clothing and Textiles Research Journal, 12,* 1–12.

THE 4-QUESTION CHALLENGE

1. In consumer psychology and marketing, the term "positioning a product" typically refers to
   (a) the highlighting of a product's benefit.
   (b) the naming of a product.
   (c) the rotation of a product as a function of a shelf-life.
   (d) a product's "shelf-esteem."

2. If one were conducting a national survey that contained an extremely lengthy list of questions, which medium would probably be best?
   (a) telephone
   (b) fax
   (c) mail
   (d) face-to-face

3. A shortcoming of Likert scales is that
   (a) the data is derived from an aggregate scaling method.
   (b) the data cannot be used with semantic differentials.
   (c) the data are not necessarily interval in nature.
   (d) None of the above

4. Tachistoscopes have been used in consumer research to assess
   (a) the visibility of consumer warning labels.
   (b) the memorability of trademarks and brand names.
   (c) projective imagery associated with kaleidoscopes.
   (d) the clarity of images used in print advertising.

Chapter 19

Computer-Assisted Psychological Assessment

To HAL, with Love

A rogue computer named HAL (who was supposed to have been christened as such by moving one letter down in the alphabet from the letters I, B, *and* M) *was a source of great consternation to the astronauts in* 2001: A Space Odyssey. *Computers are increasingly viewed as a mixed blessing in the area of psychological assessment, as thorny questions and issues regarding various aspects of their use emerge.*

Outline for Chapter 19 of Cohen et al. (1996)
COMPUTER-ASSISTED PSYCHOLOGICAL ASSESSMENT

An Overview
  The Process
  The Advantages
    Item banking
    Item branching
  The Disadvantages
    The testtaker's perspective
    The test user's perspective

Computer Input
  On-Line Test Administration
    Effects of item type
    Effects of item content
    Tests specifically designed for on-line administration
    The testtaker's attitude and emotional reaction
  Inputting Data from Tests
    Central processing
    Teleprocessing
    Local processing

Computer Output
  Scoring Reports
    Simple scoring reports
    Extended scoring reports
  Interpretive Reports
    Descriptive reports
    Screening reports
    Consultative reports
  Integrative Reports

Issues in CAPA
  Computer-Assisted Test Administration: Equivalency
  Computer-Assisted Test Interpretation: Validity
  Standards for CAPA Products
  Access to CAPA Products

CLOSE-UP:
  Designing an Item Bank

EVERYDAY PSYCHOMETRICS:
  Computer-Assisted Behavioral Assessment

EXERCISE 99
COMPUTER-ASSISTED PSYCHOLOGICAL ASSESSMENT

OBJECTIVE

To enhance understanding of computer-assisted psychological assessment.

BACKGROUND

Computer-based scoring and interpretation of psychological tests has been with us since the 1950s; those were the days of the number 2 pencil and the blackened answer grid that got sent off to some far-away mainframe. With the advent of the personal computer and the development of test administration/scoring/interpretation software, the practice of inoffice, computerized administration, scoring and interpretation of psychological tests has burgeoned.

The proliferation of computer technology and psychological test disks (where there were once test booklets) has brought with it new concerns and questions regarding professional standards in psychological testing. Some of the questions and concerns amount to "new wine in old bottles." As an example, consider the problem of safeguarding the security of a test that is written on a disk. In a fashion parallel to the way a responsible psychologist might strive to safeguard the security of a test question booklet, so would the disk have to be protected from theft, tampering, and the like.

Some of the questions and concerns that have been raised with respect to computer-assisted psychological assessment are new and unique to this method of administering, scoring, and interpreting psychological tests. For example, how might you deal with the problem of a testtaker who receives one score on a computer-administered test and a significantly different score on an equivalent form of the same test when it is administered by paper and pencil? If the discrepancy in scores was found to be due, for example, to factors inherent in the computer administration of the test, the problem could be addressed by elimination of such factors. If such factors could not be eliminated, the problem might be addressed in the long run by either (1) a weighting of scores achieved by means of the two types of administration in order to make them equivalent or (2) the development of separate norms for computer-administered and paper-and-pencil-administered versions of the test.

YOUR TASK

You have been invited to speak before a local organization of psychologists in independent practice called the "Traditional Clinicians Club" (TCC). The TCC is aware of your reputation and contributions in the field of computerized testing and has asked you to make a presentation entitled "Going Computer." Your talk will be designed to convey to the clinicians some of the benefits and liabilities as well as concerns and issues that attend the initiation of office-based computerized test administration, scoring, and interpretation. Using the material in your textbook, and the reprinted article that follows, as well as any other sources (including your own experience), prepare a 5-minute presentation entitled "Going Computer" (and be prepared to actually present it in class). Make sure to include the following in your talk:

- an engaging introduction to the subject matter;
- a description of the process of computer-based assessment;
- a listing of some of the potential benefits of "going computer";
- a listing of some of the potential problems inherent in "going computer"; and
- a mention of some of the issues and concerns that still exist in the field.

Each "Going Computer" presentation by a class member could be followed by a 5-minute question-and-answer session in which the audience plays "devil's advocate" and challenges the presenter's views; the audience of "traditional clinicians" extols the virtues of paper-and-pencil testing and it is the presenter's role to convince them otherwise.

EXERCISE 100
COMPUTER-ASSISTED EDUCATIONAL ASSESSMENT: THE CASE OF THE GRE

OBJECTIVE

To note differences between the paper-and-pencil and computerized versions of the Graduate Record Examination.

BACKGROUND

The ritual known as the taking of the Graduate Record Examination (GRE) was once performed with great regularity at 8:00 A.M. on the first Saturday of February, April, June, October, or December. Graduate school hopefuls would gather at designated testing centers with trusty and sharpened #2 pencils in hand. People residing some distance from the test site either arrived the day before or set their alarm clocks for the crack of dawn— or earlier. The group assembled at the test site and almost immediately all of the testtakers felt a common bond; never mind that it was mass anxiety, it was a bond nonetheless. You could hear a pin drop as a proctor addressed the masses, extolling the virtues of entirely blackening printed grids on answer sheets.

In fall 1992, the days of this ritual became numbered as the GRE General Test became available on-line. It was spring 1995 when the GRE Subject Tests followed suit. Before long, the paper-and-pencil version of the GRE would become something of a museum curiosity.

Like its predecessor, the computerized GRE is given only in controlled and monitored settings. Educational Testing Service (ETS), which administers the test, has contracted with Sylvan Technology Centers to conduct most of the administrations. Still, some academic institutions continue to participate, and ETS continues to administer the GRE at its field offices in Princeton, New Jersey, and Evanston, Illinois.

For testtakers, the primary advantage of the computerized GRE may be convenience. One can go to any of some 250 testing centers nationwide and take the test by appointment. A second advantage is immediate feedback. Rather than waiting five or six weeks for a first-class letter from ETS, testtakers can learn their scores before they leave the administration center. Of course, there is a premium to be paid for technology. At this writing, it costs $96 to take the computerized test versus $56 for the pencil-and-paper test.

First administered in October 1992, the computerized GRE was simply the existing GRE but in an automated format. Multiple-choice items were listed one after the other. In fall 1993, the test evolved into an adaptive format, complete with item branching. The items placed at the beginning of the test were of intermediate difficulty. The difficulty of subsequent items for the individual testtaker will be based on the nature of that testtaker's performance on earlier items.

Taking the computerized GRE requires different test-taking strategies as compared to the paper-and-pencil version (GRE 1994–1995 General Test Descriptive Booklet, 1994). For example, in the past, examinees could skip questions, either with the intent of leaving them blank or in the hope of returning to them at a later point. Skipping questions cannot be done in the computerized format. Also, testtakers may not go back to earlier questions to change answers. In the event that a testtaker makes one or two careless errors, the computer program will recognize that by noting that other questions at the same difficulty level were answered correctly. The computerized GRE, like its predecessor, is timed. However, a difference here is that a set number of questions must be answered on the computerized test in order for a score to be calculated. Scores on the traditional format could be obtained even if testtakers answered only a few items.

The GRE General Test involves three subtests: Verbal, Quantitative, and Analytical. The paper-and-pencil version had six components, two covering each of these three subtests. The computerized GRE has only three components, one covering each of the subtests. Presumably, this reduction is a consequence of the switch to an adaptive test format, and the need for fewer items to estimate ability.

Contrary to what one might suspect, the adaptive format of the GRE does not yield a significant savings in time over the paper-and-pencil administration. Both formats take about four hours to complete, including initial instructions and scheduled breaks in testing. This is partly because a tutorial session is given before computerized testing. To minimize the impact of experience with computers in general, and with IBM-compatible machines having a mouse interface, a 20- to 25-minute orientation to the computer is required of all testtakers.

At this writing, ETS is experimenting with new item formats, taking advantage of some of the things that one can do on computers but not easily in a paper test booklet. For example, a graph may be manipulated on the computer screen. In contrast to a purely selected-response format, ETS is also experimenting with constructed-response items, such as those involving essay or short-answer writing (Bridgeman, 1992; Bridgeman & Rock, 1993). Students who have taken the computerized GRE have already seen some of these kinds of items. However, the items were experimental and did not count toward their scores (GRE 1994–95 Bulletin, 1994). The format of the computerized GRE, then, is still evolving. It will continue to evolve as new technology makes possible new item formats.

Although ETS has argued that the computerized GRE is equivalent to the traditional format (GRE 1994–95 Bulletin, 1994), a number of questions remain as yet unanswered regarding possible differences between the two formats. For example, does pressure to complete a sufficient number of items within the time limit affect one's scores? Might variance in scores on items with constructed response formats be too dependent on the testtaker's keyboarding skills? What differences might there be in test scores as a result of having three variables measured by only one component of the test each, as compared to having the same three variables each measured by two components of the test? Are computer-anxious people differentially affected by the test format? Does computer experience make a difference? Are different subgroups of the population (e.g., men compared with women) differentially affected by the format changes? If there are differences, what is their cause?

And so the computerized GRE continues to evolve. The winds of change still blow, but where will they take us? Nobody knows.

YOUR TASK

1. From the perspective of a testtaker, discuss whether you would prefer to take the computerized or pencil-and-paper GRE.

2. From the perspective of the test user, discuss whether you would prefer to administer the computerized or paper-and-pencil GRE.
3. Describe in general terms what you believe are the key issues regarding paper-and-pencil and computerized tests.

EXERCISE 101
PICK-A-TEST:
COMPUTER-ASSISTED TEST PRODUCTS

OBJECTIVE

To learn more about a computer-assisted test product not reviewed in the textbook.

BACKGROUND

The approach in your textbook is to highlight only a few of the many tests that exist in any given area. For every test covered in your textbook there may well be dozens of other tests designed to measure the same attribute(s). The Pick-A-Test exercise represents an opportunity to learn more about a particular test not covered in your textbook.

YOUR TASK

A list of computer-assisted test products along with a brief description of each follows below in Table 19-1. From this list, select one test that you think you would like to know more about. Then use all of the resources at your disposal to answer the following:

Table 19-1

Some Computer-Assisted Tests

Test	Description
Beck Computer Scoring	Computerized administration, scoring, and interpretation of four scales developed by Aaron Beck: Beck Depression Inventory, Beck Hopelessness Scale, the Beck Anxiety Inventory, and the Beck Scale for Suicidal Ideation.
Jesness Inventory Computer Program	Computerized administration, scoring, and interpretation of the Jesness Inventory of Adolescent Personality, a test designed to predict asocial tendencies in testtakers age 8 to 18.
Differential Aptitude Tests: Computerized Adaptive Edition	Computerized administration and scoring of the DAT in an adaptive format with immediate reporting of results.
Psychiatric Diagnostic Interview-Revised	Computer-assisted interview with item-branching, followed by interpretation, and written report.
Rorschach Interpretive Assistance Program	Computation of scores based on coded responses entered by the test user. A feature is that specific responses can be added or deleted in order to determine how much the score is influenced.
Shipley Institute of Living Scale	Computerized administration, scoring, and interpretation of this test designed to provide an estimate of intellectual functioning in various domains.
Suicide Probability Scale	Computerized scoring and interpretation is designed to provide an estimate of suicide risk.
The Marriage Counseling Report	A computerized analysis of two individuals' 16 PF profiles designed to focus on the individual and joint strengths and weaknesses of the couple.
The Computerized Boston	For scoring and recording of assessment with the Boston Diagnostic Aphasia Examination, this software provides profiles classifications and performance printouts to aid in the diagnosis of aphasia.
CVLT Administration and Scoring System	Scores and helps interpret the California Verbal Learning Test whether or not the computer-assisted administration system is used. In computer-assisted administration system, the examiner enters responses directly into the computer.
State-Trait Anxiety Inventory Computer Program	Computerized administration, scoring, and graphic representation of results on scales designed to measure the trait of anxiety (defined in terms of anxiety proneness) and the state of anxiety (defined in terms of the current level of anxiety being experienced).
Chemical Dependency Assessment Profile	A self-report interview administered via computer or paper-and-pencil, along with a computer-generated interpretive report that organizes information in terms of chemical dependency history, beliefs about use and dependency, patterns and dimensions of use, self-concept, and interpersonal relations.

1. Describe what the test measures.
2. Who would be most apt to use this test? Why? Include in your answer sample questions the test user might hope to answer through the use of this test.
3. Who would be most apt to take this test? Why?
4. Describe the full range of people it would be appropriate to administer this test to, including comments about who would be inappropriate.
5. Describe what is known about the test's reliability.
6. Describe what is known about the test's validity.
7. Imagining that you are a measurement consultant, would you recommend this test to clients who are test users? Why or why not? If a traditional (paper-and-pencil) version of the test exists, explain why you would or would not prefer to administer the computerized version.

REFERENCES

Bridgeman, B. (1992). A comparison of quantitative questions on open-ended and multiple-choice formats. *Journal of Educational Measurement, 29,* 253–271.

Bridgeman, B., & Rock, D. A. (1993). Relationships among multiple-choice and open-ended analytical questions. *Journal of Educational Measurement, 30,* 313–329.

GRE 1994–95 bulletin. (1994). Princeton, NJ: Educational Testing Service.

GRE 1994–95 General Test descriptive booklet. (1994). Princeton, NJ: Educational Testing Service.

THE 4-QUESTION CHALLENGE

1. As used in the Cohen et al. text, the term "computer-assisted psychological assessment" implies that
   (a) an assessee is entering data by computer.
   (b) an assessor is interpretating data by computer.
   (c) an assessor is using a computer in measurement.
   (d) All of the above
2. The term "item bank" refers to
   (a) a large collection of computer-stored test questions.
   (b) "branches" of "question trees" in a computerized test.
   (c) retrieval methods for assessment-related data.
   (d) a system of penalties for early withdrawal.
3. Which is an issue regarding the equivalency of computerized and more traditional formats of tests?
   (a) the effect of item type
   (b) the effect of item content
   (c) the testtaker's attitude and emotional reaction
   (d) All of the above
4. Test user control and flexibility in terms of inputting data from computerized tests are best associated with
   (a) central processing.
   (b) local processing.
   (c) teleprocessing.
   (d) actuarial processing.

Appendix A

The Mid-Pawling Personality Inventory (MPPI)

(see Exercise 68)

1. Much like most everyone else, I have my vices.
2. People think I'm a good dancer.
3. I could have breakfast in bed 7 days a week.
4. No amount of money can buy happiness.
5. All handguns should be banned.
6. I refrain from taking medication if I can help it.
7. Everyone who meets me likes me.
8. I really should be behind bars or otherwise institutionalized.
9. I am intolerant of just about everything and everyone.
10. I smell things that other people do not.
11. In general, I respect the rights of other people.
12. I feel I am making a statement with my hair.
13. I find myself getting too agitated when driving.
14. I have a fear of snakes.
15. My love of food has led to a real problem with my weight.
16. I enjoy watching soap operas.
17. I experience weakness at the sight of laundry.
18. I tend to be a very outgoing person.
19. One learns more on the street than at school.
20. People consider me to be very adventuresome.
21. I don't feel like I'm being hugged often enough.
22. There is not the slightest shred of bias, prejudice, or ill will toward anybody in myself or any of my close friends.
23. I count miniature golf among my hobbies.
24. I have never looked forward to wearing dentures.
25. More often than not, music played on elevators is maddening.
26. In general, the police would be more mellow if they drank more cappucino and less coffee.
27. I love shopping for shoes and could do it quite often.
28. I am a firm believer in "Child on Board" signs.
29. With regard to my temperament, I experience low "lows" and "highs."
30. Death is in the very distant future.
31. Satanic cults hold no appeal to me at all.
32. I will only wear sweaters on Tuesdays.
33. I love costume parties like the kind you go to on Halloween.
34. I think I would look good in high-heeled shoes.
35. I recently bought tickets to a state-run lottery.
36. I think I am too absorbed in the past.
37. I enjoy traveling on my own.
38. I inevitably have problems with people in authority.
39. I have never considered cosmetic surgery.
40. I take a bubble bath at least once a day, every day.
41. I think I would be very good at gardening.
42. I enjoy hearing the sound of my own voice on tape.
43. I always buckle my seatbelt in a car or van.
44. In many ways, I am very traditional.
45. I have a brother in the federal witness protection program.
46. I organize a party for a friend at least once a year.
47. I enjoy listening to the radio, even if there is only static on.
48. I could stand being a bit more "macho."
49. I wish I had more close friends.
50. People think I'm very neat.
51. I seldom make reservations for restaurants.
52. I have always wanted a pen pal.
53. I consider myself "computer-phobic."
54. Few people have anything really important to say.
55. I hear voices commanding me to do certain things.
56. I have a fear of heights.
57. My videotape collection includes over 100 episodes of *Wheel of Fortune*.
58. Other families members can't believe I'm part of the family.
59. I could take a nap almost anytime, anywhere.
60. I need to take better care of myself.
61. I do not enjoy soap operas.
62. My dreams are probably much like most other people's dreams.
63. Some day I would like to be a toll-taker.
64. I avoid large crowds of people.
65. I find it easy to "tick-off" other people.
66. I would never consider getting a tattoo.
67. I feel as if I am in touch with occult phenomena.
68. My thoughts are as pure and as good as can be.
69. I do not consider myself traditional in any way.
70. A supermarket is a good place to meet new people.
71. In comparison to most other people, I am not particularly muscular.
72. I enjoy public speaking.
73. I need to laugh more than I do.

74. Most hunting is unnecessary and should be banned.
75. I sometimes experience strange, unexplainable sensations.
76. I enjoy working with computers.
77. I stutter when I get nervous.
78. Vampires exist in movies, but not in real life.
79. I see myself as very different from other people.
80. I have seen *The Rocky Horror Picture Show* more than once.
81. I enjoy sampling new varieties of sushi.
82. I feel uncomfortable at parties.
83. I consider myself a role model for others.
84. I really love when someone sends me flowers.
85. As a youngster, I got along well with other children.
86. I probably watch too much television.
87. The sight of blood has no effect on me.
88. I prefer reading to watching television.
89. I walk away from fights.
90. Only the best is good enough for me.
91. At one time or another, I have considered growing a mustache.
92. I like to drive cars that are faster than most.
93. Happiness is financial security.
94. I do not believe in gun control.
95. There is something frightening about intimacy.
96. I have absolutely no interest in learning to speak French.
97. I think I would enjoy living the rest of my life on some faraway island.
98. The respect of other people is important to me.
99. I frequently order off the menu in restaurants.
100. I look forward to the day when I can just sit home all day and watch television or do whatever else I want.

Appendix B

A Glossary
of Measurement Terms

Blythe C. Mitchell, *Consultant, Test Department, The Psychological Corporation*

This glossary of terms used in educational and psychological measurement is primarily for persons with limited training in measurement, rather than for the specialist. The terms defined are the more common or basic ones such as occur in test manuals and educational journals. In the definitions, certain technicalities and niceties of usage have been sacrificed for the sake of brevity and, it is hoped, clarity.

The definitions are based on the usage of the various terms as given in the current textbooks in educational and psychological measurement and statistics, and in certain specialized dictionaries. Where there is not complete uniformity among writers in the measurement field with respect to the meaning of a term, either these variations are noted or the definition offered is the one that the writer judges to represent the "best" usage.

academic aptitude. The combination of native and acquired abilities that are needed for school learning; likelihood of success in mastering academic work, as estimated from measures of the necessary abilities. (Also called *scholastic aptitude, school learning ability, academic potential*)

achievement test. A test that measures the extent to which a person has "achieved" something, acquired certain information, or mastered certain skills—usually as a result of planned instruction or training.

age norms. Originally, values representing typical or average performance for persons of various *age* groups; most current usage refers to sets of complete score interpretive data for appropriate successive age groups. Such norms are generally used in the interpretation of mental ability test scores.

alternate-form reliability. The closeness of correspondence, or correlation, between results on alternate (i.e., equivalent or parallel) forms of a test; thus, a measure of the extent to which the two forms are consistent or reliable in measuring whatever they do measure. The time interval between the two testings must be relatively short so that the examinees themselves are unchanged in the ability being measured. See RELIABILITY, RELIABILITY COEFFICIENT.

anecdotal record. A written description of an incident in an individual's behavior that is reported objectively and is considered significant for the understanding of the individual.

aptitude. A combination of abilities and other characteristics, whether native or acquired, that are indicative of an individual's ability to learn or to develop proficiency in some particular area if appropriate education or training is provided. Aptitude tests include those of general academic ability (commonly called mental ability or intelligence tests); those of special abilities, such as verbal, numerical, mechanical, or musical; tests assessing "readiness" for learning; and prognostic tests, which measure both ability and previous learning, and are used to predict future performance—usually in a specific field, such as foreign language, shorthand, or nursing.

Some would define "aptitude" in a more comprehensive sense. Thus, "musical aptitude" would refer to the combination not only of physical and mental characteristics but also of motivational factors, interest, and conceivably other characteristics, which are conducive to acquiring proficiency in the musical field.

arithmetic mean. A kind of average usually referred to as the *mean*. It is obtained by dividing the sum of a set of scores by their number.

average. A general term applied to the various measures of central tendency. The three most widely used averages are the arithmetic mean (mean), the median, and the mode. When the term "average" is used without designation as to type, the most likely assumption is that it is the *arithmetic mean*.

battery. A group of several tests standardized on the same sample population so that results on the several tests are comparable. (Sometimes loosely applied to any group of tests administered together, even though not standardized on the same subjects.) The most common test batteries are those of school achievement, which include subtests in the separate learning areas.

bivariate chart (bivariate distribution). A diagram in which a tally mark is made to show the scores of one [**bivariate chart (bivariate distribution),** continued.] individual on *two variables*. The intersection of lines determined by the horizontal and vertical scales form cells in which the tallies are placed. Such a plot provides frequencies for the two distributions, and portrays the relation between the two variables as a basis for computation of the product-moment correlation coefficient.

ceiling.   The upper limit of ability that can be measured by a test. When an individual makes a score which is at or near the highest possible score, it is said that the test has too low a "ceiling" for him; he should be given a higher level of the test.

central tendency.   A measure of central tendency provides a single most typical score as representative of a group of scores; the "trend" of a group of measures as indicated by some type of average, usually the *mean* or the *median*.

coefficient of correlation.   A measure of the degree of relationship or "going-togetherness" between two sets of measures for the same group of individuals. The correlation coefficient most frequently used in test development and educational research is that known as the Pearson or *product-moment r*. Unless otherwise specified, "correlation" usually refers to this coefficient, but *rank, biserial, tetrachoric,* and other methods are used in special situations. Correlation coefficients range from .00, denoting a complete absence of relationship, to +1.00, and to −1.00, indicating perfect positive or perfect negative correspondence, respectively. See CORRELATION.

composite score.   A score which combines several scores, usually by addition; often different weights are applied to the contributing scores to increase or decrease their importance in the composite. Most commonly, such scores are used for *predictive* purposes and the several weights are derived through multiple regression procedures.

concurrent validity.   See VALIDITY (2).

construct validity.   See VALIDITY (3).

content validity.   See VALIDITY (1).

correction for guessing (correction for chance).   A reduction in score for wrong answers, sometimes applied in scoring true-false or multiple-choice questions. Such scoring formulas (R − W for tests with 2-option response, R − $\frac{1}{2}$W for 3 options, R − $\frac{1}{3}$W for 4, etc.) are intended to discourage guessing and to yield more accurate rankings of examinees in terms of their true knowledge. They are used much less today than in the early days of testing.

correlation.   Relationship or "going-togetherness" between two sets of scores or measures; tendency of one score to vary concomitantly with the other, as the tendency of students of high IQ to be above average in reading ability. The existence of a strong relationship—i.e., a high correlation—between two variables does not necessarily

indicate that one has any causal influence on the other. See COEFFICIENT OF CORRELATION.

criterion.   A standard by which a test may be judged or evaluated; a set of scores, ratings, etc., that a test is designed to measure, to predict, or to correlate with. See VALIDITY.

criterion-referenced (content-referenced) test.   Terms often used to describe tests designed to provide information on the specific knowledge or skills possessed by a student. Such tests usually cover relatively small units of content and are closely related to instruction. Their scores have meaning in terms of *what* the student knows or can do, rather than in their relation to the scores made by some external reference group.

criterion-related validity.   See VALIDITY (2).

culture-fair test.   So-called culture-fair tests attempt to provide an equal opportunity for success by persons of all cultures and life experiences. Their content must therefore be limited to that which is equally common to all cultures, or to material that is entirely unfamiliar and novel for all persons whatever their cultural background. See CULTURE-FREE TEST.

culture-free test.   A test that is free of the impact of all cultural experiences; therefore, a measure reflecting only hereditary abilities. Since culture permeates all of man's environmental contacts, the construction of such a test would seem to be an impossibility. Cultural "bias" is not eliminated by the use of non-language or so-called performance tests, although it may be reduced in some instances. In terms of most of the purposes for which tests are used, the validity (value) of a "culture-free" test is questioned; a test designed to be equally applicable to all cultures may be of little or no practical value in any.

curricular validity.   See VALIDITY (2).

decile.   Any one of the nine points (scores) that divide a distribution into ten parts, each containing one-tenth of all the scores or cases; every tenth percentile. The first decile is the 10th percentile, the eighth decile the 80th percentile, etc.

deviation.   The amount by which a score differs from some reference value, such as the mean, the norm, or the score on some other test.

deviation IQ (DIQ).   An age-based index of general mental ability. It is based upon the difference or deviation between a person's score and the typical or average score for persons of his chronological age. Deviation IQs from most current scholastic aptitude measures are standard scores with a mean of 100 and a standard deviation of 16 for each defined age group.

diagnostic test.   A test used to "diagnose" or analyze; that is, to locate an individual's specific areas of weakness or strength, to determine the nature of his weaknesses or deficiencies, and, wherever possible, to suggest their cause. Such a test yields measures of the components or subparts of some larger body of information or skill. Diagnostic achievement tests are most commonly prepared for the skill subjects.

difficulty value.   An index which indicates the percent of some specified group, such as students of a given age or grade, who answer a test item correctly.

discriminating power.   The ability of a test item to differentiate between persons possessing much or little of some trait.

discrimination index.   An index which indicates the *discriminating power* of a test item. The most commonly used index is derived from the number passing the item in the highest 27 percent of the group (on total score) and the number passing in the lowest 27 percent.

distractor.   Any incorrect choice (option) in a test item.

distribution (frequency distribution).   A tabulation of the scores (or other attributes) of a group of individuals to show the number (frequency) of each score, or of those within the range of each interval.

equivalent form.   Any of two or more forms of a test that are closely parallel with respect to the nature of the content and the number and difficulty of the items included, and that will yield very similar average scores and measures of variability for a given group. (Also referred to as *alternate, comparable,* or *parallel* form.)

error of measurement. See STANDARD ERROR OF MEASUREMENT.

expectancy table ("expected" achievement). A term with two common usages, related but with some difference:

(1) A table or other device for showing the relation between scores on a predictive test and some related outcome. The outcome, or criterion status, for individuals at each level of predictive score may be expressed as (a) an average on the outcome variable, (b) the percent of cases at successive levels, or (c) the probability of reaching given performance levels. Such tables are commonly used in making predictions of educational or job success.

(2) A table or chart providing for an interpretation of a student's obtained score on an achievement test with the score which would be "expected" for those at his grade level and with his level of scholastic aptitude. Such "expectancies" are based upon actual data from administration of the specified achievement and scholastic aptitude tests to the same student population. The term "anticipated" is also used to denote achievement as differentiated by level of "intellectual status."

extrapolation.   In general, any process of estimating values of a variable beyond the range of available data.

As applied to test norms, the process of extending a norm line into grade or age levels not tested in the standardization program, in order to permit interpretation of extreme scores. Since this extension is usually done graphically, considerable judgment is involved. Extrapolated values are thus to some extent arbitrary; for this and other reasons, they have limited meaning.

f.   A symbol denoting the *frequency* of a given score or of the scores within an interval grouping.

face validity.   See VALIDITY.

factor. In mental measurement, a hypothetical trait, ability, or component of ability that underlies and influences performance on two or more tests and hence causes scores on the tests to be correlated. The term "factor" strictly refers to a theoretical variable, derived by a process of *factor analysis* from a table of intercorrelations among tests. However, it is also used to denote the psychological interpretation given to the variable—i.e., the mental trait assumed to be represented by the variable, as verbal ability, numerical ability, etc.

factor analysis.   Any of several methods of analyzing the intercorrelations among a set of variables such as test scores. Factor analysis attempts to account for the interrelationships in terms of some underlying "factors," preferably fewer in number than the original variables, and it reveals how much of the variation in each of the original measures arises from, or is associated with, each of the hypothetical factors. Factor analysis has contributed to an understanding of the organization or components of intelligence, aptitudes, and personality; and it has pointed the way to the development of "purer" tests of the several components.

forced-choice item.   Broadly, any multiple-choice item in which the examinee is *required* to select one or more of the given choices. The term is most often used to denote a special type of multiple-choice item employed in personality tests in which the options are (1) of equal "preference value," i.e., chosen equally often by a typical group, and are (2) such that one of the options discriminates between persons high and low on the factor that this option measures, while the other options measure other factors. Thus, in the *Gordon Personal Profile,* each of four options represents one of the four personality traits measured by the *Profile,* and the examinee must select both the option which describes him *most* and the one which describes him *least.*

frequency distribution.   See DISTRIBUTION.

g.   Denotes *general* intellectual ability; one dimensional measure of "mind," as described by the British psychologist Spearman. A test of "*g*" serves as a general-purpose test of mental ability.

grade equivalent (GE).   The grade level for which a given score is the real or estimated average. Grade-equivalent

[grade equivalent (GE), continued.]
interpretation, most appropriate for elementary level achievement tests, expresses obtained scores in terms of *grade* and *month of grade,* assuming a 10-month school year (e.g., 5.7). Since such tests are usually standardized at only one (or two) point(s) within each grade, grade equivalents between points for which there are data-based scores must be "estimated" by *interpolation.* See EXTRAPOLATION, INTERPOLATION.

grade norms. Norms based upon the performance of pupils of given grade placement. See GRADE EQUIVALENT, NORMS, PERCENTILE RANK, STANINE.

group test. A test that may be administered to a number of individuals at the same time by one examiner.

individual test. A test that can be administered to only one person at a time, because of the nature of the test and/or the maturity level of the examinees.

intelligence quotient (IQ). Originally, an index of brightness expressed as the ratio of a person's mental age to his chronological age, MA/CA, multiplied by 100 to eliminate the decimal. (More precisely—and particularly for adult ages, at which mental growth is assumed to have ceased—the ratio of mental age to the mental age normal for chronological age.) This quotient IQ has been gradually replaced by the deviation IQ concept.

It is sometimes desired to give additional meaning to IQs by the use of verbal descriptions for the ranges in which they fall. Since the IQ scale is a continuous one, there can be no inflexible line of demarcation between such successive category labels as very superior, superior, above average, average, below average, etc.; any verbal classification system is therefore an arbitrary one. There appears to be, however, rather common use of the term *average* or *normal* to describe IQs from 90–109 inclusive.

An IQ is more definitely "interpreted" by noting the normal percent of IQs within a range which includes the IQ, and/or by indicating its percentile rank or stanine in the total national norming sample. Column 2 of Table 1 shows the normal distribution of IQs for M = 100 and S.D. = 16, showing percentages within successive 10-point intervals. (For IQs whose S.D. is greater than 16, the percentages for the extreme IQ ranges will be larger, and those for IQs near the mean will be smaller, than those shown in the table.) Table 1 indicates that 47 percent, approximately one-half of "all" persons, have IQs in the 20-point range of 90 through 109; an IQ of 140 or above would be considered as extremely high, since fewer than one percent (0.6) of the total population reach this level, and fewer than one percent have IQs below 60. From the cumulative percents given in Column 3, it is noted that 3.1 percent have IQs below 70, usually considered the mentally retarded category. This column may be used to indicate the percentile rank (PR) of certain IQs. Thus an IQ of 119 has a PR of 89, since 89.4

Table 1

Normal Distribution of IQs with Mean of 100 and Standard Deviation of 16

(1) IQ Range	(2) Percent of Persons	(3) Cumulative Percent
140 and above	0.6	100.6
130–139	2.5	99.4
120–129	7.5	96.9
110–119	16.0	89.4
100–109	23.4 } 46.8	73.4
90– 99	23.4 }	50.0
80– 89	16.0	26.6
70– 79	7.5	10.6
60– 69	2.5	3.1
Below 60	0.6	0.6
Total	100.0	

percent of IQs are 119 or below; an IQ of 79 has a PR of 10.6, or 11. See DEVIATION IQ, MENTAL AGE.

internal consistency. Degree of relationship among the items of a test; consistency in content sampling. See SPLIT-HALF RELIABILITY.

interpolation. In general, any process of estimating intermediate values between two known points. As applied to test norms, it refers to the procedure used in assigning interpretive values (e.g., grade equivalents) to scores between the successive average scores actually obtained in the standardization process. Also, in reading norm tables it is necessary at times to interpolate to obtain a norm value for a score between two scores given in the table; e.g., in the table shown here, a percentile rank of 83 (from $81 + \frac{1}{3}$ of 6) would be assigned, by *interpolation,* to a score of 46; a score of 50 would correspond to a percentile rank of 94 (obtained as $87 + \frac{2}{3}$ of 10).

Score	Percentile Rank
51	97
48	87
45	81

inventory. A questionnaire or check list, usually in the form of a self-report, designed to elicit non-intellective information about an individual. Not tests in the usual sense, inventories are most often concerned with personality traits, interests, attitudes, problems, motivation, etc. See PERSONALITY TEST.

inventory test. An achievement test that attempts to cover rather thoroughly some relatively small unit of specific instruction or training. An inventory test, as the name suggests, is in the nature of a "stock-taking" of an individual's knowledge or skill, and is often administered prior to instruction.

item. A single question or exercise in a test.

item analysis.   The process of evaluating single test items in respect to certain characteristics. It usually involves determining the difficulty value and the discriminating power of the item, and often its correlation with some external criterion.

Kuder-Richardson formula(s).   Formulas for estimating the reliability of a test that are based on *inter-item consistency* and require only a single administration of the test. The one most used, formula 20, requires information based on the number of items in the test, the standard deviation of the total score, and the proportion of examinees passing each item. The Kuder-Richardson formulas are not appropriate for use with speeded tests.

mastery test.   A test designed to determine whether a pupil has mastered a given unit of instruction or a single knowledge or skill; a test giving information on *what* a pupil knows, rather than on how his performance relates to that of some norm-reference group. Such tests are used in computer-assisted instruction, where their results are referred to as content- or criterion-referenced information.

mean (M).   See ARITHMETIC MEAN.

median (Md).   The middle score in a distribution or set of ranked scores; the point (score) that divides the group into two equal parts; the 50th percentile. Half of the scores are below the median and half above it, except when the median itself is one of the obtained scores.

mental age (MA).   The age for which a given score on a mental ability test is average or normal. If the average score made by an unselected group of children 6 years, 10 months of age is 55, then a child making a score of 55 is said to have a mental age of 6–10. Since the mental age unit shrinks with increasing (chronological) age, MAs do not have a uniform interpretation throughout all ages. They are therefore most appropriately used at the early age levels where mental growth is relatively rapid.

modal-age norms.   Achievement test norms that are based on the performance of pupils of normal age for their respective grades. Norms derived from such age restricted groups are free from the distorting influence of the scores of underage and overage pupils.

mode.   The score or value that occurs most frequently in a distribution.

multiple-choice item. A test item in which the examinee's task is to choose the correct or best answer from several given answers or options.

N.   The symbol commonly used to represent the number of cases in a group.

non-language test.   See NON-VERBAL TEST.

non-verbal test.   A test that does not require the use of words in the item or in the response to it. (Oral directions may be included in the formulation of the task.) A test cannot, however, be classified as non-verbal simply because it does not require reading on the part of the examinee. The use of non-verbal tasks cannot completely eliminate the effect of culture.

norm line.   A smooth curve drawn to best fit (1) the plotted mean or median scores of successive age or grade groups, or (2) the successive percentile points for a single group.

normal distribution.   A distribution of scores or measures that in graphic form has a distinctive bell-shaped appearance. Figures 1 and 2 show graphs of such a distribution, known as a *normal, normal probability,* or *Gaussian* curve. (Difference in shape is due to the different variability of the two distributions.) In such a normal distribution, scores or measures are distributed symmetrically about the mean, with as many cases up to various distances above the mean as down to equal distances below it. Cases are concentrated near the mean and decrease in frequency, according to a precise mathematical equation, the farther one departs from the mean. *Mean* and *median* are identical. The assumption that mental and psychological characteristics are distributed normally has been very useful in test development work.

norms. Statistics that supply a frame of reference by which meaning may be given to obtained test scores. Norms are based upon the actual performance of pupils of various grades or ages in the standardization group for the test. Since they represent average or typical performance, they should not be regarded as standards or as universally desirable levels of attainment. The most common types of norms are deviation IQ, percentile rank, grade equivalent, and stanine. Reference groups are usually those of specified age or grade.

objective test.   A test made up of items for which correct responses may be set up in advance; scores are unaffected by the opinion or judgment of the scorer. Objective keys provide for scoring by clerks or by machine. Such a test is contrasted with a "subjective" test, such as the usual essay examination, to which different persons may assign different scores, ratings, or grades.

omnibus test. A test (1) in which items measuring a variety of mental operations are all combined into a single sequence rather than being grouped together by type of operation, and (2) from which only a single score is derived, rather than separate scores for each operation or function. Omnibus tests make for simplicity of administration, since one set of directions and one overall time limit usually suffice. The Elementary, Intermediate, and Advanced tests in the *Otis-Lennon Mental Ability Test* series are omnibus-type tests, as contrasted with the *Kuhlmann-Anderson Measure of Academic Potential,* in which the items measuring similar operations occur together, each with its own set of directions. In a *spiral-omnibus* test, the easiest items of each type are presented

[**omnibus test,** continued.]
first, followed by the same succession of item types at a higher difficulty level, and so on in a rising spiral.

percentile (P). A point (score) in a distribution at or below which fall the percent of cases indicated by the percentile. Thus a score coinciding with the 35th percentile (P_{35}) is regarded as equaling or surpassing that of 35 percent of the persons in the group, and such that 65 percent of the performances exceed this score. "Percentile" has nothing to do with the percent of correct answers an examinee makes on a test.

percentile band. An interpretation of a test score which takes account of the measurement error that is involved. The range of such bands, most useful in portraying significant differences in battery profiles, is usually from one standard error of measurement below the obtained score to one standard error of measurement above it.

percentile rank (PR). The expression of an obtained test score in terms of its position within a group of 100 scores; the percentile rank of a score is the percent of scores equal to or lower than the given score in its own or in some external reference group.

performance test. A test involving some motor or manual response on the examinee's part, generally a manipulation of concrete equipment or materials. Usually *not* a paper-and-pencil test.

(1) A "performance" test of mental ability is one in which the role of language is excluded or minimized, and ability is assessed by what the examinee *does* rather than by what he says (or writes). Mazes, form boards, picture completion, and other types of items may be used. Examples include certain *Stanford-Binet* tasks, the Performance Scale of *Wechsler Intelligence Scale for Children, Arthur Point Scale of Performance Tests, Raven's Progressive Matrices.*

(2) "Performance" tests include measures of mechanical or manipulative ability where the task itself coincides with the objective of the measurement, as in the *Bennett Hand-Tool Dexterity Test.*

(3) The term "performance" is also used to denote a test that is actually a *work-sample;* in this sense it may include paper-and-pencil tests, as, for example, a test in bookkeeping, in shorthand, or in proofreading, where no materials other than paper and pencil may be required, and where the test response is identical with the behavior about which information is desired. *SRA Typing Skills* is such a test.

The use of the term "performance" to describe a type of test is not very precise and there are certain "gray areas." Perhaps one should think of "performance" tests as those on which the obtained differences among individuals may *not* be ascribed to differences in ability to use verbal symbols.

personality test. A test intended to measure one or more of the non-intellective aspects of an individual's mental or psychological make-up; an instrument designed to obtain information on the affective characteristics of an individual—emotional, motivational, attitudinal, etc.—as distinguished from his abilities. Personality tests include (1) the so-called *personality* and *adjustment inventories* (e.g., *Bernreuter Personality Inventory, Bell Adjustment Inventory, Edwards Personal Preference Schedule*) which seek to measure a person's status on such traits as dominance, sociability, introversion, etc., by means of self-descriptive responses to a series of questions; (2) *rating scales* which call for rating, by one's self or another, the extent to which a subject possesses certain traits; and (3) *opinion or attitude inventories* (e.g., *Allport-Vernon-Lindzey Study of Values, Minnesota Teacher Attitude Inventory*). Some writers also classify interest, problem, and belief inventories as personality tests (e.g., *Kuder Preference Record, Mooney Problem Check List*). See PROJECTIVE TECHNIQUE.

power test. A test intended to measure level of performance unaffected by speed of response; hence one in which there is either no time limit or a very generous one. Items are usually arranged in order of increasing difficulty.

practice effect. The influence of previous experience with a test on a later administration of the same or a similar test; usually an increased familiarity with the directions, kinds of questions, etc. Practice effect is greatest when the interval between testings is short, when the content of the two tests is identical or very similar, and when the initial test-taking represents a relatively novel experience for the subjects.

predictive validity. See VALIDITY (2).

product-moment coefficient (r). Also known as the Pearson r. See COEFFICIENT OF CORRELATION.

profile. A graphic representation of the results on several tests, for either an individual or a group, when the results have been expressed in some uniform or comparable terms (standard scores, percentile ranks, grade equivalents, etc.). The profile method of presentation permits identification of areas of strength or weakness.

prognosis (prognostic) test. A test used to predict future success in a specific subject or field, as the *Pimsleur Language Aptitude Battery.*

projective technique (projective method). A method of personality study in which the subject responds as he chooses to a series of ambiguous stimuli such as ink blots, pictures, unfinished sentences, etc. It is assumed that under this free-response condition the subject "projects" manifestations of personality characteristics and organization that can, by suitable methods, be scored and interpreted to yield a description of his basic personality structure. The *Rorschach* (ink blot) *Technique,* the *Murray Thematic*

Apperception Test and the *Machover Draw-a-Person Test* are commonly used projective methods.

quartile.   One of three points that divide the cases in a distribution into four equal groups. The lower quartile (Q_1), or 25th percentile, sets off the lowest fourth of the group; the middle quartile (Q_2) is the same as the 50th percentile, or median, and divides the second fourth of cases from the third; and the third quartile (Q_3), or 75th percentile, sets off the top fourth.

r.   See COEFFICIENT OF CORRELATION.

random sample.   A sample of the members of some total population drawn in such a way that every member of the population has an equal chance of being included —that is, in a way that precludes the operation of bias or "selection." The purpose in using a sample free of bias is, of course, the requirement that the cases used be representative of the total population if findings for the sample are to be generalized to that population. In a *stratified* random sample, the drawing of cases is controlled in such a way that those chosen are "representative" also of specified subgroups of the total population. See REPRESENTATIVE SAMPLE.

range.   For some specified group, the difference between the highest and the lowest obtained score on a test; thus a very rough measure of spread or variability, since it is based upon only two extreme scores. Range is also used in reference to the possible spread of measurement a test provides, which in most instances is the number of items in the test.

raw score.   The first quantitative result obtained in scoring a test. Usually the number of right answers, number right minus some fraction of number wrong, time required for performance, number of errors, or similar direct, unconverted, uninterpreted measure.

readiness test.   A test that measures the extent to which an individual has achieved a degree of maturity or acquired certain skills or information needed for successfully undertaking some new learning activity. Thus a *reading readiness* test indicates whether a child has reached a developmental stage where he may profitably begin formal reading instruction. *Readiness* tests are classified as *prognostic* tests.

recall item.   A type of item that requires the examinee to supply the correct answer from his own memory or recollection, as contrasted with a *recognition item,* in which he need only identify the correct answer.

Columbus discovered America in the year _____ is a *recall* (or *completion*) item. See RECOGNITION ITEM.

recognition item.   An item which requires the examinee to recognize or select the correct answer from among two or more given answers (options).

Columbus discovered America in
(a) *1425*   (b) *1492*   (c) *1520*   (d) *1546*

is a *recognition* item.

regression effect.   Tendency of a predicted score to be nearer to the mean of its distribution than the score from which it is predicted is to its mean. Because of the effects of regression, students making extremely high or extremely low scores on a test tend to make less extreme scores, i.e., closer to the mean, on a second administration of the same test or on some predicted measure.

reliability.   The extent to which a test is consistent in measuring whatever it does measure; dependability, stability, trustworthiness, relative freedom from errors of measurement. Reliability is usually expressed by some form of *reliability coefficient* or by the *standard error of measurement* derived from it.

reliability coefficient.   The coefficient of correlation between two forms of a test, between scores on two administrations of the same test, or between halves of a test, properly corrected. The three measure somewhat different aspects of reliability, but all are properly spoken of as reliability coefficients. See ALTERNATE-FORM RELIABILITY, SPLIT-HALF RELIABILITY COEFFICIENT, TEST-RETEST RELIABILITY COEFFICIENT, KUDER-RICHARDSON FORMULA(S).

representative sample.   A sample that corresponds to or matches the population of which it is a sample with respect to characteristics important for the purposes under investigation. In an achievement test norm sample, such significant aspects might be the proportion of cases of each sex, from various types of schools, different geographical areas, the several socioeconomic levels, etc.

scholastic aptitude.   See ACADEMIC APTITUDE.

skewed distribution.   A distribution that departs from symmetry or balance around the mean, i.e., from normality. Scores pile up at one end and trail off at the other.

Spearman-Brown formula.   A formula giving the relationship between the reliability of a test and its length. The formula permits estimation of the reliability of a test lengthened or shortened by any multiple, from the known reliability of a given test. Its most common application is the estimation of reliability of an entire test from the correlation between its two halves. See SPLIT-HALF RELIABILITY COEFFICIENT.

split-half reliability coefficient.   A coefficient of reliability obtained by correlating scores on one half of a test with scores on the other half, and applying the Spearman-Brown formula to adjust for the doubled length of the total test. Generally, but not necessarily, the two halves consist of the odd-numbered and the even-numbered items. Split-half reliability coefficients are sometimes referred to as measures of the *internal consistency* of a test; they involve content sampling only, not stability

[split-half reliability coefficient, continued.]
over time. This type of reliability coefficient is inappropriate for tests in which speed is an important component.

standard deviation (S.D.). A measure of the variability or dispersion of a distribution of scores. The more the scores cluster around the mean, the smaller the standard deviation. For a normal distribution, approximately two thirds (68.3 percent) of the scores are within the range from one S.D. below the mean to one S.D. above the mean. Computation of the S.D. is based upon the square of the deviation of each score from the mean. The S.D. is sometimes called "sigma" and is represented by the symbol σ. (See Figure 1.)

standard error (S.E.). A statistic providing an estimate of the possible magnitude of "error" present in some obtained measure, whether (1) an *individual* score or (2) some *group* measure, as a mean or a correlation coefficient.

(1) standard error of measurement (S.E. Meas.): As applied to a single obtained score, the amount by which the score may differ from the hypothetical true score due to errors of measurement. The larger the S.E. Meas., the less reliable the score. The S.E. Meas. is an amount such that in about two-thirds of the cases the obtained score would not differ by more than one S.E. Meas. from the true score. (Theoretically, then, it can be said that the chances are 2:1 that the actual score is within a band extending from *true score minus 1 S.E. Meas.* to *true score plus 1 S.E. Meas.;* but since the true score can never be known, actual practice must reverse the true-obtained relation for an interpretation.) Other probabilities are noted under (2) below. See TRUE SCORE.

(2) standard error: When applied to group averages, standard deviations, correlation coefficients, etc., the S.E. provides an estimate of the "error" which may be involved. The group's size and the S.D. are the factors on which these standard errors are based. The same probability interpretation as for S.E. Meas. is made for the S.E.s of group measures, i.e., 2:1 (2 out of 3) for the 1 S.E. range, 19:1 (95 out of 100) for a 2 S.E. range, 99:1 (99 out of 100) for a 2.6 S.E. range.

standard score. A general term referring to any of a variety of "transformed" scores, in terms of which raw scores may be expressed for reasons of convenience, comparability, ease of interpretation, etc. The simplest type of standard score, known as a z-score, is an expression of the *deviation* of a score from the mean score of the group *in relation to* the standard deviation of the scores of the group. Thus:

$$\text{standard score (Z)} = \frac{\text{raw score (X)} - \text{mean (M)}}{\text{standard deviation (S.D.)}}$$

Adjustments may be made in this ratio so that a system of standard scores having any desired mean and standard deviation may be set up. The use of such standard scores does not affect the relative standing of the individuals in the group or change the shape of the original distribution. T-scores have a M of 50 and a S.D. of 10. Deviation IQs are standard scores with a M of 100 and some chosen S.D., most often 16; thus a raw score that is 1 S.D. above the M of its distribution would convert to a standard score (deviation IQ) of 100 + 16 = 116. (See Figure 1.)

Standard scores are useful in expressing the raw scores of two forms of a test in comparable terms in instances where tryouts have shown that the two forms are not identical in difficulty; also, successive levels of a test may be linked to form a continuous standard-score scale, making across-battery comparisons possible.

standardized test (standard test). A test designed to provide a systematic sample of individual performance, administered according to prescribed directions, scored in conformance with definite rules, and interpreted in reference to certain normative information. Some would further restrict the usage of the term "standardized" to those tests for which the items have been chosen on the basis of experimental evaluation, and for which data on reliability and validity are provided. Others would add "commercially published" and/or "for general use."

stanine. One of the steps in a nine-point scale of standard scores. The stanine (short for *standard-nine*) scale has values from 1 to 9, with a mean of 5 and a standard deviation of 2. Each stanine (except 1 and 9) is $\frac{1}{2}$ S.D. in width, with the middle (average) stanine of 5 extending from $\frac{1}{4}$ S.D. below to $\frac{1}{4}$ S.D. above the mean. (See Figure 2.)

survey test. A test that measures general achievement in a given area, usually with the connotation that the test is intended to assess group status, rather than to yield precise measures of individual performance.

Figure 1

Normal curve, showing relations among standard deviation distance from mean, area (percentage of cases) between these points, percentile rank, and IQ from tests with an S.D. of 16.

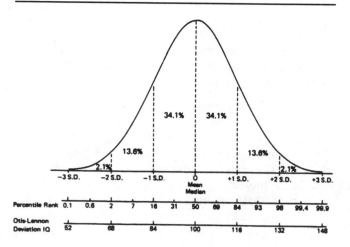

Figure 2

Stanines and the normal curve. Each stanine (except 1 and 9) is one half S.D. in width.

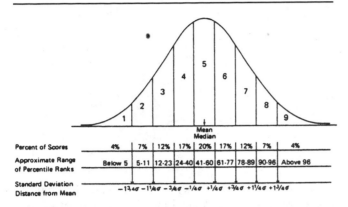

Percent of Scores	4%	7%	12%	17%	20%	17%	12%	7%	4%
Approximate Range of Percentile Ranks	Below 5	5-11	12-23	24-40	41-60	61-77	78-89	90-96	Above 96
Standard Deviation Distance from Mean		$-1\frac{3}{4}\sigma$	$-1\frac{1}{4}\sigma$	$-\frac{3}{4}\sigma$	$-\frac{1}{4}\sigma$	$+\frac{1}{4}\sigma$	$+\frac{3}{4}\sigma$	$+1\frac{1}{4}\sigma$	$+1\frac{3}{4}\sigma$

t.   A critical ratio expressing the relationship of some measure (mean, correlation coefficient, difference, etc.) to its standard error. The size of this ratio is an indication of the significance of the measure. If *t* is as large as 1.96, significance at the .05 level is indicated; if as large as 2.58, at the .01 level. These levels indicate 95 or 99 chances out of 100, respectively.

taxonomy.   An embodiment of the principles of classification; a survey, usually in outline form, such as a presentation of the objectives of education.

test-retest reliability coefficient.   A type of reliability coefficient obtained by administering the same test a second time, after a short interval, and correlating the two sets of scores. "Same test" was originally understood to mean identical content, i.e., the same form; currently, however, the term "test-retest" is also used to describe the administration of different forms of the same test, in which case this reliability coefficient becomes the same as the alternate-form coefficient. In either case (1) fluctuations over time and in testing situation, and (2) any effect of the first test upon the second are involved. When the time interval between the two testings is considerable, as several months, a test-retest reliability coefficient reflects not only the consistency of measurement provided by the test, but also the stability of the examinee trait being measured.

true score.   A score entirely free of error; hence, a hypothetical value that can never be obtained by testing, which always involves some measurement error. A "true" score may be thought of as the average score from an infinite number of measurements from the same or exactly equivalent tests, assuming no practice effect or change in the examinee during the testings. The standard deviation of this infinite number of "samplings" is known as the *standard error of measurement*.

validity.   The extent to which a test does the job for which it is used. This definition is more satisfactory than the traditional "extent to which a test measures what it is supposed to measure," since the validity of a test is always specific to the purposes for which the test is used. The term validity, then, has different connotations for various types of tests and, thus, a different kind of validity evidence is appropriate for each.

(1) content, curricular validity. For achievement tests, validity is the extent to which the *content* of the test represents a balanced and adequate sampling of the outcomes (knowledge, skills, etc.) of the course or instructional program it is intended to cover. It is best evidenced by a comparison of the test content with courses of study, instructional materials, and statements of educational goals; and often by analysis of the processes required in making correct responses to the items. *Face validity,* referring to an observation of what a test appears to measure, is a non-technical type of evidence; apparent relevancy is, however, quite desirable.

(2) criterion-related validity. The extent to which scores on the test are in agreement with (*concurrent validity*) or predict (*predictive validity*) some given criterion measure. Predictive validity refers to the accuracy with which an aptitude, prognostic, or readiness test indicates future learning success in some area, as evidenced by correlations between scores on the test and future criterion measures of such success (e.g., the relation of score on an academic aptitude test administered in high school to grade point average over four years of college). In concurrent validity, no significant time interval elapses between administration of the test being validated and of the criterion measure. Such validity might be evidenced by *concurrent* measures of academic ability and of achievement, by the relation of a new test to one generally accepted as or known to be valid, or by the correlation between scores on a test and criteria measures which are valid but are less objective and more time-consuming to obtain than a test score would be.

(3) construct validity. The extent to which a test measures some relatively abstract psychological trait or construct; applicable in evaluating the validity of tests that have been constructed on the basis of an analysis (often factor analysis) of the nature of the trait and its manifestations. Tests of personality, verbal ability, mechanical aptitude, critical thinking, etc., are validated in terms of their construct and the relation of their scores to pertinent external data.

variability. The spread or dispersion of test scores, best indicated by their standard deviation.

variance.   For a distribution, the average of the squared deviations from the mean; thus the square of the standard deviation.

Sources

Chapter 2

Malpractice cases excerpted from Ronald Jay Cohen (1979) *Malpractice: A Guide for Mental Health Professionals* published by The Free Press, a division of Macmillan, Inc. © 1979 The Free Press and reproduced by permission.

Chapter 4

"Methods of Expressing Test Scores." Test Service Notebook #148. Reproduced by permission. The Psychological Corporation, San Antonio, Texas.

"Stanines and Their Computation for Local Use." Test Service Notebook #123. Reproduced by permission. The Psychological Corporation, San Antonio, Texas.

"Interpreting Percentile Scores," "Interpreting Stanine Scores," "Interpreting SAT and ACT Scores" and "Interpreting Grade-Equivalent Scores" from J. R. Hills, *Hills' Handy Hints*. Washington, DC: National Council on Measurement in Education, 1986. Reprinted by permission of the National Council on Measurement in Education.

Figure 4-1 Copyright © 1988 Ronald Jay Cohen, Ph.D. All rights reserved. Reproduced by permission of Ronald Jay Cohen, Ph.D.

Chapter 6

Table from "A Quantitative Approach to Content Validity" by C. H. Lawshe, *Personnel Psychology*, 1975, *28*, 563–575. Reprinted by permission of Personnel Psychology, Inc.

"Fairness and the Matter of Bias" by Lois E. Burrill and Ruth Wilson. Test Service Notebook #36. Reproduced by permission. The Psychological Corporation, San Antonio, Texas.

Chapter 7

"Constructing the Puerto Rico Self-Concept Scale: Problems and Prospects" by H. Abadzi and S. Florez from *Applied Psychological Measurement*, 1981, *5*, 237–243. Copyright 1981 Applied Psychological Measurement Inc. Reproduced by permission of Applied Psychological Measurement Inc.

Chapter 8

"Interpreting IQ Scores" from J. R. Hills, *Hills' Handy Hints*. Washington, DC: National Council on Measurement in Education, 1986. Reprinted by permission of the National Council on Measurement in Education.

Chapter 10

"Assessing School Ability" by Ruth Wilson. Test Service Notebook #35. Reproduced by permission. The Psychological Corporation, San Antonio, Texas.

"Selection and Provision of Testing Materials" by Roger T. Lennon. Test Service Notebook #99. Reproduced by permission. The Psychological Corporation, San Antonio, Texas.

"Some Things Parents Should Know About Testing." Test Service Notebook #34. Reproduced by permission. The Psychological Corporation, San Antonio, Texas.

"On Telling Parents About Test Results." Test Service Notebook #154. Reproduced by permission. The Psychological Corporation, San Antonio, Texas.

"How a Standardized Achievement Test Is Built" by Lois E. Burrill. Test Service Notebook #125. Reproduced by permission. The Psychological Corporation, San Antonio, Texas.

"Reporting Standardized Achievement Test Results to the Community" by Lois E. Burrill. Test Service Notebook #60. Reproduced by permission. The Psychological Corporation, San Antonio, Texas.

Chapter 14

"Socially Reinforced Obsessing: Etiology of a Disorder in a Christian Scientist" by Ronald Jay Cohen and Frederick J. Smith from *Journal of Consulting and Clinical Psychology,* 1976, *44,* 142–144. © 1976 by the American Psychological Association. Reprinted by permission of the publisher. Further reproduction without the express written permission of the APA and the author is prohibited.

"Socially Reinforced Obsessing: A Reply" by Ronald Jay Cohen from *Journal of Consulting and Clinical Psychology,* 1977, *45,* 1166–1171. © 1977 by the American Psychological Association. Reprinted by permission of the publisher. Further reproduction without the express written permission of the APA and the author is prohibited.

Appendices

Mid-Pawling Personality Inventory © 1995 Ronald Jay Cohen. All rights reserved. Reprinted by permission.

"A Glossary of Measurement Terms." Test Service Notebook #13. Reproduced by permission. The Psychological Corporation, San Antonio, Texas.

Notes

Notes

Notes

Notes

Notes

Notes

Notes

Notes